RENÉ GIRARD

Things Hidden
since the Foundation
of the World

Research undertaken in collaboration with
Jean-Michel Oughourlian and Guy Lefort

Translated by
Stephen Bann (Books II and III)
Michael Metteer (Book I)

continuum
LONDON • NEW YORK

Continuum

The Tower Building	15 East 26th Street
11 York Road	New York
London SE1 7NX	NY 10010

© 1978 Editions Grasset & Fasquelle
English translation © 1987 The Athlone Press
This paperback edition published 2003 by Continuum

British Library Cataloguing-in-Publication Data
A catalogue record for this book is available from the British Library

ISBN 0-8264-6853-5

Library of Congress Cataloging-in-Publication Data
A catalog record for this book has been requested

Typeset by Rapidset and Design Ltd, London
Printed and bound in Great Britain by
The Cromwell Press, Trowbridge, Wiltshire

Foreword

The texts collected in this work derive from research undertaken at Cheektowaga University in 1975 and 1976, and at Johns Hopkins in 1977.

They were subsequently reworked and complemented by a number of earlier writings by René Girard which have been interpolated here and there, in particular, extracts from a discussion published in the journal *Esprit* in 1973, from an essay entitled 'Malédictions contre les pharisiens' which appeared in the *Bulletin du Centre protestant d'études* of Geneva, and from 'Violence and Representation in the Mythical Text', published in *MLN* in December 1977.

We quite deliberately left out all the concessions to the reader which it is customary, and wise, to make in the presentation of so ambitious a thesis. We did so in order to make the texts less heavy and to preserve the character of the discussion. The reader is asked to bear this in mind.

We are keen to express our gratitude to the State University of New York at Buffalo, the Johns Hopkins University, Cornell University, and all those who have made our task easier in a number of different ways: Cesareo Bandera, Jean-Marie Domenach, Marc Faessler, John Freccero, Eric Gans, Sandor Goodhart, Josué Harari, Joseph Oughourlian, Georges-Hubert de Radkowski, Oswald Rouquet, Raymund Schwager, Michel Serres.

We are specially thankful for the collaboration of Martine Bell and the patience of our wives.

R.G., J.-M.O., G.L.

Note to the English-language edition: For this English-language edition, Professor Girard has taken the opportunity to make revisions to the original French text (*Des Choses cachées depuis la fondation du monde*, Editions Grasset et Fasquelle, Paris, 1978).

Table of Contents

BOOK II: THE JUDAEO-CHRISTIAN SCRIPTURES

BOOK III: INTERDIVIDUAL PSYCHOLOGY

BOOK I

FUNDAMENTAL ANTHROPOLOGY

Man differs from the other animals in his greater aptitude for imitation.
Aristotle, *Poetics*, 4

I saw a vision of us move in the dark:
all that we did or dreamed of
Regarded each other, the man pursued the woman,
the woman clung to the man, warriors and
kings
Strained at each other in the darkness, all
loved or fought inward, each one of the lost
people
Sought the eyes of another that another should
praise him; sought never his own but
another's; the net of desire
Had every nerve drawn to the center, so that
they writhed like a full draught of fishes,
all matted
In the one mesh; when they look backward they
see only a man standing at the beginning,
Or forward, a man at the end; or if upward, men
in the shining bitter sky striding and
feasting,
Whom you call Gods

Robinson Jeffers, *The Tower Beyond Tragedy*

BOOK I

FUNDAMENTAL ANTHROPOLOGY

CHAPTER ONE

The Victimage Mechanism as the Basis of Religion

J.-M. O.: As psychiatrists, our first questions concerned the problem of desire. You objected to this as premature. You assert that we must begin with anthropology, and furthermore that only an investigation of the founding of religion will yield the secret of man.

The consensus today is that a true science of man is impossible, yet you speak of a science of religion. How would you justify such a view?

R. G.: It will take some time. . .

Science is the distinctive achievement of the modern mind. In each incontestable scientific conquest, the same process is repeated: what had been an age-old, dark and formidable mystery is transformed into an enigma.

There is no enigma, however complex, that cannot finally be solved. For centuries religion has been declining in the West and its disappearance is now a global phenomenon. As religion recedes and allows us to consider it in perspective, what was once an insoluble mystery, guarded by formidable taboos, begins to look more and more like a problem to be solved. Why the belief in the sacred? How can one explain the ubiquitous existence of rites and prohibitions? Why, before our own, has there never been a social order that was not thought to be dominated by a supernatural being?

With its comparative method and its vast accumulation of material on dying or dead religions, ethnological research has hastened the transformation of religion into a scientific problem, without ever resolving that problem. Ethnologists have devoted much of their theorizing to the questions of religious origins and the nature of religion. Roughly from 1860 to 1920, the solution seemed excitingly close. One can detect a common desire to be the first to write an ethnological equivalent to *On the Origin of Species*; an 'Origin of Religions' would play the same decisive role in the human and social sciences that Darwin's great book has played in the life sciences.

Years passed but no single book proved authoritative. One after another 'theories of religion' appeared, but none produced the hoped-for revolution in knowledge. Gradually the idea took hold that it was a mistake to view religion as a soluble problem. Some suggested that questions bearing on religion as a whole, religion as such, were too large to be addressed scientifically. But where would the contemporary science of biology be if it had ever been persuaded by that kind of argument?

G. L.: Others, such as George Dumézil, maintain that the only contemporary method capable of producing results is the 'structural' method, and that this method can operate only with material already symbolized, with structures of language, and not with over-generalized principles such as the sacred, etc.

R. G.: But we encounter these general principles in the form of words like *mana* and *sacer* in each particular culture. Why should such words be excluded from research and not others?

The evacuation of religion, in the sense in which religion constituted a theoretical problem fifty years ago, is the most characteristic trait of contemporary ethnology. To judge from the passion with which certain ethnologists attempt to make this evacuation final and definitive, something very important must be at stake. According to E. E. Evans-Pritchard, for example, there never has been nor ever will be any value in theories of religion. This eminent ethnologist treats all such theories with a degree of disdain that makes one wonder why he devoted a book to them, a work entitled *Theories of Primitive Religion*.[1] The author does not hesitate to include even future theories in what amounts to a major excommunication. Thoughts as yet unborn are condemned without appeal. When a scholar disregards the simplest courtesy in scientific matters, we can suppose that passion had the upper hand.

J.-M. O.: One could offer so many examples of such categorical prophecies being quickly refuted by experience! In fact, this type of negative prediction is repeated so frequently that one might ask if it is not prompted by the very proximity of the discovery that one solemnly proclaims will never take place. In every period, any important discovery will threaten *some* organization of knowledge.

R. G.: It is certainly natural for a question, as question, to become suspect if it remains unanswered for a long time. Scientific progress can take the form of the disappearance of questions when their non-pertinence has finally been recognized. People attempt to convince themselves that this is the case with religion, but I believe they are mistaken. If one compares the many admirable monographs on individual cultures accumulated by ethnologists since Malinowski, particularly by the English, one can see that ethnology does not possess a coherent terminology for investigating religion. This explains the repetitive character of descriptions. In true sciences, previously described objects or accomplished proofs can always be replaced with a label, a symbol, or a bibliographic reference. In ethnology this is impossible because no one agrees on the definition of the most elementary terms, such as ritual, sacrifice, mythology, etc.

Before proceeding with our discussion, it would perhaps be advisable to comment briefly on the current situation in the human sciences, since we want to justify the liberties we intend to take with the beliefs of our time.

The period that is now coming to a close has been dominated by structuralism. I believe that in order to understand structuralism it is necessary to take into account the climate of intellectual scepticism fostered by the failure of broad theorizing. By the middle of the twentieth century there was no longer any doubt as to the failure of the great theories. Durkheim is no longer prominent. No one ever took *Totem and Taboo* seriously. It was in this context that structuralist ethnology was born, specifically from the encounter of Claude Lévi-Strauss, in New York during the war, with the structural linguistics of Roman Jakobson.

Cultural phenomena, for Lévi-Strauss, are like languages in that they are composed of signs that signify nothing if isolated from one another. Signs signify by means of other signs; they form systems endowed with an internal coherence that confers individuality on cultures or on institutions. And the task of ethnologists is to describe a particular systematic coherence and individuality. Symbolic forms should be deciphered from within, and the great traditional questions, which simply reflect the illusions of our own culture and would have no meaning except as a function of the system in which we operate, should be forgotten. We must limit ourselves to the reading of symbolic forms, Lévi-Strauss tells us; meaning must be sought where it resides and not elsewhere. 'Ethnological' cultures do not ask themselves about religion as such.

What Lévi-Strauss advocates, in sum, is that ethnology and the other sciences of man undertake a major strategic retreat. Because we are prisoners of our symbolic forms, we can do little more than reconstruct the operations that generate meaning, not only for ourselves, but for other cultures also; we are unable to transcend particular meanings in order to inquire about man himself, his destiny, etc. The most we can do is to recognize man as the one who produces symbolic forms, systems of signs, and who then confuses them with 'reality' itself, forgetting that in order to make reality meaningful he interposes an always particular system of signs between reality and himself.

J.-M. O.: Structural anthropology has obtained remarkable results in some areas. Far from being arid and dehumanized, as some of its critics have charged, the structuralist's rigour has produced a remarkable poetry in its reading of forms; we appreciate the specificity of forms of culture as we never have in the past.

R. G.: I believe that the structuralist's renunciation of the 'great questions', those posed before Lévi-Strauss in the context of an impressionistic humanism, constituted the only viable path for ethnology at the moment when Lévi-Strauss in some sense took charge of the field and radically transformed it.

Nothing has been more essential for ethnology than learning to apprehend meaning only where it resides and being able to demonstrate the inane character of certain traditional questions concerning man. Structural anthropology has definitively discredited an entire set of problems inherited from the nineteenth century.

G. L.: That is why the post-structuralists have proclaimed that after God, man himself is about to die, or is already dead; it is as if there can no longer be much question of man.

R. G.: On that point, however, I no longer agree; the question of man persists and will become more acute in the future.

The notions *man* and *humanity* will remain at the centre of a complex of questions and responses for which there is no reason to renounce the name 'science of man'. But a displacement is occurring, due in part to new disciplines, such as ethology, and due in part to structuralism itself, insofar as it designates for us, however negatively, the precise domain in which the question of man will be asked, and is in fact being explicitly asked. This domain is that of the origin and genesis of signifying systems. It is already recognized as a definite problem in the life sciences, although of course it is encountered there in a somewhat different form; it is the problem of what is called the process of hominization. We know that the problem is far from being solved, but no one doubts that science, one day, will succeed in resolving it. No single question has more of a future today than the question of man.

Acquisitive Mimesis and Mimetic Rivalry

J.-M. O.: In order to think concretely about the process of hominization, it would be necessary to move beyond the mutual incomprehension of structural ethnology on the one hand, and of the life sciences, such as ethology, on the other hand.

R. G.: I believe this is possible, but in order to succeed one must take up an old problem, one not fashionable at the moment, and radically rethink it. In the science of man and culture today there is a unilateral swerve away from anything that could be called mimicry, imitation, or mimesis. And yet there is nothing, or next to nothing, in human behaviour that is not learned, and all learning is based on imitation. If human beings suddenly ceased imitating, all forms of culture would vanish. Neurologists remind us frequently that the human brain is an enormous imitating machine. To develop a science of man it is necessary to compare human imitation with animal mimicry, and to specify the properly human modalities of mimetic behaviour, if they indeed exist.

I think it can easily be shown that the silence about mimesis among contemporary schools of thought is the result of a movement that goes back to the beginning of the modern period. In the nineteenth century it proclaimed itself in romanticism and individualism; in the twentieth century it asserts itself even more strongly in the fear of researchers that they will appear too obedient to the political and social imperatives of their community. The belief is that insisting on the role of imitation would unduly emphasize the gregarious aspects of humanity, all that transforms us into herds. There is a fear of minimizing the importance of everything that tends toward division, alienation, and conflict. If we give a leading role to imitation, perhaps we will make ourselves accomplices of the forces of subjugation and uniformity.

The psychologies and sociologies of imitation that were developed at the end of the nineteenth century were indeed strongly influenced by the optimism and conformity of a triumphant *petite bourgeoisie*. This is true, for example, of the most interesting of such works, that of Gabriel Tarde, who sees in imitation the sole foundation for social harmony and 'progress'.[2]

The indifference and mistrust with which our contemporaries regard imitation is based on their conception of it, that ultimately has its source in Plato. But already in Plato the problematic of imitation is severely curtailed. When Plato speaks of imitation, he does so in a manner that anticipates the whole of Western thought. The examples he selects for us are consistently limited to *representation* – to types of behaviour, manners, individual or collective habit, as well as words, phrases, and ways of speaking.

What is missing in Plato's account of imitation is any reference to kinds of behaviour involved in appropriation. Now it is obvious that appropriation figures formidably in the behaviour of human beings, as it does in that of all living beings, and that such behaviour can be copied. There is no reason to exclude appropriation from imitation; Plato nonetheless does just this, and the omission passes unnoticed because all of his successors, beginning with Aristotle, have followed his lead. It was Plato who determined once and for all the cultural meaning of imitation, but this meaning is truncated, torn from the essential dimension of acquisitive behaviour, which is also the dimension of conflict. If the behaviour of certain higher mammals, particularly the apes, seems to foreshadow human behaviour, it does so almost exclusively, perhaps, because the role of acquisitive mimesis is so important in their behaviour, although it is not as central as it is for human beings. If one ape observes another reach for an object, it is immediately tempted to imitate the gesture. It also happens that the animal visibly resists the temptation, and if the imitative gesture amuses us by reminding us of human beings, the failure to complete it, that is to say the repression of what already can be nearly defined as a desire, amuses us even more. It makes the animal a sort of brother to us by showing it subject to the same fundamental rule as humanity—that of preventing conflict, which the convergence of two or several avid hands toward one and the same object cannot help but provoke.

It is certainly no accident that the type of behaviour systematically excluded from all discussions of imitation, from Plato onward, is one that one cannot consider for a moment without being struck by the flagrant inaccuracy and mythical character of a conception that makes imitation a 'faculty' and ascribes to it only gregarious and pacifying effects. If imitation does indeed play the fundamental role for man, as everything seems to indicate, there must certainly exist an acquisitive imitation, or, if one prefers, a possessive mimesis whose effects and consequences should be carefully studied and considered.

One might object that in children – as in animals – the existence of acquisitive imitation has been recognized by researchers. This can be verified experimentally. Place a certain number of identical toys in a room with the same number of children; there is every chance that the toys will not be distributed without quarrels.

An equivalent situation rarely occurs among adults. That does not mean that mimetic rivalry no longer exists among them; perhaps it exists more than ever, but adults, like the apes, have learned to fear and repress rivalry, at least in its crudest, most obvious and most immediately recognizable forms.

G. L.: A good part of what we call politeness consists in self-effacement before another in order to avoid mimetic rivalry. But mimetic rivalry is a persistent phenomenon and can often reappear precisely where one believes it has been successfully suppressed, as, for instance, when the self-effacement of politeness itself becomes rivalry, which is a well-known comic technique. . .

R. G.: In certain cultures this type of phenomenon can take on considerable importance, as in the potlatch, in which acquisitive mimesis is inverted into a mimesis of renunciation and is capable, like its opposite, of attaining a disastrous intensity.[3]

Even these brief remarks suggest that the repression of acquisitive mimesis must constitute a serious concern for human and also for animal societies; it is a problem whose solution could involve many more aspects of culture than we might first imagine.

Everything we have said up to this point is quite simple and banal, and as such not apt to attract the attention of our contemporaries. Simplicity and clarity are not in fashion at the moment.

The discovery of conflictual mimesis and its repression, in itself hardly very surprising, nonetheless immediately threatens various dogmas of contemporary thought. Psychoanalysis tells us that repression is a human characteristic *par excellence*, and that the Oedipus complex makes it possible. Yet we have just mentioned that in certain animals one can observe the provocation and almost immediate repression of an incipient desire, as, for example, when two animals approach the same object. If a psychoanalyst observed the same behaviour in a human being he would automatically associate it with 'Oedipal ambivalence'. Ethologists, however, do not attribute such behaviour to an 'Oedipus' of the apes. Their observations, which can be reproduced experimentally, do not require any speculation based on a problematic 'unconscious'.

The Function of the Law: Prohibiting Imitation

R. G.: I think that the conflict generated by acquisitive mimesis can illuminate a fundamental question in ethnology, that of the prohibition.

J.-M. O.: You believe it is possible to assign a common denominator to all primitive prohibitions? Contemporary ethnology has obviously decided that any such attempt is not worthwhile. No one, so far as I know, would bother to look for an Ariadne's thread in this issue. Of course psychoanalysts believe they have found it, though they no longer convince many people.

R. G.: Previous failures are responsible for the general pessimism. These failures have confirmed researchers in their beliefs about the absurdity and gratuitousness of religion. In reality, however, we will not understand religion until we bring to it the respect now accorded the less overtly religious forms of *la pensée sauvage*. There will be no true 'rehabilitation' of primitive thought as long as the existence of religion, and therefore that of prohibitions, is not explained; religion is too much a part of all these phenomena for this not to be the case.

We should first acknowledge that the reason for certain prohibitions is obvious. There is no culture that does not prohibit violence among those who live together. All occasions or events that might give rise to real violence, even intense rivalries or forms of competition that are often tolerated or even encouraged elsewhere in society, are prohibited.

G. L.: Aside from prohibitions for which the motive is obvious, there are others that seem absurd.

R. G.: A good example of an apparently absurd prohibition is one that in many societies prohibits imitative behaviour. One must not copy the gesture of another member of the community or repeat his words.

The same concern can no doubt be seen in the prohibition of the use of proper names, or in the fear of mirrors, which are often associated with the devil in traditional societies.

Imitation doubles the imitated object and produces a simulacrum that can in turn become the object of types of magic. When ethnologists comment on such phenomena, they attribute them to a desire for protection against so-called imitative magic. And this is also the explanation they receive (from the natives) when they inquire into the *raison d'être* of prohibitions.

G. L.: All this suggests that primitive peoples recognize the relation between mimesis and violence. They know more about desire than we do, whereas our own ignorance keeps us from understanding the unity of all prohibitions.

R. G.: I agree, but we have to avoid proceeding too quickly, since precisely on this point we will meet with the incomprehension of psychologists and ethnologists, neither of whom are prepared to make the connection between conflict and acquisitive mimesis.

One can begin with a formal description of the prohibitions. Inevitably we imagine that the prohibitions covering imitative phenomena must be quite distinct from those against violence or intense rivalries. But this is not the case. What is impressive in imitative phenomena is that those who participate in them never cease imitating one another, each one transforming himself into a simulacrum of the other. Where we tend to see a difference emerge from the outcome of a conflict, the difference between victory on one side and defeat on the other, traditional and primitive societies emphasize the reciprocity of the conflict, or in other words the antagonists' mutual imitation. What strikes the primitive is the resemblance between the competitors, the identity of aims and tactics, the symmetry of gesture, etc.

An examination of our own terms, such as competition, rivalry, emulation, etc., reveals that the traditional perspective remains inscribed in the language. Competitors are fundamentally those who run or walk together, rivals those who dwell on opposite banks of the same river, etc.

The modern view of competition and conflict is the unusual and exceptional view, and our incomprehension is perhaps more problematic than the phenomenon of primitive prohibition. Primitive societies have never shared our conception of violence. For us, violence has a concep-

tual autonomy, a specificity that is utterly unknown to primitive societies. We tend to focus on the individual act, whereas primitive societies
attach only limited importance to it and have essentially pragmatic
reasons for refusing to isolate such an act from its context. This context
is one of violence. What permits us to conceive abstractly of an act of
violence and to view it as an isolated crime is the power of a judicial
institution that transcends all antagonists. If the transcendence of the
judicial institution is no longer there, if the institution loses its efficacy
or becomes incapable of commanding respect, the imitative and rep-
etitious character of violence becomes manifest once more; the imitative character of violence is in fact most manifest in explicit violence,
where it acquires a formal perfection it had not previously possessed. At
the level of the blood feud, in fact, there is always only one act, murder,
which is performed in the same way for the same reasons, in vengeful
imitation of the preceding murder. And this imitation propagates itself
by degrees. It becomes a duty for distant relatives who had nothing to
do with the original act, if in fact an original act can be identified; it
surpasses limits in space and time and leaves destruction everywhere in
its wake; it moves from generation to generation. In such cases, in its
perfection and paroxysm mimesis becomes a chain reaction of vengeance, in which human beings are constrained to the monotonous repetition of homicide.[4] Vengeance turns them into *doubles*.

J.-M. O.: In your view, then, prohibitions are evidence of a knowledge that we lack. Our inability to see their common denominator corresponds to our ignorance of the primary role of mimetic behaviour in
human conflict. Reciprocal violence is an escalation of mimetic rivalry,
and the more divisive it is, the more *uniform* its result.

R. G.: Of course. We can interpret prohibitions when we take into
account what we have just said concerning imitation and appropriation.

Certainly the assertion that primitive prohibitions demonstrate more
knowledge of human violence than does our social science is somewhat
paradoxical, the more so since certain prohibitions are truly absurd,
such as the one regarding twins, or the fear of mirrors. The simple il-
logicality of the prohibition, however, confirms rather than weakens
our thesis, for in the light of mimetic conflict one can very well understand why certain absurd prohibitions should exist, or, in other words,
why certain primitive societies judge twins and mirrors to be nearly as
dangerous as vengeance. In the case of vengeance, as in the former ex-

amples, two phenomena reproduce themselves mimetically in a way analogous to two individuals that imitate one another, and any mimetic
reproduction suggests violence or is seen as a possible cause of violence.
The proof that the primitive thinks this way is the kind of precaution
taken to insure against any mimetic propagation of twins. They are
eliminated as non-violently as possible so that the response to the mimetic seduction of these doubles is held to a minimum. The parents and
sometimes the neighbours of twins are subject to strictures that clearly
reveal the fear of spreading violence.[5]

G. L.: How do you account for the obvious concern in many primitive religions with natural catastrophes, such as floods or droughts?
They have nothing to do with mimetic desire.

R. G.: Prohibitions are intended to keep distant or to remove anything that threatens the community. The most external and unpredictable
threats, such as droughts, floods, or epidemics, are roughly equated –
often on the basis of resemblances in their ways of spreading and propagating – with the deterioration of human relations at the heart of the
community and with a shift toward reciprocal violence. The rising of
flood water, for example, the gradual spreading of the effects of a
drought, and especially the spread of contagious disease, resemble mimetic propagation.

Until now thinkers have always centred religious systems on the effects of external threats and natural catastrophes, or in the explanation
of natural and cosmic phenomena. In my opinion, mimetic violence is
at the heart of the system. We need to see what results can be obtained if
we suppose that such violence is in effect the motor of the religious system. Little effort has been made in this direction and yet the results are
surprising.

I believe that this path of inquiry will allow us to solve the enigmas
one by one. So I do not claim that the fear of natural catastrophe plays
no role whatsoever in religion. The fact that flood and epidemic serve as
metaphors for mimetic violence does not mean that real floods and epidemics are not objects of religious interpretation, but that they are perceived primarily as the result of the transgression of prohibitions
against mimetic behaviour, be it that of human beings or of the divinity
itself, which can also transgress, often in order to punish human beings
for having been the first to do so.

The point is that we must emphasize mimetic behaviour and violence in order to understand the phenomenon of prohibition as a whole, which includes the reaction to threats that have nothing to do with relations among members of the community.

J.-M. O.: Earlier you emphasized the formal unity of prohibitions; the structure of symmetrical and identical reproduction, the absence of difference, these are always perceived as terrifying. The prohibition against twins, then, would amount to a mythic translation of the relation of doubles.[6] But why should the doubles appear precisely in the guise of twins? You assert that there is a knowledge of mimetic desire at the origin of the prohibition, a knowledge that escapes us; if that is the case, what is to keep the doubles from appearing as real doubles?

R. G.: The knowledge contained in the prohibition is superior to ours, but it is nonetheless very incomplete. It is incapable of formulating itself theoretically, and, above all, it has been transfigured by representations of the sacred. Mimetic conflict is there, however, as the true common denominator of prohibitions. But it rarely appears as such; it is always interpreted as an evil manifestation of the sacred, the vengeful fury of the divinity. We will see why.

Early anthropologists perceived something of the religious character of mimesis and spoke of *imitative magic*; for instance, many primitives guard against having clippings of their hair or nails fall into the hands of potential adversaries. Any part of the body that can be detached, no matter how small or insignificant, is a potential double and therefore a threat of violence. But the presence of the *double itself* is what counts, and not the harm that might come once an enemy possesses it – like the doll figure of an adversary that one sticks with pins. In such magic we see inessential and perhaps late developments that occur at a time when the danger of a double as such has diminished and when the magician, in his relation to religion, knows almost as little as contemporary ethnology. Magic is never more than a poor use of the dangerous properties of mimesis.

If we extend our observations we see that so-called imitative magic is much too narrow an interpretation of the prohibitions that cover mimetic phenomena. One would have to study closely, in this context, those religions that prohibit *all images*, as well as many other phenomena that one would not think of relating to the primitive prohibition but that remain quite close to it nonetheless, such as the fascination and fear inspired, in many traditional societies, by the theatre and actors.

J.-M. O.: When you bring these topics together it is impossible not to think of a philosophy in which they are all related; I mean the work of Plato, of course.

R. G.: Plato's hostility toward mimesis is an essential aspect of his work and it should not be seen as confined, as it always is, to his criticism of art. If Plato mistrusts art it is because art is a form of mimesis, and not the reverse. He shares with primitive peoples a terror of mimesis that has yet to be sufficiently explained.

If Plato is unique in the history of philosophy because of his fear of mimesis, he is for the same reason closer than anyone to what is essential, closer than primitive religion itself. Yet Plato is also deceived by mimesis because he cannot succeed in understanding his fear, he never uncovers its empirical reason for being. Plato never relates conflict to acquisitive mimesis, that is, with the object that the two mimetic rivals attempt to wrest from one another because they designate it as desirable to one another.

When, in *The Republic*, Plato describes the undifferentiating and violent effects of mimesis, one can note the emergence of the theme of twins and also that of the mirror. It must be admitted that this is remarkable, but then no one has ever attempted to read Plato in the light of ethnology. And yet precisely such a reading is necessary in order truly to 'deconstruct' any 'metaphysics'. Aside from the pre-Socratics, to whom Heidegger and contemporary Heideggerean thought return, there is only religion, and one must understand religion in order to understand philosophy. Since the attempt to understand religion on the basis of philosophy has failed, we ought to try the reverse method and read philosophy in the light of religion.

G. L.: In a discussion of *Violence and the Sacred*, Philippe Lacoue-Labarthe criticizes you for presenting a Plato who does not understand what you yourself understand, whereas in reality, according to his critique, Plato understands these matters very well, and the writers to whom you attribute a superior knowledge, such as Cervantes or Shakespeare, are inscribed in a 'Platonic closure'.[7]

R. G.: Lacoue-Labarthe mistakenly assimilates the theory of mimetic desire to a Hegelian conception of desire. But one should not be surprised if Lacoue-Labarthe is unable to see where Plato fails with regard to mimetic rivalry. Where Plato fails is exactly where he fails as well, right at the heart of the matter – the origin of mimetic rivalry in acquisitive mimesis. Our point of departure is the object; we cannot stress this enough even though no one understands it, apparently. Yet it must be understood in order to make clear that we are not philosophizing.

One has only to read the episode in *Don Quixote* in which the barber's basin, because it is an object of mimetic rivalry, is transformed into Mambrino's helmet, in order to understand that Cervantes has an intuition which is entirely foreign to Plato or Hegel, the very intuition that makes literature suspect because it emphasizes, through comedy, the vanity of our conflicts. Similarly, during the classical period in England, Rymer's rationalist criticism, which was influenced by the French, reproached Shakespeare for building his tragic conflicts out of trivial events, or even out of literally nothing.[8] Such criticism sees a mark of inferiority in what constitutes the prodigious superiority of Shakespeare over most dramatists and over all philosophers.

I will not go so far as to say that Cervantes and Shakespeare reveal mimetic conflict in its entirety and leave us nothing to decipher. For the moment we can say that they know more than Plato because they place acquisitive mimesis in the foreground. Cervantes and Shakespeare therefore never experience the 'irrational' terror of mimesis (although they never underestimate it) that strikes Plato, and which is a direct inheritance from the sacred. In the sacred, of course, we will find no reflections on acquisitive mimesis and its infinite consequences.

However, we have no difficulty understanding the originary role of acquisitive mimesis, since the principal prohibitions, which we have not yet mentioned, always concern objects – the sexual or alimentary prohibitions, for example – that are nearest at hand and most accessible. These objects belong to a group living together, such as the women born into it or the food gathered by it; they are thus more susceptible to becoming a stake in rivalries that threaten the group's harmony or even its survival.

There is no prohibition that cannot be related to mimetic conflict, the principle of which we defined at the beginning of our investigations.

G. L.: Your constant use of the term *mimesis* will perhaps create certain misunderstandings.

R. G.: No doubt. It might be better to speak only of imitation. But modern theorists of imitation limit its scope to behaviours that depend on 'appearing', as Jean-Michel would say; that is, gestures, the modes of speech and behaviour, that conform to socially-recognized models. The modern use of the term, then, is restricted to modalities of imitation in which there is no risk of provoking conflict and which are representational only, on the order of the simulacrum.

This is not due to a simple 'error' or instance of 'forgetfulness'; it is rather a type of repression, the repression of mimetic conflict itself. Such repression contains something essential for all human cultures, even ours. Primitive societies repress mimetic conflict not only by prohibiting everything that might provoke it but also by dissimulating it beneath the major symbols of the sacred, such as contamination, pollution, etc. This repression is perpetuated among us, but in paradoxical ways. Instead of seeing imitation as a threat to social cohesion or as a danger to the community, we view it as a cause of conformity and gregariousness. We despise it rather than fear it. We are always 'against' imitation, though in a very different way from Plato; we have excluded it from just about everything, including our aesthetics. Our psychology, psychoanalysis, and even sociology, accommodate it only grudgingly. Our art and literature take great pains to resemble nothing and no one – mimetically. We have little idea of the possibilities for conflict contained in imitation. And neither the primitive prohibition nor Plato gives us any direct explanation of the fear of mimesis.

No one has ever seriously questioned the Platonic terror of mimesis. No one has ever asked serious questions about mimetic rivalry, even *whether it exists and in what areas*. In reality, mimesis is what the modern mind sees it as, the cohesive force *par excellence*, but it is not only that. Plato is right to see it as both a force of cohesion and a force of dissolution. But why is Plato right, if he is, and why is he never able to explain the contrary effects of one and the same force? If the question is valid, how should it be answered?

J.-M. O.: These are fundamental questions. Without mimesis there can be neither human intelligence nor cultural transmission. Mimesis is the essential force of cultural integration. Is it also the force of destruction and dissolution, as the evidence of prohibitions suggests?

R. G.: Contemporary thought unfortunately has little interest in these truly scientific questions. Critical and theoretical thought in France pursues the paradoxes of mimetic play on the level of the text with an extraordinary finesse, a dazzling virtuosity. But this is precisely where it encounters its limits. Too often French critics become intoxicated with their own verbal acrobatics, while the truly interesting questions go unasked or are even scorned in the name of purely metaphysical principles. There are better things to do at this point than endlessly amuse ourselves with paradoxes to which the great writers have already committed every resource in the domain of literature. The shimmer and play of mimesis are in themselves uninteresting. The only interesting task is to integrate all of this into a rational framework and transform it into real knowledge. This is the true vocation of thought, and in the end, after periods in which it appears to have run its course, this vocation is always reaffirmed; indeed the very abundance of material that becomes accessible to us makes it seem as though rational thought cannot cope and has become outmoded. When compared to earlier forms of religious thought, the modern use of the term *imitation* produces a corresponding but reversed and aggravated ignorance. Rather than the exhausted word *imitation*, then, I chose to employ the Greek word *mimesis*, without, however, adopting a Platonic theory of mimetic rivalry, which does not exist in any case. The only advantage of the Greek word is that it makes the conflictual aspect of mimesis conceivable, even if it never reveals its cause.

That cause, we repeat, is rivalry provoked by an object, the acquisitive mimesis which must always be our point of departure. We will see now that not only the prohibition but also ritual and ultimately the whole structure of religion can be traced back to the mechanism of acquisitive mimesis. A complete theory of human culture will be elaborated, beginning with this single principle.

J.-M. O.: To sum up, then, primitive peoples mistakenly think that the presence of twins or the pronouncing of a proper name will create violent doubles in the community, but their error is comprehensible. The error is related to something quite real, an extremely simple mechanism whose existence is undeniable and yet which gives rise to surprising complications; these, however, can be easily accounted for logically and observed in the interdividual and ethnological domains. One can understand therefore that actual prohibitions correspond to what one might expect of communities that would have experienced the full range of mimetic effects, from the most benign to the most terrible, and that would seek to avoid these effects like . . . the plague.

R. G.: Exactly.

J.-M. O.: But are not the differences between one culture and another too great to make a unified theory, such as yours, plausible? Surely some societies encourage or require precisely what others prohibit? Are there not also examples, in a single society, of actions that are normally prohibited being allowed or even required in certain circumstances?

R. G.: True, and what we have said thus far appears to be contradicted by other data. But if we are patient we will see that the contradiction can be explained. For the moment we have arrived at a fundamental principle, which is the antimimetic character of all prohibitions.

When all antimimetic prohibitions are considered as a whole, from those bearing on the most harmless act to the most terrible (the blood feud), it becomes apparent that they correspond roughly to the steps of an *escalation* of mimetic contagion that threatens more and more members of the community and tends towards progressively more aggravated forms of rivalry over objects which the community is incapable of dividing peacefully: women, food, weapons, the best dwelling-sites, etc.

Here again we observe a continuous process, and ethnologists, because they do not see the unity of the mimetic crisis and the necessity of avoiding it, tend to focus on specific prohibitions that appear to be independent of one another. In summary, prohibited objects are first of all those that might give rise to mimetic rivalry, then the behaviours characteristic of its progressively violent phases, finally individuals who appear to have 'symptoms' thought to be inevitably contagious, such as twins, adolescents at the stage of initiation, women during their menstrual period, or the sick and the dead, those excluded temporarily from the community.

G. L.: Does not ritual attest much more directly to the possibility of such a crisis?

The Function of Ritual: Imperative Mimesis

R. G.: This is indeed the point to begin a discussion of ritual. In moving from the prohibition to a consideration of this second great pillar of religion, we are able confirm our model's degree of correspondence to the concerns of religious societies; in this case the concern is not to avoid, but to reproduce the mimetic crisis. If the prohibition provides a rough sketch of the crisis, ritual places it sharply in relief. There can be no doubt that the mimetic crisis bedevils all of religious thought. In fact, as we will see later on, there are few myths that, when given a more complete description, do not make at least some allusion to it.

None of this presents much difficulty to the trained observer, for the mimetic process is literally one of culture difference being reversed, unravelled and effaced as it gives way to reciprocal violence.

G. L.: Here as before, then, we need to begin with acquisitive mimesis.

R. G.: Without hesitation. When ethnologists speak of role reversals accompanied by reciprocal parody, insults and mockery, degenerating at times into organized battle, they unknowingly describe the mimetic crisis.

G. L.: Ethnologists speak of rituals that consist in 'violating prohibitions'.

R. G.: Of course. If prohibitions are antimimetic, any ritual enactment of the mimetic crisis will necessarily consist in violating prohibitions. Keep in mind that we are describing a conflictual upheaval that destroys social organization. At the acute point in the crisis men violently dispute objects that are normally prohibited; ritual incest, meaning fornication with women one ordinarily has no right to touch, is therefore frequent.

G. L.: One can nonetheless oppose your reading of ritual by pointing to the existence of rituals that are non-violent and harmonious in character, which seem to be shaped by an aesthetic impulse.

R. G.: Certainly, but if you compare ethnological descriptions you will confirm that they offer no integrative term for the extent of variation throughout ritual, from brutality and unimaginable disorder at one extreme to serenity at the other. Yet there is little difficulty in locating all the necessary intermediary forms that together constitute a range without any break in continuity; we thus hypothesize that the development of ritual constitutes a normal evolution, because rituals consist in the paradox of transforming the conflictual disintegration of the community into social collaboration.

The expressions used by ethnologists reveal this continuity. In describing one end of the spectrum, they speak of 'mêlées', discordant clamour and frenetic charges. Then come the 'simulations of combat' and the rhythmic foot-stamping accompanied by 'war cries', which are transformed imperceptibly into 'martial songs'; there are then 'bellicose dances', which give way finally to simple dances and songs. The most delicately choreographed patterns, positions exchanged while partners remain face to face, mirroring effects – all of this can be read as the purified and schematized trace of past confrontations.

In order to reproduce a model of the mimetic crisis in a spirit of social harmony, the enactment must be progressively emptied of all real violence so that only the 'pure' form is allowed to survive. It is enough to observe such a form to conclude that it is always a matter of *doubles*, that is, partners in reciprocal imitation; the model of the most abstract ritual dances is always that of the confrontation of doubles, although it has been entirely 'aestheticized'.

This means that the least violent forms of ritual do not compromise the idea of a single conflictual model. In order to understand ritual it is necessary to begin with the most manifestly conflictual forms rather than with the most pacific; during an interregnum in certain African societies, for example, violence and anarchy lead to such a degree of social decomposition that ethnologists are unsure how to define the phenomenon and unable to decide if it should be seen as ritual repetition, a type of ordered disorder, or as an actual historic event with unforeseen consequences.

J.-M. O.: Your point, then, is that all prohibitions and rituals can be related to mimetic conflict. The common denominator is the same, but there is a paradox in that what is prohibited in one case is required in another. If the mimetic crisis is indeed as threatening as our reading of prohibitions leads us to believe, it would seem incomprehensible that the ritual should be an attempt to reproduce, often in a frighteningly realistic manner, precisely what societies fear the most in normal times, with an apparently well-justified fear.

There is no innocent, harmless mimesis, and one cannot ritually imitate the crisis of doubles without running the risk of inciting real violence.

R. G.: You have given a fine presentation of the extraordinary paradox constituted by the juxtaposition of prohibitions and rituals in all religious societies. If ethnology has until now failed to solve the enigma of religion it is because it has never completely uncovered this paradox, and the latter failure in turn is due to the fact that ethnologists have always been able to find in religion itself the means to elude or lessen the degree of paradox. This does not mean that the paradox does not exist, but rather that religious consciousness is capable of reaching a stage at which, as with us, it finds this paradox intolerable and unthinkable; it then attempts to *arrange things*, to soften the edge of contradiction, whether by making prohibitions less stringent, by moderating the ritual crisis, or by doing both things at once. Instead of minimizing the opposition between prohibition and ritual, instead of blurring the distinction – which amounts to following the procedure of religion itself, as, for example, in viewing a celebration as simply a temporary and joyous vacation from the prohibition – we ought to heighten the opposition and stress its mystery; we should admit that we simply do not understand why these things happen in this way.

Primitive societies abandon themselves, in their rituals, to what they fear most during normal periods: the dissolution of the community in the mimetic crisis.

J.-M. O.: If mimesis is a power that is at once irresistible and insidious, as both individual psychopathology and religious precautions against pollution suggest, then the ritual looks like an invitation to disaster. Either we will have to dismiss the theory of mimesis or we will have to suppose that religious systems have good reason for engaging in transgression. What could these reasons be?

R. G.: The paradox we have pointed to becomes even more extraordinary in rituals that have no fixed calendar date but are enacted in order to avert the immediate threat of a crisis.

Just as in French folklore the character Gribouille seeks shelter from the rain in a river, communities throw themselves deliberately, it seems, into the evil they fear most and believe that by doing so they will somehow escape it. Religious institutions that are ordinarily quite cautious can act with unbelievable temerity in times of crisis. They not only abandon their habitual precautions, they conscientiously mimic their own dissolution in mimetic hysteria; it is as if they believed that a simulated disintegration might ward off the real disintegration. But the distinction is dangerous: it is in effect the very difference between the original and the copy that is compromised by the religious conception of mimesis.

G. L.: Certain theories support the functional aspect of ritual. The techniques that consist in the collective mimicking of conflict might indeed have the beneficial effect of deflecting the participants' desire away from the actions that might cause real violence.

R. G.: I also believe there is a functional aspect to ritual, but then it is never guaranteed; there are rituals that give way to real disorder. Yet what must be understood above all is that the existence of an institution can never be fully explained in terms of its efficacy in any domain. We do not want to fall back into the naivety of functionalism.

The mystery is that societies that usually react to a certain danger by attempting to evade it should suddenly reverse their tactics, particularly when the danger seems acute, and take up the opposite strategy, the one that ought to terrify them the most. Whatever the answer, it is really impossible to imagine that the cradle of human cultures was once watched over, as by the legendary good fairy, by a distinguished group of ethnopsychiatrists, who, in their infinite wisdom, endowed these cultures with ritual practices and institutions.

No science or doctrine is capable of a complete invention of ritual and none would be able to construe spontaneously systems that are as constant beneath their apparent differences as are humanity's religious systems.

In order to resolve the problem we must take care not to exclude any aspect of the institution we are trying to understand. Yet in limiting our study of ritual to the mimetic crisis we have excluded something that normally takes place in rituals and often functions as their conclusion. This conclusion consists generally in the immolation of an animal or human victim.

Sacrifice and the Victimage Mechanism

G. L.: Are there no rituals that conclude without sacrifice?

R. G.: There are. The conclusion of a ritual might be limited to ritual mutilation or to exorcism, but these are always the equivalent of sacrifice. Yet there are also ritual or post-ritual forms that include no sacrifice whatsoever, not even of a symbolic kind. We ought to defer this question for the time being, however, for otherwise we risk losing our way in too many digressions. Our line of argument will not be convincing until it has been followed through to the end, so I will not be able to respond to any and every objection that occurs to you along the way. The one you have just raised is extremely important because of its relation to the problem of the disappearance of sacrifice from the cultural institutions that emerged from it and that depend on it for their very existence. We will take up this problem another time.

J.-M. O.: We were talking about sacrifice.

R. G.: If rituals conclude with sacrifice, it must be that to religious societies the sacrifice seems like the conclusion of the mimetic crisis enacted by the ritual. In many rituals everyone assembled is required to participate in an immolation that might easily be mistaken for a sort of lynching. Even when the sacrifice is performed by a single person, that person usually acts in the name of everyone involved. The community affirms its unity in the sacrifice, a unity that emerges from the moment when division is most intense, when the community enacts its dissolution in the mimetic crisis and its abandonment to the endless cycle of vengeance. But suddenly the opposition of everyone against everyone else is replaced by the opposition of all against one. Where previously there had been a chaotic ensemble of particular conflicts, there is now the simplicity of a single conflict: the entire community on one side, and on the other, the victim. The nature of this sacrificial resolution is not difficult to comprehend; the community finds itself unified once more at the expense of a victim who is not only incapable of self-defence but is also unable to provoke any reaction of vengeance; the immolation of such a victim would never create fresh conflict or augment the crisis, since the victim has unified the community in its opposition. The sacrifice is simply another act of violence, one that is added to a succession of others, but it is the final act of violence, its last word.

In certain sacrifices the victim becomes an object of such hostility one must believe that it and it alone has been held responsible for the entire mimetic crisis. It might be subject to insults and physical abuse before being killed. The real question is this: How is such unity against the victim possible in so many divers rituals? What force unites the collective against the victim?

G. L.: In *Totem and Taboo*, Freud answers that the victim is the father of the primal horde. According to Freud all ritual preserves the memory of the one murder that founded culture.

R. G.: Everything that Freud says on this subject is worthy of careful

examination; for Freud, having taken into account ethnological observations that are less outdated than people think, is unique in having
understood the necessity of real collective murder as a model of sacrifice. All the same his response is not viable. His single murder, which
occurs only once for all time, cannot explain the repetition of rituals.

Freud does a poor job of situating this murder, by the way, when he
places it at the beginning of the ritual sequence. The rituals that bear
him out are rare and are examples of a reversal of the normal order. The
normal sequence is the one we are in the process of describing. The
mimetic process occurs before the collective murder, which constitutes
at once its paroxysm and its conclusion.

The idea that a group would gather to immolate any sort of victim in
order to commemorate the 'guilt' they still feel for a prehistoric murder
is purely mythical. What is not purely mythical, by contrast, is the idea
that men would immolate victims because an original, spontaneous
murder had in fact unified the community and put an end to a real mimetic crisis. In this light, ritual becomes comprehensible as an attempt
to avert the real threat of crisis; the crisis would be reproduced not for
its own sake but for the sake of its resolution; it would be a matter of
achieving what is perceived to be the only satisfactory resolution to any
crisis, past, present or future. This would resolve the paradox confronting us. There would be no contradiction in intent between prohibitions
and rituals; prohibitions attempt to avert the crisis by prohibiting those
behaviours that provoke it, and if the crisis recurs nonetheless, or threatens to do so, ritual then attempts to channel it in a direction that would
lead to resolution, which means a reconciliation of the community at
the expense of what one must suppose to be an arbitrary victim. In fact
no individual victim can ever be responsible for the mimetic crisis.

Only an arbitrary victim can resolve the crisis because acts of violence, as mimetic phenomena, are identical and distributed as such
within the community. No one can assign an origin to the crisis or judge
degrees of responsibility for it. Yet the *surrogate victim* will eventually
appear and reconcile the community; the sheer escalation of the crisis,
linked to progressively accumulating mimetic effects, will make the
designation of such a victim automatic.

J.-M. O.: I find this hard to follow. You assert that the mimetic
crisis, an anarchy of conflict and violence in a community, not only can
but must end with a certain type of arbitrary resolution. It would mean

that the resolution is something like a natural mechanism. This seems to me to be a difficult point in your theory, one that requires clarification.

R. G.: It is necessary to think through the logic of mimetic conflict and its resulting violence. As rivalry becomes acute, the rivals are more apt to forget about whatever objects are, in principle, the cause of the rivalry and instead to become more fascinated with one another. In effect the rivalry is purified of any external stake and becomes a matter of pure rivalry and prestige. Each rival becomes for his counterpart the worshipped and despised model and obstacle, the one who must be at once beaten and assimilated.

At this point mimesis is stronger than ever but no longer exerts any force at the level of the object; the object has simply dropped from view. Only the antagonists remain; we designate them as doubles because from the point of view of the antagonism, nothing distinguishes them.

If the object is excluded there can no longer be any acquisitive mimesis as we have defined it. There is no longer any support for mimesis but the antagonists themselves. What will occur at the heart of the crisis will therefore be the mimetic substitution of antagonists.

If *acquisitive mimesis* divides by leading two or more individuals to converge on one and the same object with a view to appropriating it, *conflictual mimesis* will inevitably unify by leading two or more individuals to converge on one and the same adversary that all wish to strike down.

Acquisitive mimesis is contagious, and if the number of individuals polarized around a single object increases, other members of the community, as yet not implicated, will tend to follow the example of those who are; conflictual mimesis necessarily follows the same course because the same force is involved. Once the object has disappeared and the mimetic frenzy has reached a high degree of intensity, one can expect conflictual mimesis to take over and snowball in its effects. Since the power of mimetic attraction multiplies with the number of those polarized, it is inevitable that at one moment the entire community will find itself unified against a single individual. Conflictual mimesis therefore creates a *de facto* allegiance against a common enemy, such that the conclusion of the crisis is nothing other than the reconciliation of the community.

Except in certain cases, there is no telling what insignificant reason will lead mimetic hostility to converge on one particular victim rather than on another; yet the victim will not appear to be any less absolutely unique and different, a result not only of the hate-filled idolatry to which the victim is subject, but also and especially of the effects of the reconciliation created by the unanimous polarization.

The community satisfies its rage against an arbitrary victim in the unshakable conviction that it has found the one and only cause of its trouble. It then finds itself without adversaries, purged of all hostility against those for whom, a second before, it had shown the most extreme rage.

The return to a calmer state of affairs appears to confirm the responsibility of the victim for the mimetic discord that had troubled the community. The community thinks of itself as entirely passive *vis-à-vis* its own victim, whereas the latter appears, by contrast, to be the only active and responsible agent in the matter. Once it is understood that the inversion of the real relation between victim and community occurs in the resolution of the crisis, it is possible to see why the victim is believed to be *sacred*. The victim is held responsible for the renewed calm in the community and for the disorder that preceded this return. It is even believed to have brought about its own death.

J.-M. O.: Perhaps we ought to try to sum up your presentation. Once acquisitive mimesis has produced a sufficient degree of division and conflict it is transformed into conflictual mimesis, which tends to have the contrary effect of grouping and unifying the community. The structure of rituals the world over suggests that it is a question of a necessary rather than accidental evolution, one linked to the nature of the crisis and to that of mimesis. Is this resolution an inevitable occurrence?

R. G.: It is impossible to say, but I am inclined to think not. It is possible to think that numerous human communities have disintegrated under the pressure of a violence that never led to the mechanism I have just described. But the observation of religious systems forces us to conclude (1) that the mimetic crisis always occurs, (2) that the banding together of all against a single victim is the normal resolution at the level of culture, and (3) that it is furthermore the normative resolution, because all the rules of culture stem from it.

J.-M. O.: All of them?

R. G.: In order to understand primitive rules, prohibitions and rituals, one must postulate a mimetic crisis of such duration and severity that the sudden resolution, at the expense of a single victim, has the effect of a miraculous deliverance. The experience of a supremely evil and then beneficent being, whose appearance and disappearance are punctuated by collective murder, cannot fail to be literally *gripping*. The community that was once so terribly stricken suddenly finds itself free of antagonism, completely delivered.

It is therefore comprehensible that such a community would be henceforth wholly animated by a desire for peace, and bent on preserving the miraculous calm apparently granted to it by the fearful and benign being that had somehow descended upon it. The community will thus direct all future action under the sign of that being, as if carrying out the instructions it had left.

In summary, the community attempts to consolidate its fragile hold on things under the still strong impressions of the crisis and its resolution, believing itself to be under the guidance of the victim itself. Clearly, two principal imperatives must come into play. (1) Not to repeat any action associated with the crisis, to abstain from all mimicry, from all contact with the former antagonists, from any acquisitive gesture toward objects that have stood as causes or pretexts for rivalry. This is the imperative of the prohibition. (2) To reproduce, on the contrary, the miraculous event that put an end to the crisis, to immolate new victims substituted for the original victim in circumstances as close as possible to the original experience. This is the imperative of ritual.

Human beings do not understand the mechanism responsible for their reconciliation; the secret of its effectiveness eludes them, which is why they attempt to reproduce the entire event as exactly as possible. They realize that the saving event had not come into play until the paroxysm of the fratricidal struggle. This paroxysm and the unanimous resolution form a whole that religious thought for the most part refuses to disconnect, understanding that it is indissoluble. It is here we must look if we are to understand the conflictual madness, the cultural undifferentiation that constitutes the initial phase of many rituals, the preparation for sacrifice.

Lévi-Strauss believes that the aim of ritual is to achieve undifferentiation for its own sake. But this is far from being the case; the crisis is seen simply as a means to assure differentiation. There is no reason whatsoever to consign all rituals to the realm of nonsense, as Lévi-Strauss does. Order in human culture certainly does arise from an extreme of disorder, for such disorder is the disappearance of any and all contested objects in the midst of conflict, and it is at such a point that acquisitive mimesis is transformed into conflictual mimesis and tends toward the unification of conflict against an adversary. Lévi-Strauss is mistaken in expelling ritual from his structuralist seminar. The disorderly pupil knows more about order and disorder than the professor.[9]

In initiation rites, for example, undifferentiation is equivalent to the loss of a previous identity, a particularity that has now been annulled. The ritual at first emphasizes and aggravates this loss; in fact, it is made as complete as possible, not because of any supposed 'nostalgia for the immediate', as Lévi-Strauss would say, but in order to facilitate for the initiate the acquisition of a new identity, of a definitive differentiation. Baptismal rites clearly represent submersion in undifferentiation, from which something better differentiated then emerges. The most humble adherents of all the world's religions have always known this; it might happen that an initiate drowns but it is never in order to drown that one submits to baptism.

J.-M. O.: Are you not coming rather close to a mystical definition of ritual?

R. G.: Not at all, since I realize that the *experience* of initiation offers only a particular perspective on the mimetic crisis, and this for identifiable reasons. The aim is to make the initiate undergo as severe a crisis as possible so that *the salutary effect of sacrifice will be released for his benefit*. This is why an initiate is occasionally lost wherever rites of initiation are truly alive, and for the same reason a fear for the life of initiates is often feigned in circumstances in which the ritual has lost its power.

G. L.: There can be no doubt that your theory resolves the apparent contradiction between the antimimetic prohibitions on the one hand and the enactment of the mimetic crisis in ritual on the other hand. In the latter case the crisis is not enacted for its own sake; its purpose is to provoke the sacrificial resolution. And if the theory of mimesis is correct, there is reason behind the apparent belief, evident in all ritual, that a paroxysm of disorder is necessary if the resolution is to occur. Rituals and prohibitions can be seen as directed toward the same end, which is the renewed order and peace that emerge from the victimage mechanism; the prohibition and the ritual attempt in different ways to ensure that peace.

R. G.: Prohibitions attempt to achieve this directly by prohibiting everything that touches on or appears to touch on the crisis, whereas rituals make the same attempt through the intermediary of the collective mechanism, which they attempt to release each time. One can thus understand the recourse to ritual whenever a real crisis threatens; there is no paradox in a disease that cures a disease. It is a question of augmenting the forces of destructive mimesis in order to channel them toward the sacrificial resolution. There is no difference in this between the so-called rites of passage and other rituals. The model that functions in order to perpetuate the status quo is also the model of change, which in any case functions to bring about the return of the same. The crisis must simply be replayed in order to bring about the resolution with its desired effects. The fact that contemporary thought is unable to make sense of these mechanisms does nothing to change their existence or the fact that they have existed as long as our world has been a world. Moreover, in a certain sense this inability of contemporary thought to make sense of the crisis and its resolution does it honour and clears the way for a rational revelation that structuralism is still incapable of apprehending. In the end such limitation is preferable to any vaguely mystical syncretism or pantheism, which, in the name of 'human nature' but nonetheless as direct descendants of the gods of violence, submit themselves all too easily to the mechanism of the sacred. I understand and share Lévi-Strauss's distaste for that sort of attitude.

The Theory of Religion

J.-M. O.: It seems impossible to solve any problem in the domain of religion without sooner or later being confronted with the opposite problem. In certain religious systems the antimimetic character of prohibitions is quite evident, as is the mimetic crisis in ritual. Behind this contradiction, as you show, there is a shared intent. That much is clear so far, but it still does not explain why this contradiction, if it is as justified as it seems, is so attenuated in certain religions, or in others seems to have disappeared altogether.

R. G.: You raised this same objection not long ago, and now we are prepared to answer it. As long as the memory of the original experience is vivid, religious thought has little difficulty with the contradiction between an enforced enactment of the crisis on the one hand and the prohibition of everything associated with it on the other hand. Perhaps the contradiction is not even noticed. It will become problematic, however, as soon as the original function of the ritual begins to fade.

The elaboration of religious thought never ceases; it will tend to minimize or if possible to suppress what it comes to experience as a logical contradiction—which of course is also our experience, as long as we cannot conceive of ritual in its own context as constituted by the will to reproduce the victimage mechanism. Well before the arrival of ethnologists, then, the type of ignorance in which their thought typically thrives was already well established, and it continues to further the development of late religious thought in ways that seem to us more intelligible, logical, and even more 'natural' than what has preceded it.

Such distortions are likely to occur even at the heart of religious systems, and they will tend to *rationalize* religious practice by softening the prohibitions, by moderating the rituals, or by doing both at once. The system will tend to unify itself under the aegis of a logic that corresponds neither to its origin nor to its *raison d'être*. This evolution, proceeding on its apparently rational course, will do much to deceive ethnologists and provide them with convenient arguments for denying the kind of origin I propose and for considering even the most revelatory rituals as aberrations in that one, vast aberration that we call religion. With a little patience and observation, however, one will always be able to pick up the trail that returns to the violent origin.

J.-M. O.: Before continuing, we ought to bring up several objections to points in *Violence and the Sacred*. Someone has said, for example, that the mechanism of the 'scapegoat' is too insubstantial and insignificant to be able to account for phenomena as important as major aspects of religion.[10]

R. G.: The objection ignores a number of things. The first is the mimetic nature of conflict, which is to say the ultimate absence of any object proper to it. Nothing is more difficult than admitting the final nullity of human conflict. Of course it can be somewhat more easily done with the conflicts of others, but when it comes to our own it is nearly impossible. *All* modern ideologies are immense machines that justify and legitimate conflicts that in our time could put an end to humanity. The whole madness of the human being is there. If it is not possible to admit to the madness of human conflict today, it will never be possible. If conflict is mimetic, an equally mimetic resolution will leave no residue; an entire community can be purged of violence precisely because *there is no object*. (This is not to say that *all* human conflicts occur without the involvement of real objects.)

Some object that the reconciliatory effect of the surrogate victim can only be temporary. While this is true, there is absolutely no question of attributing everything to the scapegoat effect. Culture does not proceed directly from the reconciliation that follows victimage; rather it is from the double imperative of prohibition and ritual, which means that the entire community is unified in order to avoid falling back into the crisis, and thus orients itself on the model—and the anti-model—which the crisis and its resolution now constitute. To understand human culture it is necessary to concede that only the damming of mimetic forces by means of the prohibition and the diversion of these forces in the direction of ritual are capable of spreading and perpetuating the reconciliatory effect of the surrogate victim. Religion is nothing other than this immense effort to keep the peace. *The sacred is violence*, but if religious man worships violence it is only insofar as the worship of violence is supposed to bring peace; religion is entirely concerned with peace, but the means it has of bringing it about are never free of sacrificial violence. To see in my theory some sort of 'cult of violence', approval of sacrifice, or, at the other extreme, a blanket condemnation of human culture, is to miss the point entirely.

Religion always scandalizes in periods of decomposition because the violence that had entered into its composition is revealed as such and loses its reconciliatory power. Human beings are soon moved to make religion itself into a new scapegoat, failing to realize once more that the violence is theirs. To expel religion is, as always, a religious gesture—as much so today when the sacred is loathed and abhorred as in the past when it was worshipped and adored. All attitudes that do not recognize the founding victim are never anything more than opposing errors, doubles that eternally exchange the same gesture without ever 'hitting the mark' and collapsing the structure of sacrificial misrecognition.

G. L.: There is still another reason for the misunderstanding to which you refer. In order to shed light on the process of the founding victim, it seems that we ought to seek out phenomena that resemble the process and that might give us some insight. . .

R. G.: If these phenomena were identical to those that produce religion, they would still be producing it today and we would have no way of identifying them objectively any more than those who live within primitive religion are able to identify them. Modern society no longer produces religion in the sense of the systems that we are currently studying. For reasons that we have not yet discussed but that we shall bring up soon, the founding mechanism functions much less well than in the past, even if it has not completely ceased functioning. We speak of the 'scapegoat' not only in the sense of the ritual in Leviticus[11] and analogous rituals, but also in the sense of a spontaneous psychological mechanism. No other society, I believe, has been capable of such an insight. This unusual aptitude deserves some reflection. In fact I take this to be the essential task of ethnology, the one it has always avoided. I employ the phrase *surrogate victim* only for the spontaneous mechanism.

J.-M. O.: Our knowledge of the phenomena under discussion is increasing but remains unclear and full of controversy. Our present discussion would be impossible outside of this specifically modern situation.

R. G.: We have said that the ability of the victimage mechanism to produce the sacred depends entirely on the extent to which the mechanism is misinterpreted. In a society in which everyone knows at least vaguely what a 'scapegoat' is, given that national, ideological, or personal adversaries are constantly being accused of 'looking for a scapegoat', the mechanism is to all evidence still there but has lost much of its power to accomplish, as effectively as in the past, the role that human culture has assigned to it, or rather that it has assigned to human culture.

J.-M. O.: Your point, then, is that we can find phenomena in our midst that are *sufficiently analogous* to give us some understanding of the phenomena that must be postulated behind forms of religion, but *not enough so* to enable us to assimilate the two. In our society such phenomena are always touched with a certain self-knowledge that checks their full expression and any re-creation of true religious systems. Therefore, to assert that 'scapegoat mechanisms are not capable of founding human culture' is to misunderstand the theory. The scapegoat mechanism can be compared to the proverbial Freudian tip of the iceberg—the submerged portion is by far the more significant. But what is submerged in this case is not an individual or collective unconscious, it is rather an immemorial history, properly speaking, a diachronic dimension that remains inaccessible to modes of contemporary thought.

R. G.: I could not have put it better myself. The production of the sacred is necessarily and inversely proportional to the understanding of the mechanisms that produce it. And we must recognize that the grain of knowledge in the mechanism of the surrogate victim does not mean that there will be no more victims, for the opposite is more likely. We cannot afford to be happy optimists. The more radical the crisis of the sacrificial system becomes, the more men will be tempted to multiply victims in order to accede, finally, to the same effects.

In *Violence and the Sacred* I did not sufficiently stress the danger of vague analogies. What is interesting in our work here is not the possibility of making impressionistic applications of the theory in order to denounce any aspect of society we please; rather, our purpose is to produce a rigorous reading of prohibitions and rituals, a reading made possible by the postulate of an intact mechanism of unanimous victimage functioning at a maximum degree of its potential, which must have constituted the normal condition for humanity during most of its existence. The paradox is that this normal condition is not directly observable.

But it is precisely because this condition is not directly observable that our thesis must be defined as a hypothesis. The term does not in the least imply that 'I don't believe it myself', as a gentleman, who must never have heard of what one calls a scientific hypothesis, once suggested in *The Times Literary Supplement*.

Our hypothesis makes sense, since the functioning of the mechanism can be easily accounted for by reasoning. One can then easily verify that all religious institutions, all notions included in religion, such as the sacred, divinity, etc., correspond to what one might reasonably expect from the mechanism if the cultures misinterpret its operation along the lines we have suggested.

In order to understand the necessity of this hypothesis and in order to justify it, one must also consider the silence that in our society surrounds all intensely mimetic phenomena. Wherever social integration is only partially complete or in a state of regression, phenomena such as trance states or possession occur frequently and attain a quasi-normal status within the human group, provided that the latter agrees to accept them.

J.-M. O.: Without denying the existence of these phenomena, we tend to minimize them or to reduce them to the modern notion of *hypnosis*; we classify them as belonging to a strictly limited category consisting of medical consultation, therapeutic application, or simple entertainment. Such classification is obviously determined by what we call our individualism or our rationalism, which is to say our misunderstanding of mimesis. We will take this up again later.

R.G.: The comparative study of ritual and non-ritual trances and other religious phenomena suggests that the accelerated reciprocity of mimetic reactions within the human group can alter not only the relations among the participants, which become *interdividual*, as we will suggest, rather than *interindividual*—that is, which progress beyond the point at which ego and other can still be meaningfully distinguished—but also perception as a whole, causing mixing and interference effects that determine the composite nature of ritual *masks* as well as the monstrosity of mythological creatures. The so-called cults of possession attempt to reproduce the mimetic trance and its conclusion in victimage because they view this, justifiably it seems, as a fundamental religious experience. Hallucination and perceptual scrambling can only favour the transition from acquisitive and then conflictual mimesis to the reconciliatory mimesis centred around a single antagonist (the scapegoat). The victim polarizes and *arrests* the hallucinatory phenomena. This is why the primitive deity is quintessentially *monstrous*.

G. L.: No one ever makes a systematic attempt to relate such indices to one another. People object that they stem from too many disciplines at once: ethnology, psychopathology, group psychology, etc. There is no single discipline that can accommodate all such phenomena, which means that we are either unwilling or unable to devote genuine attention to them.

R. G.: There can be no doubt that for many of us such phenomena provoke an indefinable but certainly unwelcome feeling. Taken together they constitute the 'undifferentiation' that horrifies and exasperates the structuralist, even though he can never do without it and must make it the obligatory backdrop of all his differentiating activity.

However, there is no reason to suppose any ideological plot to 'suppress' these things, or any obscure but faultless vigilance in the inevitable 'unconscious'. It is time to abandon all these Marxist and

Freudian bogymen, who are rather worn and moth-eaten, like mythology itself, precisely because they constitute little more than a modern return to ritual monstrosity rather than its rational interpretation. I think that our world can be characterized, for reasons not yet defined but that will continue to occupy us, by a historically unprecedented release from the power of mimetic effects on individuals and even larger groups. I would emphasize that I mean a lull, and not a complete release.

This release is extremely important but remains ambiguous in all respects, particularly in the sense of the self-knowledge of which it is capable. In spite of its unusual extension, over the last three centuries especially, its character remains elusive. For if it does in fact increase our ability to observe mimetic phenomena clearly without being 'contaminated' by them, and therefore allows us to study them scientifically, it begins by making these phenomena disappear, or by changing them. It removes what is by definition most essential to the observation it has enabled us to perform.

We would assert that this release is responsible for the current prevalence of 'psychopathology' where once there was a question of ritual trance. (This does not mean that there were no pathological phenomena.) Probably an initial release of the same kind was responsible, with the Greeks, for the transition from ritual trance to the theatrical universe. In our own time one tends to interpret ritual possession as a theatrical phenomenon, as Michel Leiris does in his study of the Ethiopians. We find the reverse intuition in Shakespeare, however, one that is rare and infinitely more radical, for it locates the source of all theatrical effects or of any 'identity crisis' in violent mimetic conflict, the source common to all mythology and collective murder, even in its most historical instances, notably that of Julius Caesar, the founder of the Roman empire.

Probably no text is more decisive concerning the phenomena of violent and collective mimesis than *A Midsummer Night's Dream*, but no one has yet been able to explicate fully the extraordinary message that this text contains.

I repeat that we must beware of basing our thinking about the founding mechanisms of religion on what we know or think we know about 'scapegoat' phenomena. We must attempt the reverse. We should recognize that in contemporary phenomena of violence and collective suggestion, which are incapable of attaining the true sacred, we are confronted with remnants that, due to this incapacity, are all the more threatening in terms of violence.

Religious phenomena are essentially characterized by the double transference, the aggressive transference followed by the reconciliatory transference. The reconciliatory transference sacralizes the victim and is the one most fragile, most easily lost, since to all evidence it does not occur until the mechanism has completely 'played itself out'. We remain capable, in other words, of hating our victims; we are no longer capable of worshipping them.

It will soon be possible to gain a scientific understanding of these areas, and I want to stress its scientific nature. Even though we no longer have examples of the true sacred, it can nonetheless be observed in surviving, vestigial forms, which, although difficult to discern, allow confirmation of the actual structural processes.

In the example of people who habitually attract wide public notice, such as political leaders, celebrities, notorious criminals, etc., we can easily observe the phenomenon known in psychoanalysis as ambivalence. This so-called ambivalence consists first of all in attributing excessive responsibility for currents of public opinion and sentiment to figures who have been artificially isolated or placed in the spotlight. Without such symbolic individuality it would impossible for collective movements to crystallize or achieve any self-awareness, a process that never occurs without a certain inversion of roles in the relation between the collectivity and the individual, between the active element and the passive subject.

Because the popular imagination tends to polarize its hopes and enthusiasms, and of course its fears and anxieties, around a chosen individual, the power of the individual in question seems to multiply infinitely, for good or ill. Such an individual does not represent the collectivity in an abstract manner, but rather represents the state of turmoil, restlessness, or calm of the collectivity at any given moment of representation.

It is clear, in any case, that in our time the kinds of transference that one could call beneficent have become increasingly weak, sporadic, and ephemeral; they are also scorned by intellectuals, whereas malevolent kinds of transference have extraordinary power and are denounced only selectively. There is always a favoured malevolent transference which is exempt from criticism, and any criticism of it is even held to be immoral: it is the ideological opponent, the class enemy, the older generation or the fools that govern us, the ethnic minorities, the ethnic majority, the misinformed, etc.

There can be no question that the distinguishing features of various malevolent transferences are in the process of breaking down. The antagonism of the doubles reappears in the midst of ideologies that were once the most solidly monolithic—the Russian or Chinese, for example—and deprives millions of the certainty guaranteed by a fixed adversary, by the abominable difference that in turn made possible the integrity and specificity of the positive difference, although the latter has become increasingly secondary and tributary to the former.

J.-M. O.: For the genuine sacred, by contrast, the beneficent and reconciliatory element plays a more important role. The aggressive transference is covered almost entirely by the reconciliatory transference, but not to the extent that the former disappears entirely. This is the reason for our inability to achieve a complete understanding of ritual. I take it that in your view the same thing holds true for myth.

R. G.: Exactly the same thing. In myth, below the level of sacralization, it is easy to uncover the accusation of which the victim was the object. The accusation makes the victim responsible for the disorder and catastrophe, in other words for the crisis, that afflicts the community. The ritual mistreatment of many victims prior to their immolation is related to this. Such mistreatment demonstrates clearly that the sacrifice is never, in its ultimate purpose, a purely symbolic gesture. It is an aggressive reaction against a victim that would not be killed if it were not held responsible for the mimetic crisis.

In myth as well as in ritual, then, the victim—the hero—is killed as the one responsible for crimes that are synonymous with the disintegration of the community. Just as in ritual the central action is often the collective murder of the victim, so in myth the central scene is the murder, again often collective, of the divine hero. One wonders how students of mythology manage to ignore indications as decisive as these and assert that myth and ritual have nothing to do with one another, particularly when such an assertion runs counter to the entire ethnological tradition and, before that, to the religious tradition.[12]

G. L.: Yet there are myths that portray an individual murder.

R. G.: Certainly, but then it is almost always a matter of two brothers or enemy twins, such as Cain and Abel or Romulus and Remus, who at once mask and reveal the universal antagonism of doubles at the height of a crisis. One of the brothers must die in order for the doubles to disappear, in other words in order to provide for the reappearance of difference and the subsequent founding of the city. The murderer is individual but represents the entire community in that he has escaped the conflict of the doubles.

G. L.: There are also myths in which no murder takes place at all, such as the myth of Noah, for example.

R. G.: True, but in that myth there is a single survivor of an entire community doomed to death. In other words we are still dealing with an all-against-one structure, in this example, but reversed, and the reversal makes sense in terms of the mimetic theory in one of its most commonly inverted forms. The sacralized victim represents less of a loss of life than a return to life and the founding of a new community, which is clearly the case in the myth of the flood. The victim is the principle of survival. But let us leave mythology for the time being; we will return to a fuller discussion of it later.[13]

G. L.: The genesis of prohibitions, of rituals, of myths and of the power of the sacred is traced from an origin in the moment of founding violence. It is generally thought today that such a reduction of all religious phenomena to a single mechanism is impossible.

R. G.: Ethnologists have worked for a long time on problems connected with the sacred without achieving any decisive results. But to conclude in a peremptory way that religion cannot constitute a single enigma is simply to declare that no one shall succeed where all of ethnology has previously failed. In reality, one discovers in religion a mixture of recurring and non-recurring traits, which are nonetheless always related to one another and that suggest, to the scientific mind, possibilities of reduction.

G. L.: There are people who dislike precisely this reductive character of your theory.

R. G.: I am afraid I have no reply. On this point I am in full agreement with Lévi-Strauss. Scientific inquiry is reductive or it is nothing at all.

To these people, it seems, the diversity of sacrificial forms is as precious as the three hundred varieties of French cheese. To each his own. We are not engaged in the same intellectual enterprise. It seems to me to be a sign of decadence in the human sciences to allow an invasion by the spirit of a certain literary criticism. Yet even in literary criticism there is nothing more banal and mystifying, finally, than the obsessive emphasis on the infinite diversity of literary works, on their ineffable and inexhaustible character, on the impossibility of repeating the same interpretation—on the negation of any definite statement, in other words. I cannot see in this anything more than a huge unionization of failure. We must perpetuate at any cost the interminable discourse that earns us a living.

G. L.: A harsh judgment.

R. G.: It is certainly too harsh, but we live in an intellectual universe that is all the more conformist for its belief in possessing a monopoly on nonconformist views and methods. That much obviates any genuine self-criticism. Time is spent breaking down doors that have been wide open for centuries. This is still the modern war on prohibitions that rages on all fronts, whereas it was already ridiculous during the surrealist period. As in the Greek Buphonia, we keep stuffing the old and dried sacrificial skins with straw and standing them up in order to beat them down for the thousandth time.

J.-M. O.: This game belongs to the continuing process of the degeneration of the old sacred. In order to give it a *coup de grâce*, one has to believe it contains a *hidden* scapegoat.

R. G.: We have seen that, in the founding murder, the victim is held responsible for the crisis; the victim polarizes the growing mimetic conflicts that tear the community apart; the victim breaks the vicious cycle of violence and becomes the single pole for what then becomes a unifying, ritual mimesis.

The experience of disorder and the return to order, for which such a victim is made responsible constitute an experience too intolerable and incomprehensible to allow for rational understanding. Since the victim seems to be capable of first causing the most disastrous disorder and then of re-establishing order or inaugurating a new order, it seems legitimate to return to that victim whenever it is a question of deciding what one must and must not do, as in ritual and prohibitions, the resolution and the crisis.

This *knowledge* will then take precedence over all else. It is logical to think that the victim has shown itself only for the purpose of giving this knowledge to the community; it is logical to think that the terrifying aspect of the epiphany is designed to impress in all hearts and minds the rules that the deity wants established. The deity appears to be the founder of either a particular cult devoted to it or of the society itself. We can therefore understand why in so many myths the rules of culture spring directly from the body of the victim.

If, as a present and living member of the community the victim brought death, and if, once dead, the victim brought life to the community, one will inevitably be led to believe that its ability to transcend the ordinary limits of the human in good and evil extends to life and death. If the victim possesses a life that is death and a death that is life, it must be that the basic facts of the human condition have no hold on the sacred. In this we witness the first outlines of religious transcendence.

Our hypothesis explains not only why prohibitions and rituals exist everywhere, but also why all cultures attribute their foundation to supernatural powers which are also believed to demand respect for *the rules that they transgress*, and to sanction their transgression with the most terrible punishments.

These punishments are quite real. The transgression of religious prohibitions does in fact increase the risk of renewing the cycle of mimetic rivalry and vengeance. Religious systems form a whole in this sense, such that the infraction of any particular rule, no matter how absurd it may seem objectively, constitutes a challenge to the entire community. It becomes an act of hubris capable of provoking violence, for others will be tempted to accuse the wrongdoer or to imitate and surpass the transgression. In either case mimetic rivalry is reintroduced into the community. In societies that do not have penal systems capable of halting the spread of mimetic rivalry and its escalation into a vicious circle of violence, the religious system performs this very real function.

J.-M. O.: The return of vengeance, then, is said to be divine retribution. This would be how the religious imagination sees the deterioration in human relations resulting from a lack of respect for the religious system: that is why a divinity can be called *vengeful*.

R. G.: If the mimetic crisis and the founding murder are real events, and if in fact human communities are capable of periodically breaking apart and dissolving in mimetic violence, saving themselves finally, *in extremis*, by means of the surrogate victim, then religious systems—despite the transfigurations brought about by interpretation of the sacred—are based on a keen observation both of the kinds of behaviour that lead human beings into violence and of the strange process that puts an end to violence. These are generally the kinds of behaviour that religious systems prohibit, and it is this process, roughly, that they reproduce in ritual.

The sound empirical insight behind the supernatural disguises of prohibitions would be more readily apparent if it were not for the insipid modern fascination with transgression, the influence of which, even in the best minds, isolates and accentuates the more absurd aspects of prohibitions. The supernatural disguises themselves have a role in protecting human beings from their own violence. By linking an infraction with the notion of divine vengeance rather than with intestine rivalries, religion provides a twofold defence against them: it envelops them in an imposing mystery and guards against the mistrust and suspicions that would inevitably result from a less mythic view of the threat they pose.

J.-M. O.: The clear advantage of your interpretation is that it illuminates the effective and predictive aspects of religious rules without drawing in any of the metaphysics of the sacred. On the contrary, for the first time, this metaphysics has been *reduced* to purely human relations.

R. G.: If the sacred were nothing other than the combination of banality and nonsense, as it has been variously conceived from the Enlightenment to psychoanalysis, it would never have maintained the prodigious power it has held on humanity throughout the quasi-totality of its history. Its power derives from what it has said in real terms to human beings concerning what must and must not be done in a given cultural context, in order to preserve tolerable human relations within the community.

The sacred is the sum of human assumptions resulting from collective transferences focused on a reconciliatory victim at the conclusion of a mimetic crisis. Far from being a leap into the irrational, the sacred constitutes the only hypothesis that makes sense for human beings as long as these transferences retain their power.

The hypothesis of the sacred reflects the human mind in its recognition that it is surpassed and transcended by a force that appears to be exterior to it, since at any moment this force seems to exert its will on the entire community for reasons which, though they seem ultimately incomprehensible, seem nonetheless to be beneficent rather than malevolent.

The sacred is therefore not a concept whose contours can be clearly marked in language. Durkheim, for example, made the opposition between the sacred and the profane too absolute.[14] One must also not make the opposite error and proscribe all ethnological discussion of the sacred, as has been urged by some lately, for that would be to forbid oneself any study of religion.

G. L.: I would like to return to the principal objection to your theory, namely, that it reduces heterogeneous phenomena to a unity. It seems that unless they have lost all sense of what constitutes scientific endeavour, researchers ought to feel obligated either to refute your theory immediately or to adopt it.

R. G.: It is troubling to see people write: 'It works too well to be true' and suppose that the whole question can be settled and dismissed with this aphorism. Should one then conclude that the dominant currents of thought today work too poorly to be entirely false? There is no longer room for anything but discontinuities, incoherence, and disorder. On what basis is one to choose between rival theories? Is it really necessary to choose the least effective, most fragmentary theory, the one utterly incapable of integrating any given data? Indeed, one wonders what degree of incoherence is required for a theory before it is ready to be approved by the experts.

I am not entirely serious, of course. It would be better to assume for the time being that we all remain faithful to the principles that have assured the success of Western science for several centuries, and to show that in the context of these principles, the objections raised so far carry no weight.

Some people, for example, cannot be bothered with examining my particular analyses because they have decided in advance that it is impossible to reduce all religious systems to 'a single concept', or to 'force them' into a 'single mould'. An *a priori* decision determines that the diversity of religious phenomena is too great and that the contradictions between particulars are too striking for any unitary schema to be possible.

I do indeed describe an event that is always more or less the same, but it has nothing to do with a concept or mould or any sort of receptacle. In reality it is a question of a *model* for religious phenomena, one that puts into place certain constraints, surely, and these do correspond to constants observable in real phenomena; but the model includes the possibility of infinite variation precisely because the event it describes is never concretely observed—it is, in fact, the object of a fundamental and founding misrecognition. Such misrecognition opens the way not only for difference itself, for religious and cultural differentiation, but also for the infinite diversity of concrete forms of religion. The whole theory is based on the already *interpretive* character of religious phenomena in relation to the founding event. What critics do not see, when they accuse me of forcing the extraordinary diversity of religious phenomena into a strait-jacket, is just this element of interpretation—the interpretation is necessarily skewed but its skewedness can be traced and observed.

J.-M. O.: It seems that readers of *Violence and the Sacred* have never completely understood the nature of your theory. Even if you are not wrong to insist on the 'reductive' aspect of the theory, in distinction to the formless eclecticism that surrounds us, you still risk contributing to the misunderstanding. The theory of the surrogate victim is proffered as the only true reading of an event that has already been interpreted by all cultural texts, even those that deny its existence, since any such denial is only a particularly mystified form of interpretation. In other words, your thesis is primarily not a theory of religion but a theory of human relations and of the role that the mechanism of victimage plays in those relations. The theory of religion is simply a particularly noteworthy aspect of a fundamental theory of mimetic relations. Religion is thus one means of misinterpreting mimetic relations, but modern psychology is another, as are ethnology, philosophy, etc. In your view of fundamental human relations, the texts of a culture and their cultural interpretation are automatically interpreted and traced to forms of mimesis that have gone unnoted because of the dominance of these very forms. Your position with respect to the forms of religion is not essentially different from your position on the work of Freud. All readings remain mythic if they do not take into account the radical reading of mimesis and its consequences.

R. G.: I agree. The situation of the interpreter who has the mimetic reading of human relations at his disposal is similar to that of the historian of science who is aware of the scientific solution to a certain problem and who then considers the efforts of scientists in the past to solve it. The historian is capable of showing exactly at what point and for which reasons those who worked before the solution was found went astray in their research.

There is a difference, however, and we have already referred to it. In the issue that concerns us any step toward a real solution changes the character of the problem. This is particularly serious in the case of the sacralizing mechanism, which operates with progressively less effectiveness to the extent that one is capable of seeing in scapegoat phenomena, not a meaningless ritual but a fundamental human propensity to escape the effects of violence at the expense of a victim.

The situation of the researcher is therefore comparable, in certain respects, to that of a historian of science who might be studying ancient theories of combustion in a world in which, for some reason, the phenomenon of combustion no longer occurred. This would oddly complicate the task.

Before Priestley and Lavoisier, there was the well-known theory of phlogiston. According to this theory, phlogiston was the combustible element in any combustion, and any matter capable of burning was perceived as a mixture of flammable phlogiston and of inflammable ash.

If the phenomenon of combustion were unknown to us, the historian of science would be tempted to conclude that the theory of phlogiston had no relation whatever to reality rather than that it was an erroneous interpretation of real phenomena; it would be seen as the product of a feverish or slightly deranged imagination, like that of the alchemists.

Anyone who came to that conclusion, however, would be mistaken. Phlogiston does not exist any more than the sacred, yet the theory of phlogiston allowed for a relatively exact description of certain aspects of the real phenomenon of combustion. In order to show that the situation with the sacred is somewhat similar, it is necessary to uncover the real phenomena that the sacred transfigures, to show that such phenomena exist in reality and to construct a more exact theory of the sacred, a theory that should be related to religion itself in the way that the theory of combustion based on the discovery of oxygen is related to phlogiston. Our own oxygen is mimesis and all that accompanies it.

G. L.: At first it would seem that the task is impossible; if the phenomena that religion is unable to interpret no longer exist, how can it be proved scientifically that they once did exist? Our metaphor has to be refined if we are to show that this is not impossible. One would have to say that combustion has not completely disappeared from the world: it continues to exist in certain diminished forms, but it is still recognizable as combustion.

J.-M. O.: In that case the construction of a convincing theory would require showing why the more spectacular form of combustion had ceased to occur. I believe that in your theory, biblical *knowledge* of the victimage mechanism plays such a role.

R. G.: Correct. We have already noted that if we were to respond to every objection as it arose it would mean discussing everything at once and confusing too many issues. We would lose the thread of our ideas and not be able to understand each other or be understood by anyone else. So a discussion of the Bible will take place another day. We have to ask our readers to be patient and to reserve judgment until they have come to the end of the book. It will not be possible to evaluate our hypothesis until one has read it from cover to cover.

This is perhaps too much to ask in a time as hurried as ours, but we have no other choice. The problems are simply too complex. We will see, for example, that without our having to modify anything in the analyses we are currently conducting, the light brought to them by the Judaeo-Christian texts will provide a new and completely unexpected dimension. For the moment this dimension remains entirely hidden. As yet we are still not prepared even to allude to it.

G. L.: We will return to that subject later, then, and for now continue with that extraordinary phlogiston, the sacred. If I have understood you, you maintain that the double transference on to the victim, first that of the mimetic crisis and then that of the victim, produces not only prohibitions and rituals, but also myths; myths, in turn, are equivalent to the development of founding ancestors and titulary divinities, which also result from this transference. The victim appears to be the only active principle of the whole process of crisis and resolution, rather than a fortuitous instrument of sudden reconciliation at the end of a crisis, because collective suggestion first isolates and accuses, then exalts the victim, until both processes occur simultaneously. In the end this is why the inauguration or the renewing of a religious ordering is often attributed to the victim.

R. G.: Exactly. The true 'scapegoats' are those whom men have never recognized as such, in whose guilt they have an unshaken belief.

Up to this point it has been necessary, as well as intentional on our part, to present our fundamental hypothesis in a very schematic fashion. We can now begin gradually to add detail and substance.

CHAPTER TWO

The Development of Culture and Institutions

Variants in Ritual

J.-M. O.: You argue that ritual practices that at first sight seem diametrically opposed can be traced to the victimage mechanism. What examples can you offer?

R. G.: There are rituals that demand unanimous participation in a sacrifice, whereas others forbid such participation and even all contact with the victim. The immolation is reserved for those who specialize in sacrifice, priests or others, who are quite distinct on the religious level from the rest of the community.

The question is how could two such opposed methods of sacrifice be traced to one and the same mechanism, and above all, how could each of them, in spite of their contradiction, reveal anything accurate about this mechanism?

The death of the victim transforms relations within the community. The change from discord to harmony is not attributed to its actual cause, the unifying mimesis of collective violence, but to the victim itself. Religious thought tends to think of everything in terms of the victim, which becomes the focal point of all meaning; the actual principle in the return to order is never perceived. Religious thought conceives of a malevolent quasi-substance, the sacred, which becomes polarized around the victim and is transformed into a beneficent force through the accomplishment of the sacrifice and through the victim's expulsion from the community.

Religious thought is thus led to make the victim the vehicle and transforming agent of something sacred—mimesis—which is never conflictual or undifferentiated except in so far as it is spread throughout the community; its concentration in a victim makes it a pacifying and regulating force, the positive mimesis found in ritual.

Religious thought can on the one hand accentuate the malevolent aspect of sacrifice, the concentration of the evil sacred in the victim, or on the other hand the beneficent aspect, the reconciliation of the community. In the first case, any contact with the victim can be seen as extremely dangerous and thus is absolutely forbidden. The sacrificial immolation would then be reserved for priests, who are particularly well suited to resist the danger of contamination. No doubt these priests, after having accomplished their task, will undergo an obsessive ritual of 'decontamination'.

In the other case, in which the beneficent transformation is emphasized, the logic of the interpretation points to unanimous participation.

The two practices reveal something about the founding mechanism, but this goes unnoticed by ethnologists because they see neither the effectiveness of the surrogate victim nor the *double* transferential interpretation made by religious thought.

G. L.: Can you provide other examples?

R. G.: Here is another. Certain rituals involve often very ingenious aleatory procedures in order to deprive people of the opportunity to choose the victim, that is, to prevent any chance of disagreement.

But there are other rituals that leave nothing to chance and that make every effort to emphasize the purported specificity of the victim. Here again there is an opposition that seems to exclude a common origin. Girard doesn't see the differences, they say, or he suppresses them in order to believe in a common origin.

Once one has understood the founding mechanism, and the interpretation in terms of the sacred necessarily made by those who benefit from it, it becomes clear that one interpretation is as possible as the other. During the mimetic crisis, the victim is only one antagonist among others, a double among others, their twin enemy, until mimetic polarization succeeds in converging all the signs of crisis and reconciliation on the victim. The victim them becomes extremely significant and specific. The passage from the aleatory to the specific, from the end of doubling to the return of differentiation, occurs through the victim.

Religious thought will almost never balance the two moments simultaneously and give them equal weight. One or the other will be accentuated; in one case, then, aleatory procedures will be devised, whereas in the other the concern for specificity will dominate. Once again the two contrary practices confirm rather than contradict the violent origin, each one isolating an essential aspect of the founding mechanism as that aspect would appear in the perspective created by the transferences.

At this point we should take note of a new and extremely important point that has emerged through our analysis: this is the tendency of religious thought to exclude major elements of the object of its interpretation; it retains only one of the contrary aspects of the whole constituted by the transferences and concentrates on a single facet of an extremely complex phenomenon.

Because of the two transferences the victim becomes the source for a practically limitless range of significations. Religious thought is incapable of encompassing or of extricating itself from such a polysemous abundance; choices will therefore be made in the midst of the whole phenomenon that will propel religious systems in different directions. I see in this the principal source of institutional variation.

Religious thought seeks the stability of difference; it will concentrate on one synchronous moment of the whole operation and accentuate it, thereby neglecting the others. However 'synthetic' it might appear to the modern mind, religious thought is nonetheless analytic from the beginning when it comes to the mystery it attempts to recall and reproduce. We will see that it proceeds with a series of successive cuts and dismemberments that have a strange resemblance to the sacrificial procedure itself, constituting the intellectual equivalent of the dismembering of the victim by the participants, for it is always a process of *exclusion*. Religious thought, one might say in summary, has always been differential and 'structuralist'. It has no understanding of its origin and progressively distances itself from it.

In my view the whole of this process belongs under the sign of the prohibition. The spirit of the prohibition is no different from the spirit of differentiation that dominates all ethnological thought and that continues more than ever in our own time in structu, alism. For this type of thought reveals the contradictions between ritual practice and the demands of prohibitions.

Any realization that religion is an 'insoluble contradiction' is necessarily linked to a loss of its origin, and vice versa. For this reason the increasing realization and differentiation of human culture are also a tenacious mystification, an effacement of bloody tracks, and an expulsion of the expulsion itself.

Sacred Kingship and Central Power

G. L.: The foregoing must also apply to the incestuous and sacrificial sacred monarchies that you analysed in *Violence and the Sacred*.[15] If I follow you on this point, you claim that an understanding of monarchy is only possible on the basis of an understanding of sacrifice.

R. G.: At first there is neither kingship nor any institution. There is only the spontaneous reconciliation over and against a victim who is a 'true scapegoat', precisely because no one can identify the victim as that and only that. Like any human institution, monarchy is at first nothing but the will to reproduce the reconciliatory mechanism. One attempts to find another victim that resembles the original victim as closely as possible, which of course means not what the victim was in reality but what the victim has become through interpretation, and the latter idea is determined by the *effectiveness* of the victimage mechanism. How is one not to believe that this victim actually committed the crimes it has been accused of when it has only been necessary to kill the victim to bring about a return of order and peace? The community desires to re-play the scenario of an indubitably guilty victim capable of first disrupt-ing the entire community and then of reunifying it through the victim's death. To assure that every rule of the game is respected, what could be more simple and effective than requiring that the substitute, before ascending to the role of victim, commit all the crimes that the first vic-tim was supposed to have committed?

We do not understand sacred monarchy because we do not see that the effectiveness of the founding mechanism structures a misinterpret-ation of the victim, namely the unshakable conviction that the victim is guilty, a conviction carried over into the ritual requirement of incest and other transgressions.

We share the ignorance of primitive peoples concerning the mechan-ism which they attempt to reproduce, but they at least know that the mechanism is real and that is why they attempt to reproduce it. In short, we add our modern ignorance on to the ignorance of primitive peoples.

The rules of what we call 'royal enthronement' are those of sacrifice; they attempt to make the king a victim capable of channelling mimetic antagonism. One indication of this is that in many societies the inaugur-ation of a king is accompanied by collective threats against him, and these are required by ritual just as are the expressions of submission and adoration that follow them. The two attitudes correspond to the transferences of crisis and of reconciliation that constitute the sacred.

The king is at first nothing more than a victim with a sort of suspended sentence, and this demonstrates that the victim is made responsible for the transformation that moves the community from mimetic violence to the order of ritual. In reality the victim is passive, but because the collective transference discharges the community of all responsibility, it creates the illusion of a supremely active and all-powerful victim. Kingship stages this metaphysical and religious illusion of the victim and the founding mechanism.

J.-M. O.: What you say is true in principle of all sacrificial institutions and of all victims. However there is still an essential sociological difference. In monarchy the sovereignty of the victim is not merely theoretical. The king pronounces rules and forces his subjects to follow these rules. A transgressor is severely punished. The power of the king is entirely real and his sacrifice, most often, is nothing more than an act, or even the acting at acting. But in the case of other victims the opposite is true. Their supposed power is theoretical or imaginary and amounts to a few trivial privileges without social importance, whereas the sacrifice is quite real and the victim is actually killed.

G. L.: Your hypothesis takes into account the analogies that link institutions, but a modern observer who is not content with elegant wordplay would say that the difference between the victim and the king is more important than any resemblance and that you *neglect the specificity of institutions*.

On the one hand it is a question of an all-powerful figure, the king, who possesses real power over the community, whereas on the other hand there are individuals that count for so little that they can be murdered at any time. Such a difference is certainly essential for the sociologist, so essential in fact that it leads to the conclusion that the sacrifice of the king—as well as the power of the victim—amount to rites of little consequence. A sociologist would remind you that power always seeks to disguise itself behind religious trappings and that you are naive to take such trappings seriously.

R. G.: The sacrifice of a king: is that not the very image of power that seeks to deceive human beings and mask the arbitrariness of the tyranny imposed on them? Is monarchy not simply a sacrificial theatre or a sort of theatrical sacrifice?

To return to the starting-point of our theory, we propose that in all human institutions it is necessary to reproduce a reconciliatory murder by means of new victims. The original victim is endowed with super-human, terrifying prestige because it is seen as the source of all disorder and order. Subsequent victims inherit some of this prestige. One must look to this prestige for the source of all political and religious sover-eignty.

What must happen if ritual is to give rise to a political institution, to the power of monarchy, rather than to ordinary forms of sacrifice, those that can be 'strictly defined' as such? It is necessary and sufficient for the victim to take advantage of the lapse of time before the sacrifice and to transform veneration into real power. One might therefore expect that the interval between the selection of the victim and the sacrifice will be gradually prolonged. This extension, in turn, will permit the future victim to consolidate progressively more power over the com-munity. At some point this power and the submission of the com-munity would become sufficiently effective and extensive as to make an actual sacrifice of the monarch impossible if not unthinkable. The re-lation between sacrifice and monarchy is too intimate to be dissolved all at once, but it does change. Since sacrifice is always a question of substi-tution, it is always possible to make a new substitution and henceforth to sacrifice only a substitute of the substitute. This can proceed as far as the substitute of the substitute, as in the case, cited by Frazer, of the Tibetan Jalno acquiring too much real power to be sacrificed so that a further substitute must be found.[16] Sacrifice, in any case, becomes a progressively marginal aspect of the institution. Finally it disappears altogether. The evolution of modern monarchy, properly speaking, has then been completed.

By contrast, wherever the sovereignty of the victim has not been transformed into concrete power, the contrary evolution of sacrifice, properly speaking, will take place. The lapse in time before the sacrifice will not be prolonged, it will be foreshortened. The religious power of the victim will be gradually reduced to insignificant privileges. Finally, the privileges accorded to the one who is to die will appear to be motiva-ted by simple human sympathy, like the cigarette and glass of rum given to the prisoner in the ritual of French capital punishment.

J.-M. O.: According to your analysis, then, it is unnecessary to assert that a 'real' sacrifice of a 'real' king ever takes place, or obversely that a 'real' sacrificial victim ever possesses genuine political sovereignty.

There can be no question of the analysis being politically naive or of it lacking plausibility. A lack of plausibility would be much more pertinent in the case of those who describe a structural matrix outside of any real social context, or for those who, for the sake of a real social context, completely ignore symbolic analogies.

R. G.: We should note that the sociological point of view is never more than a variation of the idea that ritual is secondary, something added on or supplementary in relation to institutions that in the end manage to free themselves of ritual and whose existence does not in any way depend on it.

This perspective is so natural and instinctive to us that it is inscribed in the terminology we use. We say *sacred monarchy*, as if the monarchy were primary and the sacred simply a secondary modification of it, something added to a pre-existing monarchy whose origin requires no explanation.

If one observes royal power, or even what is called central power in the most modern, deritualized state, it becomes clear that such power, even at its most absolute, is nonetheless never limited to oppression pure and simple and that it puts a quite different element into play.

Royal power is situated at the very heart of society. It demands observance of the most fundamental rules; its purview extends to the most intimate and secret aspects of human existence, such as sexual and familial life; it insinuates itself into what is most personal in us and yet, in many respects, it remains independent of the rules it embodies. Like the god of St Augustine, it is at once more intimate than our intimacy and more exterior than the outermost exteriority.

The idea is much too complex to have been the invention of power-hungry individuals; it would be necessary to attribute to them a literally immeasurable intelligence and strength, which would only amount to sacralizing them. The king is not a glorified gang-leader, supported by pomp and decorum, capable of dissimulating his origin with deft propaganda concerning 'divine right'.

Even if human beings had discovered the centrality of an at once immanent and transcendent power by looking within themselves or outward to the world around them, even if they were capable of completely inventing it, one would still not be able to understand how they could have established such power among themselves, imposed it on the whole of society, and transformed it into the concrete institution and mechanism of government.

G. L.: In other words you do not see how the most abstract tyranny or the abstract good will of the 'social contract' are able to account for the institution of royalty. To all evidence, only religion can account for it; the paradox of ritual gives rise to the paradox of central power.

R. G.: The proof that such power is not simple and self-explanatory is that in many societies, particularly in those called dual societies, royal or central power has never existed and no individual has ever completely invented it.

There can be no question of denying that power can be disguised in the trappings of religion. On the contrary, once power has been genuinely consolidated it is all the more likely to adopt such disguises, given that religious forms are always already present and at the disposition of power. But a purely sociological theory can never explain why the royal theatre, supposing that it is always theatre, should always be a *sacrificial* drama. Nor can sociology ever explain why the ritual murder always accords symbols of sovereignty to the victim.

Why is it that a prisoner of the Tupinamba, before being eaten, is sometimes made an object of veneration in ways analogous to those accorded the sacred king? How can such a mystery be explained? The symbolic link between sovereignty and sacrifice exists everywhere. Royalty is only one among many forms of the same juxtaposition, one in which real social power happens to be on the side of sovereignty. An explanation that would be valid for kingship only, such as the theory of political power in disguise, is not credible. We must find, if possible, an explanation that would be valid for traits common to many institutions.

J.-M. O.: In other words, in your view an overly sociological emphasis obscures symbolic structures, just as structuralism tends to obscure sociological realities. One should not be forced to choose between these two distortions of the real. Your theory of the surrogate victim permits their reconciliation.

R. G.: I am confident that it does. The homologies between sacred monarchies and other forms of religion are too striking to be accidental or the result of superficial borrowing.

G. L.: How would one conceive of divinity in relation to monarchy?

R. G.: I think that a fundamental difference is evident. In monarchy the interpretation accentuates the interval between the selection of the victim and the immolation; it is a matter of the victim being still alive, one that has not yet been sacrificed. In the case of divinity, by contrast, the interpretation accentuates a victim that has already been sacrificed and it is a matter of the sacred having been already expelled from the community. In the former example, the power of the sacred will be above all present, alive and active in the person of the king; in the latter it will be absent, in the 'person' of the god.

This absence of the sacred principle immediately renders aspects of divinity more abstract and necessitates more extensive separations and divisions. Because the divinity is outside, for example, sacrifice cannot be the exact reproduction of the origin. Yet because sacrifice nonetheless remains the equivalent of the primordial event, it will generally evolve toward the idea of attenuated repetition; it will be thought to produce the sacred, but in lesser amounts that will in turn be expelled and so serve to *increase* and *nourish* the divinity. Such would be the source of the idea of sacrifice as an offering to a sacred power.

In monarchy, however, the origin is repeated in each reign and in each sacrifice that occurs, in principle, exactly as the first sacrifice occurred. There is thus no room for anything but this repetition. Ultimately there is not even a myth of the origin independent of the inauguration of the monarch. Royalty is a mythology in action. There is nothing to venerate beyond this king himself. This is why monarchy, as long as it remains linked to sacrifice, is a particularly revealing institution. Even some ethnologists recognize that enthronement makes the king a scapegoat. Luc de Heusch, for example, in his book on incest, cites the Ruanda ritual of enthronement, in which the king and his mother figure next to one another like two prisoners condemned to death, and the following pronouncement is made: 'I wound you with the spear, the blade, the boomerang, the gun, the club, the hook. If any man, if any woman, has ever perished from the wound of the arrow, of the lance . . . I give you these wounds.'[17]

Here it is clear that the sacred king is a 'scapegoat' and that he is a scapegoat for real violence and not for more or less fantastic or Freudian transgressions. Many ethnologists recognize that the king is certainly a scapegoat, but do not pause and dwell on this strange union of exalted sovereignty and extreme subjugation. They either see in it something completely 'natural', a function supplementary to monarchy, somewhat like that of the Grand Master of the Legion of Honour for our President of the Republic, or they dismiss the whole matter as something unthinkable or unlikely, even though such a conjunction of extremes can be noted, with more or less emphasis, in all sacred monarchies, without exception, and finally in all sacrificial institutions. The refusal to consider anything that contradicts our own notions can be remarkably tenacious.

If the principles of kingship and divinity exclude one another, at least at their origin, it is because they constitute two somewhat different responses to the basic question of ritual: How should the violent resolution to the crisis be reproduced? In kingship the dominant element is what happens *before* the sacrifice, in divinity it is what comes *after* the sacrifice. In order to understand that the two responses are equally possible we must keep in mind the polysemousness and polyvalence that were discussed earlier. The sacrificial resolution is the sole matrix of all institutions, so polyvalent that it is therefore impossible to reproduce as such and concrete rituals will always accentuate one synchronic moment at the expense of others. But the consequences of this can be predicted and one can ascertain that they do correspond to actually existing institutions.

J.-M. O.: The theory of the surrogate victim cannot be considered a fantasy once one has begun to note these correspondences. But ethnologists do not realize the plausibility of the theory because they are unaware of the extent to which they remain influenced by modes of thought that they believe they have repudiated. They persist in believing that the concept of divinity is a 'natural' one; the sacred king is held to be a kind of reversal of divinity for the sake of a political power which is supposedly independent of ritual.

R. G.: Everyone repeats that the king is a kind of 'living god' but no one says that the divinity is a kind of dead king, or at any rate an 'absent' king, which would be just as accurate. In the end there is a persistent preference for viewing the sacrifice and sacredness of the king as a secondary and supplementary idea, for we must beware of rocking our little conceptual boat. Yet what guides our interpretation is only a conceptual system dominated by the idea of divinity, a *theology*. Scepticism concerning religion does not abolish this theological perspective. We are forced to reinterpret all religious schemata in terms of divinity because we are unaware of the surrogate victim. If one examines psychoanalysis and Marxism closely it becomes evident that this theology is indispensable for them. It is indispensable for all modes of contemporary thought, which will collapse whenever what we have said concerning the king and the god is finally understood.

The Polyvalence of Ritual and the Specificity of Institutions

J.-M. O.: If institutions that are quite different when viewed from a sociological perspective but quite analogous structurally, go back to a common origin, there must have been a time in human culture when they had not yet separated. Perhaps there are still some indications of such an absence of distinction in the data of ethnology, say phenomena, to which terms of kingship and sacrifice are equally applied, or institutions that are so ambiguous they remain beyond the reach of the rigid and overly specialized vocabulary of our cultural Platonism.

R. G.: I think that such institutions exist or rather once existed and that some of them have been described, however inadequately, in revealing ways. As you might expect, contemporary ethnology takes a very dim view of such institutions, for they hardly respect the laws of differential thought. In fact the books that describe them have become scapegoats and have been dismissed as being more or less fantasy.

In the work of writers like Frazer one sometimes comes across descriptions that correspond well enough to what our theory requires. But rather than citing a particular example, I think it would be preferable to offer a comprehensive summary. Frazer describes a rather strange type of kingship in which those who hold power succeed one another through a type of election or lottery process. All the young men of the village are eligible, but rather than compete with one another and dispute the sexual and other privileges enjoyed by the monarch, the candidates flee at top speed into the bush. In the end the next chosen one is only the candidate who was slowest on his feet, the first to let himself be caught during an epic chase in which the entire community takes part. Absolute power lasts only for a moment and its attraction is never sufficient to counterbalance the certainty of being finally massacred by one's own subjects.

Contemporary ethnology rejects this kind of description because it can find no way to apply its favourite techniques of differentiation and classification. It is certainly possible to describe the event in terms of 'kingship', and because earlier authors did so they judged it to be a sort of parody. The event appears much less funny if one replaces kingship with sacrifice, but there is no reason to adopt one term rather than the other. If we will only examine it closely, we will see that the institution constantly offers new perspectives. Once we stop smiling about the sexual privileges and consider the phenomenon as one of transgression, the monarch suddenly becomes a condemned man who will die for the sins of the community, a 'scapegoat' in the accepted sense of the term. And if in the end the king is eaten, which also happens, he bears some resemblance to a sacrificial animal. One can see in him a kind of priest or supreme initiate whose office demands in principle that he sacrifice himself voluntarily for the community—in practice, however, he sometimes needs a little persuasion.

J.-M. O.: Forms like these that resist classification are no doubt much more numerous than one would gather from the reports of ethnologists. It is possible, in fact, that the most interesting observations in this sense have been unconsciously scanned and corrected under the influence of the cultural Platonism that you mentioned. By cultural Platonism we mean the unexamined conviction that human institutions have been and are what they are for all eternity, that they have little need to evolve and none whatsoever to be engendered. Human culture is an immutable idea that is immediately available to any human being who begins to think. To grasp it one has only to look within oneself where it resides, innate, or otherwise outside of oneself, where it can be found legibly inscribed in the heavens, as in Plato.

R. G.: This Platonism needs to be shaken to its foundations; its influence is such that the genetic model we have proposed, which begins with a single ritual matrix, seems scandalous and inadmissible to most minds. To say that I neglect the specificity of institutions is to ignore my explanation for the cause of that specificity through the victimage mechanism. It is necessary to find the common line and the successive bifurcations that have led from the origin to the seemingly irreducible diversity of cultural forms.

It is quite evident how a universal Platonism manages to obscure any phenomena that contradict it. If one classifies our example of an ambiguous ritual as kingship, one will immediately tend to minimize any aspect, beginning with sacrifice, that does not correspond to one's preconceived idea of kingship. One will treat that aspect as a bizarre anomaly or perhaps as an error in observation that need not be taken seriously. If, on the other hand, the ritual is defined in terms of sacrifice, other aspects of the institution will tend to be relegated to a secondary position, and these will be the same ones that would be considered primary if the decision were made in terms of kingship.

In all undefinable rituals there is as yet no difference between the throne and the sacrificial altar. It is always a question of placing another sovereign victim on the altar for the sake of a reconciliatory, because unanimous, murder. If this union, which is so striking in our example, of supreme power and collective victim seems monstrous to us, if we cannot find the words to define the scandal, it is because we are not yet willing to think the matter through to its conclusion. We are not as far removed as we think from those who consider the victim to be monstrous and who place it beyond humanity in that they prostrate themselves in front of it before proceeding to kill it.

G. L.: Should one decide, then, that it is not necessary to account for bizarre forms of ritual, that they are 'aberrations' without theoretical importance, or represent the inventions of particularly 'repressive' ethnologists, it would be tantamount to acting somewhat like those who performed the sacrifice itself. It amounts to expelling the unnamable from the well-tempered and differentiated ethnology that is deemed suitable for contemporary taste.

R. G.: Since this sort of thing does not yet pose a serious threat to our way of thinking, the expulsion is made by means of laughter. At one time we laughed at actors in a farce, and these were Frazer's primitive savages. We now laugh at our predecessors in ethnology and consider them naive to have passed off fables for theory. We believe ourselves liberated from their 'ethnocentrism', but we are more lost in it than ever because of our inability to explain religious thought, which is at the heart of so-called primitive thinking. Laughter expels ritual, and ritual itself is nothing but a more primary form of expulsion. The monster is always expelled in sacrificial rituals, first in person, and later in purely intellectual operations; for it is a waste of time, we are told, to think what is contrary to the laws of thought.[18]

J.-M. O.: The more any ritual escapes our habitual labels, the more it becomes undefinable and elusive; the closer it comes to the original intent of ritual, the more apt it is for the kind of interpretation proposed here.

R. G.: Wherever institutions do not possess the degree of specificity that we would like them to have, we manage to impute it to them in our observation. This need not be intentional; one has only to rely on firmly established habits, which are apparently impervious to criticism to the degree that they stem directly from the prolongation of late developments in religious thought. In other words, wherever the spontaneous Platonism of institutional development has not been fully realized, the Platonism inherent in ethnological thinking steps in and completes the process of evolution. This Platonism is the heir of a powerful tradition that makes any independence extremely difficult. The mind that seeks progressively finer distinctions everywhere, that seeks to classify institutions in accordance with a predetermined schema, *necessarily believes* the procedure to be the correct one; it completes a process which is that of all cultural evolution. We are therefore the victims of intellectual mechanisms so deeply engrained that we cannot see the necessity of a radical revision of ethnological thought.

The unconscious decision to impute structure to ambiguous institutions is somewhat similar to the decision we allow to intervene when we are confronted with the figures that Gestalt psychology once used to illustrate its theories. If we look at the lines of a cube traced on a blackboard, perception can structure the figure as projecting inward or outward from the surface. But once one of the possibilities has become stable, our perception remains its prisoner and cannot easily switch to the other. The same is true in ethnology once we have decided that an institution has one meaning rather than another or several others.

If it is difficult to move from one structuration to another it is even more difficult to reject both solutions and remain open to the two at once, in other words to see the figure as a matrix of possible structures each of which is relevant to specific cultural forms but ultimately deceptive in that they all exclude one another.

G. L.: An ethnology that relies entirely on classification and seeks to sort and arrange institutions the way a postal employee sorts mail, an ethnology for which the last word in science is the exactness of a difference, is unable or unwilling, in the name of pseudo-rationality, to envisage the possibility of a common structural matrix. It simply refuses to consider any institution that seriously challenges its own order of certainty. The desire to classify everything leads ethnology to an unconscious attempt to forget or discredit anything that eludes its appetite for such classification. Such an ethnology is blind to the perspectives that are now opening up. The most disturbing institutions in terms of classification are the most interesting because they show us a condition prior to an already attained degree of specificity.

R. G.: There is no question of confounding everything, of seeking out mystical ecstasy or a cult of violence. Nor is there any question of destroying specificities; rather, they must be 'deconstructed' as Derrida would say, though we must not follow his self-defeating taboo on the search for an origin. Once the mechanism of the surrogate victim has been recognized, the beginning and the end of the 'deconstruction' are at hand, since its accomplishment amounts also to a 'reconstruction' which begins at the common matrix. The genetic and structural perspectives are joined in a type of analysis that transcends the limits of previous methods.

Rather than constantly projecting evolution toward cultural specificity, we must realize that evolution often remains incomplete, that indeed it has hardly begun in the example we have been referring to. The description does not seem implausible because of any intrinsic impossibility. Our own intellectual taboos make it seem so. Such descriptions are, on the contrary, quite likely to be reasonably valid because they have been made in spite of these taboos; they present tableaux in which one can show theoretically and schematically, with reference to the scapegoat mechanism, that they have in many respects a necessary correspondence to a certain stage in the development of human culture.

Traces of the polyvalence of ritual are to be found almost everywhere, and an observer ought to gather them carefully rather than contribute to their effacement. Rather than judging such vanishing elements as superfluous or supplementary, we should realize that they can be combined with the dominant elements of an institution in a whole that will always include the same ingredients but in different proportions, at least ideally. If one juxtaposes institutions that have not been completely deritualized and rituals that are not yet completely institutionalized, one discovers everywhere that the most humble position is linked to the most exalted one. One discovers a trace of subjection in domination and vice versa.

Phenomena of this type should not be made the basis for asserting, as do Frazer and Lévy-Bruhl, that primitives confuse their own categories; nor is it necessary to say, with Lévi-Strauss, that ritual is a deliberate refusal of thought and language. The scandal should be recognized rather than rejected. But this does not mean that we must embrace the scandal in the manner of religious or philosophical thought. There can be no question of returning to mystical formulations or their philosophical counterparts, such as the 'coincidentia oppositorum', the magical power of the negative, and the value of the Dionysian. There can be no question of returning to Hegel or Nietzsche.

We should not allow the last-ditch efforts of classificatory rationalism, which amount to the opposite of reason, to divert our attention from the essential paradox. For in most ritual institutions the structural elements that 'contradict' one another are such that, given differences in concentration, emphasis, and practical importance, it is always possible to deny, with only a slight effort at obfuscation that any paradox or contradictions exist. It can always be maintained that they are the inventions of theologians and philosophers. This temptation has accompanied the sciences of man, with few exceptions, since their beginning; one can always manage to smooth over contradictions somehow and the temptation to do so should be resisted.

The supposedly no-nonsense dismissal of the vestiges of ritual in human institutions, with its accompanying note of mocking scepticism, is the direct descendent of theology. Once religious belief is no longer a factor, the refusal to conceive of an institution's origin will necessarily take such a form, for there is no other possibility. The Voltairean interpretation, which is still dominant, makes religion the widespread conspiracy of priests to take advantage of *natural* institutions, and this view directly follows religious thought in its refusal to think through the origin of these institutions. The refusal is the same, but it necessarily takes the form of scepticism once the cults of sacrifice and the more primitive forms of mythology have died out.

Durkheim was the first firmly to oppose the sceptical obscurantism concerning religion, which is certainly why the narrowest empiricists accuse him of being a mystic. And they will no doubt claim that I am even more of a mystic, despite the rigorously rational character of the genetic model that we have begun to elaborate.

J.-M. O.: The 'deconstruction' can be completed once we have explained the genetic mechanism; we see the alpha and omega of human culture when we understand the surrogate victim as the result of the mimetic process.

R. G.: The discovery of the scapegoat as the mechanism of symbolic thought, human thought itself, justifies a deconstructive discourse and at the same time completes it. It can also explain the characteristic aspects of this contemporary discourse. Because much of contemporary thought is still without an anthropological basis, it remains given to verbal acrobatics that will ultimately prove to be sterile. The master tropes are not what it lacks; it is only too well endowed with words, but the mechanisms behind the word are still not sufficiently apparent. If you examine the pivotal terms in the finest analyses of Derrida, you will see that beyond the deconstruction of philosophical concepts, it is always a question of the paradoxes of the sacred, and although there is no question of deconstructing these they are all the more apparent to the reader.[19]

This is also true for a reading of Heidegger. Everything that he says concerning being can also be said of the sacred, but philosophers will hardly admit this since they have no desire to go back beyond Plato and the pre-Socratics to consider Greek religion.

This still partial deconstruction confounds our present philosophical and cultural crisis with a radical impotence of thought and language. One no longer believes in philosophy but one keeps rehearsing the same old philosophical texts. And yet beyond the current crisis there are possibilities of a rational but no longer philosophical knowledge of culture. Instead, deconstruction seems content with a pure mirroring of the sacred that amounts to nothing, at this stage, but a purely literary effect; it risks degenerating into pure verbalism. And what the literary critics and academic disciples of deconstruction do not realize is that as soon as one seeks nothing but the essence of literature it disappears. If there is really 'something' to Derrida, it is because there is something beyond: precisely a deconstruction that reaches the mechanisms of the sacred and no longer hesitates to come to terms with the surrogate victim.

J.-M. O.: With an understanding of the surrogate victim, in sum, a true structuralism might begin, one that would be not only synchronic in orientation but diachronic through and through in its understanding of the composition and decomposition of structures.

R. G.: Because contemporary structuralism cannot even conceive of such a possibility, there is the risk that we will be misunderstood as advocating a return to discredited historical explanations. We need to emphasize that we are not speaking of any single event or of a chronology; our scheme is able to explain the functioning of mechanisms of composition and decomposition—its relevance and applicability are a function of the uniquely rational and elegant solution it proposes for understanding the transition from ritual to non-ritual institutions.

The analysis of institutions does not reveal the particular moment at which any given development took place, but it does indeed show that these developments occurred in time as part of a real history. And this history continues all around us, one example being the ethnological record itself. Western thought continues to function as the effacement of traces. But the traces of founding violence are no longer the ones being expelled; rather, the traces of a first or second expulsion, or even of a third or fourth, are now submitted to expulsion. In other words we are dealing with traces of traces of traces, etc. We might note here that Derrida has substituted what he calls 'the trace' for Being in the work of Heidegger. But even more revealing is a phrase in Freud's *Moses and Monotheism* that Sandy Goodhart has pointed out to me. The gist of it is that the supreme difficulty is not the committing of a murder, but the effacement of all traces of that murder.[20]

Given this series of effacements, this enormous effort of culture, it should come as no surprise that most people are unable to understand what we have been saying. It will probably remain a dead letter for a number of years. Yet at the same time, as part of an interesting paradox that we will discuss later, everything we are saying is already inscribed metaphorically or even explicitly in contemporary discourse. The interesting paradox is that the effacement of traces leads back to the founding murder. Pilate and Macbeth can wash their hands, but the traces reappear nonetheless; they reappear even more often and point to the founding murder.

G. L.: Our readers will believe that you are speaking metaphysically. I am sure you can show, however, that this is not the case. You can point to precise examples of the effacement of traces in ethnological writing.

R. G.: I hope to. We can begin by attempting to show how traces of founding violence begin to be effaced in an example of sacred kingship, that of the Shilluk. In a work on the subject, E. E. Evans-Pritchard describes a procedure of enthronement that is in some ways unique, although it is part of the general scheme of sacred monarchies.

It begins as a kind of civil war between two moieties of the kingdom, each having been transformed into a double of the other. Far from coming from the victorious side, as a political or sociological perspective would lead one to expect, the king comes from the defeated side. At the very moment when he falls into the hands of his adversaries, who are gathered to deliver him a final blow—at the moment, in other words, when he represents the crushed and humiliated victim—the *spirit* of the monarchy enters into him and he actually becomes the king of his people.[21]

The spirit of kingship is the unanimous reconciliation that once occurred spontaneously at the expense of a victim the king is now called upon to replace. The enthronement is nothing more than the repetition of the founding mechanism; as always, the king reigns in his quality as reconciliatory victim. Once this has been well understood it becomes clear how common the occurrence is; the procedure of the Shilluk is simply one variant among many others. To an observer who has grasped the symbolic function of the institution, the example of the Shilluk conforms too closely to the general picture of sacred monarchy and is too unique in its details to be anything other than extremely significant. Evans-Pritchard never relates this to other data that he refuses to take seriously, namely the many reports of kings that die by strangulation, suffocation, or by being buried alive. He accepts these as unverifiable rumours, and considers it unnecessary to take them into account in any way. Evans-Pritchard does recognize that the theme of regicide probably has a symbolic value bearing on the unity and disunity of various segments of the community, but he is so preoccupied with avoiding the error of Frazer and his 'cult of vegetation' that he minimizes the importance of the symbolism and is unable to grasp its unity, as indicated by the signs of victimage in the so-called sacred royalty. Yet the correspondence is clear when the aspects of enthronement are related to stories of the suffocated king, stories he encounters everywhere and constantly rejects as 'unverifiable'. As if the symbolism of the sacrificial king were not in itself extraordinarily interesting as symbolism. The same ethnologists who consider many kinds of symbolism interesting and important are unconcerned when it comes to the sacrificial king. As for the latter, the only issue that is regarded as significant is the reality or unreality of a murder that is 'always alleged but insufficiently documented'.

The same intellectual prejudice had already forced Frazer, whenever he came across stories of a king or god who had also been a 'scapegoat', to conclude that the natives must have come to confuse two institutions that were once distinct. Again, the same prejudice forces Lévi-Strauss, in the final chapter of *l'Homme nu*, to banish ritual from his structural ethnology. Once more ritual is accused of combining everything that ought to be kept separate.

G. L.: You argue that the unwillingness to acknowledge the paradox of the sovereign victim tends to efface exactly what the victim represents, the truth of the founding violence. But there must be some ethnologists who accept the paradox.

R. G.: There are, certainly. In the German school of ethnology, for example, we can cite Adolf Jensen or Rudolf Otto. Yet they accept the paradox with a quasi-religious spirit of submission or at times even enthusiasm, as if its irreducible character conferred on it a kind of value and intelligibility. In an attempt to make the mystery of violence and the sacred, of the sovereign victim and the sacrificial king, acceptable, Otto proposes his famous concept of the *numinous*. Despite what my critics maintain, I have absolutely no sympathy for that sort of attitude. But I refuse to share in the rationalist's blindness, as exemplified in Evans-Pritchard or Lévi-Strauss. Somehow it must be possible to analyse primitive religion thoroughly without becoming its accomplice along with the irrationalists or dismissing it along with the rationalists. I find Otto's lyrical description of the procession of the *pharmakos* through the streets of Athens rather odious. It was Nietzsche, in his *Birth of Tragedy*, who inaugurated the style of the Dionysian.

G. L.: But how does someone like Evans-Pritchard manage to ignore evidence that is as clear as can be?

R. G.: Whenever it is confronted with recalcitrant material, rationalist ethnology adopts the strategy employed by Horatius against the three Curiatii. The adversaries must first be isolated from one another, which then makes it easier to eliminate each one in turn. When we discover something that contradicts our cherished notions, the easiest thing to do is to consider it suspect. An error must have slipped into a picture that is otherwise quite trustworthy. But if one goes back and compares the data that have been successively discarded one will find that they have much in common. As dubious as any one given fact might appear when considered in isolation, such facts will turn out to be too numerous not to be taken seriously. An ethnologist has to ask himself if what he takes to be critical discernment does not often amount to discarding anything that threatens his view of the world and of ethnology.

J.-M. O.: This reminds me of the passage from Proust that you quote in *Deceit, Desire and the Novel*. Marcel's aunt has decided that Swann is after all nothing but the son of a modest stockbroker, a neighbour one can receive without ceremony, and she manages to ignore everything that points to the exceptional social position Swann does in fact possess. The empirical evidence is not deceptive, but discovery favours the prepared mind. By themselves, the facts are rarely enough to dislodge preconceived ideas.

R. G.: Evans-Pritchard nonetheless should be praised for the care he takes to report everything from his sources, even though he refuses to take much of it seriously. Evans-Pritchard's book, despite the disclaimers, does convey the fundamental principle of African monarchies. It still allows us to recognize and reconstruct that principle. If the present trend toward minimizing religion continues, we can look forward to the disappearance of any significant evidence. This is all the more likely in that the societies themselves are evolving on a course similar to that of ethnology. Traditional religion is in the process of disappearing.

It will soon be possible to believe, as a result, that the earlier ethnologists were dreaming, that they had let themselves be taken in by fanciful informers who were anxious to make fun of the ethnologists' ethnocentric and colonialist prejudices. Thus while we assume that we are refining our critical methods we will have doubled our naivety, and ethnological knowledge will be increasingly impoverished rather than enriched.

The evolution of theory in ethnology tends to repeat and exaggerate the tendencies of all the cultural forms that preceded it, from ritual to 'idealized' religion to philosophy. The question of religion animated and directed research up to Durkheim and Freud; currently it is hardly discussed at all. After having been expelled from all other areas, religion appeared suddenly and was of immense interest in what was the new discipline of ethnology—but here again it has been gradually neutralized and expelled.

The Domestication of Animals and Ritual Hunting

J.-M. O.: In your view, then, every human institution descends from ritual, or in other words, from the surrogate victim. In *Violence and the Sacred* you attempted to show that institutions such as the festival or initiation rites are variants of the same scheme and that our notions of leisure and of education also stem from ritual.[22] This was essentially the project of Durkheim, which can be continued and completed thanks to our knowledge of the victimage mechanism. Can you continue from this point and bring in cultural phenomena you have not yet discussed?

R. G.: We might consider the domestication of animals. Everyone believes that the principle of domestication is economic. In reality, however, this is unlikely. Even though the process of domestication is quite rapid compared with periods of time normally required by evolution, the time it does require is certainly beyond any limit that the utilitarian motive would require had it been uppermost for those who began the process. What we see as a point of departure can only be the result of a long development. The domestication of animals requires that men keep them in their company and treat them, not as wild animals, but as if they were capable of living near human beings and leading a quasi-human existence.

What could be the motive for such behaviour toward animals? The final consequences of the act could not have been foreseen. At no time would men have been able to say: 'We shall treat the ancestors of the cow and the horse as if they were already domesticated, and at some point in the future our descendants will enjoy the advantages of domesticated animals.' An immediate motive was necessary, one powerful and permanent enough to encourage treating animals in such a way as to ensure their eventual domestication. The only motive could have been sacrifice.

The 'monstrous' qualities attributed to the victim allow us to suppose that its replacements might as easily have been sought among animals as among men. The victim will serve as a mediator between the community and the sacred, between the inside and the outside.

The religious mind knows that in order to polarize effectively the malevolent aspects of communal life, the victim must differ from members of the community but also resemble them. With animals, it is therefore necessary for the victim to live among members of the community and adopt their customs and characteristic habits. This explains the delay, in many rituals, between the time of choosing the victim and the time of the sacrifice. This delay, as the example of the king has demonstrated, can play an enormous role in cultural development. It is no doubt responsible for the existence of domestic animals, just as it is for so-called political power.

All species of domesticated animals have been used or are still used as sacrificial victims. The process of domestication must have come about through the cohabitation of animals and human beings over many generations and would have produced the effects of domestication in the species commonly used for sacrifice.

The results of practising sacrifice turn out to be so valuable that they produce unforeseen changes in those that benefit from them. They take man, the sacrificial creature, and create man, the economic creature. The economic motive is not sufficient to explain domestication, but sacrifice can result in economic practices that gradually become independent of their origin, as in the political development of kingship, though in the former case the practice of immolation persists. Here immolation offers no obstacle to the non-ritual development of domestication; on the contrary, it is always necessary to kill the victim before eating it.

Modern observers think that domestication must have preceded the use of animals for sacrifice, but only the reverse order is conceivable. In every instance modern man minimizes the role of religion.

G. L.: Religion is implicated in every cultural institution. If we truly reject the idea of religion as a universal parasite of human institutions, the conspiracy of Voltaire's 'deceitful and greedy' priests, the only other plausible theory is Durkheim's: religion must be the origin of all institutions.

R. G.: In order to understand better how the domestication of animals originated in sacrifice, we can relate what we have just said to sacrificial practices in which species incapable of domestication have been and continue to be treated as domestic animals.

Consider, for example, the well-known bear ceremony of the Ainu. A bear cub is captured and raised among the children of the community; it plays with them and a woman serves as its nurse. At a specified time, the animal is taken with the utmost courtesy and ceremony and ritually immolated; it is then consumed by the entire community and considered to be a god.[23]

This institution is like what occurs with other sacrificial animals, and therein lies its strangeness. In certain pastoral societies, cattle are seen as hardly distinct from human beings; the animal have their kinship system and are treated with respect. They are never eaten except on sacrificial occasions and in ceremonies analogous to the bear ceremony, yet we view these occasions differently because to us, although we never admit it, sacrifice and domestication go hand in hand and reciprocally justify one another.

The bear ceremony disturbs us precisely because it tends to reveal the secret of domestication—it suggests that we might violate the powerful taboo that guards the creative role of sacrifice in human culture.

The bear is not domesticated because bears cannot be domesticated. One can therefore suppose that domestication is only a secondary effect, a sub-product of a ritual practice that is nearly identical in every case. The practice of sacrifice has been extended to extremely diverse species, including human beings, and only chance, the accident of selecting a certain species in combination with its given aptitude, has made for the success of domestication in some cases and its failure in others. In this sense sacrifice became a means for exploring the world. It operated somewhat like scientific research operates in the modern world. There are those who are fortunate and proceed in promising directions, whereas others, without suspecting it, start off toward dead ends. The destiny of many cultures must have been influenced by similar accidents.

J.-M. O.: You mentioned the impression of strangeness produced by the bear ceremony. The same impression is intensified by reports of ritual cannibalism among the Tupinamba, as related by early explorers.[24] Once again it is not the uniqueness of the structure that is surprising, but the fact of recognizing something very familiar in cannibalism, namely the same structure that has been our topic all along.

The future victims—prisoners of war—are made a part of the community; they work, they marry and have children. They are treated with the kind of double standard accorded the purifying and sacred scapegoat. They are driven to commit certain transgressions and are then persecuted and honoured, insulted and esteemed. Finally they are ritually murdered and devoured, like the bear cub of the Ainu or the animals kept by pastoral societies.

R. G.: The cannibalism of the Tupinamba is simply an extraordinary variant of widespread sacrificial forms. In Central America, for example, the future victims in certain rituals have the privilege or obligation to commit certain transgressions, sexual or otherwise, during the interval of time between their selection and immolation.

G. L.: As we begin to understand the creative power of ritual on all levels, the inadequacy of other theories on the subject, particularly those that subordinate religion to some other factor, becomes much more evident. Once other interpretations have been evaluated and set aside, one will recognize that the structure of all ritual is identical to that of the institution we have called 'sacred kingship'.

R. G.: Sacrificial delay again plays the crucial role. If the victim is a human being, the delay can give rise to political power, just as it can produce domestication if the victim belongs to a species amenable to domestication. It is also possible that no real development will take place, which is what we witness in the case of the bear. The ritual becomes immobilized but is no less revealing than examples of the evolution of ritual: the example provides us with the 'control' necessary for the validation of our hypothesis.

J.-M. O.: Sacrifice affords us such constant and persistent structural elements in the background of institutions derived from it that their presence always deserves some attention, whether they are salient or reduced to a kind of trace. If attempts to construct a unified interpretation have been unsuccessful up to this point, it is not because their success is impossible; they simply overlooked the mechanism capable of providing a universal key, one that accounts equally well for institutions that seem totally unrelated to one another without disregarding their most singular characteristics.

When we take into account the derivative character of all differentiated institutions, such as monarchy, human sacrifice, animal sacrifice, animal worship, cannibalism, etc., the structural elements become prominent to such a degree that one can only conclude that they derive from a single, ubiquitous intention to reproduce reconciliation by means of sacrifice, which in turn is the process that eventually produces cultural institutions.

In animal domestication we reach back towards prehistorical institutions. Is it possible to proceed even further back toward the very origins of the human species?

R. G.: Before domestication, at a time when man was perhaps not yet what we call man, hunting was already practised. The hunt has an invariably ritual character in primitive societies. Here again, most theorists implicitly or explicitly take the ritual aspect of hunting for a sense-

less embellishment and remain unperturbed by the fact that it constitutes the sole invariant among infinitely diverse techniques. Yet
these too are related so closely and intimately to aspects of ritual that the
religious element in hunting cannot be the mere intruder and interloper
we always take it to be, even if we are careful not to lessen its role.

Specialists tell us that the human digestive tract has remained that of
the mainly vegetarian omnivore, the kind of system that preceded ours
in the course of evolution. Man is not naturally a carnivore; human
hunting should not be thought of in terms of animal predation.

To understand what might have impelled human beings to set off in
pursuit of the largest and most dangerous animals or to devise the strategies necessary for prehistoric hunting, it is necessary and sufficient to
recognize that hunting, at first, was actively linked to sacrifice. The
object of the hunt is seen as a substitute for the original victim in its
monstrous and sacred aspects. What impelled men to hunt was the
search for a reconciliatory victim. The ritual character of hunting is entirely compatible with an activity demanding complex technique and
the co-ordination of many individuals.[25]

Even today the religious nature of hunting, the ritual distribution of
roles, and the sacrificial character of the victim, suggest such an origin.
Some prehistoric evidence, from the magnificent cave paintings in the
Dordogne to the geometrical arrangements of bones and human and
animal skulls found in some areas, could also be cited. Furthermore,
many myths of the hunt suggest its ritual origin, particularly those
stories in which the roles of the hunter and the hunted are reversed, in
which everything turns on an act of collective murder. The common
denominator is the collective murder, whether attributed to animals or
men, rather than the hunted species or various techniques employed.

Sexual Prohibitions and the Principle of Exchange

J.-M. O.: The dynamic of this cultural process is essential—we need
to develop it in further examples.

R. G.: The only possible examples at this stage are other fundamental
customs; those said to distinguish the human from the animal, such as
the prohibition of incest.

We know by now that we cannot consider human sexual customs in
terms of the nuclear family or the incest prohibition *as we ourselves con-*

ceive them. Neither can we begin with the positive rules of exchange, as Lévi-Strauss does in his *Elementary Structures of Kinship*.[26] Clearly, something more than the passion for order or the desire to play at structuralism was required to induce an animal to refrain completely from the nearest and most available females. What is good for ethnologists is not necessarily sufficient for primates in the process of hominization.

Strangely, it was Freud, with his characteristic genius for observation, who defined the true domain of the prohibition in primitive societies. He noted that the women who were forbidden were those born to the group; these women were therefore the most accessible and were constantly 'at hand', so to speak, or at the disposition of all male members of the group.[27]

If Freud had fully developed his observation he would have realized that it destroys every hypothesis ever proposed as an explanation for human sexual customs, including the psychoanalytic hypothesis.

Before Freud's observation can be correctly understood it must be considered in the context of alimentary prohibitions found in certain so-called totemic societies, such as those in Australia. Cohabitant groups are forbidden to eat a particular food except during certain rituals.[28] The totemic food is more or less identified with a 'divinity' or sacred principle.

J.-M. O.: As soon as you cite a primitive custom, someone else will certainly be able to cite a contrary custom. It can be pointed out that the prohibition against eating a totemic food is ambiguous. In many cases, apparently, abstinence is not absolute; the totemic food is eaten on certain occasions. There are also examples of the food being eaten regularly, albeit in small quantities, in 'moderation'. One is finally confronted with such varied evidence that it becomes impossible to draw any conclusion that would not be subject to contradiction.

R. G.: Our theory is quite capable of accommodating such a situation. We can conceive of an absolute prohibition because of the totem's link to the sacred, but a relaxation of this prohibition is also quite conceivable. The notion that the sacred food can be eaten in moderate amounts, for instance, is one that might well evidence a keener knowledge of prohibitions than that of ethnologists. The concern with moderation means simply that it is necessary to avoid any overly possessive or aggressive behaviour concerning the totem, which might lead to mimetic conflict. If one considers each of the variations of the 'totemic' alimentary prohibitions individually, including ritual transgression, it becomes evident not only that all the variations can be interpreted in the light of our hypothesis—this includes, of course, the complete effacement of the prohibition—but that the variations themselves form a structural configuration that our hypothesis alone can account for.

The paradox is that the group sub-divisions that normally abstain from eating their totemic food, or that eat it moderately, nevertheless have more intimate and constant contact with it than all other sub-divisions. Each sub-division is in some way 'specialized' in the production and manipulation of its totem; it will be in charge of hunting or of cooking, depending on the particular circumstances. But generally these activities are carried out for the benefit of other groups. Each group gives the product of its work over to the collective and receives in exchange those foods that other groups abstain from because they are the ones who produce and handle them.

Now if we compare alimentary prohibitions with the incest prohibition, we observe that they function in exactly the same manner. In both cases, in fact, the prohibition falls not on rare, distant, or inaccessible objects, but on those that are nearest and most abundant, since the group has a sort of monopoly on their production.

Alimentary and sexual prohibitions are in some sense identical. Only the object of the prohibition is different. We can therefore conclude that the prohibition, whether alimentary or sexual, should not be analysed and defined in terms of its object. It is impossible to construct an adequate interpretation from the perspective of objects, whether it be the economic or sexual object, as in Marxism or psychoanalysis; any such interpretation will be determined by an erroneous schematization of culture and will force one to discard as inessential phenomena that are entirely homologous with those that have been arbitrarily deemed essential.

The structuralism of Lévi-Strauss does away with the false priorities established by the object; it prepares a solution to the enigma but cannot itself provide the solution. It remains fascinated by its own discovery, by the structural homologies it reveals, which are considered to be sufficient, in themselves, to provide their own explication.

As much as structuralism differs from functionalism, in the final analysis it succumbs to the same type of error—it mistakes the stating of the problem for its resolution. When the structures of exchange are placed in a more radical context it becomes immediately apparent that they are anything but self-explanatory; one such context is animal behaviour, which we will consider from this point on.

Animals never renounce the satisfaction of their alimentary or sexual needs *within* their own group; non-dominant males must limit themselves to the females left to them by the dominant males or they must abstain from sexual activity. Occasionally, frustrated males attempt to achieve dominance in another group, but an exogamous system is never established; animals never renounce the most available satisfaction of their needs and appetites, and will never seek at a distance what can be had in their immediate environment; they will never turn away from the most available object.

An extraordinary force would have been required to make such a renunciation the general condition for humanity, but the force cannot be the Freudian desire for incest, which presupposes the law, or the Lévi-Straussian desire for structuralism, which also presupposes the law. Lévi-Strauss follows the procedure of transforming the problem to be explained into the explanatory principle, but he does recognize, as did Mauss before him and as does Hocart, that the principle of exchange operates in all domains and not simply in those of sexuality and economics.

J.-M. O.: What could have led the animal in the process of hominization to defer the satisfaction of its needs and to transfer the possibility of this satisfaction from the nearest objects to those that are more distant and apparently less accessible?

It could only have been fear, the fear of mimetic rivalry and of a return to interminable violence.

R. G.: Of course. But if the members of the group simply feared one another, they would end up by killing each other off. Past violence in some way has to be embodied in a reconciliatory victim; a kind of collective transference must already have occurred and made the return of the victim something to be feared—as if the return meant vengeance and was such a terrifying prospect that the whole group gathered with the intention of preventing it.

The most available and accessible objects are prohibited because they are most likely to provoke mimetic rivalries among members of the group. Sacred objects, totemic foods, female deities—these have certainly been the cause of real mimetic rivalries in the past, before they were made sacred. That is the reason they were. Therefore they become the objects of strict prohibitions. Some of them, in totemic groups, are completely assimilated to the surrogate victim.

Hocart notes that ultimately not a single need or appetite is allowed satisfaction within the group or among its members; any vital function has been effectively banned. Members of the same group are unable to do very much of anything for one another because they feel themselves to be perpetually threatened by mimetic rivalry. This is true even of funeral rites. In certain societies a moiety never buries its own dead; it is expressly forbidden to participate in the funeral rites of a member of one's own group. It is not forbidden, however, to hold funeral rites for members of the other moiety, for those who are all but strangers. This explains why the two moieties mutually perform a service for one another that neither moiety can perform for itself.[29]

The weakness of theories that emphasize too exclusively the gift and exchange, like those of Mauss and Lévi-Strauss, is particularly evident in the rituals surrounding death. Should we conclude that moieties exchange their respective dead in order to perpetuate the game of exchange, the way they exchange women and food? No. All the evidence suggests that human beings fear their own dead even more than the dead of others and that such fear has nothing metaphysical in its origin. Each group 'produces' its own dead, and the activity is still more dangerous than the production of women or foodstuffs. Thus in many societies the responsibility for a death is assigned to another group or to a member of that group. This transference on to another group explains the practice of exchanging the dead; the problem is the same, really, as that of explaining the ritual character of funeral rites and ultimately of all human institutions.

Cohabitant groups are paralyzed by prohibitions; in fact if there were nothing but prohibitions these groups would perish from inactivity. But the imperative of ritual forces the members of these same groups out beyond the group domain in search of victims. The foundations of human culture, particularly the modes of matrimonial exchange, the initial economic exchanges, etc., are built on the ritual of sacrifice.

J.-M. O.: Let me interrupt at this point. If the surrogate victim is a member of the community, why should the intent to reproduce its murder turn the group toward the outside and lead it to enter into contact with other groups? If the aim is to reproduce everything exactly as it occurred the first time, why not select new victims from within the group?

R. G.: Human behaviour is determined not by what really happened but by the interpretation of what happened. The double transference guides such interpretation. It transforms the victim into something radically other than, and transcendent to, the community. The community belongs to the victim but the victim does not belong to the community. In general, then, the victim will appear to be more foreign than native; as in many myths, the victim is a *visitor* that has come from an unknown world.[30] Even when the victim does not appear in the guise of a stranger, it will be seen as coming or returning from the outside, especially as returning to the outside at the moment when the community expels it.

The fact that sacrificial victims, even when they are human, are chosen from outside the community suggests that the interpretation that makes the victim exterior to the community—while nonetheless placing the victim at the centre and origin of the community—must have been prevalent throughout the course of human history, including the most rudimentary stages of symbolizing the victim. It is thus reasonable to suppose that the imperative of ritual-led groups to search for victims outside the group at the very moment when the imperative of the prohibition made any vital interaction among members of the group impossible. Under the influence of these two imperatives that, we must not forget, have a common origin in the same mechanism—that of the double transference on to the victim—a new type of social interaction would have arisen between originally separate groups or between groups recently divided by the mimetic crisis itself. This new type of interaction would take shape as a series of exchanges regulated and symbolized by sacrificial ritual, that is to say by the ritual repetition of the mimetic crisis and of victimage, and would substitute itself for the immediate interactions of animal behaviour.

We can therefore see why it is that in all primitive cultures the institutions and rituals surrounding death, marriage, hunting, child rearing, and initiation present themselves as a 'mimetic crisis' that concludes with the sacrifice of a victim.

At first it may seem unthinkable that all human institutions could arise from a practice as negative and destructive, it seems, as sacrifice. In every case it ultimately results in the murder of a victim. But finally the number of victims is small, whereas before the sacrifice the crisis can be re-enacted with a large number of partners, permitting all the sexual, alimentary and funeral activities that are now prohibited to take place inside cohabitant groups.

In many primitive cultures the fundamental modes of exchange are not only accompanied by sacrifice but retain aspects of ritual violence from the mimetic crisis. Mauss notes this, although he is unable to explain it, in his *Essay on the Gift*.[31] In many South American cultures the word designating the brother-in-law is also the word for ritual enemy, the enemy twin of myth and the sacrificial victim of the anthropophagous meal.[32]

In most cases the utilitarian aspect of an institution comes to dominate once a system of exchange has been established and ritual hostility and sacrifice become marginal or even disappear. We have observed this process in all our analyses. It is also possible that the original violence persists in the form of ritual warfare, the rites of headhunters or the kinds of cannibalism that depend on capturing prisoners, which always operate more or less like a system of exchange between groups.

In examining these types of institutions we find that their structure is essentially that of marriage or of economic exchange, with the difference that the destructive and violent elements are paramount, in our eyes at any rate. But as usual ethnologists are influenced by their 'rational' conception of 'useful' institutions to an extent that they are unable to perceive structural homologies and to draw the radical conclusions that these homologies so visibly demand.

Whether warriors are killed alternatively by one side or the other, prisoners are captured, or women are 'exchanged', there can be little difference between institutions that establish agreement for the sake of hostility (assuring, for example, that neither of two sides will be deprived of ritual enemies) and institutions that promote hostility for the sake of agreement, providing for the exchange of women or goods that cannot be kept within the group. The 'cathartic' function dominates in the first whereas the economic function dominates in the second, but the two functions are not truly distinct. It is only by means of *a posteriori* rationalization that we manage to obscure the common origin of all institutions, which is the reproduction of generative violence.

Death and Funeral Rites

R. G.: It might at first seem incredible to claim that all significant oppositions in cultural phenomena take shape both as a function of the victimage process and as an interpretation of that process, yet our analysis suggests this not only as a possibility but as the only likely hypothesis. It is the only one that can make sense of certain specifically human modes of behaviour that until now have remained perfectly mysterious, such as our attitude toward the dead and the fact that once something like humanity exists there also exists the strange behaviour toward the dead that we call funerary: the refusal to see death naturalistically, as merely the cessation of life, with the cadaver no more than a sort of irreparably broken, useless object. Far from being 'innate', the naturalistic view of death is a relatively recent development that is alien to the greater part of humanity.

For modern thought, the religious conception of death constitutes a sublimation, an idealization of what is held to be the only 'natural' attitude toward death, which is of course our own, a naturalist and functionalist conception of life and death that is thought to precede all others. This view is unable to account for the universally ritual character of funeral rites. We can account for this, however, if we recognize that the interpretation of death is determined by the victimage process; death is always intimately linked with life.

In his essay on mourning, Freud characteristically comes very close to a truth that nonetheless escapes him entirely. He recognizes the reconciliatory power of any death but does not see that for society, at a certain level, such reconciliation is never separate from life itself. Freud felt it necessary to assume the naturalistic conception of death as a basis for his insights and to suppose it to be earlier than all other conceptions. But if we discard this assumption as a gratuitous postulate and thereby radicalize the Freudian insight, it becomes clear that the reconciliatory aspect of mourning, the mourning that rejuvenates and invigorates all cultural activity, is in fact the essence of human culture. The mechanism of mimetic reconciliation polarized around the victim is simply a more elementary and effective form of a process that Freud, with his marvellous aptitude for observation, recognizes everywhere in its subtlest manifestations and most intimate echoes, although he is unable to bring about the 'Copernican revolution' that would truly reorganize this thought around his essential insight.

The proof that human beings identify all death with the reconciliatory victim and the power of the sacred is that what is called the *cult of the dead*, unlike the naturalistic conception of death, appears to underlie all other forms of religion.

It is clear that if human beings not only create all their institutions but also discover all their 'ideas' on the basis of the victimage mechanism, their attitude toward death is not determined by an unconscious desire to repress a naturalistic conception of death that primitive peoples, 'deep within themselves', supposedly know to be true but do not possess the courage and determination, which we reserve for ourselves, to confront directly. Only ethnocentrism or perhaps the most naive moderno-centrism is capable of such a view.

In reality, the human discovery of what we call death and the discovery of what we call life can only be one and the same, because these concepts are only developed, to repeat, on the basis of the victimage mechanism; one has only to consider the elements of this process and the misinterpretation to which it is necessarily subject to see that the conjunction of what is most dead and most alive is not any more a 'confusion' of two ideas than it is the surpassing insight of some absolute spirit.

At the moment when violence ceases and peace has been established, the community has the whole of its attention fixed on the victim it has just killed; it discovers the first cadaver, in other words. But how could this discovery be made in our habitual sense of naturalistically conceived death when the cadaver signifies the return of peace for the entire community, the beginning of the very possibility of culture, which means, for human beings, the very possibility of life? The reconciliatory powers of the surrogate victim are responsible for the human discovery that joins, over one cadaver, all that can be called death and all that can be called life. The religious conception of death can be understood if we recognize that it extends to any member of the community who dies, for one reason or another, the whole of the dynamic and signifying complex based on the surrogate victim.

As Malraux has said, man is certainly the only animal who knows that he will die. But this knowledge does not take the irremediable, materialist form that, for the most part, it takes for us. If that had been the case, humanity in its period of gestation would never have survived the disintegrative power of such knowledge. There is little merit in the idea that intolerable truths are in themselves sufficient to explain the development of cultural patterns that mask these truths. Such a notion is philosophical, which is to say a substitute for the sacred, one that begins, once again, by considering death as if it were productive of life—in other words, death is once again covertly deified.

The time has come to abandon any view of religion that remains part of the retroactive perspective, that sees in religion only what is added on, superimposed on basic realities that always turn out to be identical to our own consciousness. And this includes any view of religion as an idealization or sublimation, as something logically or chronologically subordinate to modern ideas. The advantage of our theory consists precisely in the fact that it allows us to set aside such egregious misrepresentations of religion; it provides a concrete reality and confirms, at the level of minute detail, the greatest anthropological intuition of our time; Durkheim's intuition of the identity of the social and religious domains, which means, ultimately, the chronological precedence of religious expression over any sociological conception. What is creative and fertile at the cultural level is not the naturalistic conception of death, or my desire to escape the belief, which henceforth inhabits me, in that conception of death (a belief that produces nothing but the macabre caricatures that surround us), but rather it is the revelation of death as sacred, that is to say, as an infinite power ultimately more beneficent than fearful, more of an object of worship than of terror.

If the idea of death gains its potency from sacralized victims, if every god, ultimately, conceals a dead man, then it becomes comprehensible that there should be societies in which no one dies without becoming a god. Freud shows that the basic elements of that perpetual metamorphosis remain present among us; every death gives rise to a unifying phase of mourning, and every death, in society, becomes a major resource for life.

There is indeed an element of terror in funeral rites, and it corresponds to the process of physical decay. Yet the latter is not related to a physical and chemical process but to the mimetic crisis. This element is therefore never anything more than a preparation for a sacrificial reconciliation and a return to life. This is certainly why the element of terror figures in funeral rites, which of course reproduce the schema of all other ritual.

G. L.: The dead and the living are inextricably intertwined; here one can conceive, on the basis of animal nature, what precedes their differentiation.

R. G.: What is essential is the cadaver as talisman, as the bearer of life and fertility; culture always develops as a *tomb*. The tomb is nothing but the first human monument to be raised over the surrogate victim, the first most elemental and fundamental matrix of meaning. There is no culture without a tomb and no tomb without a culture; in the end the tomb is the first and only cultural symbol.[33] The above-ground tomb does not have to be invented. It is the pile of stones in which the victim of unanimous stoning is buried. It is the first pyramid.

J.-M. O.: We might well consider funeral rites to be the first design and model of all subsequent culture. Everything is based on a death at once transfigured, sacralized, and dissimulated. We can see how, beginning with the victimage mechanism and the first steps toward sacralization, which tend to include all deaths in the community, the animal's indifference to the cadaver gives way to a keen, fascinated attentiveness, leading men to regard their dead not so much as living beings as beings who have transcended life and death and have, for better or worse, become all-powerful; they might be ritually eaten so that their power is absorbed, or they might be treated as if they were alive or waiting for another life, and thus be given an appropriate abode.

We understand that temples, fortresses, and palaces that have victims buried in their foundations to assure their long life are never anything more than transfigured tombs—but how can you argue that the whole of human culture comes from sacralized victims? Is that not an interminable, impossible task?

CHAPTER THREE

The Process of Hominization

Posing the Problem

J.-M. O.: We are at the point of asking just how far back in human or pre-human history the victimage mechanism should be situated. If this mechanism is the foundation for everything that is human in man, for humanity's most ancient institutions, such as hunting or the incest prohibition, the question then becomes the process of hominization, or in other words the transition from animal to man.[34]

R. G.: We are indeed moving toward that question. But in order to pose it properly we first need to consider its current status, the way it is addressed today. Either the question is resolved in a purely verbal way, by invoking words so burdened with meaning that they end up conveying none at all—'culture' for example, and of course 'evolution'—or the transition from animal to man is conceived concretely, in which case one encounters a series of insoluble contradictions. Along either route one soon reaches an impasse.

The brain of the human infant is already so large at birth that delivery would be impossible for the female without the enlargement of the pelvis, which does not take place in other primates. Yet the brain undergoes the greatest amount of post-natal growth. In order to permit that growth it is necessary for the bone structure of the skull to complete its development only well after birth. The human infant is more vulnerable and helpless than the offspring of other mammals and it remains this way for an extremely long period—much longer, relatively, than for any species in the animal kingdom.

G. L.: Premature birth, the 'neoteny' of the human infant, is a factor of adaptation; it is no doubt responsible for the post-natal growth of the brain and thereby makes possible not only the power but also the extraordinary suppleness of human intelligence. Instead of being limited to instinctual patterns, we are capable of learning the most diverse lessons of culture. All of this contributes to the human being's superiority over other species.

R. G.: Certainly. This superiority is beyond doubt once the system is in place, but it is still unclear how the system reached that particular point. In order to protect an infant as vulnerable as the human infant, certain adaptations in behaviour must be made, and these concern not only the female, who must nourish the infant, sometimes for years, and carry it with her when she moves, but also the male. This remains true even if one grants the misleading character of certain idyllic images of the prehistoric couple. The lengthy time the infant must stay with the female necessarily creates an obstacle to the male's relations with the female; a minor impediment, perhaps, but nonetheless real.

In many species any encounter between the adult male and the infants may result in the extermination of the infants. The period of infant dependence among animals is commonly short, and periods of oestrus are distributed in such a way that any interference of maternal and sexual functions is non-existent or reduced to a minimum.

G. L.: Among anthropoid monkeys, however, the dependence of the infant lasts much longer.

R. G.: This is true, although the period is nonetheless shorter than it is for human beings, and sexual excitation is perhaps not permanent among those higher mammals. The latter, at any rate, are for the most part peaceable omnivores that are apparently analogous in many ways to those preceding us in the history of evolution. During the process of hominization, however, our ancestors very rapidly became carnivores and hunters. Strong discharges of adrenaline are necessary at the critical moment of the hunt and these can occur in different conditions, as in the middle of a family group, for example, under the effect of any sort of disturbance.

In order to appreciate the problem of controlling violence, we must also consider that strange activity we call war, which, along with cannibalism, must have appeared early in human or pre-human groups. According to the evidence, primitive warfare takes place among proximate, neighbouring groups, which is to say among men who cannot be distinguished objectively in terms of race, language, or cultural habits. There is no real difference between the external enemy and the internal friend, and it is difficult to imagine how an external pattern could account for the difference in behaviour.

J.-M. O.: The proof that such difference is not instinctual is that it can be abolished. Intrafamilial murder exists. It is not sufficiently frequent to endanger the institution of the family, but it is too frequent to allow the conclusion that the absence of violence in human social groups is a matter of instinct.

R. G.: It is important to realize that extreme rage becomes centripetal once it has been given free rein; it is never naturally centrifugal. The more exasperated rage becomes, the more it tends to turn toward those who are closest and most cherished, those who are most protected in normal circumstances by the rule against violence. The centripetal tendency of violence is not something to be treated lightly. Certain researchers are well aware of the enormous problem this poses. Sherwood L. Washburn, for example, recognizes the necessity of mastering rage but he cannot tell us how or why rage was ever effectively mastered:

> One of the essential conditions for the organization of men in cooperative societies was the suppression of rage and of the uncontrolled drive for first place in the hierarchy of dominance.[35]

J.-M. O.: In your view, then, the best studies of hominization contain a recognition of the problem but not the means of resolving it. Ethologists speak of instinct with reference to phenomena so opposed to one another that the word becomes meaningless, whereas ethnologists take prohibitions as givens that require no explanation. Freud himself does this when he relates prohibitions to repressed desire, or in other words to what is already a prohibition. When the problem is considered in the context of animal behaviour, some of Freud's brilliant observations come to the foreground but psychoanalytic theory pales by comparison.

R. G.: Freud does not realize that the control of sexual relations is part of the more fundamental question of violence. To realize just how fundamental this question is, one has only to consider the very simple but indisputable fact of the use of stone and weapons. The reduction of canine teeth to their current dimensions occurred a long time before the appearance of *homo sapiens*, suggesting that stones had replaced dentition in most of their uses, including inter-species combat.[36]

Animals are capable of engaging in rivalry and combat without fighting to the death because instinctual inhibitions assure the control of *natural* weapons, the claws and teeth. One can hardly believe that the same type of control was automatically extended to stones and other artificial weapons the day that hominids began to use them. The violence that goes unchecked by instinctual inhibitions because it represents no threat to disarmed adversaries will become fatal the moment these same adversaries are armed with rocks.

If instead of throwing branches at one another as they sometimes do, chimpanzees were to learn to throw stones at one another, their social life would be radically shaken. Either the species would disappear, or like humanity it would have to impose its own prohibitions. But how does one go about imposing one's own prohibition?

G. L.: Some see the key to the human order in permanent sexuality, the lure that keeps the male in the female's company and 'cements the union of the couple'.

R. G.: Nothing suggests that sexuality itself has this power. Among mammals the periods of sexual excitation are marked by rivalries between males. The animal group at this time is particularly vulnerable to external threats. There is no reason to view permanent sexuality as a factor of order rather than disorder.

J.-M. O.: All the basic elements present at the origin of human culture, considered together, seem more than capable of assuring the destruction of previous systems of behaviour; yet none of them seems at all promising as elements facilitating the creation of a new system. This is the case with stones and weapons as well as with the increased aptitude for violent action necessitated by hunting and warfare, to say nothing of the prolonged and more vulnerable period of infancy. If the process of hominization is decomposed into its analysable elements, we confront an ensemble of factors each of which, in itself, could easily have destroyed the species. It must be that each of these impossibilities was in one way or another transformed into a resource, because together, by some 'mysterious alchemy', they brought about progressively humanized forms of culture and biological processes.

At the moment when the propensity for rage is systematically cultivated and developed on the outside by an animal that arms itself with stones and tools, it becomes more and more necessary to master this rage on the inside, where this same animal is confronted with familial and social tasks that become constantly more delicate and absorbing. Instinctual inhibitions are unable to account for this double, contradictory evolution. Canalizing rage toward the exterior would have required a level of cultural organization that already would have been analogous to those we see around us.

R. G.: Certainly this has been understood by all those researchers who invoke 'culture' in order to explain these remarkable transformations. There is very little risk of error in asserting that 'culture' has resolved all problems. Of course culture is an unavoidable term in this context, but its use more often situates the problem than resolves it.

We have absolutely no idea what early 'cultural' processes consist of, how they interlock with 'natural' processes, and how they act on the latter to create more and more humanized forms. We recognize that the stages of biological evolution are too rapid not to implicate cultural elements, but we have no idea whatsoever of how that reciprocal relation functions. Everyone today agrees in hypothesizing that the volume of the brain has grown much too quickly to be attributed to a normal process of biological evolution.

Many of these problems are so perplexing that contemporary science has adopted the habit of treating the statement of the problem as if it were the solution. This accounts for the unreal, fairy-tale style in so many purportedly scientific descriptions. Evolutionists answer the supreme confidence of the creationists with their own supreme confidence, yet the level of argument is often very similar on both sides. This sort of exercise has resulted only in alienating ethnologists and has contributed to a regrettable rupture between cultural research and research oriented toward biology.

Much like the legendary good fairy, Lady Evolution surmounts all obstacles with such ease and so predictably that we soon lose interest. With the slightest touch of her wand, the most uniquely human cultural forms, such as symbolic institutions, appear when summoned and parade before us like brave little tin soldiers. Just as the crab needs its pincer and the bat its wings, which the always benevolent and attentive Lady Evolution has provided for them, so man has need of 'culture', which he duly receives served on a silver platter from this new, universal Great Mother.

For some time now, however, researchers in areas of evolution have attempted to react against such simplifications and locate more concrete problems. Weston La Barre, for instance, protests against the so-frequently-expressed idea that the very vulnerability of the human infant must have brought about the formation of the family group to protect it. Unfortunately he does this by falling back into a kind of modified Freudianism that is worth little more than what he criticizes:

> It is footling to say, as have two recent authors, that 'the prolonged helplessness of human infants conduces to the formation of a family group', for this is to suppose that results achieved are the dynamic causes. Besides, just how does helplessness do any conducing? On the contrary, the existence of a family group based upon identifiable drives is the enabling factor behind the development of prolonged infantile helplessness.[37]

Ethology and Ethnology

J.-M. O.: Until now you have not mentioned the fundamental element in all your analyses, acquisitive mimesis.

R. G.: There is no question of forgetting it. As an element that animals possess in common with human beings, it will play an even more fundamental role from this point on. The advantage of our hypothesis over psychoanalysis or Marxism lies in the elimination of the false specificities of the human being. If you begin with the incest prohibition, the economic motive, or socio-political oppression, you can never really pose the problem of hominization and the origin of symbolic systems on the basis of animal nature, whereas precisely this needs to be done if we are to renounce once and for all providing ourselves with answers in advance of every problem we confront. The notion of the father does not exist among apes. Subdominant animals will let themselves die of hunger rather than challenge dominant animals for their food. If we can manage to think through the process of hominization, beginning with acquisitive mimesis and the conflicts it provokes, we will escape the legitimate objection of using a vicious circle to determine an origin, a problem Lévi-Strauss raises with reference to *Totem and Taboo*. At the same time we will transcend the evolutionist fairy-tale and finally be able to approach some concrete problems.

G. L.: Ethologists, unlike ethnologists and other specialists in human culture, take an interest in mimesis. For example, they study the role of imitation in specific behaviours. It is common knowledge today that a young bird would never be able to reproduce exactly the song of its species if it had not heard adults of the same species at a determined stage of its development.

R. G.: Mimesis appears to be present in all forms of life, but in the so-called higher mammals and particularly in man's nearest relatives, the anthropoid apes, it manifests itself in some quite spectacular forms. In certain species the propensity to imitate and what we would call a quarrelsome, bickering mood are one and the same thing; it is a question of acquisitive mimesis.

Yet ethologists would never dream of relating the question of animal mimesis with that of rivalries attributed to the factor of prestige and the resulting relations of subordination. These relations of subordination, the *dominance patterns* as they are referred to by English-speaking researchers, play a crucial role in the social life of animals.

The notion of prestige, at this point, needs to be examined closely. It refers simply to the mimetic content of the rivalry, to the fact that the object cannot suffice to explain the intensity of the conflict. One can remove the object and the rivalry will continue. What interests us directly is the role of mimetic conflict in the establishment of animal societies. The individual that cedes first will always cede thereafter; it will yield the first place, the best food, and the females of choice to the victor without dispute. The relationship can be called into question again but generally it maintains a certain stability. Otherwise there would be little reason to speak of an animal society.

J.-M. O.: Currently there has been a heated debate between ethologists and structural or cultural ethnologists. The former insist on the resemblances between forms of animal and human sociality; the latter would rather not hear about animals. What is your position on this debate?

R. G.: I believe there are some important insights on both sides, along with some shortcomings. Our approach to mimesis should permit us to appropriate these intuitions and eliminate the shortcomings.

Let us first take up the ethological contribution and consider it from the perspective of mimesis. The stabilization of dominance patterns checks dissension within the animal group; it keeps mimetic rivalries from perpetuating themselves interminably. Ethologists are right to assert that dominance patterns play a role analogous to that of certain differentiations and subdivisions, which are sometimes, though not always, hierarchical in human societies; it becomes a question of canalizing desire in divergent directions and making acquisitive mimesis impossible.

In some mammal species the single individual or several individuals that dominate the rest of the group frequently occupy a central position. They are constantly observed and imitated by the other males, who remain on the periphery. This means that imitation applies to all attitudes and behaviours of the dominant animals *except for acquisitive behaviours.* I believe this to be a fact of fundamental importance that has not been sufficiently emphasized.

Once banned from an area in which it provokes rivalry, imitation increases in all other areas and becomes fixed on the most powerful animal, the one most capable of assuring the protection of the group, and who can act in the capacity of leader and model for the others; he will determine the group's character, give a signal for attack or flight, etc. Many researchers think that this kind of arrangement guarantees that a group, for example of baboons, will have a cohesion and efficacy within the group and *vis-à-vis* any external enemy that it would lack in the absence of dominance patterns.

J.-M. O.: There is a resemblance between this kind of organization and the activities derived from ritual, which provide group members with models that are in accord with social ends and that if adhered to will assure the perpetuation of the society.

R. G.: Indeed. The strength of ethology lies in its ability to uncover indubitable resemblances between animal sociality and human sociality. It has good grounds for objecting to the extraordinary insularity of cultural and structuralist ethnology, to their absolute refusal to re-situate human culture in nature, and to the wholly metaphysical conception of symbolic structures.[38]

Ethnologists are nonetheless justified in objecting that ethologists have been somewhat simplistic. In animal societies there is nothing outside of the relations between the dominant and the dominated. The systematic character of the whole is never apprehended as such. The positions do not exist outside of the individuals that occupy them. The ethologists themselves are the ones who disclose the system while observing the animals and 'verbalizing' their observations.

Ethnologists are capable of acting in this way because the *representation* of their own social system is an essential characteristic of human societies. Men who submit to the authority of a king, of a president of a republic, or of the executive officer of a corporation, act somewhat like subdominant animals *vis-à-vis* the dominant animal, but, unlike the animals, they are also capable of talking about monarchy, the presidency and similar notions. The system that was implicit among animals has become explicit. It is also much more complicated. The representation and the memory of the representation allow the system a considerable field of extension, as well as a perpetuation over several generations, without notable changes, or, on the contrary, with changes that we are capable of observing and registering, which means that we have a *history*.

The fact that as a general rule human beings do not fill vacant positions by means of mimetic combat between the candidates is evidently linked to the possibility of representing the system. There are often vestiges of mimetic combat in forms of *ritual* that surround selection procedures but these selection procedures themselves are almost never based on real mimetic rivalry, as in the case with animals. They can be based on principles as diverse as filiation, election, the drawing of lots, etc.

J.-M. O.: But in our society competition plays a formidable role and it always has an undeniably mimetic character.

R. G.: What I have just said should in fact be nuanced by distinguishing between primitive and traditional societies, and even societies as a whole, from what we see around us now. In primitive and traditional societies the status of the individual and the functions he will fulfil are very often determined before birth. This is much less so in modern society, and its the trend is continuing. Competition flourishes in many areas that extend from artistic creation, to scientific research, to economic enterprise. The rather unstable hierarchies of 'merit' and 'success' are established through the intermediary of antagonisms that are not carried through to death, at least as a rule.

Such a state of affairs can prevail because of a local effacement of the symbolic barriers that characterize primitive societies and discourage rivalries. As a consequence modern society has more of a resemblance, at least in certain respects, to animal societies than do primitive societies, in which real competition among individuals plays a much weaker role.

Clearly this recent development has contributed to the very creation of the new discipline of ethology and to the type of interpretation it characteristically advances. For in arguing for the proximity of animal sociality to human sociality it relies almost always on examples drawn from our society. Cultural ethnology, by contrast, and the disciplines that tend to stress the absolute difference between symbolic thought and everything else, prefer the support of primitive societies with their rigid and highly developed positional systems.

In support of the ethnological argument, it should be observed that in contemporary society, human beings enter into rivalry for highly symbolized objects and that the very existence of these rivalries is made possible by symbolic institutions. In other words, if mimetic conflict in our society does not normally degenerate into a fight to the death, the reasons for this are not those that obtain in animal society. It is not a matter of instinctual inhibition; instead an extremely powerful symbolic framework makes possible the relative 'desymbolization' and non-differentiation of the competitive domains. The fact that the equilibrium of the two domains seems to us to be constantly threatened does not in the least invalidate this point.

The Victimage Mechanism and Hominization

G. L.: In sum, because our society is extremely refined and developed in the symbolic sense—if I understand you here—it can permit and encourage the growth, as it sees it, of mimetic rivalries that are normally forbidden to man.

R. G.: That is exactly the point. Mimetic rivalries are normally forbidden to men; primitive prohibitions, as we have seen, are essentially concerned with these rivalries. In other words, forms of human sociality, unlike animal forms, cannot develop *directly* out of mimetic rivalries, but they do develop indirectly from them through the intermediary of the surrogate victim. Of course we know this already; until now, however, we have not attempted an analysis of human society in the context of animal society. Yet if we examine our preceding analyses, reconsider the impossibilities of hominization, and then bring the mimetic process and victimage mechanism to bear on all of this, we will see that we are already well under way on a path of discovery.

J.-M. O.: We are indeed proceeding in a new direction because of our attempt to analyse the most fundamental human institutions, such as hunting or incest prohibitions, from the point of view of the founding victim. The difference between man and animal is already at stake.

R. G.: It should be possible, on the basis of what we have accomplished so far, to think through the process of hominization in a truly radical way, that is, by beginning with animal nature itself and by making no use of anything that has been falsely claimed to be specifically human. We have to show that the intensification of mimetic rivalry, which is already very much in evidence at the level of primates, destroyed dominance patterns and gave rise to progressively more elaborate and humanized forms of culture through the intermediary of the surrogate victim. At the point when mimetic conflict becomes sufficiently intense to prohibit the direct solutions that give rise to the forms of animal sociality, the first 'crisis' or series of crises would then occur as the mechanism that produces the differentiated, symbolic, and human forms of culture.

In order for us to suppose that things did in fact happen this way it will be necessary and sufficient to show that mimetic power must increase not only during the process of hominization but even prior to its being set in motion, and to a degree great enough to set the process in motion.

This has already been shown, if we accept Jacques Monod's account of the human brain in *Chance and Necessity*, and assume that it applies to the brain in the process of hominization:

> It is the powerful development and intensive use of the simulative function that, in my view, characterizes the unique properties of man's brain. And this at the most basic level of the cognitive functions, those on which language rests and which it probably reveals only incompletely.[39]

There is reason to believe that the power and intensity of imitation increase with the volume of the brain along the entire line that leads to *homo sapiens*. In the primates closest to man the brain is relatively more voluminous than in any other animal species. It must have been the increasing power of imitation that initiated the process of hominization, rather than the reverse, even if the process subsequently served to accelerate that growth and made a prodigious contribution to the remarkable power of the human brain.

The considerable role of mimetic incitation in human sexuality, in excitation and the role of voyeurism, for example, suggests that the transition from periodic sexuality of the animal type to the permanent sexuality of human beings might well have been brought about through an intensification of mimesis. We will soon see that human desire consists of the grafting of mimesis on to instinctual patterns and the over-activation, aggravation, and disorganization of the latter. This essential link with mimesis assures that human sexuality will be even more conflictual than animal sexuality and makes sexuality itself incapable of being a factor of stability in human relations or even between sexual partners.

Human societies are obviously not based on dominance patterns, and we can see why: mimetic rivalry among human beings results easily in madness and murder. It would be a mistake, however, to attribute this increase of violence in human beings to an opaque, mute instinct; we would not only miss its real character but also ignore a more interesting explanation for it: it is part of the growth of mimetic activity linked to the increase in brain size.

We know that the ineradicable character of mimetic rivalry means that the importance of any object as a stake in conflict will ultimately be annulled and surpassed and that acquisitive mimesis, which sets members of the community against one another, will give way to antagonistic mimesis, which eventually unites and reconciles all members of a community at the expense of a victim. Beyond a certain threshold of mimetic power, animal societies become impossible. This threshold corresponds to the appearance of the victimage mechanism and would thus be the threshold of hominization.

J.-M. O.: The victimage mechanism would then begin and with it the forms of culture founded and mediated by it would take over from animal forms of behaviour. The problems encountered in this process are the same at all levels and can be solved by variations in the mechanism, which of course are simpler the nearer they are to animal behaviour.

R. G.: At this point we are forced to describe the victimage mechanism in such primitive and simple terms that it becomes difficult even to imagine it, but this is not a crucial problem. We have all the elements that make the mechanism possible and even statistically probable. The mechanism would have exercised palliative and preventive effects on rivalries in a manner analogous and proportional to what it achieves through the intermediary of fully humanized prohibitions and rituals. Up to now it was recognized that the rapid increase in brain size, as well as other phenomena, required an interaction between biological and cultural factors, but what has been missing is a model for the organizing and driving factor in the process, a motor for this strange machine. The victimage process gives us this motor. We can conceive of hominization as a series of steps that allow for the domestication of progressively increasing and intense mimetic effects, separated from one another by crises that would be catastrophic but also generative in that they would trigger the founding mechanism and at each step provide for more rigorous prohibitions within the group, and for a more effective ritual canalization toward the outside. In this sense it becomes conceivable that human infancy could become more and more vulnerable and prolong itself for a period corresponding to the growth of the brain without bringing about the simple annihilation of the species in the course of the latter's development. One can also see that at each step more and more elaborate institutions would favour a new mimetic level, which would bring about a new crisis and thus continue on in a spiral movement that would progressively humanize the anthropoid.

G. L.: Given the victimage mechanism, one can understand how cohabitant groups could have become sanctuaries of relative non-violence at a point when, on the outside, violence developed to an extreme. One can understand how the primate in the process of hominization, this hypersexual animal armed with stones, always disposed to hunting and war, could have transformed the extreme threat of self-destruction that hung over him in the crucial phases of his biological and cultural evolution into a force for cultural development.

R. G.: There is an element of truth to *Totem and Taboo*, and it consists in tracing humanity's origin to a collective murder. We might add that there are many founding myths that do the same. But, with the genius peculiar to him, Freud understood—in the face of all the futility of his time and of ours—that all such seemingly unconnected and irrelevant clues, which are nonetheless concordant on all essential points, have to be regarded with more seriousness and attention than anthropology has been able to muster. Freud, however, was unable to free himself from the mythological elements that encumber his theory. His father of the primitive horde is the last god of violence, and because it is in the process of dying today, along with the psychoanalytic religion founded on it, we are able to pursue our inquiry in different ways.

J.-M. O.: You can take up Freud's aims and give *Totem and Taboo* the recognition it deserves without falling back on the implausible elements in Freud's theory. The unique and incredible drama that Freud composed is the distorted allegory of processes that must repeat themselves over millions of years if necessary—the period of time would be determined by our empirical knowledge of pre-human history and will depend also on whatever new discoveries might be made.

R. G.: We can take a stand in the quarrel between ethnologists and ethologists. There will always be simultaneous rupture and continuity between all social forms, from animal to pre-human, and finally to human. The problematic nature of mimesis and the victimage mechanism allows us to understand that there will always be social forms based on imitation, even among animals, and that these forms must collapse in mimetic crises before they can generate new and more complex forms based on the surrogate victim. Between what can be strictly termed animal nature on the one hand and developing humanity on the other there is a true rupture, which is collective murder, and it alone is capable of providing for kinds of organization, no matter how embryonic, based on prohibition and ritual. It is therefore possible to inscribe the genesis of human culture in nature and to relate it to a natural mechanism without depriving culture of what is specifically, exclusively, human.

Of course we have no mode of access to the phenomena in question. Everything we can learn directly or indirectly about ritual belongs to a fully humanized universe. We are confronted with a gap of literally several million years. I will be criticized for exceeding the limits of the possible when I propose that the victimage mechanism is the origin of hominization. I am aware of how abstractly theoretical we must be. And yet we already have considerable evidence from the domain of human ritual; if we now examine what ethologists call animal rites we will find more evidence to buttress our hypothesis.

In certain species there are stereotyped behaviours that play a role in sexual seduction and in the establishment of relations of privilege with a partner of the same or opposite sex.[40]

Paradoxically, these rites of alliance most closely resemble aggressive behaviour. They reproduce the latter mimetically; an advance will take the form of an attack directed at the individual the assailant wishes to befriend, but at the last moment the assailant will turn aside and substitute a third animal or even an inanimate object for its goal.

The favoured individual will necessarily respond mimetically. It in turn will behave aggressively, but its aggressiveness can be directed at the assailant, which will be prepared for this possibility, or at the third, imaginary enemy, in which case it will join the other in a common cause constituted by the fictive attack. It is in achieving a 'common cause' of this kind that the alliance consists.

The repetitive character of these animal behaviours is not the only factor that recalls human ritual; the sequence foreshadows two fundamental moments of religious ritual, the moment of the 'mimetic crisis', of internal discord, and that of reconciliation against a surrogate victim. Here of course there is no sacrifice. The place of the victim is already indicated, however, and the victimage 'function' has been sketched in, although animal rites never proceed as far as immolation.

Animal rites of this kind provide us with everything necessary for an understanding of the transition, based on sacrificial religion, from animal sociality to human sociality. We need only postulate a greater mimetic intensity and the resulting rivalries that would release the actual victimage mechanism foreshadowed in the animal rites. All the evidence suggests that a catastrophic aggravation of the conflict would correspond, toward the end of the process, to a strengthening of the 'scapegoat' mechanism that remains embryonic in scapegoat rituals. If the intensity of the first moment is increased, the next moment would be correspondingly radicalized, and the violence directed at the third individual might well bring about its death.

One essential difference between human ritual and the animal rites I have just mentioned is that the latter, so far as I know, never involve a sufficient number of partners to resemble the fundamental rituals of humanity, which always gather the whole of a social group. Indeed that would be the only partially justifiable reason for objecting to the term 'rite' for the kind of animal behaviour we have been discussing.

The more intense mimesis becomes, the more the conflicts it provokes and their subsequent resolutions become 'contagious'. We can therefore suppose that as mimetic rivalries intensify they involve an increasing number of participants and that these are the ones eventually united around the sacralized victim and subjected to the double imperative of prohibition and ritual. The human community is nothing but such an assembly and can exist only as a function of it.

G. L.: Human ritual must thus be seen as the transformation of animal ritual; one finds the same elements in both, although these will be influenced in human ritual by the fight to the death and by sacrificial immolation, which are effects of easily observable causes that we have every reason to think intervened during the process of hominization.

The Transcendental Signifier

J.-M. O.: The real ambition of your theory is to overcome the opposition separating ethology from ethnology and to put an end to the schism that weakens anthropological research by dividing it into two enemy camps. In order to succeed you have to show that the hypothesis truly resolves problems on either side of the line; it is therefore necessary to relate the surrogate victim not only to problems of violence and to rituals that canalize mimesis toward the cultural institutions of humanity, but also to the question of signs and communication.

R. G.: We need to show that it is not possible to resolve the problem of violence with the surrogate victim without at the same time elaborating a theory of the sign and signification.

I think that even the most elementary form of the victimage mechanism, prior to the emergence of the sign, should be seen as an exceptionally powerful means of creating a new degree of attention, the first noninstinctual attention. Once it has reached a certain degree of frenzy, the mimetic polarization becomes fixed on a single victim. After having been released against the victim, the violence necessarily abates and silence follows the mayhem. This maximal contrast between the release of violence and its cessation, between agitation and tranquillity, creates the most favourable conditions possible for the emergence of this new attention. Since the victim is a common victim it will be at that instant the focal point for all members of the community. Consequently, beyond the purely instinctual object, the alimentary or sexual object or the dominant individual, there is the cadaver of the collective victim and this cadaver constitutes the first object for this new type of attention.

J.-M. O.: Would this already be a sacred victim?

R. G.: To the extent that the new type of attention is awakened, the victim will be imbued with the emotions provoked by the crisis and its resolution. The powerful experience crystallizes around the victim. As weak as it might be, the 'consciousness' the participants have of the victim is linked structurally to the prodigious effects produced by its passage from life to death, by the spectacular and liberating reversal that has occurred at that instant. The double transference will determine the only possible meaning to take shape under the circumstances, and this will constitute the sacred and confer total responsibility for the event on to the victim. It is necessary to conceive of stages, however, which were perhaps the longest in all human history, in which the signifying effects have still not truly taken shape. One would have to answer your question by saying that once the victim has appeared, however dimly, the process leading toward the sacred has begun, although concepts and representations are not yet part of it.

There is no need to assume that the mechanism of awakening attention works right away; one can imagine that for a considerable period it produced nothing at all, or *next to nothing*. Nonetheless, even the most rudimentary signifying effects result from the necessity of controlling excessive mimesis; as soon as we grant that these effects can be in the slightest degree cumulative, we will have recognized them as forerunners of forms of human culture.

J.-M. O.: But what you need is a theory of the sign, and as far as I understand some of our contemporary theorists, the sign only exists within a system; any beginning therefore requires at least two signs that signify one another. Given your general schema, I cannot see how you will engender the binary opposition of structural linguistics.

R. G.: There is no need to engender this particular binary opposition. It has a purely synchronic and static character. One cannot imagine starting with a structuralist system containing two differential elements that have the same degree of value. There is a simpler model that is uniquely dynamic and genetic—but also completely ignored. This is the model of the exception that is still in the process of emerging, the single trait that stands out against a confused mass or still unsorted multiplicity. It is the model of drawing lots, of the short straw, or, of the bean in the Epiphany cake. Only the piece that contains the bean is truly distinguished; only the shortest straw, or the longest, is meaningful. The rest remain indeterminate.

This is the simplest symbolic system, and yet no one considers it worthy of mention or consideration, *even though it is frequently associated with ritual.* The types of selection by chance I just alluded to have their origin in ritual. They are part of the aleatory processes that, as we have seen, are sometimes used to select a sacrificial victim. This model can be found in ritual because it is based, along with all other ritual institutions, on the operation of the victimage mechanism. As a model of the most rudimentary form of symbolism, it can therefore be exceptionally instructive for us.

It seems clear that this model served as the basis for the invention of what are called games of chance. In order to have a game of chance, strictly defined, all that is required is that men forget the ritual conclusion to the aleatory procedure and make the latter an end in itself. Exactly the same kind of development takes place, in sum, as in the examples we have previously analysed. All of these institutions seem to us to be so naturally cultural or so culturally natural that we never dream of imagining a religious origin for them—that is, until we grasp their essential proximity to ritual.

J.-M. O.: If you are correct then, there must be something more specifically human in games of chance than in other types of games.

R. G.: That is exactly the opinion of Roger Caillois in a remarkable book entitled *Les Jeux et les Hommes.* Caillois divides games into four categories and these correspond to the four principal phases of the ritual cycle.[41] I will list these in the order corresponding to the unfolding of the founding process rather than in the order given by Caillois.

There are first of all games of imitation: mime, masquerades, theatre, etc. (Caillois uses the English word *mimicry*).

Then there are games of competition or struggle (*agon*), like racing, boxing, etc. These correspond to the antagonism of the doubles.

There are games of vertigo that Caillois designates with the Greek word *ilinx*, games that consist in turning very rapidly in one place, like the cabriole, etc. These games correspond to the hallucinatory paroxysm of the mimetic crisis.

These are finally games of chance, which correspond to the sacrificial resolution. Caillois observes with due astonishment that Huizinga does not even mention them in a work entitled *Homo ludens*, whereas these are the only games that are truly specific to man. All the other forms of play have precedents among animals. This fact corresponds perfectly to the difference we noted earlier between human and animal rites. The only thing 'lacking' in animal rites is the sacrificial immolation, and the only thing an animal needs to become human is the surrogate victim.

Even in the most attenuated forms of drawing lots one can observe multiple signs of the sacred, polarized around the winner or chosen one. In 'drawing kings' the one who finds the bean is immediately surrounded by the ritual opposites. He becomes a target for mockery and a kind of scapegoat, yet he represents the group from which he has been excluded. In a sense, then, he has transcended himself: he certainly is the king. This comic mini-sacralization foreshadows a sort of transcendental signifier. This alone ought to answer the criticism that the polyvalence of ritual is unthinkable or that it amounts to nothing more than nostalgia for the 'immediate' and is foreign to the real structures of human thought and culture!

G. L.: As long as one knows how to look, then, the outline of the founding mechanism can be observed in many areas.

R. G.: Exactly. In the founding mechanism reconciliation is achieved against and around the victim. What we said earlier about the victim appearing to designate himself as the origin and cause of everything was not incorrect but is insufficient; a more radical formulation is appropriate at this point. We must attempt to set aside the whole context of acquired meanings in order to understand that at the most primitive levels the victimage mechanism is already at work and generates the most basic strata of meaning.

Because of the victim, in so far as it seems to emerge from the community and the community seems to emerge from it, for the first time there can be something like an inside and an outside, a before and after, a community and the sacred. We have already noted that the victim appears to be simultaneously good and evil, peaceable and violent, a life that brings death and a death that guarantees life. Every possible significant element seems to have its outline in the sacred and at the same time to be transcended by it. In this sense the victim does seem to constitute a universal signifier.

J.-M. O.: Are you referring to the idea of a transcendental signifier, which has been energetically rejected by current thought?

R. G.: I am not saying that we have found the *true* transcendental signifier. So far we have only discovered what functions in that capacity for human beings.

J.-M. O.: Should not the reference be to a transcendental signified rather than signifier?

R. G.: The signifier is the victim. The signified constitutes all actual and potential meaning the community confers on to the victim and, through its intermediacy, on to all things.

The sign is the reconciliatory victim. Since we understand that human beings wish to remain reconciled after the conclusion of the crisis, we can also understand their penchant for reproducing the sign, or in other words for reproducing the language of the sacred by substituting, in ritual, new victims for the original victim, in order to assure the maintenance of that miraculous peace. The imperative of ritual is therefore never separate from the manipulation of signs and their constant multiplication, a process that generates new possibilities of cultural differentiation and enrichment. The processes that we have described in the preceding pages in relation to hunting, the domestication of animals, sexual prohibitions, etc., might all be described as the manipulation and differentiation of the sign constituted by victimage.

There is no difficulty in explaining why ritual is repeated. Driven by sacred terror and wishing to continue life under the sign of the reconciliatory victim, men attempt to reproduce and represent this sign; this attempt consists first of all in the search for victims who seem capable of bringing about the primordial epiphany, and it is there that we find the first signifying activity that can always be defined, if one insists, in terms of language or writing. The moment arrives when the original victim, rather than being signified by new victims, will be signified by something other than a victim, by a variety of things that continue to signify the victim while at the same time progressively masking, disguising, and failing to recognize it.

Articulated language and the exchange of words, like all other kinds of exchange, surely must also have its basis in ritual, in the screams and cries that accompanied the mimetic crisis and that must be reproduced by ritual because they precede and perhaps condition the reconciliatory immolation. It seems possible, during the ritual around the victim, that cries at first inarticulate should fall into a rhythm and become ordered like steps in a dance, particularly since in ritual centred around the sacrificial act a spirit of collaboration and agreement pervades the re-enactment of all aspects of the crisis. There is no culture on earth that does not hold its sacred vocables or words to be primary and fundamental in the order of language.

CHAPTER FOUR

Myth: The Invisibility of the Founding Murder

The 'Radical Elimination'

R. G.: I believe I can show that in spite of its apparent absence, indeed in spite of the total silence that surrounds it in our time, the thesis of the founding murder takes shape everywhere, even among those who are the most refractory to the kinds of analysis I pursue. I can show you analyses in the work of Lévi-Strauss that concern the founding murder itself, that reveal the principal structural traits involved, without demonstrating any awareness of what is being shown or any understanding of the fact that they are in the process of revealing the generative mechanism of all mythology.

J.-M. O.: Since you have hardly spoken of mythology at all so far and since mythology, in principle, is a privileged domain for the application of structuralism—the domain of pure language removed from all the anti-linguistic intrigue of religious perversity (Lévi-Strauss *dixit*)—it would be helpful, I believe, to go into detail and analyse a passage from Lévi-Strauss as closely as possible.

R. G.: The analysis should be based, from beginning to end, on the analyses of Lévi-Strauss himself, on his own discourse, beginning with the two myths that will occupy most of our attention.

In *Totemism* Lévi-Strauss juxtaposes two myths that come from two societies very distant from one another, the Ojibwa Indians from the northern Great Lakes region in North America and the Tikopia, of the Pacific ocean.[42] First the Ojibwa myth:

The five 'original' clans are descended from six anthropomorphic supernatural beings who emerged from the ocean to mingle with human beings. One of them had his eyes covered and dared not look at the Indians, though he showed the greatest anxiety to do so. At last

he could no longer restrain his curiosity, and on one occasion he partially lifted his veil, and his eye fell on the form of a human being,
who instantly fell dead 'as if struck by one of the thunderers'.
Though the intentions of this dread being were friendly to men, yet
the glance of his eye was too strong, and it inflicted certain death. His
fellows therefore caused him to return to the bosom of the great
water. The five others remained among the Indians, and 'became a
blessing to them'. From them originate the five great clans or totems
(p. 19).

Now the Tikopia myth; the text is once again taken from Lévi-Strauss:

> A long time ago the gods were no different from mortals, and the
> gods were the direct representatives of the clans in the land. It came
> about that a god from foreign parts, Tikarau, paid a visit to Tikopia,
> and the gods of the land prepared a splendid feast for him, but first
> they organized trials of strength and speed, to see whether their guest
> or they would win. During a race, the stranger slipped and declared
> that he was injured. Suddenly, however, while he was pretending to
> limp, he made a dash for the provisions for the feast, grabbed up the
> heap, and fled for the hills. The family of gods set off in pursuit;
> Tikarau slipped and fell again, so that the clan gods were able to re-
> trieve some of the provisions, one a coconut, another a taro, another
> a breadfruit, and others a yam. Tikarau succeeded in reaching the
> sky with most of the foodstuffs for the feast, but these four vegetable
> foods had been saved for men (pp. 25-26).

In both myths, we can see the schema of the mimetic crisis and a
violent destructuring that releases the victimage mechanism. The initial confusion between the divine and the human is part of that crisis. It
is not said explicitly that the confusion is conflictual; the noxious effects
of the crisis are immediately attributed to the victim, who, as always,
appears to be responsible for them. In the first myth the sudden death
of an Indian is supposedly caused by the simple gaze of the future victim. In the second myth the future victim, Tikarau, is held responsible
for the theft of the whole cultural system. The experienced observer
will also recognize an indication of the conflictual situation in the 'trials
of speed and strength' organized by the humano-divine consortium.
We are not surprised to find a ritual connotation in the 'contests' or

organized trials. The myth presents the crisis as 'always already' ritualized and as a non-ritual event simultaneously, since the games lead directly to the spontaneous collective violence, the *model* of all ritual.

Just as in Euripides' *The Bacchae*, where the bacchanal, in principle already a ritual, leads directly to the murder of Pentheus, here the contests of strength and skill lead to the chase of the god and end, clearly enough, in a murder. If the future god had at first pretended to fall and limp, by the end of the chase he 'took a real fall'.* There is something sinister in that phrase. You might object that my obsession with lynching has got the better of me and that Tikarau makes out well enough with his escape into the sky, but I would refer you to the work of Raymond Firth—not to the book that Lévi-Strauss uses in *Totemism*, but to a second book by the same author that appeared several years later, in 1967, entitled *Tikopia Ritual and Belief*.[43]

According to this book Tikarau tries to evade his pursuers by climbing a hill. The hill ends in an abrupt cliff. Raymond Firth writes that Tikarau 'bolted to the edge of the cliff, and being an *atua* [a spirit or god] launched himself into the sky and set off for the far lands with his ill-gotten gains'.

It seems clear enough that if Tikarau had not been an *atua* he would have fallen off the cliff and probably would not have got up again. Perhaps this explains the insistence of the myth in presenting the fall as real rather than as a feint. But Tikarau is an *atua* and he takes off into the air. Underlying the sacralization that makes the reconciliatory victim into an immortal divinity is the account of a mortal fall; the word-for-word account in the text on this point is extremely suggestive.

In many societies lacking a judicial system the event not quite described but indubitably alluded to by the fall of Tikarau constitutes the favourite mode of capital punishment, given, of course, an appropriate topography. The prisoner is led up the slopes that lead to the cliff, and the community, forming an arc, advances slowly, blocking any path of escape except of course for the one leading to the cliff edge. Nine times out of ten, panic will probably force the unfortunate to throw himself off the cliff without it being necessary to lay a hand on him. The famous Tarpean rock is only one example among others of the same custom. The advantage of the procedure, in the religious sense, is that the entire community participates in the execution and no one is exposed to 'pol-

---

* Lévi-Strauss's text reads, 'cette fois, Tikarau tomba pour de bon' [trans.].

lution' or contact with the victim. This same advantage figures in other types of capital execution in archaic societies.

These kinds of ritual execution were not invented *ex nihilo*; they are visibly copies of a model that varies a great deal in its details but is always structured in the same way, and this, of course, is the event described for us in the myth about Tikarau—the murder of the first victim that was reconciliatory because it was spontaneously unanimous, the generative mechanism of ritual execution as of all other institutions, whether totemic or not.

Collective murder is part of the Ojibwa myth also, but it is described more rapidly than in the myth about Tikarau: after one of the six supernatural visitors had killed an Indian by raising the corner of the blindfold tied over his eyes and looking at the Indian, his five companions *'caused him to return to the bosom of the great water'*. In one case the victim dies crushed on the rocks, in the other death is by drowning. If a human group has a cliff at its disposal, the cliff may be used. If it has a lake, you have the Ojibwa situation. If it has neither cliffs nor lakes, it probably has stones, and the victim will be stoned. If it does not have stones, it may have trees, and the victim will be hanged or crucified, etc.

J.-M. O.: In both myths, in sum, the victim is considered divine because it appears responsible for the disorder culminating in a unanimous gathering against it and for the return to order assured by that unanimity itself. The community is unable to see in the victim only an occasional and passive instrument of its own metamorphosis, a catalyst for its instant transition from collective hysteria to tranquility. It supposes that the original criminal cannot have really died in the unfortunate event that his crimes eventually led to, because he has suddenly been transformed into an all-powerful benefactor. How could he be dead when it was he who gave to the community the gift of life and of its so-called totemic order?

G. L.: This reading of the two myths has of course been ours and not that of Lévi-Strauss. Let us now move on to his commentary.

R. G.: We should note first of all that Lévi-Strauss is in agreement with us, or rather we are in agreement with him, since it concerns a discovery he has made, in recognizing in the myth a movement from 'undifferentiation' to differentiation.

J.-M. O.: But his linguistic *a priori* keeps him from recognizing in the myth what we believe to have discovered there, namely a mimetic and violent reciprocity that destroys all cultural differences *in reality* and *that does not exist only in the text.*

R. G.: In the linguistic perspective of Lévi-Strauss, the 'un-differentiated' or the 'continuum' is nothing but a 'patching over' of distinctions that have already been made in language, and thus constitutes a deception whose presence the ethnologist comes to deplore, particularly in ritual, because he sees in it, as we have already mentioned, a perverse refusal of differential thought. In the analyses contained in *Totemism*, the presence of this same 'undifferentiated' seems justified by the fundamental aim of mythology, which according to him consists in representing, in a necessarily inexact but nonetheless suggestive manner, the birth and development of the only thing that interests him—differential thought. A representation of difference as such, of the discontinuous as such, can only be made against the background of the continuum, the undifferentiated.

G. L.: According to Lévi-Strauss, then, myth is nothing more than the fictive representation of cultural development, whereas in your view it is the transfigured account of a real violence.

Mythic thought supposedly confuses a purely intellectual process, the differential, with a real process, a sort of drama that took place 'at the beginning of the world' among completely wondrous characters.

R. G.: For structuralism, in other words, the actual dramatic elements of mythology have no intrinsic interest, and Lévi-Strauss disdains any researcher who considers them important. He is too good an observer, however, not to see that certain recurrent patterns demand an explanation.

Lévi-Strauss thus notes that there are *several common points that should be emphasized* in the Ojibwa and Tikopia myths (*Totemism*, p. 26).

How does Lévi-Strauss define these common points, how does he see the mythic drama? In a purely logical manner, of course, but in a mode that will be of interest to us, since it comprises a logic of exclusion and elimination. Here are some examples:

> In both cases, totemism as a system is introduced as *what remains* of a diminished totality.

In each case, discontinuity is achieved by the radical elimination of certain fractions of the continuum. Once the latter has been reduced, a smaller number of elements are free to spread out in the same space, while the distance between them is now sufficient to prevent them overlapping or merging into one another.

For the five great clans from which the Ojibwa believe their society to have sprung to be established, six supernatural personages had to be reduced to five through the elimination of one. The four 'totemic' plants of Tikopia are the only ones that the ancestors hung on to, when a strange god stole the feast that the local divinities had prepared in his honour.

In all these instances, therefore, a discrete system is produced by the destruction of certain elements or their removal from the original whole.[44]

The above are a collection of passages from *Totemism* and from *The Raw and the Cooked*, where the same sort of analysis is taken up and extended.

In Lévi-Strauss's interpretation, as you can see, terms such as *removal*, *destruction*, and *radical elimination* return constantly but never refer to real violence done to a real individual. The eliminated elements are the anthropomorphic divinity who is 'chased' in the Ojibwa myth and, in the other, the totemic plants carried off by Tikarau *rather than Tikarau himself*. The fact that in the second myth there is also the elimination of an 'anthropomorphic' deity, as Lévi-Strauss would say, constitutes another common point between the two myths, but one that Lévi-Strauss does not mention.

In his perspective, then, the radical elimination of one or of several fragments—the expulsion of a god, the destruction of living beings or of particular foods—never amounts to anything more than various solutions 'to resolve the problem of the transition from continuous to discrete quantities'. The undifferentiated state that dominates at the beginning of the myth is interpreted as an excessive congestion in a given field. In order to distinguish things, thought requires that there be interstices between them so as to permit its movement; according to Lévi-Strauss, such interstices are still lacking at the beginning of the myth. The problem, in sum, for this dramatization of nascent thought would be *to make room*, to separate things from one another in order to differentiate them, and Lévi-Strauss tells us that the elimination of even a single fragment is supposed to accomplish this.

With its emphasis on difference, structuralism necessarily sees things in terms of spacing, so that according to Lévi-Strauss, mythic thought, with its invention of fantastic stories, is attempting simply to spatialize difference, to represent metaphorically the process of differentiation. Primitive thought, in sum, is already structuralism; it is a primitive structuralism, however, that confuses the process of differentiation with a real event because it is unable to achieve a sufficient level of abstraction. The myth still has something to learn but it is on the right track—that of Lévi-Strauss himself.

One can show without difficulty that such an interpretation is indefensible. If the story derives from a procedure of disencumbering a mythic domain, then it would be necessary for the eliminated fragments to have been part of the domain from the beginning. If by chance they were not present at the beginning, if they were introduced into the domain later *as foreign elements*, their elimination would not provide any more space than was in the initial situation.

But in my view this is just what happens in the two myths, since in both cases the eliminated fragment was the deity, and in neither the Ojibwa text nor the Tikopia text was the deity part of the original mythic domain—the god is represented as a *visitor*. Lévi-Strauss's topological schema collapses.

J.-M. O.: Yet according to you the surrogate victim is very much a part of the community.

R. G.: When the victim is real, certainly, but not as it is represented in the myth. The representation is determined by the violent reconciliation and the resulting sacralization. The victim is thus represented with all the attributes and qualities of the sacred. Fundamentally, then, the victim does not belong to the community; it is the community that belongs to the victim. The myth will sometimes represent the victim as a visitor from the outside, sometimes as a member of the community, and again this is because it must choose from too rich a matrix of meaning. The victim can appear to be foreign or native because it seems to move constantly from the outside to the inside and from the inside to the outside in accomplishing its role of saving and refounding the community.[45]

Contrary to what some of my critics have asserted, I never confuse religious representations with their 'referent'. We are still dealing strictly with representations.[46] Clearly, the topological schema is being proposed as the correct interpretation of what in reality is a represen-tation of collective violence, a description of a lynching. This becomes clearer still when the Lévi-Straussian schema is applied to myths or adaptations of myths in which the representation of the lynching is even more explicit than it is in the Ojibwa and Tikopia myths.

At the beginning of Euripides' *The Bacchae*, the chaotic bacchanal can be interpreted as an encumbered field, as an excessive density that impedes the functioning of thought. Fortunately the Bacchantes are able to eliminate the unfortunate Pentheus, and although it is not handled in an altogether logical style, the elimination is definite and quite 'radical'; Dionysian 'thought' then begins to function, and the divine order is inaugurated.

Of course one cannot deduce the reality of a collective murder or lynching from its representation. And that is certainly not what I have been doing. However, it is already somewhat troubling to observe that Lévi-Strauss's topological schema is nothing but a transposition of the representation of collective murder and that Lévi-Strauss himself, ob-viously, has not recognized that representation for what it is.

There is every likelihood that this transposition is an error, not only because in certain cases it does not correspond to the evidence in myths, but because it is unlikely that mythology should make consistent use of as troubling and striking a representation as collective murder for something as respectable, academic, and ultimately even insignificant as structuralism's view of the immaculate conception of human thought. Why should myths so frequently represent collective violence in order to express something that has no relation to it? Lynching or camouflaged lynching is represented so frequently that at some point or other one has to ask why it should be so. Why is the all-against-one of collective violence so evident in mythology?

'Negative Connotation', 'Positive Connotation'

R. G.: The rub is that Lévi-Strauss is quite aware of this *all-against-one*, which he recognizes as one of the common elements of the two myths; but for him it becomes the occasion to illustrate one of the bi-nary oppositions to which he devotes the clearest of his analyses. None-theless, he points with complete lucidity to the decisive elements of the process: 'Firstly,' he writes, 'the same opposition will be noted between individual and collective conduct, the former being negatively regarded and the latter positively in relation to totemism. In the two myths, the individual and maleficent conduct is that of a greedy and inconsiderate god (a point on which there are resemblances with Loki of Scandinavia, of whom a masterly study has been made by Georges Dumezil)' (*Totemism*, p.26).

In the Ojibwa myth the individual and negatively qualified behaviour is that of the one supernatural being who imprudently raises a corner of his blindfold and kills an Indian with a single glance. In the Tikopia myth it is Tikarau's theft of the totemic plants.

The collective and positively qualified behaviour consists, in the Ojibwa myth, in the intervention of the five other gods, who chase the one delinquent back into the ocean. In the Tikopia myth, the positive act is the entire community's chase of Tikarau. The positively qualified collective action, in sum, is always collective violence, the lynching of the victim.

We would therefore see the negative qualifications as nothing but an *accusation* made against the victim. Since no one doubts the truth of the accusation and since it is adopted by the entire community, it becomes an urgent and legitimate motive for getting rid of the victim. The scapegoat of the Objiwa has time enough to kill a single Indian only because the rapid intervention of the five other gods keeps the gaze that is 'too strong' from further ravaging the community. In the same way Tikarau's theft of the totemic foods justifies the violent expulsion of the god.

If the reasons for a given 'negative qualification' are examined closely, it becomes clear that together they constitute a potential or current threat to the community as a whole. The parricide and incest of Oedipus are not a private matter because they bring the plague to all the Thebans. The impiety of Pentheus is not a personal or even purely familial affair—and we can very well see why if we suppose that the myth represents an event that actually occurred, a lynching that really took place but that neither Lévi-Strauss nor any other interpreters of mythology have succeeded in recognizing because it is represented from the perspective of the murderers themselves. Such a perspective transforms a fantastic accusation into an indubitable truth in the eyes of the community; therefore in the myth it becomes a representation among other representations and the interpreters of mythology do not distinguish it from others. They are unable to recognize it as an accusation transformed into a certainty by the unanimous agreement of the community, by the vengeful reconciliation against a necessarily more or less random victim.

What seems to justify Lévi-Strauss's cavalier treatment of the all-against-one motif in these two myths is that in spite of its crucial character this relation is also quite susceptible to inversion, displacement, countless metamorphoses, and even, in some myths, complete disappearance. As we have seen there are some myths in which the victim is the sole survivor who, after having caused the downfall of an entire community, brings the latter back into being in a selective and differentiated manner. In *The Raw and the Cooked* Lévi-Strauss cites one such (Bororo) myth, which he relates to the Ojibwa and Tikopia myths (p. 51).

G. L.: Lévi-Strauss accords all mythic representations the same status and considers them all equally suspect, but a paradoxical consequence of this scepticism pairs it with religious faith as far as the founding violence is concerned. It makes a truly radical critique, one that would reveal that violence impossible. Curiously, the modern attitude has the same effects as religious faith, and this is not surprising in that one and the other give equally uniform treatment to all recurrent representations. In the end, belief in all representations and belief in none amount to the same thing. In order to form a true criticism of myth and to forge an instrument of analysis that will break through its deceptive appearance and reveal the secret of its genesis, one must refuse, as you do, all *a priori* theories of representation.

J.-M. O.: The question is whether we should see in the innumerable lynchings in mythology the superfluously dramatic representation of pure discrimination, a fundamental process in human thought that should have no need of such violence in order to exist, or should we rather see in all discrimination the result of collective murder? That would be the crucial question. In the end you do agree with Lévi-Strauss on an essential point, namely that there is a relation between mythology (or, for you, all forms of religion) and the engendering of human thought. For Lévi-Strauss, however, the relation is purely representational, with mythology giving an inevitably fantastic version of the innocent development of human thought.

R. G.: The elements common to the two myths, or now to all three, are certainly those pointed out by Lévi-Strauss: the negative connotation of the eliminated fragment, the positive connotation given to the elimination itself, which is generally presented as a collective expulsion. But Lévi-Strauss is unable to explain the conjunction of all these traits, and for good reason. He does not even offer an explanation. It is not clear why, in the context of the logical and topological schema he proposes, the eliminated fragment should become the object not only of a negative connotation, but, following that, of the supremely positive connotation as well, the one that characterizes the divinity. Lévi-Strauss has even more trouble explaining this than he has with the rest, and seems willing to pass the problem on to Georges Dumézil, who has also not solved it.

Lévi-Strauss has succeeded no more than other interpreters in perceiving the prodigious possibilities suggested by the conjunction of all the elements that he himself has singled out, a conjunction that is too common to be due to chance. If the radical elimination *is* collective violence and if that violence is justified by some misdeed or flaw attributed to the victimized fragment, then there is no difficulty in making all elements equally intelligible or in explaining the conjunction of the two groups of elements that Lévi-Strauss points to but whose universal juxtaposition he is unable to explain. There is one and only one perspective capable of making lynching a positive action—since it sees the victim as a real threat that must be dealt with by any means available—and this is the perspective of the lynchers themselves, the perspective of the lynchers on their own lynching.

The advantage of this thesis is that it resolves all the problems created by the common significations. It allows us to understand why disorder prevails at the beginning of the myth; why the victim, at the moment of being driven out by the community, is considered guilty of having committed a crime that poses an immediate or long-term threat to the community. It allows us to understand why the lynching of this victim appears to be a just and good act. Only the perspective of the lynchers and of their descendants through the ages, the religious community, can explain with unshakable certainty that the victim is genuinely malevolent and all-powerful and ought to be destroyed—or in other words that the lynching is justified. Only the perspective of the lynchers, who have been reconciled by the very unanimity of the transference but who are unable to understand the mimetic mechanism of that reconciliation, can explain why the victim, by the end of the operation, is not only execrated but deified: the victim and not the lynchers themselves will be held responsible for the reconciliation. Deification reveals the efficacy of lynching because it can rest only on a total inability to recognize the transference of which the victim is the object, and it is certainly to this unanimous transference that the community owes its reconciliation; this is why the return to peace and order is attributed to the victim. Our hypothesis not only clarifies the paradoxical structure of the myth, it makes so many details intelligible that it must surely carry conviction. Think, for example, of the fantastic aspects of the accusation that weighs on the victim. The god in the Ojibwa myth lifts the corner of his blindfold and the Indian he sees drops dead. In many societies one would say that the Ojibwa god has the evil eye, the Sicilian *malocchio*. The fantastic element in mythology is not as free and unpredictable as some say it is. It belongs to a well-determined type. The various efforts to determine the character of this type—psychoanalytic, aesthetic, mystic—have never revealed the essential. It is a question of something social and collective, although someone like Jung, with his rosewater archetypes, will never help us explain it.

The evil eye is a banal cultural trait; it is found in numerous communities that until recently were habitually called 'backward', precisely because of the presence of cultural traits like the evil eye and the widespread popular belief they inspire. We attach little or no importance to this kind of thing; we view it as 'vestigial magic' that has no serious consequences for human relations. We cannot overlook the fact, however, that accusations of this type almost always result in real ostracism, and at times in the persecution and death of those who are singled out.[47]

Belief in the evil eye allows any individual to be held responsible for whatever adverse event might occur in the community. Since the evil eye can function at the will of the one who possesses it, the victim of this terrible accusation can say nothing of his 'friendly intentions', as Lévi-Strauss puts it, that cannot be turned against himself; there is no witness to call on. It is absolutely impossible to prove one's innocence. There is nothing, from minor inconveniences to major disasters, that one cannot impute to the evil eye, and this includes catastrophes that transcend all individual responsibility, as with an epidemic, for example. One need only think of Oedipus. . .

The evil eye is the mythic accusation *par excellence*; it is related to many well-known cultural traits that can be traced back to it, although the connection is not clear to us because they appear in the transfigured and literally sacralized context of classical culture. The strange power possessed by Oedipus in bringing the plague to the Thebans is clearly nothing but a traditional variant of the evil eye. In *The Bacchae* the supposed *mala curiositas* of Pentheus, that is, his perverse desire to spy on the bacchae, is what provokes their rage. Before looking for the psychoanalytic meaning of Pentheus's supposed voyeurism, we would do better to place the phenomenon back into its true collective and sociological context. The terror of the 'evil eye' is present in all societies in which a propensity for collective violence continues to ferment, and is manifest as an apparently rational fear of the indiscreet observer, of the prying or penetrating gaze; in times of war this becomes the *espionite*, a kind of mass phobia of spies. I am sure that in the southern United States there is a connection between the perpetuation of lynching and the obsession with the Peeping Tom that, until recent years, remained quite striking for any visitor.

If the evil eye enjoys some sort of privilege among all types of mythic accusation, it is ultimately because of the conflictual power of mimesis that comes into play, and that power, which requires the look or gaze to be exercised, is projected entirely on to the surrogate victim. These days the accusation of the evil eye can take subtle forms, but it will always tempt any human group in the grip of intolerable tensions and seemingly insurmountable conflicts; the temptation consists in projecting what is inexpressible and insoluble in these tensions on to a victim who will of course have no choice or say in the matter. In sum, we find the same fantastic aspects of the mythic accusation in groups that remain subject to the more elementary and brutal forms of collective violence.

Even if we acknowledge that representations of accusations and violence are sometimes not sharply drawn, as in the Ojibwa myth, for example, or even in the Tikopia myth, and that in these cases the blindness of observers is aided by attenuating circumstances, the evident connection between myths in which lynching is half concealed and those in which it is plainly visible, as *in all episodes, without exception, in the cycle of Dionysus*, ought finally to illuminate even those observers who are intent on seeing nothing at all. More or less explicit lynching certainly figures in the majority of myths on the planet. It is the most frequent action in myths and by far the most characteristic, and yet one would search in vain for any reference to it in the index of Lévi-

Strauss's *Mythologiques* or in any other specialized works. Even if the representation is gratuitous, who will explain its astounding recurrence to us?

G. L.: Since science, according to Lévi-Strauss, is the study of recurrent phenomena, we are obliged to ask the question concerning radical elimination that he refuses to bring up. . .

R. G.: I want to emphasize again that the representation of lynching, in itself, is not what leads me to any conclusion concerning the reality of lynching. Nor is it the fact that the victim is marked with accusations as significant as those related to the evil eye. But what will persuade an observer who works in the scientific spirit to conclude that lynching must be real is the *constant conjunction of these two types of representations*. The very kind of lack of verisimilitude that characterizes mythic accusations strengthens the verisimilitude of representations of collective violence, and vice versa. There is only one satisfying explanation for the conjunction of these two types of representations, and that is real lynching; why would one constantly encounter the perspective of the lynchers if there were no lynching to provoke it? The particular combination of themes that we find in mythology, the signs of crisis and the signs of reconciliation against and around the victim can be explained, perfectly and completely, only by the presence of a necessarily real lynching behind the myth.

J.-M. O.: If lynching has reconciled a community that had been in a state of crisis and disorder, and this event is recorded by the community itself and passed on by later members, it can only be communicated to us in the transfigured perspective that is a necessary part of the reconciliatory effect. Everything that we call mythology is simply the evidence of that perspective on the textual level, in the same way that what we call ritual is nothing more than the quite understandable wish on the part of the lynchers to reproduce, rather than simply to remember, the reconciliatory event in real sacrificial acts.

R. G.: There are two groups of common traits in our three examples. On the one hand there is the 'radical elimination', which is 'positively qualified', and on the other hand there is the 'negative connotation' (in reality a double connotation, negative and positive) of the 'eliminated fragment'. In Lévi-Strauss these two groups remain separate. Only the hypothesis on the founding murder allows them to be brought back together and integrated properly.

This is what makes our theory so strong. It alone can account for the combination of verisimilitude and the lack of verisimilitude that we find in myths.

To reject my hypothesis on the grounds that *structuralism has taught us not to confuse representations with their referents* is to misunderstand completely the reasons that necessitate my postulating the reality of lynching behind mythology. The representation of lynching in myths is always found in a context that necessitates the inference of its reality, because only that inference can illuminate that myth as a whole and in all its details.

G. L. Let us then itemize:
(1) the theme of violent undifferentiation, that is to say the type of social context that tends to provoke collective violence;
(2) accusations characteristic of collective violence as it occurs in the pogrom, the lynching, etc.;
(3) the representation of collective violence;
(4) the theme of the founding or refounding of culture, which implies the pacific effects of lynching and its choice as a model of ritual action;
(5) the essential factor, which at first throws everyone off on to the wrong track but which becomes revelatory once it has been understood, namely: that the accusation against the mythic hero is not taken as a simple accusation, but as an absolute given, an incontestable fact.

J.-M. O.: We need to emphasize the paradox; the trait that becomes decisive proof once it has been truly understood is the same one that has always misled everyone, namely the 'negative connotation' of the mythic hero.

R. G.: Our reading reveals considerable possibilities once it is truly understood. I will not hesitate to assert that this is the first truly 'hard' finding in the explication of mythology, not only because obscurity is dispelled, because all elements become intelligible and coherent, but also because we can now understand why first the believers and after them the non-believers have always been so close to and yet so far from the concealed yet truly simple truth of mythology. The first were blinded by their unquestioning acceptance of all mythic representations; the second were equally blinded by their substitution of equally unquestioning and abstract distrust, in that all mythic representations were given the same status. In the earlier interpreters, if a myth signifies something, it had to be something other than what it addresses directly, be it Freud's complexes or the abstract birth of thought in Lévi-Strauss.

The unlikely, indeed fantastic character of Lévi-Strauss's ideas is never sufficiently noted. It is neither reasonable nor even thinkable to read behind all of mythology to Paul Valéry's project in *La Jeune Parque*: to describe thought in its nascent condition, the first conception—which is immaculate, of course—of human thought.

As surprising at it seems at first, the hypothesis of the founding murder has much more plausibility than that of Lévi-Strauss. I cannot see why mythology should have the incredible poetico-philosophic project that structuralism attributes to it. Its real project is that of recalling the crises and the founding murder, the sequences in the realm of events that have constituted or reconstituted the cultural order. What is accurate and profound in Lévi-Strauss's thought is the idea that myth in some way deals with the birth of thought. Indeed this is more central to myth than structuralism has ever imagined because there is no human thought that was not born of the founding murder. Lévi-Strauss is wrong, however, as wrong as Paul Valéry, when he mistakes that birth for an immaculate conception. He sees in the constantly repeated lynching a simple *fictive* metaphor for an intellectual operation that is alone real. In reality everything here is concrete; from the moment one realizes this, the imbrication of all elements in myth becomes too striking to leave the least doubt.

Physical Signs of the Surrogate Victim

J.-M. O.: Tikarau limps like Oedipus, even if he is only pretending at first. I am struck by the physical peculiarities, which are often infirmities, that in many cases are attributed to the mythic hero. There are many contradictory interpretations. What, in your view, is the best way of reading these distinctive signs?

R. G.: Many well-known figures limp, including the Jacob of Genesis, Hephaestos, and so on. Lévi-Strauss has his own interpretation of all these abnormal or handicapped heroes. Naturally he has to formulate the problem in terms of his topological model and the inevitable problem of a 'transition from continuous quantity to discrete quantity':

In all these [myths] . . . a discrete system is produced by the destruction of certain elements or their removal from the original whole. In all these cases, too, the originator of the reduction is himself in a sense reduced: the six Ojibwa gods were blind from choice and exiled their companion who had been guilty of removing the bandage over his eyes. Tikarau, the thieving Tikopia god, pretended to limp in order to be better able to get possession of the banquet. . . . Mythological figures who are blind or lame, one-eyed or one-armed, are familiar the world over; and we find them disturbing, because we believe their condition to be one of deficiency. But just as a system that has been made discrete through the removal of certain elements becomes logically richer, although numerically poorer, so myths often confer a positive significance on the disabled and the sick, who embody modes of mediation. We imagine infirmity and sickness to be deprivations of being and therefore evil. However, if death is as real as life, and if therefore everything is being, all states, even pathological ones, are positive in their own way.[48]

It should be noted that the figure Lévi-Strauss calls 'the originator of the reduction' is also the one by whom the totality has been diminished, who has been cut out of the community and who is, in other words, the victim. But Lévi-Strauss prefers to see things in the perspective of our literary criticism and treat the matter as a *mise en abîme* of his topological allegory. Even a very superficial acquaintance with mythology shows us that the augmented or supplementary organ or limb plays exactly the same role as the lacking or diminished ones. The hunchback is also a well-known mythological hero, and his hump is regarded as an addition rather than a subtraction. Limping itself must be counted in this category when it is defined, not by a shortened leg, but by the 'swollen foot' of the son of Laios.

Lévi-Strauss's reading is obviously wrong. A Freudian reading at least has the advantage of recognizing that infirmity can be marked by augmentation as well as by diminution. One can always relate the good old phallic symbol, in other words, to anything involving castration, and vice versa. There is, however, one mythological theme that puts psychoanalysis at a great disadvantage and this is the explicitly sexual theme. The psychoanalytic theory of the symbol demands that the sexual element be repressed before it can be transposed. The hump of Punch, studied by Ernest Jones, is perfectly suited for this kind of analysis. In many myths, on the other hand, the object that should be hidden is too evident to be explained by a theory based on repression. What can one do, for example, with the North American myths in which the trickster possesses an organ of such extraordinary length that he has to carry it rolled around his neck, at least until he disposes of it in a definitive manner, sometimes in having it cut off, sometimes in cutting it himself, but always in a manner deplorably explicit with regard to the castration complex. I need not remind you that only the complex, and not castration itself, is ever expected to show itself.

The Freudians of the Paris school are much too clever, of course, to allow themselves to be daunted by this sort of objection. They have discovered the imposing abyss that divides the penis from the phallus and other fine articles that render them impervious to any conceivable criticism and that permit them to say absolutely anything they please. Certainly this is why their most brilliant intellectual performances have ultimately little import in terms of knowledge. The gradual exhaustion of any grand theory in its decadent phase is characterized by more and more acrobatic and subtle attempts to shore up the whole, but finally they prove nothing except that the time has come to move on to other things. In this sense the Lacanian theories of the symbol resemble the Lévi-Straussian theory of infirmity in myth as a *mise en abîme* of the topological model. Eventually this degree of preciosity will have its numbing effect and inevitably lead to the sort of absolute scepticism that we can see spreading everywhere.

J.-M. O.: What is particularly troubling is that for those who are maturing in this debilitating intellectual climate, the truly revolutionary insights that sooner or later will make so much current verbiage irrelevant will appear too *simple* to deserve any attention.

R. G.: The search for more and more subtle interpretations blinds interpreters to what is literally right in front of them. We can always gain more understanding in these matters if we consider the more backward or closed societies. Wherever there are no racial or religious minorities to polarize the majority, the selection of the victim is still not necessarily left to chance. There are other factors that can orient mimesis and these are physical characteristics, anything that might make an individual less well adapted than others to social life, or that would keep one from being inconspicuous. For this reason the role of infirmity in myth goes far beyond the subtraction or addition of limbs that we have considered so far. The speech defect of Moses plays the same role as the swollen foot of Oedipus. There is also the putrid odour that emanates from certain heroes in myths that Lévi-Strauss has analysed.

J.-M. O.: I think that infirmity in itself represents a difference and that as such it polarizes mimesis. For example, I have observed that if in a group of children there is one who stutters or limps, the others will be drawn irresistibly to imitate the characteristic, and that only secondarily, because of the reaction of the model, is the imitation experienced as mockery, and then as persecution.

R. G.: The reference to children is very suggestive. I have often thought that, in order to understand myths, one has only to observe the behaviour of groups of children. Their favourite targets for persecution are the same as those of adults but are simply more obvious: strangers, late comers, or, if necessary, a member of the group who has some infirmity or other distinctive physical sign that attracts the attention of the others. Think for a moment of the habitual characteristics of the common social outcast, among the most diverse human groups, and you will realize that all of these characteristics can be found in mythology from all over the planet. If only we look at things clearly and unflinchingly we will realize that infirmity in myth is one more proof of what we have been discussing since the beginning; the only difference between mythology and other intelligible modes of persecution is our immemorial inability to decipher it, our tenacious desire to ignore violence and its generative power until the very end, even where it thrusts itself on us with the greatest impudence and, one is tempted to say, innocence.

In order to clear the field of useless neo-Freudian or structuralist subtleties and also make the debate less acrimonious, we need to recognize that the question of physical signs is of a much 'lower' order than one thinks, so 'low' in fact that it has a precedent in animal life. The role played by infirmity or deformity in mythology certainly bears some relation to the way beasts of prey hunt down one animal out of a large group composed of numerous identical individuals. The chosen animal always differs from the general uniformity in some way, and the visual difference is caused by exceptional youth, age, or some infirmity that prohibits the chosen individual from moving exactly like the others or being identical to the others in all modes of behaviour. If it is true that, as ethologists claim, this type of selection contributes to maintaining an ecological balance, then we would have one more example of the relative interpenetration of a natural kind of equilibrium and the sacrificial equilibrium of human societies.

G. L.: It seems that Lévi-Strauss must have some presentiment of this point, in that he advises his readers not to let themselves be 'disconcerted'.

R. G.: The greatest weakness of modern thought consists in the false identification that is constantly made between scientific thought and the effacement of all human relationships, their reduction to the simple objectivity of things. Lévi-Strauss succumbs to that illusion more than ever when he equates victims with 'fragments', their death with 'logical elimination', and the effects of that death with the transition from the 'continuous' to the 'discontinuous'. He believes that he has attained a higher level of scientific objectivity whereas in reality, as with all myths before his, he has done nothing but invent a new jargon in which to transfigure the representation of lynching.

In any case, honesty compels us to acknowledge that the language of structuralism in the example of Lévi-Strauss is certainly superior to the approaches that preceded it. It *advances* inquiry in that it does reveal a certain logical structure that is in fact there. In the same way the fourth part of *Totem and Taboo* advances inquiry by revealing the structural presence of the collective murder at the centre of mythology.

J.-M. O.: Lévi-Strauss is therefore closer to Freud than he thinks. One has only to read the logical model in the perspective of the murder Freud discusses, or else place the murder in the logical perspective of Lévi-Strauss, to arrive at the hypothesis we are in the process of formulating.

R. G.: That is in fact just what we are doing. And we can confirm once again that even though our hypothesis breaks radically with everything that precedes it on a number of points, it is nonetheless also a direct development of many ethnological insights that have preceded it. We would be doing the hypothesis an injustice if we were to present it as an entirely new invention; it is important to recognize its place in the ethnological tradition.

I think it was necessary, therefore, to show what kind of relation the hypothesis has with the kind of model Lévi-Strauss developed for mythology. The relation can be summed up, perhaps, by our inability to keep from exclaiming—while reading a structuralist version of *The Bacchae*, for example—in the words of Molière: 'Ah! qu'en termes galants ces choses-là sont mises!'

G. L.: We can smile here, certainly, but your reading of Lévi-Strauss is not primarily negative and polemical. It is clear that the 'main points' in question are put in too precious a language for an understanding of what is essential, but it is more important that the main points are there in the first place and that lynching can be made manifest in the Lévi-Straussian discourse itself; that is, the truly scientific element can be revealed in the metaphoric scientism of topo-structuralism. With Lévi-Strauss as with Freud, then, something of substance is there and thus Molière's words have a positive sense.

R. G.: In closing it will be interesting, although also somewhat disturbing, to reflect on the real 'connotations', as the structuralists would say, of the topological model invented by Lévi-Strauss. The model is one of encumberment. How to diminish this encumberment, how to reduce the excessive crowding of the field so that one might get on there more easily? That is the question that is constantly posed. Behind the appearance of the coolest logic we can sense a fear of the spectre of over-population, which certainly has many psycho-sociological implications; one can detect it almost everywhere at the present time. It is the greatest fear of the so-called developed countries.

The tragic situation of humanity today is stated not only in terms of a total destruction that has to be avoided, but also of the selective destruction that must be based on choice—which is precisely what has become impossible at a time when any selective destruction runs the risk of becoming total destruction. The question, then, is one of reducing the population without annihilating it entirely. This is actually a sacrificial question and surely the 'topological' model of Lévi-Strauss reflects it. The model also brings to mind the many urban situations of overcrowding, such as those of traffic or of a bus that is so full that ejecting a single passenger eases the congestion. In our own time the question of the scapegoat hides easily behind statistics and the specifically modern anguish caused by excessive growth.

CHAPTER FIVE
Texts of Persecution

Persecution Demystified: The Achievement of the Modern and Western World

R. G.: When considered as a whole, modern research (of which our own project constitutes only a new, more advanced stage), can be seen as part of a much larger dynamic, that of the first society to become capable of deciphering a causal sequence and revealing it to be one of arbitrary violence—whereas in the history of all humanity this causal sequence has never appeared in any form other than that of mythology.

Much suggests that there exists nowadays a question about human beings as such that results from our growing ability to decipher phenomena of collective violence and then to produce texts of persecution rather than myths. The question of human existence and the question of violence as ignorance take on their true significance when each question is seen as a function of the other. The discovery of the founding mechanism as a mechanism not only of religion but of culture and of hominization itself is a decisive step. The fact that these three questions have finally become a single question is not the result of modern thought and of the sciences of man alone; all must be placed in the much larger context of a society that for centuries has been able at first to abate and then to halt altogether—in its areas of influence, which has come to mean most of the planet—the production of myth and ritual or the sacred transfiguration of violence.

A society that replaces myth by an awareness of persecution is a society in the process of desacralization. We are not the first to note that the one and the other are related, but we are the first to understand the necessity of their relatedness.

The whole of our discussion can be related to a victimage mechanism that is progressively less obscured by ignorance. To illustrate this we can use a spatial metaphor, though of course it can have no other application or value. One could say that outside our society the mechanism is invisible because it is constantly in retreat; it keeps a position *behind* human beings. In Judaeo-Western society, on the other hand, it has gradually come forward again and is more and more visible. This growing visibility has innumerable consequences, but for the moment we should emphasize the religious and epistemological consequences. In so far as light is shed on the victimage mechanism, concepts like violence and unjust persecution become thinkable and begin to play a larger role in cultural institutions. The production of myth and ritual simultaneously declines and eventually disappears entirely.

Although this process of discovery includes phases of intensity and periods of sudden acceleration, such as ours in particular, and although this process is more or less advanced in different groups and individuals, one should beware of defining it as an instantaneous 'awakening of consciousness' or as the privilege of a certain elite. One should beware of giving it too 'intellectual' an interpretation.

We should be well aware, for example, that the medieval texts of persecution, like anti-semitic texts, records of the Inquisition, or witch trials, even if they still contain elements that are very close to mythology, in that the perspective they employ remains definable by a type of distortion close to that of myth, can be situated in an intermediary zone between mythology and the more radial demythification of which we ourselves are capable. These texts are much easier to decipher than myths because the transfiguration of the victim is much less powerful and complete than in myth. In texts of persecution that have already been interpreted the victim has not been sacralized or has undergone only a vague attempt at sacralization. That certainly makes interpretation much easier. We might therefore conclude that the path leading to this particular interpretive ability extends back a long way and is not incompatible—far from it—with the practice of violence, perhaps even a considerable augmented and multiplied violence, to the extent that it becomes more clearly recognized and its 'unconscious' power of mimetic polarization diminishes along with its power of reconciliation.

In other words, the process that leads to the discovery of the victimage mechanism cannot possibly be a smooth, peaceful process. At this point we already know enough about the paradoxical and violent cultural remedies for violence to understand that any increase in our knowledge of the victimage mechanism, anything that tends to disengage or reveal violence, represents considerable progress, at least potentially, in intellectual and ethical respects, but that also, in the short term, it will mean a terrible recrudescence of that same violence, often in odious and atrocious forms, since sacrificial mechanisms become progressively less efficient and less capable of renewal. One can imagine that human beings, confronted with this situation, will be tempted to restore the lost effectiveness of the traditional remedy by forever increasing the dosage, immolating more and more victims in holocausts that are meant to be sacrificial but that are progressively less so. The always arbitrary but culturally real difference between legitimate and illegitimate violence will weaken. Its power of illusion diminishes, and henceforth there are only enemy brothers to confront one another in its name, which all will claim to embody but which in reality no longer exists; cultural difference will be distinguished less and less from the mimetic crisis to which it returns. Any sense of legality will be lost.

G. L.: Your emphasis on the sacrificial and violent character of cultural protections against violence is clearly not based on any approbation of sacrificial societies or a desire to regress toward them. People who read you in this way can only see a reprise, which would be quite banal, of theories about the cathartic nature of ritual and culture in general. What they do not seem to understand is the importance of the role of distortion and misinterpretation in the victimage mechanism, which is essential if the mechanism is to have its generative and productive effects.

Perhaps this is because generally they do not read beyond the first chapter in *Violence and the Sacred*, or because this is the most easily misunderstood point in your theory.

R. G.: The virtue of what we have accomplished so far in our discussions, I believe, lies in our having better defined this mechanism and in having made misunderstandings, if not impossible—they never are—at least more difficult.

From the moment when knowledge of the mechanism begins to spread, there can be no turning back. It is impossible to rehabilitate a sacrificial mechanism in the process of decomposition because growing awareness of these mechanisms is what decomposes them; any effort to interrupt or reverse the process can only be made at the cost of the knowledge being disseminated. This will always lead to an attempt to stifle this knowledge by violence; there will be an unsuccessful attempt to close the human community in on itself. I believe that this sort of undertaking characterizes all totalitarian movements and the virulent ideologies that have succeeded and battled with one another throughout the twentieth century; they are founded on a kind of monstrous but ineffective rationalization of victimage mechanisms. Entire categories of human beings are distinguished from the rest of humanity and are singled out for annihilation—the Jews, the aristocrats, the bourgeois, the faithful of such and such a religion, and miscreants of all kinds. We are always told that the creation of the perfect city, the way to terrestrial paradise, depends on the prior elimination or forced conversion of the guilty categories.

J.-M. O.: In sum, the mechanism becomes recognizable only with the development of sufficient critical intelligence to hinder its functioning. The arbitrariness of the victim becomes apparent, and a reconciliatory unanimity is no longer possible. Myth and ritual can no longer grow and spread. One can find only intermediate, mixed phenomena that are increasingly transparent to criticism; these can be read as persecution.

Spontaneous collective violence no longer possesses its founding capability and no longer plays a central role in society; it subsists as a marginal phenomenon in less advanced groups. We are able to observe it there but its degenerate state conceals its importance. Certain critics have thus been able to object that you base your anthropology on secondary phenomena that are incapable of supporting the formidable structure of your hypothesis.

G. L.: The founding murder simply cannot be witnessed. This is not then a fortuitous or accidental difficulty but a logical and practical impossibility. As we have said, the only true scapegoats are those we cannot recognize as such.

R. G.: The better we grasp the mechanism, then, the less value doing so has for us. As we tighten our grip the object in question diminishes, so that we no longer understand the crucial importance, not of the object itself, but of what it must have been before we were able to take hold of it.

J.-M. O.: This is a very important and subtle point in your theory. If there were absolutely nothing analogous to the founding mechanism in the modern world, your hypothesis would be less easy to understand, but it would be more readily received by people accustomed to Freudian theory or eager to identify hidden mechanisms in the form of a disguised individual or collective unconscious.

R. G.: The founding mechanism is at once visible and invisible. It is visible in the sense that one can observe analogous phenomena in the modern world. It is invisible in the sense that the directly observable phenomena are nothing but pale, diluted residues; even if their effects remain analogous to what they once were, their limitations as examples make them as deceptive as informative.

J.-M. O.: Our contemporary state can be thought of as intermediary between the sacralizing misinterpretation of primitive societies and the mode of knowledge your hypothesis attempts to support. This intermediary phase consists of a limited perception of victimage mechanisms, but never attains an understanding of their founding role for the whole of human culture.

R. G.: If the effectiveness of the mechanism and the richness of ritual production are inversely proportional to a community's aptitude for perceiving the functioning of this same mechanism, the very poverty of texts of persecution and the fact that the victim is barely sacralized already reflects a certain emergence of the founding mechanism, even though persecution persists and the perspective of our text is the perspective of the persecutors. The medieval communities that persecuted Jews are in many respects close to the communities that in other times and places achieved reconciliation at the cost of victims and produced the great Greek, Ojibwa, and Tikopia myths, as well as the diverse forms of religion over the entire planet. They are also quite distant, however, in that they never quite sacralize their victims and do not reorder their communities through the production of myth and ritual that issues directly from collective violence.

The text of persecution reveals an *inability* to produce true myths that characterizes the modern Western world as a whole. The modern ability to pursue and demystify subtle modes of persecution, which may be hidden not only behind very transparent accusations but also behind texts that appear to be innocent, can only correspond to a more advanced phase of an evolution that progresses in the form of a spiral, with the deciphering of cultural mechanisms leading to more decomposition, and vice versa.

The Double Semantic Sense of the Word 'Scapegoat'

J.-M. O.: You have already mentioned another sign of this more advanced phase, one constituted by the use of the term 'scapegoat'. . .

R. G.: The expression scapegoat comes from *caper emissarius*, a term in the Vulgate that is a liberal interpretation of the Greek *apopompaios*: 'one who wards off illnesses'. The latter term, in the Greek translation of the Bible known as the Septuagint, is itself a liberal interpretation from the Hebrew, the exact translation of which would read: 'destined to Azazel'. It is generally thought that Azazel is the name of an ancient demon said to inhabit the desert. In Chapter 16 of Leviticus the ritual treatment of the goat is described as follows:

> And Aaron shall lay both his hands upon the head of the live goat, and confess over him all the iniquities of the people of Israel, and all their transgressions, all their sins; and he shall put them upon the head of the goat, and send him away into the wilderness by the hand of a man who is in readiness. The goat shall bear all their iniquities upon him to a solitary land; and he shall let the goat go in the wilderness.
>
> (Leviticus 16, 21-22)

In the eighteenth century, researchers and others related the Jewish ritual of the scapegoat to other rituals that obviously resembled it. In his *Histoire philosophique*, for example, Raynal writes of the Hindus: 'They have a horse in their rites, which corresponds to the scapegoat of the Jews.'[49]

J.-M. O.: To my knowledge the word 'scapegoat' has the double semantic sense of ritual institution and unconscious, spontaneous psycho-sociological mechanism only in the languages of those societies that have been part of the long process of cultural deciphering, in other words, the Western languages from the end of the Middle Ages and many non-Western languages since. The semantic conjunction really constitutes something of a paradox. Ritual and spontaneous behaviour are generally thought of as being poles apart. How is it that they have come together in the term 'scapegoat'?

R. G.: According to the Japanese anthropologist, Masao Yamaguchi, there is no word in Japanese to translate the modern meaning of 'scapegoat'. The merit of this conjunction is that it reveals a very widespread intuition that ethnology and the sciences of man have never officially recognized: there is a relation between the forms of ritual and the universal human tendency to transfer anxiety and conflict on to arbitrary victims.

The double meaning of the English term 'scapegoat' is found in the French *bouc émissaire*, the German *Sündenbock*, and in all modern Western languages. Ultimately, everything we say here is an attempt to understand this semantic evolution of the word and evaluate its impact. Our whole hypothesis has existed silently in common language since the emergence of what is called rationalism.

Strangely, there has been no work up to this point, as far as I know, concerning this evolution. If one looks at the history of ethnology, one notes that innumerable theories of religion have been proposed. There is only one that has never been proposed, and precisely that theory has been inscribed in Western languages for at least two or three centuries.

When ethnology does turn its attention to what since Frazer have been known as 'scapegoat' rituals, something that occurs less and less often, there is usually not even an attempt to explain the phenomenon; at times it will be alluded to as a 'well-known phenomenon' that it is not necessary to define, or it will be labelled aberrant behaviour that also requires no explanation because it has no real sociological importance. In either case this amounts to closing off a line of research that might prove to be too fruitful.

One might think that ethnology had firmly decided to ignore the psycho-sociological meaning of the term scapegoat, with its allusion to a spontaneous mechanism, and further that ethnology will not permit any recourse to this second meaning of the term—one might think that a would-be scientific discipline had renounced all use of an idea that had been found to have absolutely no theoretical importance.

Yet even a superficial review of ethnological literature in the twentieth century quickly shows that this is not the case. It is only when ethnologists bring up a category of ritual, which is otherwise non-existent, like all categories—one they have baptized 'scapegoat rituals' because aspects of the malevolent transference are particularly salient in this grouping—that ethnologists refuse the modern significance and go back to the description of Leviticus, which they declare unintelligible.

As soon as there is no longer any official question of the Leviticus scapegoat, the same ethnologists have no scruples about using the expression in the sense of a spontaneous collective catharsis.

The desire to use the term in this way must certainly overtake them whenever they have the opportunity, increasingly rare today, to witness the performance of still vigorous rituals, or when they sense, in the course of a purely intellectual process, the imposing forces that are awakened in great ritual for the sole purpose of calming them and channelling them in the direction of neutral or neutralized victims.

The expression 'scapegoat' occurs spontaneously to ethnologists when they confront certain forms of sacrifice that do not belong to the category defined by Frazer. This occurs every time that contact is truly established, that the interpreter 'hits the mark' with respect to the reality of the religious phenomenon under study. That this should be so is a sign that the relation between spontaneous collective violence and the organized violence of ritual—and not only the type labelled 'scapegoat ritual'— is too intimate and fundamental to escape a good observer.

Yet when this occurs it occurs surreptitiously; any time the second meaning of the term is used it retains a metaphorical and literary character because the term has no official status in ethnology.

In a remarkable, indeed dazzling essay, the ethnologist mentioned before, Masao Yamaguchi, has gathered the principal Japanese ritual institutions such as the emperor, the geishas, the theatre, the marionettes, etc., under the heading of what he calls the scapegoat. In certain types of travelling theatre, the principal hero, who is of course the one who plays the role of the scapegoat, is so 'polluted' by the end of the performance that he has to leave the community without having contact with anyone or anything. In this sort of theatre we come upon an intermediary form between ritual expulsion and dramatic art, and if literary critics would pause for a moment to reflect they would find it has much to say about the meaning of our own theatre, about its relation to ritual, and about the well-known Aristotelian *catharsis*.

In any case, Masao Yamaguchi nowhere inquires, in the course of his article, into the precise meaning and domain of the term scapegoat, in spite of the crucial role he accords it.[50]

Neither ethnology nor the dictionary have any use for the double semantic sense, ritual and spontaneous, of the scapegoat. As one might expect, the dictionary would have us believe that the second meaning represents a *figurative* use of the term, whereas the use of the term in Leviticus would be the *proper* use of the term. How well we are instructed!

An established discipline such as ethnology has every right to call any aspect of a new hypothesis, such as mine, into question. This is an indubitable right and we have responded. Yet at a certain point the relationship becomes reciprocal. A hypothesis that has been inscribed in language for centuries has the right to put into question an ethnology that need only employ it to escape the absurd categorization of ritual that was still being used fifty years ago but shies away from a serious examination of the various connotations of 'scapegoat' as if this word could give them the plague. Indeed, I believe that it can!

The Historical Emergence of the Victimage Mechanism

G. L.: What you have just said needs to be placed in the context of your earlier statements concerning the modern and Western world as a whole. According to you, this world is entirely ordered by the diminishing efficacy of sacrifice, or, what amounts to the same thing, by an ever harsher and more revealing awareness of victimage mechanisms. Furthermore, contrary to the views of philosophical elitists like Heidegger or Nietzsche, there is no way of distinguishing in this process between the effects of scholarly and popular opinion. One often has the impression, as with the double semantic sense of the term 'scapegoat', that popular opinion is far ahead of critical reflection, and that the latter will do anything to ignore the possibilities that popular language holds right before its eyes.

In spite of such resistance, you suggest that the process continues its implacable course and that we can distinguish two phases: a world in which texts of persecution are written from the point of view of the persecutor—a phase that, unfortunately, has not yet run its course—and a later universal deciphering of these texts, a time when their meaning grows increasingly clear.

Although this second phase represents a tremendous advance, it provokes new types of resistance to the argument you have been developing. Does this mean that a universally accepted reading of all myths, religions, and cultures on the planet as texts of persecution would correspond to a new phase, a new rupture that remains frightening to most of us and that, even though we have every encouragement, most of us still refuse to cross?

R. G.: That is indeed my view. I believe we are undergoing unprecedented change, change more radical than humanity has ever been subject to before.

This change, which later on we will discuss further, does not depend on any books that we might or might not write. It is simply part of the terrifying and wondrous history of our time, which manifests itself in places other than our writings.

I do think it is necessary for us to engage in the discourse we have been pursuing here. But if we had chosen otherwise, others would have taken up this discourse. And there will be others, in any case, who will repeat what we are in the process of saying and who will advance matters beyond what we have been able to do. Yet books themselves will have no more than minor importance; the events within which such books emerge will be infinitely more eloquent than whatever we write and will establish truths we have difficulty describing and describe poorly, even in simple and banal instances. They are already very simple, indeed too simple to interest our current Byzantium, but these truths will become simpler still; they will soon be accessible to anyone.

J.-M. O.: You mean to say, then, that the gradual emergence of the victimage mechanism has already dominated our history for some time and that this will accelerate its pace in the years to come. And now you suggest that, although we all are part of this history, we often participate in it against our will and without our knowledge. Like Heidegger, you ask us to consider the possibility that this history, even though it is accomplished by human beings and by human beings alone, is not entirely human, is not only human. Can you be more precise? Everything you have said concerning modern Western society leads us to this question. The complete disintegration of the mechanisms of culture and the global expansion of modern society can be seen, according to you, as the unique vocation of this society, as a historical challenge without precedent, one that has come to involve the whole of humanity.

On this point, you once more find yourself categorically opposed to the commonplace views of our time; you attach little permanent value to the cognitive nihilism that has gained the upper hand in most places, to the belief that there is no universal history, that meaning has only a marginal existence in dispersed and relative forms, since we must acknowledge the existence of concurrent and contradictory meanings. You remain unimpressed by everything put forward as proof that ethnocentrism always undermines the universal, or that polycentrism is irreducible in contemporary culture.

R. G.: I am fully in favour of the major liquidation of philosophy and the sciences of man that is currently taking place. The grave-digger's work is necessary, for what is being buried is truly dead—even if there is too much ceremony. There is no need to exaggerate the task and make the undertaker the prototype of all future cultural life. We ought to let the dead bury the dead, and move on to other things.

The danger today, in fact, is that as the public becomes weary of these interminable funerary rites for meaning and of the funerary metaphysics it has swallowed for so long now, it will lose sight of the real accomplishments of modern thought, all of which are critical and negative. I subscribe to many facets of this criticism and find it indispensable. I simply refuse to admit that there is nothing more to be done from now on than to mull over past failures.

There is no question of advocating simple optimism or pious, wishful thinking. The completion of contemporary criticism coupled with the finally complete deconstruction of all religious and cultural mystification necessarily corresponds to an ever greater privation of sacrificial resources. Humanity is one with respect to knowledge, but of course it is not at all unified; it is no longer capable of producing idols of violence around which it might achieve unanimity. We are therefore always and everywhere confronted with conflicts of the *doubles*. All the mythologies of the 'plural' and the 'polycentric' are being hawked by doubles who hope to convince themselves of the legitimacy of their products. They devote themselves to a desperate marketing of their cherished differences. The ever more rapid advance of our society toward the truth of all culture cannot resemble a final closure of positivist knowledge as conceived by Flaubert's Mr Homais.

I think that the advent of a true science of man will correspond not to the image that most people have of any scientific achievement, but with the fall of the last illusions that have accompanied science from its beginning through its rise over the last two centuries. Science has come to look more and more like a trap that modern humanity has unknowingly held out for itself. Humanity is henceforth threatened with weapons powerful enough to annihilate it; if they are not yet quite that destructive today, they will be tomorrow. The rise of science and technology is clearly linked to the desacralization of nature in a universe in which victimage mechanisms function less and less well.

But the desacralization of nature is only a first step; the crossing of the scientific threshold by all disciplines that will truly deserve to be called sciences of man constitutes a much more difficult step and leads to a more advanced stage of desacralization. At the same time, our impression of moving into a trap we have set for ourselves will become more acute. The whole of humanity is already confronted with an ineluctable dilemma: human beings must become reconciled without the aid of sacrificial intermediaries or resign themselves to the imminent extinction of humanity.

The progressively more precise knowledge we possess concerning cultural systems and the mechanisms that generate them is not gratuitous; it is not without its counterpart. There can no longer be any question of giving polite lip-service to a vague 'ideal of non-violence'. There can be no question of producing more pious vows and hypocritical formulae. Rather, we will more and more often find ourselves faced with an implacable necessity. The definitive renunciation of violence, without any second thoughts, will become for us the condition *sine qua non* for the survival of humanity itself and for each one of us.

G. L.: The logic of what you are saying is clear. Far from corresponding to the ideological climate of scientism that has deceived us for some time, far from heralding the realization of the naive Utopias dreamed of in the nineteenth century, the emergence of a true science of man will mark the beginning of a radically new climate; it will open a universe of absolute responsibility; it has nothing to do with the 'all is permitted' of the Dostoievskian nihilist hero or with the Nietzschean will to power. If man acts as he has in the past and abandons himself to mimetic contagion, there will be no victimage mechanisms to save him.

R. G.: We know that this is not simply an opinion, an intellectual prejudice; we read in the papers every day that things have come this far. It really matters very little what means desacralized man will discover or has already discovered for realizing the infinite potential of his violence; we know that the limits of his destructive power are receding more and more and that to give way to the temptation of unleashing this power will mean the risk of total annihilation.

J.-M. O.: But I would like to return to a question that was left unanswered. I can see that everything you refer to here results from a gradual uncovering that has proceeded for centuries, perhaps for millennia, and that has now reached a decisive stage. This must be more than a simple intellectual adventure or 'research project' that modern Western man has set for himself and that he will pursue with characteristic tenacity, without any regard for the consequences.

If we conclude that we alone are the masters of this project, that it results from a decision no other society would have been capable of making before ours, will we not simply be giving way once more to Western hubris, even if we admit that the decision will turn out badly for us; are we not falling back into a Promethean romanticism—a negative romanticism, certainly—but for all that the more appropriate; does this amount to justifying the charge of ethnocentrism?

R. G.: Everything you say would be correct beyond any doubt if the process were attributed to a voluntary decision made by Western man. Certainly one would be reduced to such a hypothesis if it were not possible to proceed back beyond Western civilization itself and point straight to the real motor of the revelatory yet menacing dynamic that animates the whole of this civilization.

We have come to the most crucial point of the whole of our exposition, and to the surprise of surprises. The logic of my hypothesis forces me to seek the essential, if not exclusive, cause of the dynamic animating us in an area that by rights should be entirely excluded, not only from the perspective of modern thought, which needs to be transcended, but from the perspective that genuinely transcends it, the completely revealed perspective of the surrogate victim. The most *improbable* source of our demythologizing is religion itself, and in our world, more particularly, it would appear to be the religious tradition proper to it, the one it has adhered to blindly and is particularly incapable of subjecting to criticism. I propose that if today we are capable of breaking down and analysing cultural mechanisms, it is because of the indirect and unperceived but formidably constraining influence of the Judaeo-Christian scriptures.

You will see that I have no illusions about the originality or novelty of the propositions we have been developing. The revelation of the surrogate victim as the founding agent in all religion and culture is something that neither our world as a whole nor any one particularly 'gifted' individual can claim to have discovered. *Everything is already revealed.* This is certainly the claim of the Gospels at the moment of the Passion. To understand that the victimage mechanism constitutes an essential dimension of that revelation, we will not need to take up the comparative analyses and constant cross-references that were necessary in the examples of religions of violence; we need only give our fullest attention to the letter of the text. It speaks incessantly of everything we have said ourselves; it has no other function than to unearth victims of collective violence and to reveal their innocence. There is nothing hidden. There is no secret dimension that the interpreter must painstakingly seek to discover. Everything is perfectly transparent. Nothing is less problematic or easy than the reading we will offer. The true mystery, therefore, as far as this reading is concerned, is its absence among us.

BOOK II

THE JUDAEO-CHRISTIAN SCRIPTURES

In principio erat Verbum (John 1,1)

CHAPTER ONE

Things Hidden Since the Foundation of the World

Similarities between the Biblical Myths and World Mythology

R. G.: We have now dealt with the hypothesis of the scapegoat as an exclusively scientific one. No doubt our discussions have been far too hasty, as well as too schematic. All the same, our readers now know our gist. We must turn to other subjects. Or rather, we must investigate other, even more spectacular ways in which the same truth has come to the fore.

From this point onwards we shall take it for granted that the victimage mechanisms exist and that their role in the establishment of religion, culture and humanity itself is an established fact, no longer open to doubt. Actually, I never lose sight of the point that this is only a hypothesis. I am hardly likely to forget it, for the very reason that the material remaining to be studied here will supply us with new proofs, and increasingly striking ones.

First of all, we shall look at Judaeo-Christian scripture. After that, we shall deal with psychopathology, and this will ultimately lead us to some conclusions about our own times. People will accuse us of playing at being Pico della Mirandola—the Renaissance Man—certainly a temptation to be resisted today, if we wish to be seen in a favourable light. But in fact a very different thing is in question here. We simply cannot confine our hypothesis to the area of hominization and primitive religion. As we shall see, this hypothesis will compel us to broaden our horizons, for it can only acquire its fullest meaning in universal terms.

If we turn to the Old Testament, and particularly to the books that come first or those that may contain the oldest materials, we find ourselves immediately in familiar territory. Immediately we come upon the three great moments we have defined:

(1) Dissolution in conflict, removal of the differences and hierarchies which constitute the community in its wholeness;

(2) the *all against one* of collective violence;

(3) the development of interdictions and rituals.

To the first moment belong the very first lines of the text on the creation of the world, as well as the tale of the confusion of the Tower of Babel and that of the corruption of Sodom and Gomorrah. We also see immediately that in Exodus the ten plagues of Egypt form the equivalent of the plague at Thebes in Sophocles. The Flood, again, belongs with these metaphors of crisis. And in every case, from the first lines of Genesis, we have the theme of the warring brothers or twins: Cain and Abel, Jacob and Esau, Joseph and his eleven brothers, etc.

The second moment is no less easy to locate. It is always by violence, by the expulsion of one of the brothers, that the crisis is resolved, and differentiation returns once again.

In every one of the great scenes of Genesis and Exodus there exists a theme or a quasi-theme of the founding murder of expulsion. Obviously, this is most striking in the expulsion from the Garden of Eden; there, God takes the violence upon himself and founds humanity by driving Adam and Eve far away from him.

In the blessing that Isaac gives to Jacob rather than to his brother Esau, we are again dealing with the violent resolution of a conflict between warring brothers, and the surreptitious character of Jacob's act in substituting himself for his brother, when the act is discovered, does not compromise the outcome. It matters little, in effect, who is the victim, provided that there is one.

In Jacob's struggle with the angel, a conflict between *doubles* is in question—one that hangs in the balance for a long time because the contestants are perfectly matched. Jacob's adversary is first of all called a *man*; and it is with the defeat of this adversary and his expulsion at the hands of the victor that he becomes a God from whom Jacob demands and obtains a blessing. In other words, the combat of *doubles* results in the expulsion of one of the pair, and this is identified directly with the return to peace and order.

In every one of these scenes, the relationship between *brothers* or *doubles* has in the first instance a character of undecidability, resolved by expulsion through violence despite an arbitrary element involved, as in the case of Jacob and Esau.

Since the single victim brings reconciliation and safety by restoring life to the community, it is not difficult to appreciate that a sole survivor in a world where all others perish can, thematically, amount to the same thing as a single victim extracted from a group in which no one, save the victim, perishes. Noah's Ark, which alone is spared by the Flood, guarantees that the world will begin all over again. It is Lot and his family who are the sole survivors of the destruction of Sodom and Gomorrah. Lot's wife, who is changed into a pillar of salt, brings back into this story the motif of the single victim.

Let us now look at the third moment—at the establishment of interdictions and sacrifices, or circumcision, which comes to the same thing. Here references to this side of things can become confused with references to the founding mechanism. For instance, in the sacrifice of Isaac the necessity of sacrifice threatens the most precious being, only to be satisfied, at the last moment, with a substituted victim, the ram sent by God.

In the story of Jacob's blessing, the theme of the kids offered to the father in a propitiatory meal represents a sacrificial institution; and one detail that reveals clearly, despite its link with the other themes of the story, the way in which the sacrifice operates. It is thanks to the hair of those kids that Isaac can mistake Jacob's hide-covered limbs for Esau, and so Jacob escapes his father's curse.

In all these mythic accounts, society and even nature appear as a whole being put in order, or in which order is being re-established. In general, these belong to the end of the victimage account, the place where the logic of the hypothesis expects to be. But in the story of the creation of the world, the founding moment comes at the beginning, and no victimage is involved. For Noah, the final reorganization is implied not only in the Covenant after the Flood, but also in the confinement of prototypes of all species within the Ark; here we have something like a floating system of classification, on the basis of which the world will re-people itself in conformity with the norms of God's will. We can also cite here God's promise to Abraham after the sacrifice of the ram substituted for Isaac, as well as the rules which are prescribed for Jacob after the expulsion of his divinized double. In both cases, the change of name points to the founding character of the process.

J.-M. O.: Up to now you have only shown us the similarities between the biblical myths and the myths which you spoke about earlier. Are you not concerned with stressing the differences between these mythologies and the Bible?

R. G.: I shall shortly be talking about these differences. If I insist first of all upon the similarities, it is to demonstrate clearly that I am not embarrassed by them, and that I am not trying to spirit them away. There can be no doubt that the first books of the Bible rest upon myths that are very close to those found all over the world. What I shall try to prove to you now is that these analogies are not the end of the matter. The biblical treatment of these myths offers something which is absolutely distinctive, and this is what I shall be trying to define.

The Distinctiveness of the Biblical Myths

Cain

R. G.: First let us take the story of Cain. Here I follow the text of the Jerusalem Bible:

> The man had intercourse with his wife Eve, and she conceived and gave birth to Cain. 'I have acquired a man with the help of Yahweh' she said. She gave birth to a second child, Abel, the brother of Cain. Now Abel became a shepherd and kept flocks, while Cain tilled the soil. Time passed and Cain brought some of the produce of the soil as an offering for Yahweh, while Abel for his part brought the first-born of his flock and some of their fat as well. Yahweh looked with favour on Abel and his offering. But he did not look with favour on Cain and his offering, and Cain was very angry and downcast. Yahweh asked Cain. 'Why are you angry and downcast? If you are well disposed ought you not to lift up your head. But if you are ill disposed, is not sin at the door like a crouching beast hungering for you, which you must master?' Cain said to his brother Abel, 'Let us go out'; and while they were in the open country, Cain set on his brother Abel and killed him.
>
> Yahweh asked Cain, 'Where is your brother Abel?' 'I do not know' he replied. 'Am I my brother's guardian?' 'What have you done?' Yahweh asked. 'Listen to the sound of your brother's blood, crying out to me from the ground. Now be accursed and driven from the ground that has opened its mouth to receive your brother's blood at your hands. When you till the ground it shall no longer yield you any

of its produce. You shall be a fugitive and a wanderer over the earth.'
Then Cain said to Yahweh, 'My punishment is greater than I can
bear. See! Today you drive me from this ground. I must hide from
you, and be a fugitive and a wanderer over the earth. Why, whoever
comes across me will kill me!' 'Very well, then,' Yahweh replied, 'if
anyone kills Cain, sevenfold vengeance shall be taken for him.' So
Yahweh put a mark on Cain, to prevent whoever might come across
him from striking him down. Cain left the presence of Yahweh and
settled in the land of Nod, east of Eden.

Cain had intercourse with his wife, and she conceived and gave
birth to Enoch. He became builder of a town, and he gave the town
the name of his son Enoch. Enoch had a son, Irad, and Irad became
the father of Lamech. Lamech married two women: the name of the
first was Adah and the name of the second was Zillah. Adah gave
birth to Jabal: he was the ancestor of the tent-dwellers and owners of
livestock. His brother's name was Jubal: he was the ancestor of all
who play the lyre and the flute. As for Zillah, she gave birth to
Tubal-Cain: he was the ancestor of all metal-workers, in bronze or
iron. Tubal-Cain's sister was Naamah.

Lamech said to his wives:

> Adah and Zillah, hear my voice,
> Lamech's wives, listen to what I say:
> I killed a man for wounding me,
> a boy for striking me.
> Sevenfold vengeance is taken for Cain,
> but seventy-sevenfold for Lamech. (Genesis 4, 1-24)

When men had begun to be plentiful on the earth, and daughters
had been born to them, the sons of God, looking at the daughters of
men, saw they were pleasing, so they married as many as they chose.
Yahweh said, 'My spirit must not be for ever disgraced in man, for he
is but flesh; his life shall last no more than a hundred and twenty
years.' The Nephilim were on the earth at that time (and even afterwards) when the sons of God resorted to the daughters of man, and
had children by them. These are the heroes of days gone by, the
famous men.

Yahweh saw that the wickedness of man was great on the earth,
and that the thoughts in his heart fashioned nothing but wickedness
all day long. Yahweh regretted having made man on the earth, and

his heart grieved. 'I will rid the earth's face of man, my own creation,' Yahweh said 'and of animals too, reptiles too, and the birds of
heaven; for I regret having made them.' (Genesis 6, 1-7).

As we can see, the myth of Cain is presented in a classic fashion. One of
the two brothers kills the other, and the Cainite community is founded.

People have often asked why God, although he condemns the murder, responds to the appeal of the murderer. Cain says: 'Every one that
findeth me shall slay me.' And God responds: 'Whosoever slayeth Cain,
vengeance shall be taken on him sevenfold.' God himself intervenes,
and in response to the founding murder he enunciates the law against
murder. This intervention makes it clear, in my view, that the decisive
murder, here as elsewhere, has a founding character. And to talk in
terms of 'founding' is also to talk in terms of 'differentiating', which is
why we have, immediately afterwards, these words: 'And the Lord set a
mark upon Cain, lest any finding him should kill him.' I see in this the
establishment of a differential system, which serves, as always, to discourage mimetic rivalry and generalized conflict.

G. L.: A great number of communities attribute their own foundation to a similar type of murder. Rome, for example. Romulus kills
Remus and the city of Rome is founded. In both cases, the murder of
one brother by another has the same founding and differentiating
power. Discord between doubles is succeeded by the order of the new
community.

R. G.: There is nonetheless a difference between the two myths that
can easily be disregarded, within the normal context of statements
about mythology. In our own particular context—that is, an anthropology entirely centred on victimage mechanisms and thus open to the
proposition that to regard them as arbitrary is to misinterpret
them—this difference can acquire a great significance.

In the Roman myth, the murder of Remus appears as an action that
was perhaps to be regretted, but was justified by the victim's transgression. Remus did not respect the ideal limit traced by Romulus between the inside and the outside of the city. The motive for the killing is
at once insignificant—since the city does not yet exist—and crucial, literally fundamental. In order for the city to exist, no one can be allowed
to flout with impunity the rules it prescribes. So Romulus is justified.
His status is that of a sacrificer and High Priest; he incarnates Roman

power under all its forms at one and the same time. The legislative, the judiciary, and the military forms cannot yet be distinguished from the religious; everything is already present within the last.

By contrast, even if Cain is invested with what are basically the same powers, and even if he has the ear of the deity, he is nonetheless presented as a vulgar murderer. The fact that the first murder precipitates the first cultural development of the human race does not in any way excuse the murderer the biblical text. The founding character of the murder is signalled just as clearly, and perhaps even more clearly, than in the non-biblical myths. But there is something else, and that is moral judgement. The condemnation of the murder takes precedence over all other considerations. 'Where is Abel thy brother?'

The importance of this ethical dimension in the Bible is well-known. And yet few commentaries have sought to define it with rigour, particularly for texts that are not necessarily the most ancient, but have to deal with archaic data. In my view, Max Weber has been the most successful in this regard. In his great but incomplete work *Ancient Judaism*, he comes to the conclusion at several stages that the biblical writers have an undeniable tendency to take the side of the victim on moral grounds, and to spring to the victim's defence.[51]

Max Weber sees this observation as having a purely sociological and cultural significance. He takes the view that the propensity to favour the victim is characteristic of a particular cultural atmosphere peculiar to Judaism, and he looks for its explanation in the innumerable catastrophes of Jewish history and the fact that the Jewish people had not experienced any great historical success comparable to the successes of the empire-builders surrounding them: Egyptians, Assyrians, Babylonians, Persians, Greeks, Romans, etc.

He is therefore not at all interested in what might derive on the level of mythic and religious texts from a factor that appears to him to be in the last analysis a form of prejudice comparable to so many others, a prejudice in favour of victims. Seen in the context of the victimary anthropology centred on victimage mechanisms that we have just sketched out, this attitude of indifference is unacceptable. Suppose that the texts of mythology are the reflection, at once faithful and deceptive, of the collective violence that founds community; suppose that they bear witness of a real violence, that they do not lie even if in them the victimage mechanism is falsified and transfigured by its very efficacy; suppose, finally, that myth is the persecutors' retrospective vision of their own persecution. If this is so, we can hardly regard as insignificant a change in perspective that consists in taking the side of the victim, proclaiming the victim's innocence and the culpability of his murderers.

Suppose that, far from being a gratuitous invention, myth is a text that has been falsified by the belief of the executioners in the guiltiness of their victim; suppose, in other words, that myths incorporate the point of view of the community that has been reconciled to itself by the collective murder and is unanimously convinced that this event was a legitimate and sacred action, desired by God himself, which could not conceivably be repudiated, criticized, or analysed. If that is so, an attitude that involves rehabilitating the victim and denouncing the persecutors is not something that calls only for disillusioned and blasé commentaries. This attitude can hardly fail to have repercussions not merely on mythology itself, but on all that is involved in the hidden foundation of collective murder: forms of ritual, interdictions and religious transcendence. One by one, the whole range of cultural forms and values, even those that appear to be furthest removed from the domain of myth, would be affected.

J.-M. O.: Isn't this happening already in the Cain myth, however primitive it may be?

R. G.: If we examine the story with care, we come to see that the lesson of the Bible is precisely that the culture born of violence must return to violence. In the initial stages, we observe a brilliant flowering of culture: techniques are invented; towns spring from the desert. But very soon, the violence that has been inadequately contained by the founding murder and the legal barriers deriving from it, starts to escape and propagate. The borderline between legalized punishment, vengeance, and the blood feud is erased when Cain's seven victims become, for Lamech, seventy-seven.

G. L.: It is quite obvious that we have here a case of undifferentiated violence propagating contagiously. . .

R. G.: The Flood also results from an escalation that involves the monstrous dissolution of all differences: giants are born, the progeny of a promiscuous union between the sons of the gods and the daughters of men. This is the crisis in which the whole of culture is submerged, and its destruction is not only a punishment from God; to almost the same extent it is the fatal conclusion of a process which brings back the violence from which it originally managed to get free, thanks to the temporary benefits of the founding murder.

With reference to the violence that both founds and differentiates, the story of Cain has, in addition to its unquestionable significance as myth, a much greater power of revelation than that of non-Judaic myths. Certainly there must be, behind the biblical account, myths in conformity with the universal norms of mythology; so the initiative of the Jewish authors and their critical reappraisal must undoubtedly be credited with the affirmation that the victim is innocent and that the culture founded on murder retains a thoroughly murderous character that in the end becomes self-destructive, once the ordering and sacrificial benefits of the original violence have dissipated.

Here we are not just making a vague conjecture. Abel is only the first in a long line of victims whom the Bible exhumes and exonerates: 'The voice of thy brother's blood crieth unto me from the ground.'

Joseph

R. G.: Although it may be concealed in the Cain myth, the collective character of the persecution is fully visible in the story of Joseph.

Let us now look at the passages from the story of Joseph that are important for the purposes of our analysis:

Israel loved Joseph more than all his other sons, for he was the son of his old age, and he had a coat with long sleeves made for him. But his brothers, seeing how his father loved him more than all his other sons, came to hate him so much that they could not say a civil word to him.

Now Joseph had a dream, and he repeated it to his brothers. 'Listen,' he said, 'to this dream I have had. We were binding sheaves in the countryside; and my sheaf, it seemed, rose up and stood upright; then I saw your sheaves gather round and bow to my sheaf.' 'So you want to be king over us,' his brothers retorted, 'or to lord it over us?' And they hated him still more, on account of his dreams and of what he said. He had another dream which he told to his brothers. 'Look, I have had another dream,' he said, 'I thought I saw the sun, the moon and eleven stars, bowing to me.' He told his father and brothers, and his father scolded him. 'A fine dream to have!' he said to him. 'Are all of us then, myself, your mother and your

brothers, to come and bow to the ground before you?' His brothers
were jealous of him, but his father kept the thing in mind.

His brothers went to pasture their father's flock at Shechem. Then
Israel said to Joseph, 'Are not your brothers with the flock at
Shechem? Come, I am going to send you to them.' 'I am ready,' he
replied. . .

So Joseph went after his brothers and found them at Dothan.
They saw him in the distance, and before he reached them they made
a plot among themselves to put him to death. 'Here comes the man of
dreams,' they said to one another. 'Come on, let us kill him and
throw him into some well; we can say that a wild beast devoured him.
Then we shall see what becomes of his dreams.'

But Reuben heard, and he saved him from their violence. 'We
must not take his life,' he said. 'Shed no blood,' said Reuben to
them, 'throw him into this well in the wilderness, but do not lay violent hands on him'—intending to save him from them and to restore
him to his father. So when Joseph reached his brothers, they pulled
off his coat, the coat with long sleeves that he was wearing, and catch-
ing hold of him they threw him into the well, an empty well with no
water in it. Then they sat down to eat.

Looking up they saw a group of Ishmaelites who were coming
from Gilead, their camels laden with gum, tragacanth, balsam and
resin, which they were taking down to Egypt. Then Judah said to his
brothers, 'What do we gain by killing our brother and covering up
his blood? Come, let us sell him to the Ishmaelites, but let us not do
any harm to him. After all, he is our brother, and our own flesh.' His
brothers agreed.

Now some Midianite merchants were passing, and they drew
Joseph up out of the well. They sold Joseph to the Ishmaelites for
twenty silver pieces, and these men took Joseph to Egypt. When
Reuben went back to the well there was no sign of Joseph. Tearing
his clothes, he went back to his brothers. 'The boy has disappeared,'
he said. 'What am I going to do?'

They took Joseph's coat and, slaughtering a goat, they dipped the
coat in the blood. Then they sent back the coat with long sleeves and
had it taken to their father, with the message, 'This is what we have
found. Examine it and see whether or not it is your son's coat.' He
examined it and exclaimed, 'It is my son's coat! A wild beast has
devoured him. Joseph has been the prey of some animal and has been

torn to pieces.' Jacob, tearing his clothes and putting on a loin-cloth of sackcloth, mourned his son for a long time. All his sons and daughters came to comfort him, but he refused to be comforted. 'No,' he said, 'I will go down in mourning to Sheol, beside my son.' And his father wept for him.

Meanwhile the Midianites had sold him in Egypt to Potiphar, one of Pharaoh's officials and commander of the guard. . .

It happened some time later that his master's wife looked desirously at him and said, 'Sleep with me'. But he refused, and answered his master's wife, 'Because of me, my master does not concern himself with what happens in the house; he has handed over all his possessions to me. He is no more master in this house than I am. He has withheld nothing from me except yourself, because you are his wife. How could I do anything so wicked, and sin against God?' Although she spoke to Joseph day after day he would not agree to sleep with her and surrender to her.

But one day Joseph in the course of his duties came to the house, and there was not a servant there indoors. The woman caught hold of him by his tunic and said, 'Sleep with me'. But he left the tunic in her hand and ran out of the house. Seeing he had left the tunic in her hand and left the house, she called her servants and said to them, 'Look at this! He has brought us a Hebrew to insult us. He came to me to sleep with me, but I screamed, and when he heard me scream and shout he left his tunic beside me and ran out of the house.'

She put the tunic down by her side until the master came home. Then she told him the same tale, 'The Hebrew slave you bought us came to insult me. But when I screamed and called out he left his garment by my side and made his escape.' When the master heard his wife say, 'this is how your slave treated me', he was furious. Joseph's master had him arrested and committed to the gaol where the king's prisoners were kept.

And there in gaol he stayed (Genesis 37, 3-36; 39, 7-20).

Once again, the hypothesis that best illuminates the biblical text is also the most common one. The authors of Genesis have recast a preexistent mythology, adapting it in the spirit of their special concerns. This involves inverting the relationship between the victim and the persecuting community. From the mythological perspective, the eleven brothers would appear first of all as the passive objects of the violence

inflicted by a malevolent hero, then as the recipients of the benefits conferred by this same hero after he has been victimized and deified.
Joseph would thus be at first a cause of disorder, and a remnant of this
can be surmised from the dreams that he recounts, dreams of domination that excite the jealousy of his eleven brothers. The original
myths would no doubt have sanctioned the charge of hubris. The kid
that provided the blood in which Joseph's tunic was dipped in order to
prove to his father that he was really dead would have played a directly
sacrificial role in the pre-biblical account.

In the first part of the account, two separate sources have been combined; each one seeks to rehabilitate the victim at the expense of his
brothers, even if each is also concerned with partially exempting one of
the brothers from blame. The first source, known as 'elohist', chooses
Reuben and the second, known as 'yahwist', chooses Judah. Hence
there are two different stories, juxtaposed with one another, that account for one and the same act of collective violence.

If we take into account that Joseph's Egyptian master behaved
toward him as a father, then the accusation of the Egyptian's wife has an
almost incestuous character. Instead of corroborating the accusation, as
do so many myths (with the story of Oedipus at their head), the story of
Joseph declares that it is false!

J.-M. O.: You are quite right. But surely the myth to compare with
the story of Joseph is not the Oedipus myth but that of Phaedra and
Hippolytus?

R. G.: Of course. But you will observe that in the Greek myth, as
opposed to the Racinian version, Hippolytus is treated, if not as a guilty
party in the modern sense, at least as being justly punished: his excessive chastity has an element of hubris that offends Venus. By contrast, in
the story of Joseph the victim is simply an innocent party who is falsely
accused.

Further on in the story, there is a second account of a victim who is
falsely accused and in the end gets off free. This time, Joseph himself
uses trickery to impugn his brother Benjamin—the other favourite son
of Jacob and the only one younger than Joseph—with guilt. But on this
occasion, one of the ten brothers is not willing to accept the expulsion of
the victim. Judah puts himself forward in Benjamin's place, and Joseph
is moved by pity to make himself known to his brothers and pardon
them.

G. L.: The point that rehabilitating the victim has a desacralizing effect is well demonstrated by the story of Joseph, who ends up having no demoniac or divine aspects but simply being human. . .

J.-M. O.: Mythological culture and the cultural forms that have been grafted upon it, such as philosophy or in our own day ethnology, with a few exceptions tend first to justify the founding murder and then to eliminate the traces of this murder, convincing people that there is no such thing. These cultural forms have succeeded perfectly in convincing us that humanity is innocent of these murders. By contrast, in the Bible there is an inverse movement, an attempt to get back to origins and look once again at constitutive acts of transference so as to discredit and annul them—so as to contradict and demystify the myths. . .

R. G.: The proof that we are not entirely unaware of this inspired role played by the Bible lies in the fact that for centuries we have been accusing it of 'laying blame' on humanity, which, of course, as the philosophers assure us, has never harmed a fly in its own right. Clearly the story of Cain lays blame on Cainite culture by showing that this culture is completely based upon the unjust murder of Abel. The story of Romulus and Remus lays blame upon the city of Rome since the murder of Remus is presented to us as being justified. No one asks if the Bible is not right to lay blame as it does, and if the city of man is not in fact founded on concealed victims.

G. L.: But your analysis has up to now been restricted to Genesis. Can you show that it remains valid for other great biblical texts?

J.-M. O.: In Exodus it is the whole of the chosen people which is identified with the scapegoat, *vis-à-vis* Egyptian society.

R. G.: Yes indeed. When Moses complains that the Egyptians are not willing to let the Hebrews leave, Yahweh replies that soon the Egyptians will not only let them leave but will *expel* them.

As he himself causes the sacrificial crisis that ravages Egypt (the Ten Plagues), Moses is evidently playing the part of the scapegoat, and the Jewish community around him is associated with this role. So there is something absolutely unique in the foundation of Judaism.

In order to 'function' normally, in the sense of the myths that we have already dealt with here, Exodus would have to be an Egyptian myth; this myth would show us a sacrificial crisis resolved by the expulsion of the trouble-makers, Moses and his companions. Thanks to their expulsion, the order that Moses disturbed would have been re-established in the society of Egypt. We are indeed dealing with this kind of model, but it has been diverted towards the scapegoat, who is not only made human but goes on to form a community of a new type.

G. L.: I can certainly see that in this case there is a tendency once again to unearth the mechanism that is at the foundation of religion and to call it into question. But these great stories from Genesis and Exodus remain nonetheless inscribed within a mythic framework and retain the characteristics of myth. Are you going so far as to say that we are no longer dealing with myth at all?

R. G.: No. I believe we are dealing with mythic forms that have been subverted but still retain, as you rightly say, many of the characteristics of myth. If we had nothing but these particular texts, we would not be able to stress the radical singularity of the Bible *vis-à-vis* the mythological systems of the entire planet.

The Law and the Prophets

R. G.: Genesis and Exodus are only the beginning. In the other books of the Law and particularly in those of the Prophets, a reader who has been alerted to the role of the scapegoat cannot fail to note an increasing tendency for the victim to be brought to light. This tendency goes hand in hand with an increasing subversion of the three great pillars of primitive religion: first, mythology, then the sacrificial cult (explicitly rejected by the Prophets before the Exile), finally the primitive conception of the law as a form of obsessive differentiation, a refusal of mixed states that looks upon indifferentiation with horror.

There is no difficulty in discovering in the books of the law precepts that recall all codes of primitive law, and Mary Douglas in *Purity and Danger* has discussed at length the biblical fear of the dissolution of identities. In my opinion, she is wrong not to note the part played by fear of violence in this horrified reaction to forbidden mixtures.[52]

However this may be, in the biblical context these archaic legal prescriptions are far less important than what comes after them. The inspiration of the prophets tends to eliminate all these obsessional prescriptions in favour of their true *raison d'être*, which is the maintenance of harmonious relationships within the community. What the prophets come down to saying is basically this: legal prescriptions are of little consequence so long as you keep from fighting one another, so long as you do not become enemy twins. This is the new inspiration, and it arrives, even in the books of the law such as Leviticus, at unambiguous formulations like: *Thou shalt love thy neighbour as thyself* (Lev. 19,18).

J.-M. O.: So the three great pillars of primitive religion—myth, sacrifice and prohibitions—are subverted by the thought of the Prophets, and this general activity of subversion is invariably governed by the bringing to light of the mechanisms that found religion: the unanimous violence against the scapegoat.

R. G.: In the prophetic books, we are no longer confronted with mythical or legendary accounts, but with exhortations, threats and forecasts of the future of the chosen people. Our hypothesis highlights a common theme in the prophetic literature and the great myths of the Pentateuch. The phenomenon of the Prophets is an original response to a crisis of Hebraic society, one made worse by the great empires of Babylon and Assyria, which threatened the little kingdoms of Israel and Judah. Yet these political developments are invariably interpreted by the prophets as an exclusively religious and cultural crisis, in which the sacrificial system is exhausted and the traditional order of society dissolves into conflict. The way in which the Prophets define this crisis impels us to compare it with definition required by our hypothesis. It is precisely because a common experience is involved that our crisis can be described using themes and metaphors taken from the mythical heritage of the chosen people.

If the crisis that we must suppose to be at the origin of these mythic texts is revealed directly by the Prophets, where it is spoken of as a religious and indeed a cultural and social reality, there is reason to ask whether the specific resolution of this type of crisis—the phenomenon of collective transference, which is the core of the mechanism that engenders religion—will not be more directly apparent in these exceptional religious texts than anywhere else.

That proves to be so. In the first books of the Bible, the founding mechanism shows through the texts here and there, sometimes strikingly but never completely and unambiguously. The mechanism never really gets described as such. By contrast, the prophetic books offer us a group of astonishing texts that are all integrally related, as well as being remarkably explicit. These are the four 'Songs of the Servant of Yahweh' interpolated in the 'Book of the Consolation of Israel' in the second part of Isaiah, perhaps the most grandiose of all the prophetic books. (They are located at Isaiah 42, 1-4; 49, 1-6; 50, 4-11; 52, 13-53, 12.) Modern historical criticism has isolated these four 'Songs', recognizing their unity and their relative degree of independence from the material surrounding them. This is all the more praiseworthy in that no one has ever been able to say what gives them this singular status. Speaking of the return from Babylon authorized by Cyrus, they develop as an enigmatic counterpoint the double theme of the triumphant Messiah, here identified with the liberating prince, and the suffering Messiah, the Servant of Yahweh.

To recognize the relevance of our hypothesis to the Servant, we need only quote one or two key passages. In the first place, the Servant appears within the context of the prophetic crisis for the purpose of resolving it. He becomes, as a result of God's own action, the receptacle for all violence; he takes the place of all the members of the community:

> All we like sheep have gone astray;
> we have turned every one to his own way;
> and the Lord has laid on him
> the iniquity of us all. (Isaiah 53, 6)

All the traits attributed to the Servant predispose him to the role of a veritable human scapegoat.

> For he grew up before him like a young plant,
> and like a root out of dry ground;
> he had no form or comeliness that we should look at him,
> and no beauty that we should desire him.
> He was despised and rejected by men;
> a man of sorrows, and acquainted with grief;
> and as one from whom men hide their faces
> he was despised, and we esteemed him not. (Isaiah 53, 2-3)

If these traits make him similar to a certain type of sacrificial victim within the pagan world—for example, the Greek *pharmakos*—and if the fate he undergoes, the fate reserved for the anathema, is similar to that of the *pharmakos*, it is nonetheless no ritual sacrifice that we are dealing with. It is a spontaneous historical event, which has at once a collective and a legal character, and is sanctioned by the authorities:

By oppression and judgement he was taken away;
and as for his generation, who considered
that he was cut off from out of the land of the living,
stricken for the transgression of my people?
And they made his grave with the wicked
and with a rich man in his death,
although he had done no violence,
and there was no deceit in his mouth. (Isaiah 53, 8-9)

This event therefore has the character not of a ritual but of the type of event from which, according to my hypothesis, rituals and all aspects of religion are derived. The most striking aspect here, the trait which is certainly unique, is the innocence of the Servant, the fact that he has no connection with violence and no affinity for it. A whole number of passages lay upon men the principal responsibility for his saving death. One of these even appears to attribute to men the exclusive responsibility for that death. 'Yet we esteemed him stricken, smitten by God, and afflicted' (Isaiah 53, 4).

In other words, this was not so. It was not God who smote him; God's responsibility is implicitly denied.

Throughout the Old Testament, a work of exegesis is in progress, operating in precisely the opposite direction to the usual dynamics of mythology and culture. And yet it is impossible to say that this work is completed. Even in the most advanced texts, such as the fourth 'Song of the Servant', there is still some ambiguity regarding the role of Yahweh. Even if the human community is, on several occasions, presented as being responsible for the death of the victim, God himself is presented as the principal instigator of the persecution. 'Yet it was the will of the Lord to bruise him' (Isaiah 53, 10).

This ambiguity in the role of Yahweh corresponds to the general conception of the deity in the Old Testament. In the prophetic books, this conception tends to be increasingly divested of the violence characteristic of primitive deities. Although vengeance is still attributed to Yahweh, a number of expressions show that in reality mimetic and reciprocal violence is festering more and more as the old cultural forms tend to dissolve. Yet all the same, in the Old Testament we never arrive at a conception of the deity that is entirely foreign to violence.

J.-M. O.: So in your view there is an inconclusiveness in the Old

Testament that deconstructs all the still primitive aspects to the same degree. The myths are worked through with a form of inspiration that runs counter to them, but they continue in being. The sacrifices are criticized, but they continue; the law is simplified and declared to be identical to the love of one's neighbour, but it continues. And even though he is presented in a less and less violent form, and becomes more and more benevolent, Yahweh is still the god to whom vengeance belongs. The notion of divine retribution is still alive.

R. G.: That is right. I think it is possible to show that only the texts of the Gospels manage to achieve what the Old Testament leaves incomplete. These texts therefore serve as an extension of the Judaic bible, bringing to completion an enterprise that the Judaic bible did not take far enough, as Christian tradition has always maintained. The truth of this whole account comes to the fore when we use the scapegoat in our reading. And it comes to the fore in a form that can immediately be verified against the texts themselves, albeit in an unforeseen form that will startle all traditions, not excepting the Christian tradition, which has never acknowledged the crucial importance in the anthropological domain of what I call the scapegoat.

The Gospel Revelation of the Founding Murder

The Curses against the Pharisees

G. L.: How do you intend to show that the truth of the scapegoat is written for all to see in the text of the Gospels?

R. G.: In the Gospels of Matthew and Luke, there is a group of texts that used to be entitled the 'Curses against the Scribes and Pharisees'. This title is no longer employed because of the embarrassment the reading of these texts usually provokes. In the literal sense, of course, such a title is perfectly valid. But it does tend to restrict unduly the vast implications of the way in which Jesus accuses his audience of Pharisees. Obviously he is directing his accusations at them, but a careful examination reveals that he is using the Pharisees as an intermediary for something very much larger, and indeed something of absolutely universal significance is at stake. But then this is always the case in the Gospels. Every reading that restricts itself to particulars—however legitimate it may seem on the historical level—is nonetheless a betrayal of the overall significance.

The most terrible and meaningful 'curse' comes right at the end of the text in both Matthew and Luke. I quote first of all from Matthew:

> Therefore I send you prophets and wise men and scribes, some of whom you will kill and crucify, and some you will scourge in your synagogues and persecute from town to town, that upon you may come all the righteous blood shed on earth, from the blood of innocent Abel to the blood of Zechariah the son of Barachiah, whom you murdered between the sanctuary and the altar. Truly, I say to you, all this will come upon this generation.
>
> (Matthew 23, 34-36)

The text gives us to believe that there have been many murders. It only mentions two of them, however: that of Abel, the first to occur in the Bible, and that of a certain Zechariah, the last person to be killed in the Second Book of the Chronicles, in other words the last in the whole Bible as Jesus knew it.

Evidently mention of the first and last murders takes the place of a more complete list. The victims who belong between Abel and Zechariah are implicitly included. The text has the character of a recapitulation, and it cannot be restricted to the Jewish religion alone, since the murder of Abel goes back to the origins of humanity and the foundation of the first cultural order. Cainite culture is not a Jewish culture. The text also makes explicit mention of 'all the righteous blood shed on earth'. It therefore looks as though the kind of murder for which Abel here forms the prototype is not limited to a single region of the world or to a single period of history. We are dealing with a universal phenomenon whose consequences are going to fall not only upon the Pharisees but upon this *generation*, that is, upon all those who are contemporary with the Gospels and the time of their diffusion, who remain deaf and blind to the news that is being proclaimed.

The text of Luke is similar, but it includes, before Abel is mentioned, a further crucial detail. It identifies 'the blood of all the prophets, shed from the foundation of the world, from the blood of Abel to the blood of Zechariah' (Luke 11, 50-51). The Greek text has *apo kataboles kosmou*. The same expression comes up in Matthew when Jesus quotes from Psalm 78 in reference to himself:

> 'I will open my mouth in parables,

I will utter what has been hidden since the
foundation of the world' (Matthew 13, 35).

On each occasion the Vulgate uses the translation *a constitutione
mundi*. But *kataboles* really seems to imply the foundation of the world
in so far as it results from a violent crisis; it denotes order in so far as it
comes out of disorder. The term has a medical use to mean the on-
slaught of a disease, the attack that provokes a resolution.

We must certainly not lose sight of the fact that, for Jewish culture,
the Bible formed the only ethnological encyclopedia available or even
conceivable. In referring to the whole of the Bible, Jesus is pointing not
only at the Pharisees but at the whole of humanity. Clearly the dreadful
consequences of his revelation will weigh exclusively on those who have
had the advantage of hearing it—if they refuse to take its meaning, if
they will not recognize that this is a revelation which concerns them in
the same way as it concerns the rest of humanity. The Pharisees to
whom Jesus is speaking are the first to put themselves in this difficult
position, but they will not be the last. It can be deduced from the gospel
text that their innumerable successors will not fall under the same condemnation, even if they belong to a different religion named Christianity.

Jesus is very well aware that the Pharisees have not themselves killed
the prophets, any more than the Christians themselves killed Jesus. It is
said that the Pharisees were the 'sons' of those who carried out the kil-
lings (Matthew, 23, 31). This is not to imply a hereditary transmission
of guilt, but rather an intellectual and spiritual solidarity that is being
brought to an end (remarkable enough) through the intermediary of a
resounding repudiation—not unlike the repudiation of Judaism by the
'Christians'. The *sons* believe they can express their independence of
the *fathers* by condemning them, that is, by claiming to have no part in
the murder. But by virtue of this very fact, they unconsciously imitate
and repeat the acts of their fathers. They fail to understand that in the
murder of the Prophets people refused to acknowledge their own violence and cast it off from themselves. The sons are therefore still governed by the mental structure engendered by the founding murder. In
effect they are still saying:

'If we had lived in the days of our fathers, we would not have taken
part with them in shedding the blood of the prophets' (Matthew 23,
30).

Paradoxically, it is in the very wish to cause a break that the continuity between fathers and sons is maintained.

To understand what is decisive about the texts in the synoptic Gospels we have just been considering, we need to confront them with the text from the Gospel of John that is most directly equivalent:

'Why do you not understand what I say? It is because you cannot bear to hear my word. You are of your father the devil, and your will is to do your father's desires. He was a murderer from the beginning, and has nothing to do with the truth, because there is no truth in him. When he lies, he speaks according to his own nature, for he is a liar and the father of lies' (John 8, 43-44).

Here the essential point is that a triple correspondence is set up between Satan, the original homicide, and the lie. To be a son of Satan is to inherit the lie. What lie? The lie that covers the homicide. This lie is a double homicide, since its consequence is always another new homicide to cover up the old one. To be a son of Satan is the same thing as being the son of those whose have killed their prophets since the foundation of the world.

N.A. Dahl has demonstrated that calling Satan a homicide is a concealed reference to the murder of Abel by Cain.[53] It is undoubtedly true that Abel's murder in Genesis has an exceptional importance. But this importance is due to the fact that it is the first founding murder and the first biblical account to raise a corner of the curtain that always covers the frightful role played by homicide in the foundation of human communities. This murder is presented to us, we have seen, as the origin of the law that sanctions murder as a sevenfold reprisal, the origin of the rule against homicide within the Cainite culture, and in effect the origin of that culture.

So the synoptic Gospels refer to Abel's murder because it has an exceptional significance. But we should not wish to bring the Johannine text back at any price to the literal meaning of the synoptic text, which refers to a certain person called Abel or to a category of victims called 'the prophets'. In writing 'he was a murderer from the beginning' John's text goes further than the others in disentangling the founding mechanisms; it excises all the definitions and specifications that might bring about a mythic interpretation. John goes to the full length in his reading of the text of the Bible, and what he comes up against is the hypothesis of the founding violence.

Biblical specialists are misled on this point in much the same way as ethnologists, and all the other specialists in the human sciences, who move invariably from myth to myth and from institution to institution, from signifier to signifier in effect, or from signified to signified, without ever getting to the symbolic matrix of all these signifiers and signifieds—that is, to the scapegoat mechanism.

G. L.: It is indeed the same mistake.But there is something more paradoxical and exclusive about the blindness of the biblical experts, compared with those in the human sciences, because they have right under noses, in the text which they claim to be able to decipher, the key to the correct interpretation—the key to every interpretation—and they refuse to make use of it. They do not even notice the unbelievable opportunities staring them in the face.

R. G.: Even with John's text, the danger of a mythical reading is still present, clearly so, if we do not see that Satan denotes the founding mechanism itself—the principle of all human community. All of the texts in the New Testament confirm this reading, in particular the 'Temptations' made by Satan the Prince and principle of this world, *princeps hu jus mundi*. It is no abstract metaphysical reduction, no descent into vulgar polemics or lapse into superstition that makes Satan the true adversary of Jesus. Satan is absolutely identified with the circular mechanisms of violence, with man's imprisonment in cultural or philosophical systems that maintain his *modus vivendi* with violence. That is why he promises Jesus domination provided that Jesus will worship him. But Satan is also the *skandalon*, the living obstacle that trips men up, the mimetic model in so far as it becomes a rival and lies across our path. We shall be considering the *skandalon* further in connection with desire.

Satan is the name for the mimetic process seen as a whole; that is why he is the source not merely of rivalry and disorder but of all the forms of lying order inside which humanity lives. That is the reason why he was a homicide from the beginning; Satan's order had no origin other than murder and this murder is a lie. Human beings are sons of Satan because they are sons of this murder. Murder is therefore not an act whose consequences could be eliminated without being brought to light and genuinely rejected by men. It is an inexhaustible fund; a transcendent source of falsehood that infiltrates every domain and structures everything in its own image, with such success that the truth cannot get in, and Jesus' listeners cannot even hear his words. From the original murder, men succeed in drawing new lies all the time, and these prevent the word of the Gospel from reaching them. Even the most explicit revelation remains a dead letter.

J. -M. O.: What you have shown, in short, is that despite differences in style and tone, the Gospel of John says exactly the same thing as the synoptic Gospels. For the majority of modern commentators, the work of exegesis consists almost exclusively in trying to find the *difference* between the texts. You, on the other hand, look for the convergence, since you believe that the Gospels represent four slightly different versions of one and the same form of thought. This form of thought necessarily escapes us if we start off from the principle that only the divergences are worthy of attention.

R. G.: These divergences do indeed exist, though they are minor ones. Yet they are not without interest. In a number of cases they allow us to discover what might perhaps be called particular minor defects in respect of the entirety of the message that they are obliged to transcribe.

The Metaphor of the Tomb

R. G.: I must now come back to the 'Curses'. They testify to a concealed relation of dependence on the founding murder; they demonstrate a paradoxical continuity between the violence of past generations and the denunciation of that violence in contemporaries. Here we are getting to the heart of the matter; in the light of this mechanism—the very one that has preoccupied us from the outset of these discussions—a great 'metaphor' within the gospel text becomes clear. This is the metaphor of the *tomb*. Tombs exist to honour the dead, but also to hide them in so far as they are dead, to conceal the corpse and ensure that death as such is no longer visible. This act of concealment is essential. The very murders in which the fathers directly took part already resemble tombs to the extent that, above all in collective and founding murders but also in individual murders, men kill in order to lie to others and to themselves on the subject of violence and death. They must kill and continue to kill, strange as it may seem, in order not to know that they are killing.

Now we can understand why Jesus reproaches the Scribes and Pharisees for putting up tombs for the prophets who have been killed by their fathers. Not to recognize the founding character of the murder, whether by denying that the fathers have killed or by condemning the

guilty in the interests of demonstrating their own innocence, is to perpetuate the foundation, which is an obscuring of the truth. People do
not wish to know that the whole of human culture is based on the
mythic process of conjuring away man's violence by endlessly projecting it upon new victims. All cultures and all religions are built on this
foundation, which they then conceal, just as the tomb is built around
the dead body that it conceals. Murder calls for the tomb and the tomb
is but the prolongation and perpetuation of murder. The tomb-religion
amounts to nothing more or less than the becoming invisible of the
foundations, of religion and culture, of their only reason for existence.

> Woe to you! for you build the tombs of the prophets whom your
> fathers killed. So you are witnesses and consent to the deeds of your
> fathers; for they killed them, and you build their tombs (Luke 11,
> 47-48).

For they killed them, and you build their tombs: Jesus at once reveals
and unambiguously *compromises* the history of all human culture. That
is why he takes to himself the words of Psalm 78: *I will utter what has
been hidden since the foundation of the world*—*apo kataboles kosmou*
(Matthew 13, 35).

If the metaphor of the tomb applies to all forms of human order taken
in their entirety, it can also be applied to the individuals formed by that
order. On the individual level, the Pharisees are absolutely identified
with the system of misrecognition on which they rely as a community.

It would be foolhardy to call 'metaphorical' our usage of the term
'tomb', since we are so close to the heart of the matter. To speak of
metaphor is to speak of displacement, and yet no metaphorical displacement is involved here. On the contrary, it is the tomb that is the starting-point of the constitutive displacements of culture. Quite a number
of fine minds think that this is literally true on the level of human history as a whole; funerary rituals could well, as we have said, amount to
the first actions of a strictly cultural type.[54] There is reason to believe
that these rituals took shape around the first of the reconciliatory
victims, on the basis of the creative transference achieved by the first
communities. This also brings to mind the sacrificial stones that mark
the foundation of ancient cities, which are invariably associated with
some story of a lynching, ineffectively camouflaged.

J.-M. O.: We must turn back at this point to what we said the other day on all these subjects. We must keep them continually in mind in order to grasp what is at once the simplicity of the hypothesis and the endless wealth of applications to be drawn from it.

R. G.: Archaeological discoveries seem to suggest that people were really building tombs for the Prophets in Jesus' period. That is a very interesting point, and it is quite possible that a practice of this kind suggested the 'metaphor'. However, it would be a pity to limit the significance generated in our text by the different uses of the term 'tomb' to a mere evocation of this practice. The fact that the metaphor applies both to the group and to the individual clearly demonstrates that much more is involved than an allusion to specific tombs, just as much more is involved in the following passage than a mere 'moral' indictment:

> Woe to you, scribes and Pharisees, hypocrites! for you are like white-washed tombs, which outwardly appear beautiful, but within they are full of dead men's bones and all uncleanness (Matthew 23, 27).

Deep within the individual, as within the religious and cultural systems that fashion the individual, something is hidden, and this is not merely the individual 'sin' of modern religiosity or the 'complexes' of psychoanalysis. It is invariably a corpse that as it rots spreads its 'uncleanness' everywhere.

Luke compares the Pharisees not just to tombs but to underground tombs, that is to say, invisible tombs—tombs that are perfect in a double sense, if we can put it like that, since they conceal not only death, but also their own existence as tombs.

> Woe unto you! for you are like graves which are not seen, and men walk over them without knowing it (Luke 11, 44).

J.-M. O.: This double concealment reproduces the way in which cultural differentiation develops on the basis of the founding murder. This murder tends to efface itself behind the directly sacrificial rituals, but even these rituals risk being too revealing and so tend to be effaced behind post-ritual institutions, such as judicial and political systems or the forms of culture. These derived forms give away nothing of the fact that they are rooted in the original murder.

R. G.: So we have here a problem of a *knowledge* which is always being lost, never to be rediscovered again. This knowledge certainly comes to the surface in the great biblical texts and above all in the prophetic books, but the organization of religion and law contrives to repress it. The Pharisees, who are satisfied with what seems to them to be their success in the religious life, are blind to the essentials and so they blind those whom they claim to be guiding:

> Woe to you lawyers! for you have taken away the key of knowledge; you did not enter yourselves and you hindered those who were entering (Luke 11, 52).

Michel Serres first made me see the importance of this reference to the 'key of knowledge'. Jesus has come in order to place men in possession of this key. Within the perspective of the Gospels, the Passion is first and foremost the consequence of an intolerable revelation, while being proof of that revelation. It is because they do not understand what he proclaims that Jesus' listeners agree to rid themselves of him, and in so doing they confirm the accuracy and the prophetic nature of the 'curses against the Pharisees'.

They have recourse to violence, to expel the truth about violence:

> As he went away from there, the scribes and the Pharisees began to press him hard, and to provoke him to speak of many things, lying in wait for him, to catch at something he might say (Luke 11, 53).

Religion is organized around a more or less violent disavowal of human violence. That is what the religion that comes from man amounts to, as opposed to the religion that comes from God. By affirming this point without the least equivocation, Jesus infringes the supreme prohibition that governs all human order, and he must be reduced to silence. Those who come together against Jesus do so in order to back up the arrogant assumption that consists in saying: 'If we had lived in the days of our fathers, we would not have taken part with them in shedding the blood of the prophets.'

The truth of the founding murder is expressed first of all in the words of Jesus, which connect the present conduct of men with the distant past, and with the near future (since they announce the Passion), and with the whole of human history. The same truth of the founding murder will also be expressed, with even greater force, in the Passion itself, which fulfils the prophecy and gives it its full weight. If centuries and indeed millennia have to pass before this truth is revived, it is of little consequence. The truth is registered and will finally accomplish its work. Everything that is hidden shall be revealed.

The Passion

R. G.: Jesus is presented to us as the innocent victim of a group in crisis, which, for a time at any rate, is united against him. All the sub-groups and indeed all the individuals who are concerned with the life and trial of Jesus end up by giving their explicit or implicit assent to his death: the crowd in Jerusalem, the Jewish religious authorities, the Roman political authorities, and even the disciples, since those who do not betray or deny Jesus actively take flight or remain passive.

We must remember that this very crowd has welcomed Jesus with such enthusiasm only a few days earlier. The crowd turns around like a single man and insists on his death with a determination that springs at least in part from being carried away by the irrationality of the collective spirit. Certainly nothing has intervened to justify such a change of attitude.

It is necessary to have legal forms in a universe where there are legal institutions, to give unaniminity to the decision to put a man to death. Nonetheless, the decision to put Jesus to death is first and foremost a decision of the crowd, one that identifies the crucifixion not so much with a ritual sacrifice but (as in the case of the servant) with the process that I claim to be at the basis of all rituals and all religious phenomena. Just as in the 'Songs' from Isaiah, though even more directly this hypothesis confronts us in the four gospel stories of the Passion.

Because it reproduces the founding event of all rituals, the Passion is connected with every ritual on the entire planet. There is not an incident in it that cannot be found in countless instances: the preliminary trial, the derisive crowd, the grotesque honours accorded to the victim, and the particular role played by chance, in the form of casting lots, which here affects not the choice of the victim but the way in which his clothing is disposed of. The final feature is the degrading punishment that takes place outside the holy city in order not to contaminate it.

Noticing these parallels with other rituals, certain ethnologists have attempted—in a spirit of hostile scepticism, as you can imagine, which does not diminish, paradoxically, their absolute faith in the historicity of the gospel text—to attribute ritualistic motives to some of the actors in the Passion story. In their view, Jesus must have served as 'scapegoat' to some of Pilate's legionaries, who were caught up in some sort of saturnalia. Frazer even debated with some German researchers the precise ritual that must have been involved.

In 1898, P. Wendland noted the striking analogies between 'the treatment inflicted on Christ by the Roman soldiers and that which other Roman soldiers inflicted on the false king of the Saturnalia at Durostorum.'[55] He took the view that the legionaries would have clothed Jesus with the traditional ornaments of King Saturn in order to make fun of his pretentions to a heavenly kingdom. In a long note added to the second edition of *The Golden Bough*, Frazer declared that he had also been struck by these similarities but had not been able to take them into account in the first edition because he was incapable of offering an explanation for them. Wendland's article did not seem satisfactory to him, in the first place for dating reasons—the Saturnalia took place in December whereas the crucifixion took place at Easter—but above all because he had by this time come up with a better explanation:

> But closely as the Passion of Christ resembles the treatment of the mock king of the Saturnalia, it resembles still more closely the treatment of the mock king of the Sacaea. The description of the mockery by St Matthew is the fullest. It runs thus: 'Then released he Barabbas unto them: and when he had scourged Jesus, he delivered him to be crucified. Then the soldiers of the governor took Jesus into the common hall, and gathered unto him the whole band of soldiers. And they stripped him, and put on him a scarlet robe. And when they had platted a crown of thorns, they put it upon his head, and a reed in his right hand: and they bowed the knee before him, and mocked him, saying, Hail, King of the Jews! And they spit upon him, and took the reed, and smote him on the head. And after that they had mocked him, they took the robe off from him, and put his own raiment on him, and led him away to crucify him.' Compare with this the treatment of the mock king of the Sacaea, as it is described by Dio Chrysostom: 'They take one of the prisoners condemned to death and seat him upon the king's throne, and give him the king's raiment, and let him lord it and drink and run riot and use the king's concubines during these days, and no man prevents him from doing just what he likes. But afterwards they strip and scourge and crucify him.'[56]

However suggestive it may be in certain respects, this type of hypothesis seems untenable to us because of the conception of the gospel text it takes for granted. Frazer persists in making the Gospel no different from a historical account, or even a piece of on-the-spot reporting. It does not occur to him that the relationship between the rituals to which he refers and the Gospels could be based on anything but a chance coincidence between events; he does not take into account that there might be something much more profound on the level of the text itself—which could explain the way in which this religious and cultural document was internally organized. If this possibility is discounted, how could we account for the striking coincidence between the Saturnalia and the account that he gives of the 'mock king of the Sacaea'?

Here we are confronted with a kind of prejudice that flourished in the epoch of positivism. Although we are not going to succumb to the opposite prejudice, which is in the ascendant in our own period, we should nonetheless pay some attention to the internal organization of the text and, as a first stage, look at it independently of its potential reference.

Frazer's own thesis is not lacking in detailed observation. It is as ingenious as it is naive. The analogies traced between religious forms are not by any means restricted to those which ethnologists parade because they believe that they can explain them consistently with their own views. These analogies extend to a whole group of religious phenomena—the servant of Yahweh, for example, not to mention a host of other Old Testament texts. An ethnological critic in the Frazer style will declare analogies of this kind to be ultimately inadmissible for the very reason that the Gospels themselves claim a kinship with such texts. He will proclaim them to be non-existent, invented to serve the cause of religion, whereas in reality we are dealing with parallels very close to ones he congratulates himself about drawing to our attention. It is simply that his positivist spirit can tolerate only those analogies that he feels will discredit the claims of the Gospels, and jibes at those the Gospels themselves invoke in order to buttress those same claims.

For there to be an effective, sacralizing act of transference, it is necessary that the victim should inherit all of the violence from which the community has been exonerated. It is because the victim genuinely passes as guilty that the transference does not come to the fore as such. This piece of conjuring brings about the happy result for which the lynching mob is profoundly grateful: the victim bears the weight of the incompatible and contradictory meanings that juxtaposed, create *sac-*

redness. For the gospel text to be mythic in our sense, it would have to take no account of the arbitrary and unjust character of the violence which is done to Jesus. In fact the opposite is the case: the Passion is presented as a blatant piece of injustice. Far from taking the collective violence upon itself, the text places it squarely on those who are responsible for it. To use the expression from the 'Curses', it lets the violence fall upon the heads of those to whom it belongs:

'Verily I say unto you, All these things shall come upon this generation.'

G. L.: You prove, I believe, that these words have nothing to do with the old primitive curses that are designed to draw the vengeance of a violent god upon the cursed individual. In this case, the effect is precisely the opposite. There is a complete 'deconstruction' of the whole primitive system, which brings to light the founding mechanism and leaves men without the protection of sacrifice, prey to the old mimetic conflict, which from this point onwards will acquire its typically Christian and modern form. Everyone will now seek to cast upon his neighbour the responsibility for persecution and injustice, and, though the universality of persecution and injustice will become more and more apparent, everyone will be reluctant to admit that they are involved.

R. G.: There has to be a close connection between the revelation in words of the founding murder and its revelation on the level of action; this murder is repeated, taking as its victim the person who has revealed it—whose message everyone refuses to understand. In the Gospels, the revelation in words immediately stirs up a collective will to *silence* the speaker, which is concretized as a collective murder. In other words, the founding mechanism is reproduced once again, and, by virtue of this, the speech it strives to stifle is confirmed as true. The revelation is one and the same as the violent opposition to any revelation, since it is this lying violence, the source of all lies, that must first of all be revealed.

The Martyrdom of Stephen

R. G.: The process that leads directly from the 'curses' to the Passion can be found again in a form both compact and striking in a text which is not strictly speaking from the Gospels, but is as close as it could possibly be to at least one of the gospel accounts in which the 'curses' figure—that of Luke. I am talking about the Acts of the Apostles, which are presented, as you know, as the work of Luke himself, and may well be his.

The text I have in mind reconstitutes the sequence formed by the 'curses' and the Passion, but does so in such a compact way, articulating its elements in so explicit a fashion, that we can really envisage it as a genuine interpretation of the gospel text. I am referring to Stephen's speech and its consequences. The ending of this speech to the Sanhedrin is so disagreeable to its audience that it immediately causes the death of the person who made it.

Stephen's last words, the ones that trigger murderous rage in his public, are no more than the repetition, pure and simple, of the curses against the Pharisees. Obviously the murders already named by Jesus are joined, in Stephen's speech, by a reference to the murder of Jesus himself, which is by now an established fact and re-enacts better than anything else the founding murder.

So it is the whole formed by the prophecy and its fulfilment that the words of Stephen isolate and underline. It is the relationship of cause and effect between the revelation that compromises the community's basis in violence and the new violence that casts out the revelation in order to re-establish that basis, to lay its foundation once again.

> 'You stiff-necked people, uncircumcised in heart and ears, you always resist the Holy Spirit. As your fathers did, so do you. Which of the prophets did not your fathers persecute? And they killed those who announced beforehand the coming of the Righteous One, who you have now betrayed and murdered, you who received the law as delivered by angels and did not keep it.'
>
> Now when they heard these things they were enraged, and they ground their teeth against him. But he, full of the Holy Spirit, gazed into heaven and saw the glory of God, and Jesus standing at the right hand of God; and he said, 'Behold, I see the heavens opened, and the Son of man standing at the right hand of God.' But they cried out with a loud voice and stopped their ears and rushed together upon him. Then they cast him out of the city and stoned him (Acts 7, 51-58).

The words that throw the violence back upon those who are really guilty are so intolerable that it is necessary to shut once and for all the mouth of the one who speaks them. So as not to hear him while he remains capable of speaking, the audience 'stop their ears'. How can we miss the point that they kill in order to cast off an intolerable knowledge and that this knowledge is, strangely enough, the knowledge of the murder itself? The whole process of the gospel revelation and the Crucifixion is reproduced here in the clearest possible way.

It is worth pointing out that the Jews, like other peoples, reserve Stephen's method of execution—stoning—for the most impure of criminals, those guilty of the most serious crimes. It is the Jewish equivalent of the Greek *anathema*.

As with all forms of sacrifice, the execution must reproduce the founding murder in order to renew its beneficial effects, in this case wiping out the dangers to which the blasphemer exposes the community (cf. Deuteronomy 17, 7).

The repetition of this murder is a dangerous action that might bring about the return of the crisis which it is designed to avoid. One of the first precautions against the pollution of violence consists in forbidding any kind of ritual execution within the community. That is why the stoning of Stephen takes place—like the Crucifixion—outside the city walls of Jerusalem.

But this initial precaution is not sufficient. Prudence dictates that there must be no contact with the victim who pollutes because he is polluted. How is it possible to combine this requirement with another important requirement, which is to reproduce as exactly as possible the original murder? To reproduce it exactly implies unanimous participation by the whole community, or at any rate by all those who are present. This unanimous participation is explicitly required by the text of Deuteronomy (17, 7). How can it be arranged for everyone to strike the victim, while no one is soiled by contact with him? Obviously, stoning resolves this delicate problem. Like all methods of execution from a distance—the modern firing squad, or the community's driving Tikarau from the top of a cliff in the Tikopia myth—stoning fulfils this two-fold ritual requirement.

The only person taking part in this event whose name figures in the text is Saul of Tarsus, the future Paul. He is also, it would appear, the only person not to throw stones, although the text assures us that his heart is with the murderers. 'And Saul was consenting to his death.' Thus Saul's presence does not break the unanimity. The text makes it clear that the participants rushed upon Stephen 'with one accord'. This way of signalling the unanimity would have an almost technical ritual significance if we were not dealing with something quite different from a ritual. The unanimity that, in ritual has a compulsory and premeditated character is here achieved quite spontaneously.

The hurried aspect of this stoning and the fact that the procedures listed in the text of Deuteronomy are not all observed have led a number of commentators to judge that the execution was more or less illegal and to define it as a kind of lynching. Johannes Munck, for example, writes as follows in his edition of The Acts of the Apostles:

> Was this examination before the Sanhedrin and the following stoning a real trial and a legally performed execution? We do not know. The improvised and passionate character of the events as related might suggest that it was illegal, a lynching.[57]

Munck compares Stephen's last words to 'a spark that starts an explosion' (p.70). The fact that we are concerned here with a ritualized mode of execution and an irresistible discharge of collective fury is extremely significant. For this two-fold status to be possible, it is necessary for the ritual mode of execution to coincide with a possible form of spontaneous violence. If the ritual gesture can be to a certain extent deritualized and become spontaneous without really altering in form, we can imagine that such a metamorphosis can also take place in the other direction; the form of the legal execution is nothing more than the ritualization of a spontaneous violence. If we look carefully at the martyrdom of Stephen, we inevitably come up against the hypothesis of the founding violence.

This scene from Acts is a reproduction that both reveals and underlines the relationship between the 'curses' and the Passion. Stephen's death has the same twofold relationship to the 'curses' as the Passion itself. It verifies them because Stephen, like Jesus, is killed to forestall this verification. Stephen is the first of those who are spoken of in the 'curses'. We have already quoted from Matthew (23, 34-35). Here now is the text from Luke that also defines the precise function of this *martyrdom* which is indeed one of *witness*. Dying in the same way as Jesus died, for the same reasons as he did, the martyrs multiply the revelation of the founding violence:

> Therefore also the Wisdom of God said, 'I will send them prophets and apostles, some of whom they will kill and persecute,' that the

blood of all the prophets, shed from the foundation of the world, may be required of this generation. . . (Luke 11, 49-50).

This particular text must not be interpreted in a narrow fashion. It does not say that the only innocent victims, from now on, are to be the 'confessors of the faith' in the dogmatic, theological sense used historically by the Christian church. It means that there will be no more victims from now on who are persecuted unjustly but those persecuted will not eventually be recognized as unjust. For no further sacralization is possible. No more myths can be produced to cover up the fact of persecution. The Gospels make all forms of 'mythologizing' impossible since, by revealing the founding mechanism, they stop it from functioning. That is why we have fewer and fewer myths all the time, in our universe dominated by the Gospels, and more and more texts bearing on persecution.

The Scapegoat Text

J.-M. O.: If I understand you rightly, the process of misunderstanding that is defined in the text must also be reproduced once again in the restrictive interpretations that have always been given of it—first and foremost, of course, in the interpretations that try to limit its application to those for whom it is immediately destined.

To read the material in this way is to take an attitude full of consequences. The reading will tend to reproduce, in circumstances which are historically and ideologically different but structurally invariant, a violent transference upon the scapegoat, the very form of transference that has been in force since the dawn of humanity. So it is by no means a fortuitous or innocent reading. It transforms the universal revelation of the founding murder into a polemical denunciation of the Jewish religion. So as not to have to recognize that they are themselves involved in the message, people will claim that it only involves the Jews.

R. G.: This kind of restrictive interpretation is indeed the only way out for a type of thought that is in principle made over to 'Christianity' but is firmly resolved to divest itself of any form of violence, and so inevitably brings with it a new form of violence, directed against a new scapegoat—the Jew. In brief, what happens again is what Jesus reproached the Pharisees for doing, and since Jesus has been accepted, it can no longer be done directly to him. Once again, the truth and universality of the process revealed by the text is demonstrated as it is displaced toward the latest available victims. Now it is the Christians who say: *If we had lived in the days of our Jewish fathers, we would not have taken part with them in shedding the blood of Jesus.* If the people whom Jesus addresses and who do not listen to him fulfil the measure of their fathers, then the Christians who believe themselves justified in denouncing these same people in order to exculpate themselves are fulfilling a measure that is already full to overflowing. They claim to be governed by the text that reveals the process of misunderstanding, and yet they repeat that misunderstanding. With their eyes fixed on the text, they do once again what the text condemns. The only way of transcending this blindness consists in repudiating—as is done today—not the process that is revealed in the text and can maintain itself, paradoxically, in its shade, but the text itself; the text is declared to be responsible for the acts of violence committed in its name and actually blamed for not, up to now, mastering the old violence except by diverting it to new victims. There is at present a general tendency among Christians to repudiate this text or at any rate never to take any account of it, concealing it as if it were something to be ashamed of. There is one last trick, one last victim, and this is the text itself, which is chained to a fallacious reading and dragged before the tribunal of public opinion. It is the ultimate irony that the gospel text should be condemned by public opinion in the name of charity. Face to face with a world that is, as we well know, today overflowing with charity, the text appears to be disconcertingly harsh.

There is actually no contradiction between the choice of the Jews, as it is reaffirmed in the Gospels, and texts like those of the 'curses'. If anywhere in the world a religious or cultural form managed to evade the accusation made against the Pharisees—not excluding those that confess Jesus himself—then the Gospels would not be the truth about human culture. In order for the Gospels to have the universal significance Christians claim for them, it is necessary for there to be nothing on earth that is superior to the Jewish religion and the sect of the Pharisees. This absolute degree of representativeness is part and parcel of the status of the Jews as the chosen people, which is never disavowed by the New Testament.

Nor is there any contradiction between a revelation of violence made on the basis of biblical texts and the veneration that the New Testament never ceases to show for the Old. As we saw earlier, when we were considering the texts of Genesis and Exodus, the revelation of the founding murder and of its generative power in regard to myth become increasingly apparent in these texts. That implies that even at this early stage the inspiration of the Bible and the prophets is at work on the myths, undoing them in order to reveal their truth. Instead of invariably displacing the responsibility for the collective murder toward the victim, this form of inspiration takes a contrary path; it looks once again at the mythical elaborations and tends to deconstruct them, placing the responsibility for the violence upon those who are really responsible—the members of the community. In this way, it paves the way for the full and final revelation.

J.-M. O.: To understand that the Gospels really do reveal all this violence, we have to understand first of all that this violence engenders the mythic meanings. Now I can appreciate why you decided to place our initial discussions on Judaeo-Christian texts after the section on basic anthropology. You wanted to show that we are now in a position to get to the truth about all non-Christian religious phenomena by means of purely scientific and hypothetical procedures. Then the shift to the Judaeo-Christian texts confirms the analysis and makes it more compelling.

R. G.: What you say seems quite right to me. In fact, that is exactly why I wrote *Violence and the Sacred* in the way that I did. I am well aware of the blemishes in that work, as I am of the blemishes in what we have been saying here.

The thesis of the scapegoat owes nothing to any form of impressionistic or literary borrowing. I believe it to be fully demonstrated on the basis of the anthropological texts. That is why I have chosen not to listen to those who criticize my scientific claims and have determined to try to reinforce and sharpen the systematic character of my work, and to confirm the power of the scheme to reveal the genesis and structure of cultural phenomena.

In effect, all that I did in *Violence and the Sacred* was to retrace, with all its hesitations, my own intellectual journey, which eventually brought me to the Judaeo-Christian writings, though long after I had become convinced of the importance of the victimage mechanism. In the course of this journey, I remained for a long period as hostile to the Judaeo-Christian texts as modernist orthodoxy could wish. But I came to the conclusion that the best way of convincing my readers was not to cheat on my own experience and to reproduce its successive stages in two separate works, one of which would deal with the universe of sacred violence, and the other with the Judaeo-Christian aspect.

In the 'modern' period, Judaeo-Christian writings have become more and more alien to modern philosophy and all our 'sciences of man'. They now seem more foreign than the myths of the Ojibwa and the Tikopia. But our intellectual life is being influenced by forces that, far from taking the Judaeo-Christian scriptures further and further away, in fact bring them closer by a process whose circularity the 'sciences of man' still fail to grasp.

We can no longer believe that if it is we who are reading the Gospels in the light of an ethnological, modern revelation, which would really be the first thing of its kind. We have to reverse this order. It is still the great Judaeo-Christian spirit that is doing the reading. All that appears in ethnology, appears in the light of a continuing revelation, an immense process of historical work that enables us little by little to catch up with texts that are, in effect, already quite explicit, though not for the kind of people that we are—who *have eyes and see not, ears and hear not.*

Trusting ever more numerous and precise analogies, ethnological research has been trying for centuries to demonstrate that Christianity is just one more religion like the others and that Christianity's pretensions to absolute singularity are merely founded on the irrational attachment of Christians to the religion within which they chanced to be born. It might appear, at first sight, that the discovery of the mechanism that produces religion—the collective transference against a victim who is first reviled and then sacralized—would bring with it the final and most essential stone in the structure of 'demystification' to which this present reading, quite obviously, presents a sequel. Yet the discovery contributes, not just one more analogy, but the source of all analogies, which is situated behind the myths, hidden within their infra-structure and finally revealed, in a perfectly explicit way, in the account of the Passion.

By an astonishing reversal, it is texts that are twenty or twenty-five centuries old—initially revered blindly but today rejected with contempt—that will reveal themselves to be the only means of furthering all that is good and true in the anti-Christian endeavours of modern times: the as-yet-ineffectual determination to rid the world of the sacred cult of violence. These texts supply such endeavours with exactly what is needed to give a radically sociological reading of the historical forms of transcendence, and at the same time they place their own transcendence in an area which is impervious to any critique by placing it in the area from which a critique would derive.

Of course the Gospels also speak tirelessly of this reversal of all interpretations. After telling the parable of the labourers in the vineyard who *all came together to drive out* the envoys of the Master and then finally to kill his son so that they would be the sole proprietors, Christ offers his audience a problem in Old Testament exegesis:

> But he looked at them and said, 'What then is this that is written: "The very stone which the builders rejected has become the head of the corner" ' (Luke 20, 17).

The quotation comes from Psalm 118. People have always supposed that the question only invited 'mystical' replies, replies that could not be taken seriously on the level of the only kind of knowledge that counts. In this respect as in many others, the anti-religious person is in complete accord with the weak-kneed, purely 'idealist' religious person.

If we accept that all human religions and all human culture come down to the parable of the murderous labourers in the vineyard—that is, come down to the collective expulsion of the victim—and if this foundation can remain a foundation only to the extent that it does not become apparent, then it is clear that only those texts in which this foundation is made apparent will no longer be built upon it and so will be genuinely revealing. The words from Psalm 118 thus have a remarkable epistemological value; they require an interpretation for which Christ himself ironically calls, knowing very well that he alone is capable of giving it in the process of having himself rejected, of himself becoming the rejected stone, with the aim of showing that this stone has always formed a concealed foundation. And now the stone is revealed and can no longer form a foundation, or, rather, it will found something that is radically different.

The problem of exegesis Christ puts to his audience can only be resolved, in short, if we see in the words that he quotes the very formula for the reversal, at once an invisible and an obvious one, that I am putting forward. The rejected stone is the scapegoat, who is Christ. By submitting to violence, Christ reveals and uproots the structural matrix of all religion.

The text alerts us, in short, to its own functioning, which eludes the laws of ordinary textuality, and by virtue of this fact the warning itself eludes us, as it eluded Christ's audience. If such is indeed the movement of the text, then the claims of Christianity to make Christ the author of a universal revelation are far more securely founded than even its defenders would imagine. They fall back inevitably into ordinary textuality, blotting out once again the true point of origin, which is nonetheless clearly inscribed in scripture; they reject all over again, in a final and paradoxical form of expulsion, the stone that is Christ, and they still fail to see that this selfsame stone continues to serve them as a concealed cornerstone.

If you read the commentaries customarily written about phrases of this kind, not only by Christians but also by so-called 'scientific' exegetes, you will be amazed by the universal inability to recognize meanings that are for us by now so obvious that we are hesitant to repeat the train of reasoning which would make them explicit.

The exegetes are aware, obviously, that Christ identifies with the stone rejected by the builders, but they fail to see the formidable reverberations of this phrase on the anthropological level, and the reason why it is already present in the Old Testament.

Instead of reading myths in the light of the Gospels, people have always read the Gospels in the light of myths. In comparison with the astonishing work of demystification effected by the Gospels, our own exercises in demystification are only slight sketches, though they may also be cunning obstacles that our minds erect against the gospel revelation. But from now on the obstacles themselves must contribute to the invisible but ineluctable advance of revelation.

CHAPTER TWO

A Non-Sacrificial Reading of the Gospel Text

Christ and Sacrifice

R. G.: The Gospels only speak of *sacrifices* in order to reject them and deny them any validity. Jesus counters the ritualism of the Pharisees with an anti-sacrificial quotation from Hosea: 'Go and learn what this means, "I desire mercy, and not sacrifice" ' (Matthew 9, 13).

The following text amounts to a great deal more than ethical advice; it at once sets the cult of sacrifice at a distance and reveals its true function, which has now come full circle:

> So if you are offering your gift at the altar, and there remember that your brother has something against you, leave your gift there before the altar and go; first be reconciled to your brother, and then come and offer your gift (Matthew 5, 23-24).

G. L.: Surely the Crucifixion is still the sacrifice of Christ?

R. G.: There is nothing in the Gospels to suggest that the death of Jesus is a sacrifice, whatever definition (expiation, substitution, etc.) we may give for that sacrifice. At no point in the Gospels is the death of Jesus defined as a sacrifice. The passages that are invoked to justify a sacrificial conception of the Passion both can and should be interpreted with no reference to sacrifice in any of the accepted meanings.

Certainly the Passion is presented to us in the Gospels as an act that brings salvation to humanity. But it is in no way presented as a sacrifice.

If you have really followed my argument up to this point, you will already realize that from our particular perspective the sacrificial interpretation of the Passion must be criticized and exposed as a most enormous and paradoxical misunderstanding—and at the same time as something necessary—and as the most revealing indication of mankind's radical incapacity to understand its own violence, even when that violence is conveyed in the most explicit fashion.

Of all the reappraisals we must make in the course of these interviews, none is more important. It is no mere consequence of the anthropological perspective we have adopted. Our perspective is rooted in the Gospels themselves, in their own subversion of sacrifice, which restores the original text, disengaging the hypothesis of the scapegoat and enabling it to be transmitted to the human sciences.

I am not speaking of my own personal experience here. I am referring to something very much larger, to the framework of all the intellectual experiences that we are capable of having. Thanks to the sacrificial reading it has been possible for what we call Christendom to exist for fifteen or twenty centuries; that is to say, a culture has existed that is based, like all cultures (at least up to a certain point) on the mythological forms engendered by the founding mechanism. Paradoxically, in the sacrificial reading the Christian text itself provides the basis. Mankind relies upon a misunderstanding of the text that explicitly reveals the founding mechanism to re-establish cultural forms which remain sacrificial and to engender a society that, by virtue of this misunderstanding, takes its place in the sequence of all other cultures, still clinging to the sacrificial vision that the Gospel rejects.

J.-M. O.: Any form of sacrificial vision would contradict, I suppose, the revelation of the founding murder that you have shown to be present in the Gospels. It is obvious that bringing to light the founding murder completely rules out any compromise with the principle of sacrifice, or indeed with any conception of the death of Jesus as a sacrifice. A conception of this kind can only succeed in concealing yet again the real meaning and function of the Passion: one of subverting sacrifice and barring it from working ever again by forcing the founding mechanism out into the open, writing it down in the text of all the Gospels.

G. L.: I can see very well that a non-sacrificial reading is necessary. But at first sight it looks as though the enterprise will come up against some formidable obstacles, ranging from the redemptive character of Jesus' death to the conception of a violent God, which seems to become indispensable when you take into account themes like the Apocalypse. Everything that you say here is bound to provoke in response the famous words that the Gospels have no qualms about putting in Jesus' own mouth: 'I have come not to bring peace but a sword.' People are going to tell you that the Christian scriptures explicitly provide a reason for discord and dissension.

R. G.: None of what you say is incompatible with the non-sacrificial reading I am putting forward. It is only in the light of this reading that we can finally explain the Gospels' intrinsic conception of their action in history in particular the elements that appear to be contrary to the 'gospel spirit'. Once again, we must judge the interpretation that is being developed by the results it will offer. By rejecting the sacrificial definition of the Passion, we arrive at a simpler, more direct and more coherent reading, enabling us to integrate all the gospel themes into a seamless totality.

The Impossibility of the Sacrificial Reading

R. G.: It must be admitted that nothing in what the Gospels tell us directly about God justifies the inevitable conclusion of a sacrificial reading of the Epistle to the Hebrews. This conclusion was most completely formulated to the medieval theologians, and it amounts to the statement that the Father himself insisted upon the sacrifice. Efforts to explain this sacrificial pact only result in absurdities: God feels the need to revenge his honour, which has been tainted by the sins of humanity, and so on. Not only does God require a new victim, but he requires the victim who is most precious and most dear to him, his very son. No doubt this line of reasoning has done more than anything else to discredit Christianity in the eyes of people of goodwill in the modern world. However acceptable to the medieval mind it might have been, it has become intolerable for us, and it forms the major stumbling-block for a world that is entirely (and quite justifiably) hostile to the idea of sacrifice, even though that hostility remains tinged with sacrificial elements which no one has succeeded in rooting out.

If we keep to the passages that relate specifically to the Father of Jesus, we can easily see they contain nothing which would justify attributing the least amount of violence to the deity. On the contrary, we are confronted with a God who is foreign to all forms of violence. The most important of these passages in the synoptic Gospels formally repudiate the conception of a vengeful God, a conception whose traces can be found right up to the end of the Old Testament. Even if we discount all the explicit and implicit identifications of God with love that we find in the Gospel of John and in the Epistles attributed to the same author, we can confidently assert that in respect of the rejection of violence, the Gospels are fulfilling the work of the Old Testament. The following is the basic text, in my opinion, that shows us a God who is alien to all violence and who wishes in consequence to see humanity abandon violence:

You have heard that it was said, 'You shall love your neighbour and hate your enemy.' But I say to you, Love your enemies and pray for those who persecute you, so that you may be sons of your Father who is in heaven; for he makes his sun rise on the evil and on the good, and sends rain on the just and on the unjust (Matthew 5, 43-45).

Beside this text we can put all the texts denying that God is responsible for the infirmities, illnesses and catastrophes by which innocent victims perish—in particular, of course, for conflict. No god can be blamed for this; the immemorial and unconscious practice of making the deity responsible for all the evils that can afflict humanity is thus explicitly repudiated. The Gospels deprive God of his most essential role in primitive religions—that of polarizing everything mankind does not succeed in mastering, particularly in relationships between individuals.

It is precisely because this role is abandoned that the Gospels can pass for having established a kind of practical atheism. People who oppose the sacrificial conception often quote this passage in order to accuse the gospel text of offering what is in the last analysis a more distant and abstract conception of God than the one given by the Old Testament; at least old Yahweh was interested enough in humans to be roused to anger by their iniquities. By contrast, it looks as though the passage I have just quoted offers us a completely impassive God.

In fact, we do not meet an indifferent God in the Gospels. The God presented there wishes to make himself known, and can only make himself known if he secures from men what Jesus offers them. This is the essential theme, repeated time and time again, of Jesus' preaching: reconciliation with God can take place unreservedly and with no sacrificial intermediary through the rules of the kingdom. This reconciliation allows God to reveal himself as he is, for the first time in human history. Thus mankind no longer has to base harmonious relationships on bloody sacrifices, ridiculous fables of a violent deity, and the whole range of mythological cultural formations.

G. L.: It is easy to see why sacrifice and all that is implied in the sacrificial mentality could form an insurmountable obstacle for a God concerned with revealing himself. Between the God that emerges in your reading of the gospel text and the sacrificial deities whom you have spoken of up to now, there is a rift no less absolute than the one between the religious conception of life, seen in its totality, and the atheism of the modern world.

R. G.: I would hold that the rift is even more absolute since (as we have already seen) modern atheism is incapable of bringing the victim-age mechanisms to light; its empty scepticism about all religion con-stitutes a new method of keeping these mechanisms invisible, which favours their perpetuation. By contrast, the gospel text contains an ex-plicit revelation of the foundations of all religions in victimage, and this revelation takes place thanks to a non-violent deity—the Father of Jesus—for this revelation appears in the close association between Father and Son, in their common nature, and in the idea, repeated sev-eral times in John, that Jesus is the only way to the Father, that he is himself the same thing as the Father, that he is not only the Way, but also the Truth and the Life. Indeed, this is why those who have seen Jesus have seen the Father himself.

J.-M. O.: In order to justify the sacrificial interpretation, which is not even mentioned in the Gospels, it is necessary to presuppose that there is a kind of secret pact between the Son and the Father. According to this reading, the Father (for reasons that remain obscure) asks the Son to sacrifice himself, and the Son (for reasons that remain obscure) obeys his command. What has taken place, in effect, is a secret agree-ment about violence, such as might exist in our own times between superpowers when they are obliged to come to an understanding with-out consulting their own citizens.

R. G.: The very idea of such a pact, unbelievable as it is, is explicitly contradicted by the Gospel of John, in texts whose vital importance no Christian can miss:

No longer do I call you servants, for the servant does not know what his master is doing; but I have called you friends, for *all that I have heard from my Father I have made known to you* (John 15, 15; italics mine).

J.-M. O.: Either this is a non-sacrificial economy—the first and only non-sacrificial economy yet found in human society—or the text is still governed by the sacrificial economy and all that you are saying about the Gospel falls to the ground. In that case the radical originality of this text would be only a delusion.

As so often before, everything rests on your ability to demonstrate to us that the non-sacrificial reading you advocate is superior to the sacrificial reading advocated by the churches and their enemies. Here the stakes multiply; the proof must take place on what you hold to be the only real testing-ground for all that you have talked about so far. If the wholesale revision that you are carrying out in anthropology depends on how the gospel text unfolds and on the crumbling of the sacrificial readings that have up to now prevented its subversive potential from being realized among us, or at least from being fully realized, then it is crucial that the non-sacrificial reading should demonstrate a clear superiority to all the sacrificial readings that have been given so far.

Apocalypse and Parable

J.-M. O.: At first sight, that seems to be difficult, if not impossible, because of the close resemblance between the themes you must now make explicit and the structure of all the other great myths of violence. What are we to make of the universal threat contained in the theme of Apocalypse? How can we not see it as a regression toward a violent deity? How is it possible to reconcile this threat with the non-violent aspects of the gospel text, when it preaches the coming of God's kingdom? This contradiction is so intellectually disturbing that throughout the nineteenth century, men like Renan went to the trouble of distinguishing what were really two mutually contradictory Gospels: an original one based on the teaching of a more or less arbitrary 'historical' Jesus, and one which transfigured and falsified that teaching, making it into a theology in response to a powerful yet banal desire for power—the chief villain being, of course, the Apostle Paul. Are you not also compelled implicitly or explicitly to divide the gospel text into two unequal halves: the good, anti-sacrificial, humanist text, on the one hand, and the bad, sacrificial and theological one, on the other? Will you not have to expel the bad text from the Gospels, recalling in that very gesture the classic sacrificial practices?

R. G.: Certainly not. I am going to show you that everything can easily be accommodated within the non-sacrificial interpretation.

We must realize that the apocalyptic violence predicted by the Gospels is not divine in origin. In the Gospels, this violence is always brought home to men, and not to God. What makes the reader think that this is still the Old Testament wrath of God is the fact that most features of the Apocalypse, the great images in the picture, are drawn from Old Testament texts.

These imagines remain relevant because they describe the mimetic and sacrificial crisis. We find precisely the same structure of crisis in the Gospels, but by this time there is no longer a god to cut short the violence, or indeed to inflict it in the first place. So we have a lengthy decomposition of the city of man, in which a disorientated humanity meets in chaotic confrontation.

All the references to the Old Testament are preceded with an 'as', which suggests the metaphorical character of the mythical borrowing:

> *As* it was in the days of Noah, so will it be in the days of the Son of man. They ate, they drank, they married, they were given in marriage, until the day when Noah entered the ark, and the flood came and destroyed them all. *Likewise* as it was in the days of Lot—they ate, they drank, they bought, they sold, they planted, they built, but on the day when Lot went out from Sodom fire and sulphur rained from heaven and destroyed them all—*so* will it be on the day when the Son of man is revealed (Luke 17, 26-30; italics mine).

We have here not just an explicit comparison, but one that aims to demonstrate the non-miraculous character of the events in store for humanity. In the midst of the most outlandish phenomena, everyday concerns will come to the fore, and apathy and indifference will prevail. In the last days, we are told, 'most men's love will grow cold'. As a result, the combat between doubles will be in evidence everywhere. Meaningless conflict will be worldwide:

> And you will hear of wars and rumours of wars; see that you are not alarmed; for this must take place, but the end is not yet. For nation will rise against nation, and kingdom against kingdom. . . (Matthew 24, 6-7).

G. L.: To conclude, apocalyptic violence is always laid at the door of humanity in the Gospels, and never blamed on God. The commentators do not appreciate this, because they read the texts in the light of the apocalyptic passages of the Old Testament, in which God is indeed involved. These passages, however, serve as the basis of the New Testament passages only in so far as they exactly describe the mimetic crisis.

R. G.: One should ask whether these Old Testament texts have not been taken up in a spirit appropriate to the Gospels, one that completely desacralizes them. Modern readers are not interested in this possibility. Whether they call themselves believers or unbelievers, they still remain faithful to the medieval reading. Some of them do so because they want to keep the conception of a sinful humanity punished by a vengeful God; others because they are interested only in denouncing the first conception rather than in subjecting the texts to a genuine criticism. It never occurs to them that these texts, which are either fetishized or held up to ridicule, never really deciphered, could be rooted in a spirit that is quite different from the spirit of sacrificial religion.

J.-M. O.: You surely cannot deny that in some texts Jesus takes over Yahweh's traditional destructive violence. I have before me, for example, in the version from Luke, the parable of the murderous tenants of the vineyard, which you spoke about earlier. Let me sum it up briefly:

After renting out his vineyard to tenants, the owner goes to live elsewhere. In order to collect the fruits of the rented property, he sends a number of emissaries, the prophets, who are beaten, sent away and return with empty hands. Finally he sends his son, his heir, and the tenants put him to death. Jesus then asks his audience: What then will the owner of the vineyard do to them? And he himself answers the question: he will destroy the faithless tenants and put others in their place (Luke 20, 15-16; Mark 12, 9).

R. G.: Matthew's text is slightly different from those of Luke and Mark, and this slight difference is crucial for my answer to your objection. Matthew has the same question as Mark, and Jesus asks it. Yet this time *it is not he who replies*, but his listeners:

'When therefore the owner of the vineyard comes, what will he do to those tenants?' They say to him, 'He will put those wretches to a miserable death, and let out the vineyard to other tenants who will give him the fruits in their seasons' (Matthew 21, 40-41).

Jesus does not credit God with the violence. He allows his audience to come to their own conclusions and these represent not his thoughts but their own, thoughts that take God's violence for granted. I believe we should prefer Matthew's text. There is nothing arbitrary about the way in which Jesus entrusts his deaf and blind audience with responsibility for coming to conclusions that can only be referred back to the divine agency by listeners who remain imprisoned within the sacrificial vision. The author of Matthew is reluctant to place in Jesus' mouth a speech that makes God capable of violence, and this very point demonstrates how original the Gospel is by contrast with the Old Testament.

In Mark and Luke the sentence that attributes the violence to God is also interrogative, but Jesus both asks the question and supplies the answer. Here, it would seem, we may have simply a rhetorical effect.

But comparison with the more complex and meaningful text of Matthew shows that something quite different is at issue. The authors of Mark and Luke, or the scribes who recopied the texts, have simplified a text whose complete, meaningful form we find in Matthew. The question/answer format remains, but it no longer corresponds to the original intention, which was to let the audience take upon itself the violent conclusion of the parable.

Because they did not grasp this intention, Mark and Luke, or some scribes, allowed the element of dialogue to drop out, thinking it to be insignificant. On consideration, it turns out instead to be crucial.

As a general rule, these authors remain remarkably faithful to the disconcerting thought of the Gospels. And yet, as we have seen in the example just noted, and as other instances would confirm, minor defects have managed to creep into the text, working their way sometimes into one version and sometimes into another.

These original defects have been enlarged and multiplied by the innumerable Christian and non-Christian commentators. Posterity has always focused on the texts that tend to revert to the sacralization found in the Old Testament, if only because these texts seem the most 'characteristic' of what people think a religious spirit should be. The usual version of the apocalyptic theme, to take one example, is taken for the most part from John's Revelation, a text which is clearly less representative of the gospel inspiration than the apocalyptic chapters in the Gospels themselves (Matthew 24; Mark 13; Luke 17, 22-37; John 21, 5-37).

The intention I credited to Matthew's version of the parable of the tenants of the vineyard is certainly not at variance with the gospel spirit. To be assured of this, we need only note that it comes up again, very explicitly in the parable of the talents.

The servant who is content to bury the talent that was entrusted to him, instead of making it bear interest, also has the most frightening picture of his master. He sees in him a demanding overseer who 'reaps where he has not sown'. What happens to this servant is, in the last analysis, in exact conformity with his expectations, with the image he has constructed of his master. It does not derive from the fact that the master is really like the servant's conception of him (here the text of Luke is the most suggestive), but from the fact that men make their own destinies and become less capable of breaking away from the mimetic obstacle the more they allow themselves to be fascinated by it (Luke 19, 11-27).

In taking away from the bad servant the one talent left with him, the master is not saying, 'I am indeed as you imagined me to be', but 'since you saw in me the one who reaps where he has not sown, etc., why did you not make the talent that I left with you bear interest?' The parable does not permit us to assume that there is a god of vengeance; violence always is derived from purely human mechanisms. 'I will condemn you out of your own mouth, you wicked servant!'

That is indeed the main lesson to be drawn from this brief analysis. The notion of a divine violence has no place in the inspiration of the Gospels. But this is not the only lesson. For a while, we have been looking exclusively at the parables. And the parables are presented as explicitly metaphorical, as stopping short of the gospel truth, and, for that very reason, as more accessible to the majority of the audience (Matthew 13, 10-23), even though the audience generally makes a bad use of them.

In the parable of the sower, the gospel text attempts to define the inadequacy of the parable to Jesus' message. It does not fully succeed in the attempt, but we can now see what this inadequacy consists in. It consists in the tendency to revert to the notion of a violent god and to belief in vengeful retribution.

In order to secure the attention of his listeners, Jesus is obliged to speak their language up to a certain point and take into account illusions that cannot yet be eradicated. If his audience conceives of the deity as vengeful, then the audience can only approach the truth if it is still partly clothed in myth. This is precisely what Jesus does in the two parables we have just quoted. He indicates the violence that is in play and will redound upon humanity, and he leaves to his questioners the responsibility of making the interpretation that will sacralize this process. But his warning remains valid, since the violence in play is a real violence, and it is correctly described, even taking into account the illusion that it must have a sacred origin.

Powers and Principalities

G. L.: Yet it is not easy to accept the argument that the great descriptions of Apocalypse do not involve some supernatural elements.

R. G.: Obviously the whole theme has a cosmic breadth. The entire planet is affected; the whole foundation of human existence gives way. But the process is not directed by any divine agent; indeed the complete absence of God, up to the time of the Judgement, gives these texts their uncanny flavour, the sense that mankind as a whole is slipping from its moorings, which calls to mind the great liquid mass of the Flood:

> And there will be signs in sun and moon and stars, and upon the earth distress of nations in perplexity at the roaring of the sea and the waves, men fainting with fear *and with foreboding of what is coming on the world; for the powers of the heavens will be shaken* (Luke 21, 25-26; italics mine).

The reference to the 'powers of heaven' in this passage can be misleading. But the fact that these powers are shaken demonstrates that the passage cannot have to do with the true God, who is unshakeable. The powers of the heavens have nothing to do either with Jesus or with anything truly Christian. They are powers that have governed humanity since the world began. It we put this passage beside some other texts in the Gospels and Epistles of Paul, these worldly powers receive a wide variety of names. They may be presented as human, as angelic or as demonic and satanic; they may be called 'dominions', or the 'sovereigns of this world'. When Paul states that not God but one of his angels promulgated the Jewish law, he means that the Jewish law is still bound up with these powers, which are occasionally presented, quite significantly, as intermediaries between God and men. Depending on how we look at them and relate them to historical periods—before or after the intervention of Jesus in the affairs of this world—these 'powers of the heavens' will appear either as positive forces that maintain order and prevent men from destroying each other, in expectation of the true God, or as veils and obstacles that obstruct the fullness of revelation.

The interpretation I have just sketched out has been frequently conceded, and for a more complete account I refer you to Markus Barth's excellent commentary in his edition of the Epistle to the Ephesians.[58]

G. L.: This matter of the *powers* is certainly important. I imagine that in your view these powers are rooted in the founding murder, and we must compare the texts that speak of them with the text of John that calls *Satan a murderer from the beginning* and formulates that doctrine explicitly.

R. G.: That is indeed what I think. The Gospels are always telling us that Christ must triumph over these powers, in other words that he must desacralize them. But the Gospels and the New Testament in their entirety date from the first and second centuries of our era; that is to say, they date from a period when this work of desacralization had, quite obviously, a long way to go. That is why the authors of the Gospels cannot stop themselves from reverting, in describing these powers, to expressions contaminated by the symbolism of violence, even when they are really announcing the complete and full deconstruction of violence—the process to which we ourselves are heirs and which today enables us to seek out the mechanism of such powers.

As the Gospels tell us, Jesus engages in decisive struggle with these particular powers. And it is at the very moment when they apparently triumph—at the moment when the speech that brings them out into the open and condemns them as being basically murderous and violent has been reduced to silence by the Crucifixion, that is to say by a new murder and new violence—that these powers, believing themselves to be victorious once again, have in fact been vanquished. It is at that point, in effect, that the secret of their operations, which has never before been revealed, becomes inscribed quite explicitly in the gospel text.

Modern thought sees this merely as a kind of imaginary revenge, a kind of 'sublimation' of the Christian failure carried out by Jesus' disciples. It has never crossed people's minds that what is involved might be the absolute prototype of the intellectual mechanisms that concern them but that they believe they have discovered unaided, certainly without the kind of help the gospel text might provide. We believe that we monopolize the unmasking of all masks—while in reality our boldest thoughts in this domain are still based, however unconsciously, on the Gospels. Perhaps modern thinkers are only rediscovering—in a series of tentative and misguided steps that will presently stop appearing to be motiveless—the mechanism of the founding murder and the masking of it, which the gospel revelation has quite literally 'shattered'.

There exists in Paul a genuine doctrine of the victory represented by Jesus' apparent failure—a victory that is absolute but remains concealed. This doctrine explains the efficacy of the Cross in terms that have nothing to do with sacrifice. However, with the passage of time this doctrine was completely smothered by the sacrificial reading; on the rare occasions the commentators take note of it, they are liable to suspect it of containing unpalatable magical elements that justify the disuse into which it has fallen.

Here we have yet another example of the remarkable paradoxes with which this analysis is strewn. In effect, Paul's doctrine of the efficacy of the Cross is really quite . . . crucial. We must perceive its pertinence in the context of our reading of the Cross as a means of revealing the founding mechanism. It is possible, I believe, to show that this doctrine is much more important than all the elements in Paul that could be regarded as supportive of the sacrificial reading. It is later on, with the Epistle to the Hebrews and the other texts either inspired by it or deriving from a similar inspiration, that we see the triumph of the sacrificial interpretation, which Christian theology has not yet managed to throw off.

The text that tells us most is Colossians 2, 13-15. Here Paul writes of Christ that he has made us

> . . . alive together with him, having forgiven us all our trespasses, having cancelled the bond which stood against us with its legal demands; this he set aside, nailing it to the cross. He disarmed the principalities and powers and made a public example of them, triumphing over them in him.

The bond that stood against us with its demands is human culture, which is the terrifying reflection of our own violence. It bears against us a witness that we do not even notice. And the very ignorance in which we are plunged seats the principalities and powers upon their thrones. By dissipating all this ignorance, the Cross triumphs over the powers, brings them into ridicule, and exposes the pitiful secret of the mechanism of sacralization. The Cross derives its dissolving capacity from the fact that it makes plain the workings of what can now only be seen—after the Crucifixion—as evil. For Paul to be able to speak as he does, *it is necessary for the powers of this world to operate in the same way as the Crucifixion does*. So it is indeed the Crucifixion that is inscribed in the gospel text and is demystified by Christ, stripped for evermore of its capacity to structure the work of the human mind.

Some Greek Fathers made a great deal of this Pauline theory of the Crucifixion. For Origen, as for Paul, before Christ mankind is subservient to the yoke of the powers of evil. The pagan gods and the quality of the sacred are both identified with the evil angels, who still rule over the nations. Christ appears in the world to do battle with these 'powers' and 'principalities'. His very birth is an ominous sign that threatens the hold of these powers on human societies:

> When Jesus was born . . . the powers were weakened, their magic was countered and their effectiveness cancelled out.[59]

Time and again Origen comes back to the 'public example' or 'spectacle' of the Epistle to the Colossians and to the work of the Cross which 'leads captivity captive' (Commentary on John VI, 56-57).

It is a sign of Dante's insight into the text I have just read to you, as well as into other texts, that he was impelled, in his *Divine Comedy*, to show Satan nailed to the Cross—a picture that can only appear bizarre and out of place to those who maintain a conventional, sacrificial interpretation of the Crucifixion.

To prove that the Crucifixion is really about a hidden mechanism of masking that is conclusively demolished by the description of it in the Gospels, we have other passages from Paul that show how the wisdom of God ironically outplayed the calculations of the powers. 'None of the rulers of this age understood this; for if they had, they would not have crucified the Lord of glory' (I Corinthians 2, 8).

By resorting to the founding mechanism once again against Jesus (who had revealed the secret of their power, the founding murder), the powers of this world thought to stifle the Word of Truth for ever. They thought to triumph yet again by the method that had always allowed them to triumph in the past. What they failed to appreciate was that, in spite of the temporary consensus in which even the most faithful of the disciples cooperated, nothing like the usual mythological falsehood would appear in the Gospels. They would show, not the lie common to the religions of the entire planet, but the structural matrix in itself. Under the influence of the spirit, the disciples perpetuated the memory of the event, not in the mythic form that ought to have triumphed once again, but in a form that reveals the innocence of the just man who has suffered martyrdom. Thus they avoided sacralizing the victim as the guilty party and prevented him from being held responsible for the purely human disorders that his death was supposed to end. That is how the 'powers' played their hand, and, if they had it to play all over again, seeing that the Crucifixion has revealed their most important trick, they would play it differently. . . .

Besides, the death of Jesus had no results in the worldly sphere. By authorizing his death, the High Priest did not succeed in reaching his chosen objective, which was to *sacrifice one single victim in order that the whole nation should not perish* (John 11, 50).

In Luke's Gospel, all the same, the persecution of Jesus is not wholly without the effects that the most lucid of his persecutors were banking on:

> And Herod with his soldiers treated him with contempt and mocked him; then, arraying him in gorgeous apparel, he sent him back to Pilate. And Herod and Pilate became friends with each other that very day, for before this they had been at enmity with each other (Luke 23, 11-12).

J.-M. O.: We might say that the gospel text includes this detail in order to prove that it is not unfamiliar with the effect produced by events of which the Crucifixion is an example. But here we have no more than a temporary and minor effect. In the main, no reconciliation and reaffirmed order result from the Crucifixion.

If it were indeed a matter of yet another case of sacred violence, it would have social impact. Yet Christ tells us that it produces no effects of this kind; on the contrary, it undermines the foundations of all social, religious and even family life. Christ is not 'making threats' when he asserts this; he is spelling out the consequences that the loss of sacrificial protection will have in the long run. The gods of violence are devalued. The machine is broken, and the mechanism of expulsion will not work any more. Christ's murderers have acted in vain. Rather, they have acted in an extremely fruitful way, in so far as they have helped

Christ to record the objective truth of violence within the gospel text. This truth—however much it may be misunderstood and travestied—will make its slow way, finally achieving its disruptive effect like an insidious poison. The Christian and modern worlds produce no mythologies, no rituals, no prohibitions.

R. G.: The theme of the Christian Apocalypse involves human terror, not divine terror: a terror that is all the more likely to triumph to the extent that humanity has done away with the sacred scarecrows humanists thought they were knocking over on their own initiative, while they reproached the Judaeo-Christian tradition for striving to keep them upright. So now we are liberated. We know that we are by ourselves, with no father in the sky to punish us and interfere with our paltry business. So we must no longer look backward but forward; we must show what man is capable of. The really important apocalyptic writings say nothing except that man is responsible for his history. You wish for your dwelling to be given up to you; *well then, it is given up to you*.

Divine punishment is demystified by the gospels; its only place nowadays is in the mythic imagination, to which modern scepticism remains strangely attached. Modern indignation continues to get worked up over this mythic imagination, since it is, after all, a feature which is unequivocally reassuring. As long as the violence seems to be divine in origin, it really holds no terrors for anybody, since it is either an aid to salvation, or it doesn't exist at all. The confidence that all sacrificial religions show in the *ultimately positive* nature of violence rests inevitably upon the founding mechanism itself, whose beneficial effects can be tacitly counted on because the mechanism has not yet really been revealed. This positive aspect of violence is absent from the Gospels. If the threat continues to be truly frightening, this is because it brings with it no remedy: it offers no recourse of any sort; it has ceased to be 'divine'.

With the founding mechanism absent, the principle of violence that rules humanity will experience a terrifying recrudescence at the point when it enters its agony. To understand this, we have only to recall the paradoxical character of everything that affects mimetism and violence. Only through the mediation of the scapegoat mechanism can violence become its own remedy, and the victimage mechanism can only be triggered by the frenetic paroxysm of the 'crisis'. This means that the violence, having lost its vitality and bite, will paradoxically be more terrible than before its decline. As the whole of humanity makes the vain effort to reinstate its reconciliatory and sacrificial virtues, this violence will without doubt tend to multiply its victims, just as happened in the time of the prophets.

The Preaching of the Kingdom

G. L.: But among the consequences of the collective violence should we not take into account the essential themes of the grouping of the disciples around a Jesus who has been raised from the dead and made God? Do we not have here something analogous to other religions?

R. G.: I would like to show you that this crucial question must be answered in the negative. But before I do I must complete my explanation of the apocalyptic theme from a non-sacrificial perspective, and I must add to it a second important theme—that of the Kingdom of God—which can now be articulated (for the first time, I believe) with a logic that bears both on the Crucifixion and on the Apocalypse.

For the gospel criticism of the past two centuries, the conjunction of these two themes—the Apocalypse and the so-called preaching of the 'Kingdom of God'—has posed an insurmountable difficulty. In the middle of the nineteenth century, emphasis was placed on the Kingdom: liberal thinkers like Renan fabricated a Jesus with humanitarian and socialist traits. The apocalyptic theme was minimized. Albert Schweitzer wrote a famous essay that exposed the vanity of these attempts and once again emphasized the apocalyptic theme, which, however, he declared to be more or less unintelligible from our point of view—and foreign to the conditions of modern existence.[60] This was at the outset of the twentieth century!

Throughout the first part of Jesus' preaching, the tone is in fact quite different; there is no trace of apocalyptic prophecy; the texts mention only the reconciliation between men that is also the Kingdom of God, to which all are invited to belong.

J.-M. O.: We defined the Kingdom of God when we spoke of the attitude of the Gospels toward the Jewish law. The Kingdom is the substitution of love for prohibitions and rituals—for the whole apparatus of the sacrificial religions.

R. G.: Look again at the Sermon on the Mount. We can see that the significance of the Kingdom of God is completely clear. It is always a matter of bringing together the warring brothers, of putting an end to the mimetic crisis by a universal renunciation of violence. Apart from collective expulsion—which brings about reconciliation because it is unanimous—only the unconditional and, if necessary, unilateral renunciation of violence can put an end to the relation of doubles. The Kingdom of God means the complete and definitive elimination of every form of vengeance and every form of reprisal in relations between men.

Jesus makes all of this an absolute duty in everyday life. It is an obligation without counterpart, which makes no condition that it must be reciprocated:

> You have heard that it was said, 'An eye for an eye and a tooth for a tooth.' But I say to you, Do not resist one who is evil. But if any one strikes you on the right cheek, turn to him the other also; and if any one would sue you and take your coat, let him have your cloak as well (Matthew 5, 38-40).

Modern interpreters certainly see that everything in the Kingdom of God comes down to the project of ridding men of violence. But because they conceive of violence in the wrong way, they do not appreciate the rigorous objectivity of the methods which Jesus advocates. People imagine either that violence is no more than a kind of parasite, which the appropriate safeguards can easily eliminate or that it is an ineradicable trait of human nature, an instinct or fatal tendency that it is fruitless to fight.

But the Gospels tell quite a different story. Jesus invites all men to devote themselves to the project of getting rid of violence, a project conceived with reference to the true nature of violence, taking into account the illusions it fosters, the methods by which it gains ground, and all the laws that we have verified over the course of these discussions.

Violence is the enslavement of a pervasive lie; it imposes upon men a falsified vision not only of God but also of everything else. And that is indeed why it is a closed kingdom. Escaping from violence is escaping from this kingdom into another kingdom, whose existence the majority of people do not even suspect. This is the Kingdom of love, which is also the domain of the true God, the Father of Jesus, of whom the prisoners of violence cannot even conceive.

To leave violence behind, it is necessary to give up the idea of retribution; it is therefore necessary to give up forms of conduct that have always seemed to be natural and legitimate. For example, we think it quite fair to respond to good dealings with good dealings, and to evil dealings with evil, but this is precisely what all the communities on the planet have always done, with familiar results. People imagine that to escape from violence it is sufficient to give up any kind of violent *initiative*, but since no one in fact thinks of himself as taking this initiative—since all violence has a mimetic character, and derives or can be thought to derive from a first violence that is always perceived as originating with the opponent—this act of renunciation is no more than a sham, and cannot bring about any kind of change at all. Violence is always perceived as being a legitimate reprisal or even self-defence. So what must be given up is the right to reprisals and even the right to what passes, in a number of cases, for legitimate defence. Since the violence is mimetic, and no one ever feels responsible for triggering it initially, only by an unconditional renunciation can we arrive at the desired result:

> And if you do good to those who do good to you, what credit is that to you? For even sinners do the same. And if you lend to those from whom you hope to receive, what credit is that to you? Even sinners lend to sinners, to receive as much again. But love your enemies, and do good, and lend, expecting nothing in return (Luke 6, 33-35).

If we interpret the gospel doctrine in the light of our own observations about violence, we can see that it explains, in the most clear and concise fashion, all that people must do in order to break with the circularity of closed societies, whether they be tribal, national, philosophical or religious. There is nothing missing and there is no superfluous detail. This doctrine is completely realistic. It envisages perfectly all that is implied in going beyond the 'metaphysical closure', and it never falls into the associated errors of modern fanaticism, which misunderstands the ambiguity and the ubiquity of violence, and invariably limits its indictment either to the loss of sacrificial order or to the presence of that order, either to unruliness alone or to rules alone, in the belief that to triumph over violence is simply a matter of violently eliminating one or other—either by curbing individual impulses or by taking the opposite path and 'liberating' them in the expectation that this act will establish peace in our time.

Because they have no knowledge of violence and the role that it plays in human life, these commentators sometimes imagine that the Gospels preach a sort of natural morality that men, being naturally good, would respect of their own accord if there were no 'wicked' people to prevent them from doing so, and sometimes they imagine that the Kingdom of God is a kind of Utopia, a dream of perfection invented by some gentle dreamer who was incapable of understanding the ground rules upon which humankind has always operated.

No one can see that the true nature of violence is deduced with implacable logic, from the simple and single rule of the Kingdom. No one can see that disobeying or obeying this rule gives rise to two kingdoms which cannot communicate with one another, since they are separated by a real abyss. Mankind can cross this abyss, but to do so all men together should adopt the single rule of the Kingdom of God. The decision to do so must come from each individual *separately*, however; for once, others are not involved.

J.-M. O.: If we follow your reasoning, the real human *subject* can only come out of the rule of the Kingdom; apart from this rule, there is never anything but mimetism and the 'interdividual'. Until this happens, the only subject is the mimetic structure.

R. G.: That is quite right. . . . To complete our understanding of the Kingdom of God, we must fully grasp the context in which it is being preached. The gospels show themselves to be placed at the paroxysm of the crisis that John the Baptist defines as sacrificial and prophetic when he re-employs the opening of the second part of Isaiah: 'Every valley shall be lifted up, and every mountain and hill made low.' This is the great and tragic act of levelling, the triumph of reciprocal violence. That is why the mutual recognition of John the Baptist and Christ, which gives the seal of prophetic and messianic authenticity, consists first and foremost in the absence of any symmetrical antagonism, in the simple and miraculous fact of not succumbing to the escalating violence of the two who turn themselves into 'enemy twins', like Oedipus and Tiresias.

Throughout the prophetic period, it is invariably in the midst of such a crisis that the prophets address the chosen people and, invariably, what they advocate is the substitution of love and harmony for the sterile and symmetrical conflict of doubles—the violence that sacrifice is no longer capable of curing. The more desperate the situation, the more absurd the reciprocal violence strikes us as being, and the more the message is likely, so it would seem, to be taken seriously.

With Jesus, it is the same crisis and the same message, except for the fact that, according to the Gospels the final paroxysm has arrived. All the aspects of the dilemma are conveyed with the greatest clarity: since the resources of sacrifice have been finally exhausted and since violence is just on the point of being brought into the open, there will be no further possibility of compromise, no escape any more.

We can understand why one of the titles given to Jesus is that of 'prophet'. Jesus is the last and greatest of the prophets, the one who sums them up and goes further than all of them. He is the prophet of the last, but also of the best, chance. With him there takes place a shift that is both tiny and gigantic—a shift that follows on directly from the Old Testament but constitutes a decisive break as well. This is the complete elimination of the sacrificial for the first time—the end of divine violence and the explicit revelation of all that has gone before. It calls for a complete change of emphasis and a spiritual metamorphosis without precedent in the whole history of mankind. It also amounts to an absolute simplification of the relations between human beings, in so far as all the false differences between doubles are annulled—a simplification in the sense in which we speak of an algebraic simplification.

We saw earlier that throughout the texts of the Old Testament it was impossible to conclude the deconstruction of myths, rituals and law since the plenary revelation of the founding murder had not yet taken place. The divinity may be to some extent stripped of violence, but not completely so. That is why there is still an indeterminate and indistinct future, in which the resolution of the problem by human means alone—the face-to-face reconciliation that ought to result when people are alerted to the stupidity and uselessness of symmetrical violence—remains confused to a certain extent with the hope of a new epiphany of violence that is distinctively divine in origin, a 'Day of Yahweh' that would combine the paroxysm of God's anger with a no less God-given reconciliation. However remarkably the prophets progress toward a precise understanding of what it is that structures religion and culture, the Old Testament never tips over into the complete rationality that would dispense with this hope of a purgation by violence and would give up requiring God to take the apocalyptic solution by completely liquidating the 'evil' in order to ensure the happiness of the chosen.

J.-M. O.: To sum up: it is in the perpetuation of God's purging and violence—though in a modified form—that we can locate the differences between the apocalypses of the Old Testament and the gospel Apocalypse. Yet, confronted with the latter, all the commentators inevitably regress toward the Old Testament conceptions.

R. G.: The metamorphosis from Old Testament into Gospel is not an exclusively intellectual development; it is the crisis itself that matures. A historical moment comes about that was never possible before, a moment in which there can only be an absolute and conscious choice between two forms of reciprocity which are at once very close and radically opposed. At this moment the loosening of cultural constraints and the awareness of the truth underlying violence have matured, so that everything will soon topple over, either into a form of violence with infinite powers of destruction, or into the non-violence of the Kingdom of God, which now is alone capable of ensuring the survival of the community.

At this supreme moment, the risks have never been greater. But it has never been easier to change people's allegiance and alter their behaviour, since the vanity and stupidity of violence have never been more obvious. The offer of the Kingdom has to intervene at this very moment, which corresponds to a concept in the Gospels that is very important yet very imperfectly understood: that of the *hour* of Christ. At the beginning of the Gospels, and in particular that of John, Jesus is extremely concerned not to speak until his hour has come, and also, as we might expect, not to let slip the hour, which will not come again.

The offer of the Kingdom is no mere formality. It coincides with a possibility that has never been more accessible to the Jews, *prepared* as they are—I emphasize the term, which comes from the Gospels—by the Old Testament to throw themselves into the great adventure of the Kingdom. It is precisely because this possibility is not in the least illusory that the message of Jesus is good news here and now on this earth. For the first time, people are capable of escaping from the misunderstanding and ignorance that have surrounded mankind throughout its history. As long as there is any chance of its success, the preaching of the Kingdom has no dark counterpart and is accompanied by no pronouncements that strike fear.

By the same token, we can clarify the remarkable note of urgency that marks this initial stage of Christ's preaching—the pressing and even

impatient tone that colours his urging. The slightest hesitation amounts
to a final refusal. If the chance is lost, it will not occur again. . . . Woe
to him who looks backwards, woe to him who looks towards his neighbours and waits for them to decide, before himself deciding to follow
the example of Jesus.

J.-M. O.: So in fact it is not a question of redifferentiating the community, but of reversing the universal negative reciprocity—which
profits no one and harms everyone—into a beneficent reciprocity which
is the love and light of the true God. At the moment when violence is at
its peak, when the community is one the brink of dissolution, the
chances of succeeding are at their greatest, as are the dangers, if men
will not recognize the situation of extreme urgency in which they find
themselves.

In the light of what you say, we can grasp why the Kingdom of God is
presented as a permanent reality, which is always on offer to all men,
and also as a historical opportunity without precedent. One can understand why Jesus talks of his *hour* with such solemnity and attempts to
put across to his immediate audience the huge responsibility—but at
the same time the exceptional opportunity—that they have in living at
this hour which is absolutely unique in all human history (John 2, 4; 8,
20; 12, 23-27; 13, 1; 17, 1).

Kingdom and Apocalypse

R. G.: The events that followed the preaching of the Kingdom of
God depended entirely on the response of Jesus' audience. If they had
accepted the invitation unreservedly, there would have been no Apocalypse announced and no Crucifixion. The majority turned away in
indifference or hostility. As for the disciples, they argued among themselves about the best positions in what they imagined to be a kind of
politico-religious movement that would take its place within the Judaic
universe of the period. We find this mode of thinking again in many
modern commentators.

The more it is confirmed that the Kingdom is a failure, the darker
become the prospects for the future. In the nineteenth century, interpreters of the historical and psychological school used to attribute this
darkening to Jesus' bitterness at a reverse that had taken him by surprise. In accordance with that reasoning, the Apocalypse could be read
as an appeal to the anger of God, which seemed to verify these false

conclusions by suggesting that Jesus or his disciples must have experienced the kind of resentment that Nietzsche thinks he can detect behind everything Christian—hardly fitting the soft, humanitarian spirit they had displayed up to that point.

This reading still dominates the majority of present-day interpretations, and yet it is manifestly absurd. It is wholly generated by our inability to recognize the founding violence and the primordial role that the misunderstanding of this violence has played throughout human history—a misunderstanding that this reading perpetuates.

There is no way of getting to the real logic of the text without becoming aware of this fact. The darkening takes place in proportion to the negative attitude of those who could have helped Jesus in his mission and made the good reciprocity really catch on. To explain this change in tone, we have no need of psychological conjectures.

So we now have in our hands all the threads of the logic that transforms the announcement of the Kingdom into an announcement of the Apocalypse: if men turn down the peace Jesus offers them—a peace which is not derived from violence and that, by virtue of this fact, *passes human understanding*, the effect of the gospel revelation will be made manifest through violence, through a sacrificial and cultural crisis whose radical effect must be unprecedented since there is no longer any sacralized victim to stand in the way of its consequences. The failure of the Kingdom, from the viewpoint of the Gospels, does not amount to the failure of the mission Jesus undertakes; but it does amount to the inevitable abandonment of the direct and easy way, which would be for all to accept the principles of conduct that he has stated. It is now necessary to turn to the indirect way, the one that has to by-pass the consent of all mankind and instead pass through the Crucifixion and the Apocalypse. To sum up: the revelation is not impeded by the obstinate attachment to violence that the majority of men demonstrate *since from now on this violence has become its own enemy and will end by destroying itself*. The Kingdom of Satan, more than ever divided against itself, will be able to stand no longer. The only difference is that by remaining faithful to violence and taking its side, however little they may be aware of the fact, men have *deferred* the revelation once again and compelled it to take the terrible path of incalculable violence. It is upon men and men alone that responsibility falls for the tragic and catastrophic nature of the changes humanity is about to witness.

If the Gospels (especially that of Matthew) clearly divide into two parts, the first devoted to the preaching of the Kingdom and the second to apocalyptic predictions and the Passion, it is because between these two parts falls a negative event that is terrifying in its consequences. This is the failure of the preaching of the Gospel because of the indifference and disdain of those who are its immediate audience. Obviously they are not reacting differently from the rest of mankind. This event determines that the text will have two sides, which are opposed in content and tone, but bear a logically compatible relationship via a link of which the humanistic and historicist criticism of the nineteenth century had no inkling. All the illusions entertained by this critical tradition and those that have succeeded it rest upon the misunderstanding of this link—that is to say, upon the misunderstanding from time immemorial of the founding murder.

J.-M. O.: If redemptive virtues are in fact attributed to the Passion, they must exist on quite a *different plane*, which has no connection with the world built upon violence—the world that Jesus does not pray for, since to do so would be to pray for the cancellation of his own work, to pray against the coming of the Kingdom of God. When Jesus says: 'The world will pass away and my words will not pass away', he does not only mean that his words will endure for ever. The word of Jesus has a destructive effect on the world. Far from being consolidated, the world of Herod and Pilate, of Caiaphas and the Zealots, must be literally dissolved at the breath of this word. For this word brings the world the only truth that it cannot hear without vanishing—its own truth.

Jesus is not there in order to stress once again in his own person the unified violence of the sacred; he is not there to ordain and govern like Moses; he is not there to unite a people around him, to forge its unity in the crucible of rites and prohibitions, but on the contrary, to turn this long page of human history once and for all.

G. L.: If Jesus is occasionally compared to a second Moses, it is only because with him, as with Moses, a new and decisive stage of history begins. But it is not the same stage. In a good many respects, the mission of Jesus is opposed to that of Moses, who is concerned with arbitration and legislation (Luke 12, 13-14).

R. G.: The refusal of the Kingdom by those to whom it is first offered is still only a threat to the Jewish community, which is the only one to have benefited from the *preparation* of the Old Testament. This is the term applied, in Luke, to John the Baptist, who sums up the achievement of all the prophets prior to Jesus:

> And he [John] will go before him [the Messiah], in the spirit and power of Elijah, to turn the hearts of the fathers to the children, and the disobedient to the wisdom of the just, to make ready for the Lord a people prepared. (Luke 1, 17)

This preparation has its counterpart. It is identical to the undifferentiation that must tip over sooner or later into beneficent or malevolent reciprocity. Total destruction threatens Judaism as a religious and cultural entity in the very near future. Luke, in particular, tries hard to distinguish between a near and specifically Judaic apocalypse and a world apocalypse that will take place 'after the times of the Gentiles'—after the Gospels have been announced to the whole world and very probably rejected by it.

The Non-Sacrificial Death of Christ

R. G.: If we can rid ourselves of the vestiges of the sacrificial mentality that soil and darken the recesses of our minds, we shall see that we now have all the elements to hand for understanding that the death of Jesus takes place for reasons that have nothing to do with sacrifice. All that remained unclear in the non-sacrificial reading should have been clarified in the most comprehensive way.

As we have seen, Jesus is the direct, though involuntary, cause of the division and dissension that is stirred up by his message, by virtue of the fact that it meets with almost universal incomprehension. But all of his actions are directed toward non-violence, and no more effective form of action could be imagined.

As I have already pointed out, Jesus cannot be held responsible for the apocalyptic dimension that underlies Jewish history and ultimately all of human history. In the Jewish universe, the superiority of the Old Testament over all forms of mythology meant that the point of no return had already been reached. The Law and the Prophets, as we saw, constitute a genuine announcement of the Gospel, a *praefiguratio Christi*, as the Middle Ages testified, but could not show, unable as they were to recognize in the Old Testament a first step outside the sacrificial system, and the first gradual withering of sacrificial resources. At the very moment when this adventure approaches its resolution Jesus arrives on the scene—Jesus as he appears in the Gospels.

From now on, it becomes impossible to put the clock back. There is an end to cyclical history, for the very reason that its mechanisms are beginning to be uncovered.

G. L.: I think that the same thing happens in the pre-Socratics, at the very beginning of what we can call our history in the fullest sense of the term—in other words, at the moment when the cycles of eternal recurrence—which Nietzsche thinks wrongly that we are reverting to, in his inspired madness—open on to a future that seems to be absolutely undetermined; though they fail to disappear completely.

Empedocles gives us the splendid anti-sacrificial text that you quoted in *Violence and the Sacred*.[61] But the pre-Socratics are unable to see the ethical consequences of what they are saying in the domain of human relationships. No doubt that is why the pre-Socratics are *still* fashionable in the world of Western philosophy, whilst the Prophets *never* are.

R. G.: Let us come back to the attitude of Jesus himself. The decision to adopt non-violence is not a commitment that he could revoke, a contract whose clauses need only be observed to the extent that the other contracting parties observe them. If that were so, the commitment to the Kingdom of God would be merely another farcical procedure, comparable to institutionalized revenge or the United Nations. Despite the fact that all the others fall away, Jesus continues to see himself as being bound by the promise of the Kingdom. For him, the word that comes from God, the word that enjoins us to imitate no one but God, the God who refrains from all forms of reprisal and makes his sun to shine upon the 'just' and the 'unjust' without distinction—this word remains, for him, absolutely valid. It is valid even to death, and quite clearly that is what makes him the Incarnation of that Word. To sum up: the Christ can no longer continue to sojourn in a world in which the Word is either never mentioned or, even worse, derided and devalued by those who take it in vain—those who claim to be faithful to it but in reality are far from being so. Jesus' destiny in the world is inseparable from that of the Word of God. That is why Christ and the Word of God are, I reaffirm, simply one and the same thing.

Not only does Jesus remain faithful to this Word of Love, but he also does everything to enlighten men about what awaits them if they continue in the pathways they have always taken before. So urgent is the problem and so massive the stake that it justifies the remarkable vehemence, even brutality, that Jesus manifests in his dealings with 'those who have ears and hear not, eyes and see not'. That is indeed why—through a further paradox, which is outrageously unjust but could have been expected since we know that no mercy can be shown to the person who understands what all the world around him refuses to understand—Jesus himself stands accused of unnecessary violence, offensive language, immoderate use of polemics, and failure to respect the 'freedom' of his interlocutors.

Within a process that has lasted for centuries—indeed, since the beginnings of human history—the preaching of the Kingdom, first in the Judaic world and later throughout the world, must intervene at the very point when the chances of success are maximized: that is to say, at the very point when everything is ready to slide into a limitless violence. Jesus lucidly perceives both the threat and the possibility of salvation. He therefore has the duty to warn mankind; by announcing to all the Kingdom of God, he is doing no more than observing in his own behaviour the principles he proclaims. He would fail in his love for his brothers if he were to keep silent and abandon the human race to the destiny that it is unconsciously creating for itself. If Jesus has been called the Son of Man, this is principally, in my view, a response to a text in Ezekiel that accords to a 'son of man' a mission to warn the people that is very similar to the one conferred on Jesus by the Gospels:

> The word of the Lord came to me: 'Son of man, speak to your people and say to them, If I bring the sword upon a land, and the people of the land take a man from among them, and make him their watchman; and if he sees the sword coming upon the land and blows the trumpet and warns the people; then if any one who hears the sound of the trumpet does not take warning, and the sword comes and takes him away, his blood shall be upon his own head. . .
>
> 'So you, son of man, I have made a watchman for the house of Israel; whenever you hear a word from my mouth, you shall give them warning from me. If I say to the wicked, O wicked man, you shall surely die, and you do not speak to warn the wicked to turn from his way, that wicked man shall die in his iniquity, but his blood I will require at your hand. But if you warn the wicked to turn from his way, and he does not turn from his way; he shall die in his iniquity, but you will have saved your life.

'And you, son of man, say to the house of Israel, Thus have you said: "Our transgressions and our sins are upon us, and we waste away because of them; how then can we live? Say to them, As I live, says the Lord God, I have no pleasure in the death of the wicked, but that the wicked turn from his way and live; turn back, turn back from your evil ways; for why will you die, O house of Israel'" (Ezekiel 33, 1-11).

Jesus does all in his power to warn mankind and turn them away from paths that will be fatal henceforth—the most terrifying texts, like the 'Curses against the Pharisees', are just the most extreme and the most dangerous for the messenger of these warnings—but he also serves as the victim, once his audience has determined not to listen to him and to fall back into their old ways. He does not resist their blows, and it is at his expense that they would become reconciled and re-establish a ritualized community if that were still a possibility. On all conceivable fronts, he is always ready to take all risks upon himself; he is always ready to pay with his own person in order to spare men the terrible destiny that awaits them.

Refusing the Kingdom means refusing the knowledge that Jesus bears—refusing the knowledge of violence and all its works. In the eyes of those who reject it, this knowledge is ill-omened; it is the worst of all forms of violence. That is indeed how things must look from the perspective of the sacrificial community. Jesus appears as a destructive and subversive force, as a source of contamination that threatens the community. Indeed, to the extent that he is misunderstood he becomes just that. The way in which he preaches can only make him appear to be totally lacking in respect for the holiest of institutions, guilty of hubris and blasphemy, since he dares to rival God himself in the perfection of the Love that he never ceases to make manifest.

Certainly the preaching of the Kingdom of God reveals that there is an element of violence even in the most apparently holy of institutions, like the church hierarchy, the rites of the Temple, and even the family.

Faithful to the logic of sacrifice, those who have refused the invitation to the Kingdom are obliged to turn against Jesus. They can hardly fail to see in him the sworn enemy and corruptor of the very cultural order that they are vainly attempting to restore.

This means that violence will find in Jesus the most perfect victim that can be imagined, the victim that, for every conceivable reason, violence has the most reasons to pick on. Yet at the same time, this victim is also the most innocent.

J.-M. O.: What you mean, in other words, is that Jesus, of all the victims who have ever been, is the only one capable of revealing the true nature of violence to its utmost. Whichever way you look at it, his death is exemplary; in it the meaning of all the persecutions and expulsions in which mankind has ever engaged, as well as all the misconceptions that have sprung from them, stand revealed and represented for all time.

Jesus, in other words, provides the scapegoat *par excellence*—he is the most arbitrary of victims because he is also the least violent. At the same time he is the least arbitrary and the most meaningful, again because of being the least violent. We might say that the same reason always makes Jesus the victim *par excellence*, in whom the previous history of mankind is summed up, concluded and transcended.

R. G.: Violence is unable to bear the presence of a being that owes it nothing—that pays it no homage and threatens its kingship in the only way possible. What violence does not and cannot comprehend is that, in getting rid of Jesus by the usual means, it falls into a trap that could only be laid by innocence of such a kind because it is not really a trap: there is nothing hidden. Violence reveals its own game in such a way that its workings are compromised at their very source; the more it tries to conceal its ridiculous secret from now on, by forcing itself into action, the more it will succeed in revealing itself.

We can see why the Passion is found between the preaching of the Kingdom and the Apocalypse. It is an event that is ignored by historians, who have much more serious topics, with their Tiberius and their Caligula; it is a phenomenon that has no importance in the eyes of the world—incapable, at least in principle, of setting up or reinstating a cultural order but very effective, in spite of those who know better, in carrying out subversion. In the long run, it is quite capable of undermining and overturning the whole cultural order and supplying the secret motive force of all subsequent history.

J.-M. O.: Let me cut in with two questions. First, are you not in fact hypostatizing violence by treating it like a kind of subjective agency, which is personally hostile to Jesus Christ? Second, how are you able to reconcile all you have been saying with the real history of historical Christianity, in other words, with the failure of the gospel revelation to

affect events? You are the first person to read the Gospels in the way
that you do. However brilliant and rigorous the textual logic that you
are unfolding for our benefit, it seems to have no hold on the real history
of mankind, particularly on the history of the part of the world that
claimed to be Christian.

R. G.: I would reply to your first question by reminding you that
violence, in every cultural order, is always the true *subject* of every ritual
or institutional structure. From the moment when the sacrificial order
begins to come apart, this subject can no longer be anything but the
adversary par excellence, which combats the installation of the Kingdom
of God. This is the devil known to us from tradition—Satan himself, of
whom some theologians tell us that he is both subject and not subject at
once.

As for your second question, I cannot reply at the moment, but I shall
do so presently. For the time being, it is only necessary to point out that
we are searching for coherence in the text, and I believe that we are
finding it. We cannot concern ourselves at this stage with its possible
relationship to our history. The fact that this logic can seem abstract
and foreign to history only serves to bring out more clearly its status as a
logic, in relation to the text which we are reading—and nothing more is
required at present.

First of all, it is important to insist that Christ's death was not a sacrificial one. To say that Jesus dies, not as a sacrifice, but in order that
there may be no more sacrifices, is to recognize in him the Word of God:
'I wish for mercy and not sacrifices'. Where that word is not obeyed,
Jesus can remain. There is nothing gratuitous about the utterance of
that word and where it is not followed by any effect, where violence
remains master, Jesus must die. Rather than become the slave of violence, as our own word necessarily does, the Word of God says no to
violence.

J.-M. O.: That does not mean, if I have understood you rightly, that
Jesus' death is a more or less disguised suicide. The maudlin and morbid element which is to be found in a certain type of Christianity makes
common cause with the sacrificial reading.

R. G.: Yes indeed. Since they do not see that human community is
dominated by violence, people do not understand that the very one of
them who is untainted by any violence and has no form of complicity

with violence is bound to become the victim. All of them say that the world is evil and violent. But we must see that there is no possible compromise between killing and being killed. This is the dilemma brought out by tragic drama. But the majority of mankind do not accept that it is truly representative of the 'human condition'. Those who do gain a reputation for 'exaggerating', for 'taking things tragically'. There are a thousand different ways, so it would seem, of escaping from such a dilemma, even in the darkest times of history. All well and good. But people fail to understand that they are indebted to violence for the degree of peace that they enjoy.

How can non-violence become fatal? Clearly it is not so in itself; it is wholly directed toward life and not towards death! How can the rule of the Kingdom come to have mortal consequences? This becomes possible and even necessary because others refuse to accept it. For all violence to be destroyed, it would be sufficient for all of mankind to decide to abide by this rule. If all mankind offered the other cheek, no cheek would be struck. But for that to be possible, it would be necessary for each person separately and all people together to commit themselves irrevocably to the common purpose.

If all men loved their enemies, there would be no more enemies. But if they drop away at the decisive moment, what is going to happen to the one person who does not drop away? For him the word of life will be changed into the word of death. It can be shown, I believe, that there is not a single action or word attributed to Jesus—including those that seem harshest at first sight and including the revelation of the founding murder and the last efforts to turn mankind aside from a path that will henceforth be fatal—that is not consistent with the rule of the Kingdom. It is absolute fidelity to the principle defined in his own preaching that condemns Jesus. There is no other cause for his death than the love of one's neighbour lived to the very end, with an infinitely intelligent grasp of the constraints it imposes. 'Greater love has no man than this, that a man lay down his life for his friends' (John 15, 13).

If violence is genuinely the ruling factor in all cultural orders, and if circumstances at the time of the preaching of the Gospel are as the text proclaims them to be—involving, that is to say, the paroxysm of paroxysms within one single vast prophetic crisis experienced by Judaic society—then the refusal of the Kingdom by Jesus' listeners will logically impel them to turn against him. Moreover, this refusal will issue in the choice of him as a scapegoat, and in apocalyptic violence, by virtue of the fact that this last of victims, despite having been killed by unanimous consent, will not produce the beneficial effects that were produced before.

Once it has been possible to detect the operations of violence and the logic underlying them—or, if you prefer, the logic of violent men—confronted by the logic of Jesus, you will realize that Jesus never says a word that cannot be deduced from the events that have already taken place within the perspective of these two types of logic. Here and elsewhere, the 'gift of prophecy' is nothing but the detection of these two logics.

So we can understand why it is that from the moment when the failure of the Kingdom becomes a certainty, the Gospels repeatedly announce through Jesus' mouth both the Crucifixion and the Apocalypse. The old historical school interpreted these announcements as *ex post facto* prophecies destined to mask the impotence of the political leader in the face of an unexpected disaster.

The reason modern interpreters speak in this way is that they are unable to detect the two types of logic I have distinguished. Although the logic of violence provisionally has the last word, the logic of non-violence is superior, since it comprehends the other logic in addition to itself—which the logic of violence is incapable of doing. This superior logic of non-violence may be in the grip of illusions. But it exists and it must be detected and understood. Modern commentators fail to do so, and attribute to the Gospels objectives as futile as those of modern advertising or political propaganda because they do not even suspect the existence of such a logic.

This incomprehension can be identified with the attitudes stigmatized by the text. It simply reproduces and extends the reactions of Jesus listeners, including the reactions of his disciples. There are those who believe that Jesus will kill himself, and there are those who believe in his wish for power. Not one of the positions taken up by modern criticism has not already been sketched within the gospel text itself, so clearly that we might claim direct borrowing. Yet we must conclude that modern criticism is actually unable to see these positions in their original context. Interpreters never notice that they are themselves invariably understood and explained by the text that they pride themselves on understanding and explaining to us.

G. L.: So we can say that Jesus does nothing but obey, right up to the end, the promptings of the love that he declares has come from the

Father and is directed toward all mankind. There is no reason to suppose that the Father has devised for him alone duties that he would not require of all mankind: 'I say to you: Love your enemies, pray for your persecutors; so you will be sons of your Father which is in Heaven.' All the world is called to become sons of God. The only distinction—though of course it is a crucial one—is that the Son hears the Word of the Father and himself conforms to it right to the end; he makes himself perfectly identical with the Word, while other people, even if they hear it, are incapable of conforming to it.

R. G.: So Jesus is the only man who achieves the goal God has set for all mankind, the only man who has nothing to do with violence and its works. The epithet 'Son of Man' also corresponds, quite clearly, to the fact that Jesus alone has fulfilled a calling that belongs to all mankind.

If the fulfilment, on earth, passes inevitably through the death of Jesus, this is not because the Father demands this death, for strange sacrificial motives. Neither the son nor the Father should be questioned about the cause of this event, but all mankind, and mankind alone. The very fact that mankind has never really managed to understand what is involved reveals clearly that the misunderstanding of the founding murder is still being perpetuated, as is our inability to hear the Word of God.

That is indeed why people are constrained to invent an irrational requirement of sacrifice that absolves them of responsibility. According to this argument, the Father of Jesus is still a God of violence, despite what Jesus explicitly says. Indeed he comes to be the God of unequalled violence, since he not only requires the blood of the victim who is closest to him, most precious and dear to him, but he also envisages taking revenge upon the whole of mankind for a death that he both required and anticipated.

In effect, mankind is responsible for all of this. Men killed Jesus because they were not capable of becoming reconciled without killing. But by this stage, even the death of the just no longer had the power to reconcile them. Hence they are exposed to a limitless violence that they themselves have brought about and that has nothing to do with the anger or vengeance of any god.

When Jesus says: 'your will be done and not mine,' it is really a question of dying. But it is not a question of showing obedience to an incomprehensible demand for sacrifice. Jesus has to die because continuing to live would mean a compromise with violence. I will be told that 'it comes to the same thing'. But it does not at all come to the same thing. In the usual writings on the subject, the death of Jesus derives, in the final analysis, from God and not from men—which is why the enemies of Christianity can use the argument that it belongs within the same schema as all the other primitive religions. Here we have the difference between the religions that remain subordinated to the powers and the act of destroying those powers through a form of transcendence that never acts by means of violence, is never responsible for any violence, and remains radically opposed to violence.

Presentations of Christ's Passion as obedience to an absurd sacrificial order disregard the texts that show it involves, of necessity, the love of one's neighbour, demonstrating that only death can bring this love to its fullest expression:

> We know that we have passed out of death into life, because we love the brethren. He who does not love abides in death. Any one who hates his brother is a murderer, and you know that no murderer has eternal life abiding in him. By this we know love, that he laid down his life for us; and we ought to lay down our lives for the brethren (1 John 3, 14-15).

Not to love one's brother and to kill him are the same thing. Every negation of the other leads, as we have shown, toward expulsion and murder. The basis for all of this lies in the fundamental human situation of a mimetic rivalry that leads to a destructive escalation. That is the reason why killing and dying are simply one and the same thing. To kill is to die, to die is to kill—for both stay within the circle of evil reciprocity, in which reprisals inevitably take place. Not to love is to die, therefore, since it is to kill. Cain—who is mentioned in the Epistle a few lines earlier—said: 'Now that I have killed my brother, everyone can kill me.' Everything that could be taken for a rupture in the text that we are following is in reality part and parcel of all the rest within the terms of the gospel logic. There must be no hesitation about giving one's own life in order not to kill, so as to break out, by this action, from the circle of murder and death. It is quite literally true, when we are concerned with the confrontation of *doubles*, that he who wishes to save his life will lose it; he will be obliged, in effect, to kill his brother, and that means dying in a state of fatal misunderstanding of the other and of himself.

He who agrees to lose his life will keep it for eternal life, for he alone is not a killer, he alone knows the fullness of love.

J.-M. O.: There is also a contradiction between what Jesus says about his relations with the Father, which do not involve any violence or any concealed element, and the assertion of a need for sacrifice that has its origin in the Father and requires the obedience of the Son. This economy of violence, which is not human but divine, can only be rooted, from the standpoint of the Gospel, in a projection of human violence on to God.

The Divinity of Christ

R. G.: The Gospels tell us that to escape violence it is necessary to love one's brother completely—to abandon the violent mimesis involved in the relationship of doubles. There is no trace of it in the Father, and all that the Father asks is that we refrain from it likewise.

That is indeed why the Son promises men that if they manage to behave as the Father wishes, and to do his will, they will all become sons of God. It is not God who sets up the barriers between himself and mankind, but mankind itself.

G. L.: Does not that amount to eliminating any barrier between God and humanity—which would be the same as making humans godlike, in the same way as Feuerbach and the nineteenth-century humanists did?

R. G.: To hold that view you have to believe that love, in the Christian sense of the term—Nygren's *agape*[62]—is like common sense for Descartes: the thing that is, of all others, most common among human beings. In effect, love of this kind has been lived to its end only by Jesus himself. On this earth, therefore, only the Christ has ever succeeded in equalling God in the perfection of his love. Theologians do not take note of the founding murder and the way in which everyone is trapped by violence, in complicity with violence; that is why they are fearful of compromising divine transcendence by taking the words of the gospels at face value. They have no need to worry. Nothing in these words risks making the divine too accessible to humankind.

You shall love the Lord your God with all your heart, and with all your soul, and with all your mind. This is the great and first commandment. *And a second is like it*, You shall love your neighbour as yourself (Matthew 22, 37-39; Mark 12, 28-31; Luke 10, 25-28).

The two commandments are like one another because love makes no distinctions between beings. Jesus himself says this. And we can repeat it after him with no fear of 'humanizing' the Christian text overmuch. If the Son of Man and the Son of God are one and the same, it is because Jesus is the only person to achieve humanity in its perfect form, and so to be one with the deity.

The gospel text, especially John but also to a certain extent the synoptic Gospels, establish beyond any doubt the fact that Jesus is both God and Man. The theology of the Incarnation is not just a fantastic and irrelevant invention of the theologians; it adheres rigorously to the logic implicit in the text. But it only succeeds in becoming intelligible if we read the text in non-sacrificial rather than sacrificial terms. This is, in effect, the only time that this notion of a fullness of humanity that is also a fullness of divinity makes sense in a context that is as 'humanist' as it is 'religious'. If Jesus is the only one who can fully reveal the way in which the founding murder has broadened its hold upon mankind, this is because at no point did it take hold upon him. Jesus explains to us mankind's true vocation, which is to throw off the hold of the founding murder.

The non-sacrificial reading allows us to understand that the Son alone is united with the Father in the fullness of humanity and divinity. But it does not imply that this union is an exclusive one, or prevent us from envisaging the possibility of mankind becoming like God through the Son's mediation. Indeed, this process could only take place through him, since he is the only Mediator, the one bridge between the Kingdom of violence and the Kingdom of God. By remaining absolutely faithful to God's Word, in a world that had not received the Word, he succeeded in transmitting it all the same. He has managed to inscribe in the gospel text the reception that mankind in its slavery to violence was obliged to offer him—a reception that amounted to driving him out. If we go beyond this point, we would become involved in questions of *faith* and *grace*, which our anthropological perspective is not competent to address.

The non-sacrificial reading is not to be equated with a humanist reading, in the ordinary sense, one which would try to cut the distinctively religious aspects out of the gospel text. Although it brings to light the powerful demystificatory aspect of the Gospels, it has no difficulty in drawing attention to the religious aspects as well and in demonstrating their crucial importance, just as it draws attention to the great canonical statements about Jesus' divinity and his union with the Father.

Far from eliminating divine transcendence, the non-sacrificial reading shows it to be so far from us, in its very closeness, that we did not even suspect it to be there. Invariably, it has been concealed and covered up by transcendent violence—by all the powers and principalities that we have stupidly identified with it, to some extent at least. To rid ourselves of this confusion, to detect transcendent love—which remains invisible beyond the transcendent violence that stands between—we have to accept the idea that human violence is a deceptive worldview and recognize how the forms of misunderstanding that arise from it operate.

This differentiation between the two forms of transcendence appears negligible and absurd from the point of view of the violent mentality that possesses us—a mentality concerned with detecting the structural similarities between the gospel enactment and the basic workings of all other religions: workings that we have ourselves been concerned to expose. These analogies are real ones, just as are analogies between the evil reciprocity of violence and the benevolent reciprocity of love. Since both surpass all cultural differences, the two structures, paradoxically, amount to very much the same thing, which is why it is possible to pass from one to the other by means of an almost instantaneous conversion. But at the same time, there is also a radical, an abysmal opposition between them, something that *no form of structural analysis can detect*: we see in a mirror, darkly, *in aenigmate*.

J.-M. O.: Precisely because the revelation of violence has always been greeted with incomprehension, it becomes easier to understand why the Christian text puts before us someone who triumphs over violence by not resisting it, and as the direct emissary of the God of non-violence, shows his message emanating directly from him.

Within the human community, which is the prisoner of unanimous violence and of mythical meanings, there is no opportunity for this truth to be entertained, let alone to carry the day.

People are most open to the truth at the stage when false differences melt away, but this is also the point when they are most in the dark, since it is the point at which violence becomes even more intense.

Whenever violence starts to reveal itself as the basis of the community, it is accompanied by the manifestations one might expect at an acutely violent crisis, when mankind lacks the least vestige of lucidity. It almost seems as if violence is always able to conceal the truth about itself, whether by causing the mechanism of transference to operate and re-establish the regime of the sacred, or by pushing destruction as far as it will go.

Either you are violently opposed to violence and inevitably play its game, or you are not opposed to it, and it shuts your mouth immediately. In other words, the regime of violence cannot possibly be brought out into the open. Since the truth about violence will not abide in the community, but must inevitably be driven out, its only chance of being heard is when it is in the process of being driven out, in the brief moment that precedes its destruction as the victim. The victim therefore has to reach out at the very moment when his mouth is being shut by violence. He has to say enough for the violence to be incited against him. But this must not take place in the dark, hallucinatory atmosphere that characterizes other religions and produces the intellectual confusion that helps conceal their founding mechanism. There must be witnesses who are clear-sighted enough to recount the event as it really happened, altering its significance as little as possible.

For this to happen, the witnesses must already have been influenced by this extraordinary person. They themselves will not escape the hold of the collective violence; but it will be temporary. Afterwards, they will recover and write down in a form that is not transfigured the event that is primarily a transfiguration.

This unprecedented task of revealing the truth about violence requires a man who is not obliged to violence for anything and does not think in terms of violence—someone who is capable of talking back to violence while remaining entirely untouched by it.

It is impossible for such a human being to arise in a world completely ruled by violence and the myths based on violence. In order to understand that you cannot see and make visible the truth except by taking the place of the victim, you must already be occupying that place; yet to take that place, you must already be occupying that place; yet to take that place, you must already be in possession of the truth. You cannot become aware of the truth unless you act in opposition to the laws of violence, and you cannot act in opposition to these laws unless you already grasp the truth. All mankind is caught within this vicious circle.

For this reason the Gospels and the whole New Testament, together with the theologians of the first councils, proclaim that Christ is God not because he was crucified, but because he is God born of God from all eternity.

J.-M. O.: To sum up: the proclamation of Christ's divinity, in the sense of non-violence and love, is not in any way a sudden disconnection or a break in the logic of the texts that we are elucidating. In fact, it forms the only possible conclusion to this logic.

R. G.: The authentic knowledge about violence and all its works to be found in the Gospels cannot be the result of human action alone. Our own inability to grasp knowledge that has been waiting there for two millennia confirms theological intuitions that are no less certain for being incapable of setting out explicitly their foundations in reason. These rational foundations can only become intelligible if we proceed beyond the sacrificial version of Christianity, and are guided by the non-sacrificial reading which can emerge when the other one has fallen away.

G. L.: So theology is not being hyperbolic when it proclaims the divinity of Jesus. The belief is not just an excessive piece of praise, the product of a kind of rhetorical overkill. It is the only fit response to an inescapable constraint.

R. G.: To recognize Christ as God is to recognize him as the only being capable of rising above the violence that had, up to that point, absolutely transcended mankind. Violence is the controlling agent in every form of mythic or cultural structure, and Christ is the only agent who is capable of escaping from these structures and freeing us from their dominance. This is the only hypothesis that enables us to account for the revelation in the Gospel of what violence does to us and the accompanying power of that revelation to deconstruct the whole range of cultural texts, without exception. We do not have to adopt the hypothesis of Christ's divinity because it has always been accepted by orthodox Christians. Instead, this hypothesis is orthodox because in the first years of Christianity there existed a rigorous (though not yet explicit) intuition of the logic determining the gospel text.

A non-violent deity can only signal his existence to mankind by having himself driven out by violence—by demonstrating that he is not able to establish himself in the Kingdom of Violence.

But this very demonstration is bound to remain ambiguous for a long time, and it is not capable of achieving a decisive result, since it looks like total impotence to those who live under the regime of violence. That is why at first it can only have some effect under a guise, deceptive through the admixture of some sacrificial elements, through the surreptitious re-insertion of some violence into the conception of the divine.

The Virgin Birth

R. G.: Let us turn to the gospel themes that are on the surface most mythical in character, like the virgin birth of Jesus as it appears in Matthew and Luke. We notice at once that behind a superficial appearance of recounting fabulous events, the Gospels are always giving us a message exactly opposite to the one conveyed by mythology: the message of a non-violent deity, who has nothing in common with the epiphanies of the sacred.

Everything that is born of the world and of the 'flesh', as the prologue to John's Gospel puts it, is tainted by violence and ends up by reverting to violence. Every man is the brother of Cain, who was the first to bear the mark of this original violence.

In innumerable episodes of mythical birth, the god copulates with a mortal woman in order to give birth to a hero. Stories of this kind always involve more than a hint of violence. Zeus bears down on Semele, the mother of Dionysus, like a beast of prey upon its victim, and in effect strikes her with lightning. The birth of the gods is always a kind of rape. In every case we rediscover various structural features that have already been touched upon; in particular, the feature of monstrosity. In every case we find the doubling effects, the mad oscillation of differences, and the psychotic alternation between all and nothing. These monstrous couplings between men, gods and beasts are in close correspondence with the phenomenon of reciprocal violence and its method of working itself out. The orgasm that appeases the god is a metaphor for collective violence.

G. L.: And not the other way round, as psychoanalysis would have us believe!

R. G.: Monstrous births provide mythology with a way of alluding to the violence which always haunts it and that gives rise to the most varied meanings. The child whose birth is at the same time human and divine is a particularly relevant metaphor for the thunderous resolution of reciprocal violence as it passes into a unanimous, reconciliatory violence and gives birth to a new cultural order.

To put its message across, no doubt the virgin birth of Jesus still resorts to the same 'code' as do the monstrous births of mythology. But precisely because the codes are parallel, we should be able to understand the message and appreciate what is unique to it—what makes it radically different from the messages of mythology.

No relationship of violence exists between those who take part in the virgin birth: the Angel, the Virgin and the Almighty. No one here is playing the role of the *mimetic antagonist*, in the sense of the 'enemy twins': no one becomes the fascinating obstacle that one is tempted to remove or shatter by violence. The complete absence of any sexual element has nothing to do with repression—an explanation thought up at the end of the nineteenth century and worthy of the degraded puritanism that produced it. The fact that sexuality is not part of the picture corresponds to the absence of the violent mimesis with which myth acquaints us in the form of rape by the gods. This idol—what we have called the model-obstacle—is completely absent.

In fact, all the themes and terms associated with the virgin birth convey to us a perfect submission to the non-violent will of the God of the Gospels, who in this way prefigures Christ himself:

'Hail, O favoured one, the Lord is with you!' (Luke 1, 28)

The unprecented event brings no scandal with it. Mary does not set up any obstacle between herself and the Word of God:

'Behold I am the handmaid of the Lord; let it be to me according to your word' (Luke 1, 38).

The various episodes around the birth of Christ, make palpable the humble beginnings of the revelation, its complete insignificance from the standpoint of the mighty. Right from the start the child Jesus is excluded and dismissed—he is a wanderer who does not even have a stone on which to lay his head. The inn has no room for him. Informed by the Magi, Herod searches everywhere for him in order to put him to death.

Throughout these episodes, the Gospels and the Christian tradition,

taking their cue from the Old Testament, place in the foreground beings foredoomed to play the part of victim—the child, the woman, the
pauper and domestic animals.

The Gospels can make use of a mythological code in this account of
the birth of Jesus without being brought down to the level of the clumsy
mystification and 'mystical naivety', which our philosophers customarily see in them.

Our own period's summary dismissal of them is in fact quite revealing, because reactions have become outmoded for the violent mythologies. We may congratulate ourselves on having made some progress,
but this still leaves the message of non-violence out of account—among
all the others, the Christian message alone is universally despised and
rejected.

G. L.: So the only religion it is still permissible to disdain and ridicule, in intellectual circles, is also the only one that expresses something
different from violence and a failure to come to terms with violence. We
can hardly fail to ask ourselves what such a blind spot might imply in a
world dominated by nuclear weapons and industrial pollution. Are the
beliefs of our intellectuals as out of tune as they themselves like to think
with the world that has brought them into being?

R. G.: There is no more telling feature than the inability of the
greatest minds in the modern world to grasp the difference between the
Christian crib at Christmas-time and the bestial monstrosities of
mythological births. Here, for example, is what Nietzsche writes in *The
Anti-Christ*, after he has drawn attention, as a good follower of Hegel, to
what he terms the 'atemporal symbolism' of Father and Son that in his
view dominates the Christian text:

> I am ashamed to recall what the Church has made of this symbol-
> ism: has it not placed an Amphitryon story at the threshold of the
> Christian 'faith'?[63]

We could well ask why Nietzsche might be *ashamed* to discover in the
Gospels something he acclaims enthusiastically when he comes across it
somewhere else. After all, the Amphitryon myth is one of the most
splendidly Dionysiac myths of all. The birth of Hercules seems to me to
square very well with the will to power, and indeed it contains all the

elements that Nietzsche praises in *The Birth of Tragedy* and other writings.

It is important to try and explain the reasons for this *shame*. It tells us a good deal about the double standard that all modern thought—taking after Nietzsche and his rivals—applies to the study of Christian 'mythology'.

A great many modern theologians succumb to the terrorism of modern thought and condemn without a hearing something they are not capable of experiencing even as 'poetry' any more—the final trace in the world of a spiritual intuition that is fast fading. So Paul Tillich dismisses in the most peremptory way the theme of the virgin birth because of what he calls 'the inadequacy of its internal symbolism'.[64]

In Luke the theme of the virgin birth is not all that different when you come down to it, from the Pauline thesis defining Christ as the second Adam, or the perfect Adam. Saying that Christ is God, born of God, and saying that he has been conceived without sin is stating over again that he is completely alien to the world of violence within which humankind has been imprisoned ever since the foundation of the world: that is to say, ever since Adam. The first Adam was himself also without sin, and it was he who, in becoming the first sinner, caused humankind to enter the vicious circle from which it has never been able to break out. Christ is thus in the same situation as Adam, facing the same temptations as he did—the same temptations as all humanity, in effect. But he wins the struggle against violence; he wins, on behalf of all humankind, the paradoxical struggle that all people, in the succession of Adam, have always been fated to lose.

If Christ alone is innocent, then Adam is not the only one to be guilty. All men share in this archetypal state of blame, but only to the extent that the chance of becoming free has been offered to them and they have let it slip away. We can say that this sin is indeed *original* but only becomes actual when knowledge about violence is placed at humanity's disposition.

CHAPTER THREE

The Sacrificial Reading and Historical Christianity

Implications of the Sacrificial Reading

R. G.: I feel that the non-sacrificial reading brings all the great canonical dogmas back into play, making them intelligible by articulating them more coherently than has been possible up to now.

I also believe that the sacrificial interpretation of the Passion and the Redemption cannot legitimately be extrapolated from the text of the New Testament—though an exception must perhaps be made in the case of the Epistle to the Hebrews.

Without in any way seeking to 'justify' this interpretation, we shall know how far it is predictable and necessary within the economy of revelation that systematically gives more and more striking proofs of the deafness and blindness of those 'who have ears and hear not, eyes and see not'.

G. L.: If I follow you correctly, this revelation consistently makes the sacrificial Christians play a role like that of the Pharisees confronted with the first preaching of the Kingdom of God.

R. G.: Yes, indeed. The task is to show that the Christian sons have repeated, even aggravated, all the errors of their Judaic fathers. The Christians have condemned the Jews, but they themselves are condemned by Paul's statement in the Epistle to the Romans: 'In passing judgement upon him you condemn yourself, because you, the judge, are doing the very same things' (Romans 2, 1).

In a remarkable paradox, but one that accords well with the sacrificial course of mankind, the sacrificial reading (that is, the logic of the violent Logos) refashions the mechanism that has been revealed and thus of necessity annihilated—if the revelation were genuinely accepted—into a kind of sacrificial cultural foundation. This is the foundation that both 'Christianity' and the modern world have rested upon, right up to our own time.

J.-M. O.: That is certainly true. Historical Christianity holds a number of structural features in common with all other cultural forms: for example, the 'scapegoating' of the Jews. We have shown how this expulsion works on the textual level. But of course it is not merely a textual mechanism, and terrible historical consequences have arisen from it.

R. G.: I believe it is possible to demonstrate that historical Christianity took on a persecutory character as a result of the sacrificial reading of the Passion and the Redemption.

All the features of the sacrificial reading cohere. The very fact that the deity is reinfused with violence has consequences for the entire system, since it partially absolves mankind from a responsibility that ought to be equal and identical for all.

Reducing the responsibility enables one to particularize the Christian event, to diminish its universality, and to search for the guilty men who would absolve humankind of guilt—the role the Jews fulfill. At the same time, violence continues to have repercussions, as we have seen, in the apocalyptic destruction that traditional readings still project upon the deity.

What turns Christianity in on itself, so that it presents a hostile face to all that is not Christian, is inextricably bound up with the sacrificial reading. That reading cannot possibly be *innocent*. It is not difficult to demonstrate the close connections between resacralization and the historical development of Christianity—which is structurally parallel to that of all cultures being characterized, like them, by the gradual exhaustion of sacrificial resources, amid the increasing disintegration of all cultural formations.

Because Christians have been incapable of understanding the relationship of Christ to his own death, they have followed the Epistle to the Hebrews and taken up the term 'sacrifice'. They have seen only the structural analogy between the Passion and the sacrifices of the Old Law, and in doing so they have failed to take into account an incompatibility. They have not noticed that the sacrifices of the Jewish religion and the sacrifices of all other religions simply *reflect* what the words of Christ, and his subsequent death, actually *reveal*: the founding death of the scapegoat.

This initial mistake also accounts for the blindness of the anthropologists, who are convinced that precise tabulation of these particular analogies will refute the Christian text's claims to universality.

Modern anti-Christianity is merely the reversal of sacrificial Christianity and as a result helps to perpetuate it. On no occasion does this anti-Christian movement return to the text in any real sense and seek to expose it to radical re-thinking. It remains piously in awe of the sacrificial reading, and it cannot operate in any other way, since that is where it directs its criticism. Sacrifice is what atheistic humanism wishes to see in Christianity, and sacrifice is what it denounces as an abomination. As far as sacrifice goes, I share this opinion. But I think that the anti-Christian critique never understands what sacrifice actually is. If it were to give serious attention to this question, it would discover that it was not alone in feeling repugnance to the sacrificial; rather, all the feelings it takes pride in would turn out to be Christian feelings that have been falsified, deformed and to some extent neutralized by the deep-rooted presence within us of the very thing from which we believed ourselves free—that is, sacrifice. It would come to the conclusion that Christianity has already made this critique, and that it alone has the capacity to follow it through to the end.

The word 'sacrifice'—sacri-fice—means making sacred, producing the sacred. What sacrifices the victim is the blow delivered by the sacrificer, the violence that kills this victim, annihilating it and placing it above everything else by making it in some sense immortal. Sacrifice takes place when sacred violence takes charge of the victim; it is the death that produces life, just as life produces death, in the uninterrupted circle of eternal recurrence common to all the great theological views that are grafted upon sacrificial practices—those that do not acknowledge the demystifying effect of the Judaeo-Christian tradition. It is not by chance that Western philosophy begins, and up to a certain point ends, in the 'intuition' of the Eternal Recurrence that the pre-Socratics and Nietzsche hold in common. This is the sacrificial intuition *par excellence*.

The sacrificial reading is basically a form of regression—slight but consequential—to the notions of the Old Testament. To clarify this claim, we need only recall the texts by the second Isaiah quoted in an earlier discussion—those 'Songs of the Servant of Yahweh' in which the Gospels and then the whole Christian tradition saw the most striking *figura Christi* of the Old Testament. They were right to do so, since we have here a scapegoat that has already been partially revealed. The fact that the community has banded together unanimously against the Servant in order to persecute and kill him does not alter the victim's innocence, or the community's guilt. Already in this text everything is Christian, with the reservation that Yahweh still bears a certain responsibility for the death of the Servant. There can be no question of attributing this divine responsibility to a later interpretation that falsifies the text. It figures quite explicitly in the text itself, which includes sentences like the following: 'He was cut off out of the land of the living, stricken for the transgression of my people' (Isaiah 53, 8), and again: 'Yet it was the will of the Lord to bruise him' (Isaiah 53, 10).

I believe we have here an intermediate form of religion, which lies between the purely sacrificial norms of 'primitive' religions, as conveyed in the myths we have commented upon, after Lévi-Strauss, and the radically non-sacrificial Gospels. The truth of the scapegoat is almost at the point of being expressed, but it is neutralized by formulas that involve God in the process. We have, therefore, an unstable combination, some of whose elements announce the God of the Gospels and all that we have called the transcendence of love, while others still belong to the universal religion of the past. Religious thought is already on the path that leads to the gospel text, but it has not yet succeeded in freeing itself completely from concepts that derive their structure from transcendent violence.

The sacrificial theology of Christianity does not correspond to the Gospels, but it does correspond exactly to the 'Songs of the Servant of Yahweh'. Although medieval thinkers always affirmed the essential difference between the two Testaments, they never succeeded in defining exactly what this difference was—and this is hardly surprising. We have already spoken of the tendency of medieval and modern exegesis to read the New Testament in the light of the Old: for example, John 8, 43-44 is read in the 'light' of Cain and Abel. People who claim to be reading the Old Testament in the light of the New are doing the reverse much of the time, without being aware of it, for they have not yet recovered the 'key to science' that had been already lost by the Pharisees.

The Epistle to the Hebrews

J.-M. O.: Yet one text in the New Testament advocates a sacrificial interpretation of the Passion. This is the Epistle to the Hebrews, a text whose place in the canon was, as I understand it, long disputed.

R. G.: The author of the Epistle to the Hebrews interprets Christ's death on the basis of the sacrifices under the Old Law. The new bond with God, like the old one, is inaugurated in blood. But as it is perfect, is is no longer the blood of animals which is 'powerless to remove sins', but the blood of Christ. Since Christ is perfect, his blood suffices to accomplish once and for all what the sacrifices of the Old Law could not:

> . . . Indeed, under the law almost everything is purified with blood, and without the shedding of blood there is no forgiveness of sins. Thus it was necessary for the copies of the heavenly things to be purified with these rites, but the heavenly things themselves with better sacrifices that these. For Christ has entered not into a sanctuary made with hands, a copy of the true one, but into heaven itself, now to appear in the presence of God on our behalf. Nor was it to offer himself repeatedly, as the high priest enters the Holy Place yearly with blood not his own; for then he would have had to suffer repeatedly since the foundation of the world. But as it is, he has appeared once for all at the end of the age to put away sin by the sacrifice of himself. . .
>
> And every priest stands daily at his service, offering repeatedly the same sacrifices, which can never take away sins. But when Christ had offered for all time a single sacrifice for sins, he sat down at the right hand of God, then to wait until his enemies should be made a stool for his feet. For by a single offering he has perfected for all time those who are sanctified (Hebrews 9, 22-26; 10, 11-14).

According to this Epistle, there is certainly a difference between Christ's Passion and the sacrifices that have gone before. But this difference is still defined within the context of the sacrificial, and consequently the real essence of the sacrificial is never examined. Like all the variants that are to follow, this first attempt at a sacrificial theology is based on analogies between the form of the Passion and the form of all other sacrifices, but it allows the essential feature to escape.

Certainly the believer rightly sees an enormous difference between Christianity and the sacrifices of the Old Testament. But he can give no justification for this difference as long as he continues to define everything in sacrificial terms. He may well say that Christ's sacrifice is, by contrast with the others, unique, perfect and definitive. But in reality he can see only continuity with previous sacrifices, if he takes no account of the scapegoat mechanism. As long as the Christian difference is defined in sacrificial terms, as all former differences among religions have been defined, it will eventually be effaced.

This is exactly what has happened. The difference that was arbitrarily held to exist within the institution of sacrifice has given way to a regime of continuity and identity between sacrifices that comprises not just the Old Law but the entire planet. The modern preoccupation with 'demystifying' the Christian message and proving to Christians that there is nothing original in their religion is a product of the process of wear and tear in the sacrificial institution, and it still has its basis—by virtue of this fact—in the reading advocated by the Epistle to the Hebrews. It carries the implications of the Epistle to a further stage, while retaining its basis in the Epistle's failure to see anything but irrational structural analogies among the whole range of sacrifices, including the one attributed to Christ.

The criticism of comparative anthropology is effective. But it only works against the Epistle to the Hebrews and the innumerable readings to which it has given rise. The whole enterprise of demystification is based, like the sacrificial conception of Christianity, on a confusion between the Epistle to the Hebrews and the Gospels. Anti-Christians show no sign of wanting to relinquish this reading, any more than so-called traditionalist Christians do. Both groups regard the sacrificial definition as providing the final, essential meaning of the Christian text. All these disputes between *doubles* require preliminary agreement on the manner in which the fundamental problem must be defined.

To justify its sacrificial reading, the Epistle to the Hebrews invokes Psalm 40, which it puts into Christ's own mouth. This is how the version of the psalm quoted in the Epistle reads:

> Sacrifices and offerings thou hast not desired,
> but a body hast thou prepared for me;
> in burnt offerings and sin offerings thou hast taken no pleasure.
> Then I said, 'Lo, I have come to do thy will, O God,'
> as it is written of me in the roll of the book (Hebrews 10, 5-7).

The Epistle interprets this text as if it were a sacrificial dialogue between God and Christ, with mankind excluded. But the Judaic reading rightly stresses that this psalm is addressed to all the faithful. If God is no longer content with sacrifices—if worship has lost its efficacy—then the wish to obey Yahweh puts all the faithful under a new set of obligations. There are no longer any restrictions on what is required by the Law.

What if we have here a summons that is addressed to all the faithful, not to a single person, but only one just man responds to it? For this Just Man, the fact that sacrifices have become completely useless and that the Law is being radically reinterpreted, must produce a situation in which the only path open to him is the supreme . . . 'sacrifice'. The rest of the psalm demonstrates the point well. If there is a special bond between Yahweh and the Just Man, and if this bond threatens to bring about the latter's death, then this is not because Yahweh and the Just Man are joined in a sacrificial pact from which all others are excluded. It is not an agreement from which all others have been barred *a priori*. On the contrary, they have excluded themselves by refusing to listen to God's summons. The rest of the psalm makes the consequences of this deafness obvious. Because they refuse to obey Yahweh, men conspire together against the Just Man; they treat him as a collective victim:

> Be pleased, O Lord, to deliver me!
>   O Lord, make haste to help me!
> Let them be put to shame and confusion altogether
>   who seek to snatch away my life;
> let them be turned back and brought to dishonour
>   who desire my hurt!
> Let them be appalled because of their shame
>   who say to me, 'Aha, Aha!' (Psalm 40, 13-15).

This psalm is genuinely close to the Gospels because it is close to the Kingdom and the rule of the Kingdom. This is so because it recognizes, like all the great texts of the Old and New Testament, that when the crisis reaches its paroxysm, the person who lends his ear to the commandment of love—the person who interprets the Law with rigour—will be confronted with the choice of killing or being killed.

Certainly the psalm is *christological*. But the Epistle to the Hebrews excises a number of the most important actors in a scene whose consequences are fully developed only in the Gospels, though it is sketched in the psalm: the scene of the collective murder of the Just Man.[65]

The author of the Epistle to the Hebrews would, of course, be the first to acknowledge that Christ was unjustly put to death. But his sacrificial reading takes little account of human responsibility for the death of Christ. The murderers are merely the instruments of divine will; it is hard to see how they could be found guilty. Here we have the most familiar ground for objecting to sacrificial theology, and there is no doubt that it must and can be answered.

It is the murderers who carry on the sacrifices and holocausts that Yahweh no longer wishes to hear of. It is from their perspective that the Passion can still be seen as a sacrifice—not from that of the victim, who understands that God holds all sacrifices in abomination and that he is dying because he will have nothing whatsoever to do with them. *Sacrifice and offering thou dost not desire. . . Holocaust and victim thou hast not required*.

To sum up: the Epistle to the Hebrews re-enacts what is re-enacted in all earlier formulations of sacrifice. It discharges human violence, but to a lesser degree. It restates God's responsibility for the death of the victim, it also leaves a place, though indeterminate, for human responsibility. Sacrificial theology is on the same level as the theology implied in the second Isaiah.

Like all the oppositions that proliferate in and around the Judaeo-Christian scriptures, Judaism and historical Christianity are fundamentally in agreement here. Both fail to find a place for the revelation of human violence. They skirt this revelation without ever understanding that they are *doubles* one of another—that the only thing separating them is what, at the same time, unites them.[66]

The Death of Christ and the End of the Sacred

J.-M. O.: Would you say then that your critique of the sacrificial reading impels you to deny that there is any sacred—in the sense of violent—element in Jesus' death?

R. G.: Yes, indeed. I think that it is necessary to rid ourselves of the sacred, for the sacred plays no part in the death of Jesus. If the Gospels have Jesus pronounce on the Cross those words of anguished impotence and final surrender, 'Eli, Eli, lama sabachtani'—if they allow three symbolic days to elapse between death and resurrection—this is not to diminish faith in the resurrection or in the all-powerful Father. It is to make quite clear that we are dealing with something entirely different from the sacred. Here life does not come directly out of the violence, as in primitive religions. Christ is not born again from his own ashes like the phoenix. He does not play with life and death like a kind of Dionysus. That is what the theme of the empty tomb is designed to show.

In this case, death no longer has anything at all to do with life. The naturalistic character of this death is underlined, together with human powerlessness before death—aggravated by the crowd's hostile bearing and ironically emphasized by those who confuse Jesus' references to the deity with the primitive *mana*, the power that comes from sacred violence. The crowd challenges Jesus to provide them with an unmistakable sign of his power: to come down from the Cross and distance himself from the sufferings and humiliation of his long and inglorious agony:

> And those who passed by derided him, wagging their heads and saying, 'You who would destroy the temple and build it in three days, save yourself! If you are the Son of God, come down from the cross.' So also the chief priests, with the scribes and elders, mocked him, saying, 'He saved others; he cannot save himself. He is the King of Israel; let him come down now from the cross, and we will believe in him. He trusts in God; let God deliver him now, if he desires him; for he said, 'I am the Son of God'. And the robbers who were crucified with him reviled him in the same way (Matthew 27, 39-44).

The controversies to which the 'Eli, Eli, lama sabachtani' has given rise among believers and unbelievers demonstrate how difficult it is to escape from the sacred and the violent. Unbelievers have always regarded this phrase as the *little true fact* that 'gives the game away' and controverts the falsifications of the theologians. Believers reply that these words are a scriptural quotation, from the beginning of Psalm 22. And they tend to regard this quotation as merely decorative, rather like a sentence from Plutarch that crops up in a page of Montaigne. Some people have even claimed that the act of quoting from the scriptures proves that Jesus retained complete mastery of himself, right up to the point of death. I mention commentaries of this kind only to show that believers as well as unbelievers still entertain the same magical, sacrificial conception of the deity—treating Christ like a hero from Corneille.

In *La Chute*, Albert Camus makes his central character observe that

'Eli, Eli, lama sabachtani' has been 'censored' by two Gospels out of four.[67] But Simone Weil shows herself to be incomparably more profound when she takes the presence of this particular sentence in the other two Gospels as a striking sign of their supernatural origin. To take upon itself so radically the naturalistic character of the death, the gospel text must be founded upon the unshakable certainty of a form of transcendence that leaves this death completely behind.

J.-M. O.: Your reading has been judged to be humanist because you attached great importance to 'Eli, Eli, lama sabachtani' when you entered into a debate published in *Esprit* in 1973. Modern thought places itself *in between* transcendence by violence—which it has not yet succeeded in demystifying completely—and what you call sur-transcendence through love, which violence still manages to conceal from us. People fail to see that it is not a question of controverting or undermining this sur-transcendence (as Christian commentators fear, and anti-Christian commentators hope), since everything that demythologizes the transcendence of violence reinforces and glorifies the sur-transcendence of love.

R. G.: What gives rise to the confusion, of course, is the habit of tracing structural analogies between the Passion and the sacrifices instituted by all other religions. The sacrificial reading, is capable only of seeing such analogies of this kind, and as we have shown, all anti-Christian arguments remain committed to this superficially structural reading. One can only escape these seductive analogies and detect the signs that point unequivocally to the opposition between the two forms of transcendence by realizing that the gospel text has achieved its anthropological fulfilment in the revelation of the founding mechanism.

To sum up: if Jesus' death were sacrificial, the Resurrection would be the 'product' of the Crucifixion. But this is not so. Orthodox theology has always successfully resisted the temptation to transform the Passion into a process that endows Jesus with divinity. In orthodox terms, Christ's divinity—though it is obviously not external to his humanity—is not dependent on the events of his earthly life. Instead of making the Crucifixion a *cause* of his divinity—which is a constant temptation for Christians—it is preferable to see it as a *consequence* of the latter. For the power of the Resurrection, it would be better to use a word other than 'sacred', if we reserve this word, as I do, for the religions of the hidden scapegoat.

Behaving in a truly divine manner, on an earth still in the clutches of violence, means not dominating humans, not overwhelming them with supernatural power; it means not terrifying and astonishing them in turn, through the sufferings and blessings one can confer; it means not creating difference between doubles and not taking part in their disputes. 'God is no respecter of persons.' He makes no distinction between 'Greeks and Jews, men and women, etc.'. This can look like complete indifference and can lead to the conclusion that the all-powerful does not exist, so long as his transcendence keeps him infinitely far from us and our violent undertakings. But the same characteristics are revealed as a heroic and perfect love once this transcendence becomes incarnate in a human being and walks among men, to teach them about the true God and to draw them closer to Him.

Our first concern has been to bring the founding mechanism out into the open. All the rest flows directly from that, not because the gospel texts can be reduced to a purely anthropological content, but because we cannot come to terms with their true religious content as long as we remain incapacitated, as we have been since time immemorial, to understand their anthropological content.

G. L.: But only in John are the scenes of the Crucifixion totally cleansed of any sign of the miraculous. And yet you attach equal importance to all four Gospels. How do you explain the element of the miraculous which gets into the synoptic Gospels? Does it not override your arguments?

R. G.: In Mark and Luke, there is only one such sign, which has a remarkable symbolic import. It is the rending of the Temple veil from top to bottom. The veil of the Temple conceals the mystery of sacrifice—it makes material and concrete the misrecognition at the basis of the sacrificial system. For the veil to be rent, therefore, is tantamount to saying that by his death Jesus has triumphed over this mis-recognition (Mark 15, 38; Luke 23, 45).

In Matthew, the miraculous effects of the Crucifixion are more spectacular. But the most notable of them returns us once again, in spite of first appearances, to the anthropological, demystificatory significance of the Passion:

> . . . the tombs also were opened, and many bodies of the saints who had fallen asleep were raised, and coming out of the tombs after his

resurrection they went into the holy city and appeared to many (Matthew 27, 52-53).

We are not making the Resurrection an exclusively religious theme if we recognize that it is homologous with the essential task of scripture, which is bringing to light all the victims buried by mankind—not in the interests of death but in the interests of life. These are the victims who have been assassinated since the foundation of the world, who begin to return upon this earth and make themselves known.

Sacrifice of the Other and Sacrifice of the Self

R. G.: We have now clearly detected and defined the error implicit in the sacrificial definition and the innumerable consequences which it brings with it. We can see that it provokes misinterpretation of the texts and again veils revelation. Now we must examine some of the other features of this definition and realize its significance for those who claim to abide by it, even today.

Its significance remains, of necessity, everything all previous religions meant when they had recourse to sacrifice. Although they are incapable of understanding the real significance of what has taken place, men of good faith are aware that something real has happened, something beyond ordinary humanity. Faced by this unprecedented event, it seems natural and no doubt inevitable to have recourse to the sacrificial terminology that has always sufficed.

So many people remain attached to this terminology because they can see no other signifiers that will enable them to affirm the transcendent character of the gospel revelation against those who try to purge Christianity of sacrifice by methods that are still sacrificial, in effect, since they consist in totally excising its transcendental dimension.

People who believe that they can defend transcendence while retaining sacrifice are misguided in my opinion. The sacrificial definition, which has always been sedulously preserved by anti-Christian critics, facilitates today's atheism and all the talk about the death of God. What is in fact finally dying is the sacrificial concept of divinity preserved by medieval and modern theology—not the Father of Jesus, not the divinity of the Gospels, which we have been hindered—and still are hindered—from approaching, precisely by the stumbling block of sacrifice. In effect, this sacrificial concept of divinity must 'die', and with it the whole apparatus of historical Christianity, for the Gospels to be able to rise again in our midst, not looking like a corpse that we have exhumed, but revealed as the newest, finest, liveliest and truest thing that we have ever set eyes upon.

The word 'sacrifice' has evolved considerably in the course of its long history, particularly under the influence of the Old Testament. It has expressed a number of attitudes and forms of behaviour essential to every form of communal life. But from the earliest times, religions have emphasized not the expiatory and propitiatory aspects of sacrifice, but the sacrificers' renunciation of the sacrificed creature, the object that is destroyed or consumed without any form of material compensation. Even the most 'primitive' forms of religion have tended to endow sacrifice with an ethical dimension, which extends beyond prohibition because it cannot be reduced to abstention, to behaving in a negative way. The offering of sacrifices creates an ethic appropriate to itself.

The interaction between prohibition and ritual seems to lie at the root of the social attitudes that can be described as ethical. These attitudes and the reflection that they stimulate fall under the same rubric as all other cultural attitudes and indeed all human thought. Everything that touches humans is a product of religion: that is to say, it derives from the interaction of imperatives that can be traced back to the victimary unanimity. Here we are simply restating what we have already tried to demonstrate in the preceding discussions on anthropology.

In Judaism and Christianity sacrificial morality achieves its most refined expression. Christianity opposes all sacrifices of an object to the *self-sacrifice* exemplified by Christ—a type of sacrifice that ranks as the noblest possible form of conduct. It would of course be excessive to condemn everything put forward in this language of sacrifice. But in the light of our analyses, we are bound to conclude that any procedure involving sacrifice, even and indeed especially when it turns against the self, is at variance with the true spirit of the gospel text. The Gospels never present the rule of the Kingdom under the negative aspect of *self-sacrifice*. Far from being an exclusively Christian concept, which would form the summit of 'altruism' by contrast with an 'egoism' prone to sacrifice the other with gay abandon, self-sacrifice can serve to camouflage the forms of slavery brought into being by mimetic desire. 'Masochism' can also find expression in self-sacrifice, even if a person has no knowledge of this, and no wish to reveal it. What might be concealed here is the desire to sacralize *oneself* and make *oneself* godlike—which quite clearly harks back to the illusion traditionally produced by sacrifice.

The Judgement of Solomon

R. G.: Taking up my argument against the sacrificial reading of the Passion, I would like to invoke one of the finest texts in the Old Testament, the Judgement of Solomon.

The language of the Bible seems to me to combat sacrifice more effectively than does the language of modern philosophy and criticism. All the commentators who love the Bible go to it in the first place in order to understand it better. We shall follow their example:

> Then two harlots came to the King, and stood before him. The one woman said, 'Oh, my lord, this woman and I dwell in the same house; and I gave birth to a child while she was in the house. Then on the third day after I was delivered, this woman also gave birth; and we were alone; there was no one else with us in the house, only we two were in the house. And this woman's son died in the night, because she lay on it. And she arose at midnight, and took my son from beside me, while your maidservant slept, and laid it in her bosom, and laid her dead son in my bosom. When I rose in the morning to nurse my child, behold, it was dead; but when I looked at it closely in the morning, behold it was not the child that I had borne.' But the other woman said, 'No, the living child is mine, and the dead child is yours.' The first said, 'No, the dead child is yours, and the living child is mine.' Thus they spoke before the king.
>
> Then the king said, 'The one says, "This is my son that is alive, and your son is dead"; and the other says, "No; but your son is dead, and my son is the living one."' And the king said, 'Bring me a sword.' So a sword was brought before the king. And the king said, 'Divide the living child in two, and give half to the one, and half to the other.' Then the woman whose son was alive said to the king, because her heart yearned for her son, 'Oh, my lord, give her the living child, and by no means slay it.' But the other said, 'It shall be neither mind nor yours; divide it.' Then the king answered and said, 'Give the living child to the first woman, and by no means slay it; she is its mother.' And all Israel heard of the judgement which the king had rendered; and they stood in awe of the king, because they per-

ceived that the wisdom of God was in him, to render justice (I Kings 3, 16-28).

We have no trouble in recognizing that this text brings in the whole question of the mimetic crisis and the rivalry of doubles. The fact that both of the women are described as 'harlots' underlines the lack of differentiation between them.

Throughout the quarrel that leads to the king's brilliant stratagem, the text makes no distinction between the two women. It refers to them merely as 'one woman' and 'the other woman'. In effect, it does not matter in the slightest who is speaking, since both of them are saying precisely the same thing: 'No, the living child is mine, and the dead child is yours.' To which the other replies: 'No, the dead child is yours, and the living child is mine.' The symmetry is obvious, and it represents the very essence of human conflict—and there is nothing more to say. That is why the text only adds: 'thus they spoke before the king. . .'.

The only commentary that the king offers is an exact repetition of the words of the two women, which underlines once again their symmetry, the identity of their discourses, and confirms that the judge is powerless to make a rational decision in favour of one or the other.

As he cannot decide the case on any genuine basis, the king pretends to have decided to divide the child itself in two; being incapable of setting the antagonists apart, he decides to divide the object of the litigation. The Latin word *decidere* means etymologically to divide by the sacrificial knife, to cut the throat of a victim.

There is an element of logic and justice in this royal decision. But the justice, which is purely formal conceals a terrible injustice, since the child is not an object that can be divided in two. To do so would kill the child. By this murder the true mother will be deprived of her living child.

'Bring me a sword', commands the king, and the sword is brought to him. He then says, 'Divide the living child in two, and give half to the one and half to the other.' The king proposes to follow through his respect for the symmetry of the doubles; the symmetry of the terms used corresponds to the complete equality with which the two women are treated.

By accepting the king's proposal, the second woman reveals her lack of any genuine love for the child. The only thing that counts for her *is possessing what the other one possesses.* In the last resort, she is ready to accept being deprived of the child as long as her opponent is deprived of it in the same way. Quite clearly, mimetic desire impels her to speak and act; things have reached such a pitch of exasperation with her that the object of the quarrel, the living child, no longer counts; all that counts is her fascination with the hated model and rival—her feeling of resentment that impels her to involve this model in her own downfall, if it proves impossible to achieve any other triumph over it.

The scene Solomon stages is both a possible solution to the dilemma and a stratagem designed to bring real motherly sentiments to the fore, if they are present in either of the two women. By arranging things in this way, he inevitably recalls an important theme in the historical and prophetic books: the theme of child sacrifice, a custom that seems to have persisted until a relatively late date, if we are to judge by the repeated condemnations to which it gave rise. What would happen if the two women agreed to accept the decision of the king? Though the king does not 'put the child through flame', it is hard to read the text without picking up echoes of this custom, which still bore the title of 'abomination'.

No doubt the custom continued not just under the influence of neighbouring tribes but because it took its place among the legitimate forms of sacrifice for the Hebrews themselves, at a date that cannot easily be pinpointed. It therefore has the character of an historical survival. Many of the scenes from Genesis and Exodus are apparently concerned, on the historical level, with a state of transition from a world in which human sacrifice was practised on a regular basis, particularly the sacrifice of the first-born, to a world in which the only legitimate blood rites are circumcision and the burning of animal victims (Jacob's blessing, the sacrifice of Abraham, the circumcision of Moses's son, and so on).

There is no lack of texts to back up this hypothesis. From our standpoint its advantage is that it allows us to view the Bible permeated by a single, dynamic movement away from sacrifice. We can distinguish a number of very different stages—differing in their content and the results they produced—which are nonetheless identical in general bearing and form. This form always involves the preliminary disintegration of a pre-existing system, a catastrophic crisis that ends happily when the victimage mechanism provides a mediation, and the subsequent establishment of a sacrificial system that became more and more humane.

The first stage is the transition from human sacrifice to animal sacrifice in the so-called patriarchal period; the second, in Exodus, is the institution of Passover, which accentuates the common meal rather than the burnt sacrifice and can hardly claim to be a sacrifice at all in the proper sense of the term. The third stage is represented by the prophets' wish to renounce all forms of sacrifice, and this is only carried out in the Gospels.

I am speculating here, but however well-founded these thoughts may be, I do not need them to support my reading of the Judgement of Solomon. Even if the stratagem devised by Solomon has no connection whatsoever with child sacrifice, the way in which it is presented gives it a putative sacrificial function. Its point is to reconcile the doubles—to get beyond the king's incapacity to distinguish between them—by offering them the victim that would suffice to bring their quarrel to an end, since they would be able to share it, whereas they cannot share the living child.

So the 'solution' proposed by the king and accepted by one of the two women should be defined as sacrificial in the broad sense. But of course it would not be fair—in fact, it would be an abominable misconception—to use *the same term* to characterize the attitude of the good mother, the one who demonstrates the possession of maternal feelings and rejects the sacrificial solution with horror.

We cannot interpret the good mother's renunciation in terms of 'self-sacrifice'. We cannot say that the sacrifice, with her, has been turned back on itself—that it has been totally transformed from a transitive to a reflexive level, or from an objective to a subjective one. The abyss between the conduct of the two women cannot be measured in terms of a simple reversal. A simple reversal does not do justice to the radicalism of the difference.

I would not deny that when modern religious ethics refers to sacrifice by the real mother it is trying to put its finger on something genuine. The real mother is the only one with any rights in the child, and she is ready to 'sacrifice' them. We could even say that she puts herself forward as a sacrifice, in the sense that she can have no advance knowledge of how things will turn out. She cannot be sure that her sudden decision to renounce the child will not be interpreted *unfavourably to her*, as if she were incapable of keeping up her daring lie any longer in the presence of his majesty. She has no means of anticipating the monarch's 'divine wisdom'. So she risks her own life.

I can understand why the commentators are anxious to use a sacrificial vocabulary here. At the same time, I believe that this vocabulary misses the essential point and introduces confusion where there is most need of clear distinctions. Not only does it play down the difference between the ways in which the two women behave, but—for the second woman—it also transfers to the foreground what is of secondary importance: that is, the act of renunciation and the personal risk to which it exposes the real mother. The sacrificial definition relegates to the secondary level what is most important for the real mother—that her child should live.

The sacrificial definition always emphasizes renunciation, death, and split subjectivity; that is to say, it emphasises the values that belong to the bad mother, including the element of mimetic desire, which is identical with what Freud calls the death instinct.

Sacrificial language can only betray the values of the second woman, which are not directed toward suffering and death, not subordinated to a form of subjectivity that is both mimetic and solipsistic (the two always go together), and instead directed positively toward her neighbour and toward life. Sacrificial discourse cannot do justice to the crucial importance of life and the living in the very language of the text—to the fact that the child over whom the two women are quarrelling is always described as *the living child*.

The good mother has absolutely no inclination to 'sacrifice herself' in the abstract. She wishes to go on living to take care of her child. But she is ready to renounce her child for ever, even to renounce her own life if necessary, *in order to save his life*. This is her only motive and there is nothing 'sacrificial' about it.

This text can easily be applied to Christ's position in the stages leading up to the Passion. Those who read sacrificially do not appreciate the threat that weighs on the community, and since they cannot understand the implications of their own attitude, they are incapable of seeing that all of Christ's words and deeds—from the offer of the Kingdom to the Passion, not excepting the explicit disclosure of the founding murder—are determined by his will to save a humanity unable to see that all the old sacrificial solutions are now bankrupt and completely empty.

Christ's conduct parallels at every point that of the good harlot. She offers the most perfect *figura Christi* that can be imagined. Christ agrees to die so that mankind will live. We must beware of calling his action sacrificial, even if we then have no words or categories to convey its meaning. The very lack of appropriate language suggests that we are dealing with a type of conduct for which there is no precedent in the realm of mythology or philosophy, or indeed in the pragmatic sphere. Like Judah at the end of the Joseph story, the good harlot agrees to substitute herself for the sacrificial victim, not because she feels a morbid attraction to the role but because she has an answer to the tragic alternative: kill or be killed. The answer is: be killed, not as a result of masochism, or the 'death instinct', but *so that the child will live*. Christ himself—reaching the situation that reveals the ultimate basis of human community—also adopts an attitude that will necessarily expose him to the violence of a community unanimously bent on retaining sacrifice and repressing the radical significance of what is being put to it.

We have not yet exhausted the significance of the Judgement of Solomon as a prefiguration of the mission of Christ. It is important to recognize that the family setting to which the account seems to be confined and the maternal character of the love that it reveals are only secondary elements. The woman who cries: 'Give her the living child and by no means slay it' is presented to us as the true mother in the biological sense, which resolves the matter within a family context. But this is only one of the possible contexts. The rivalry of doubles can take place outside this context, and it has no need of Solomon or his sword to bring about the destruction of the object of litigation—or indeed, in the last resort, of any conceivable object. All that is needed is for the conflict to get more and more embittered—for there to be nothing or no one capable of halting the destructive escalation.

From this broader point of view we must ask about the motives that lie behind the Passion—recognizing in them a rule of conduct that is closely parallel to that of the good harlot. In order to understand the attitude of Jesus' Father, we have only to reflect on the feelings that pass through the king's mind throughout the affair. The king does not wish to sacrifice the child—the child does not in fact die—nor does he wish to sacrifice the mother—she is given the child, so that both of them can live together in tranquillity. In the same way, the Father does not wish to sacrifice anyone. But, unlike Solomon, he is not on earth to put an end to the conflicts between doubles; on earth, there is no King Solomon who can bring about the rule of true justice. The human situation, at its most basic level, depends on there being no Fathers and all-wise kings to ensure the rule of justice for a humanity that continues in a state of eternal infancy. So the only way of doing the will of the

Father, on earth as it is in heaven, is by behaving like the good harlot, by taking the same risks as she did—which should be done not in a spirit of sacrificial gloom or morbid preoccupation with death but in a spirit of love for true life, so that life may triumph.

The non-sacrificial reading I am advocating places the emphasis where it really belongs in the Gospels, on those passages that show us the death of Christ in terms of his absolute devotion to the disciples and to all mankind: 'Greater love has no man than this, that a man lay down his life for his friends' (John 15, 13). But we should note yet again that the Gospels never present Christ's witness as a form of sacrifice. In Paul, the most common expressions used are 'work of love' or 'work of grace'. The rare examples of sacrificial language can be taken as metaphorical in view of the absence of any specific theory of sacrifice comparable to that of the Epistle to the Hebrews or the range of theories that develop later.

By using the example of the Judgement of Solomon, we find it possible to treat with deserved contempt the accusation of masochism that the demystification merchants cast at the Christian concept of devotion unto death.

G. L.: I believe *Antigone* can be related to the Judgement of Solomon, and its heroine compared to the 'good harlot'.

R. G.: At the beginning of *Antigone* we are confronted with what we 'usually' find in the prophets and tragedians: the paroxysm of reciprocal violence. This is what is presented symbolically, or taken out of the realm of symbols, by the simultaneous deaths of Eteocles and Polyneices, who even in death remain undifferentiated. Nothing can be affirmed or denied about one of the two brothers without it being necessary immediately to affirm or deny the same thing about the other. The whole problem of reciprocal violence can be summed up in that. Here we have the reason why Creon claims to distinguish between the two brothers. But, strikingly at the outset of his first speech in *Antigone*, Creon uses a formula that is close to those found also in Aeschylus and Euripides—one that asserts the impossibility of making distinctions:

In their double destiny, the two brothers have perished in a single day, giving and receiving blows from their unjust arms.

Euripides, for his part, concludes the description of a combat in the *Phoenician Women* in the following way:

> . . . dust in their teeth, and each one murderer of the other, they lie side by side, and power is not discriminated between them.

Like Ulysses in *The Odyssey* and Caiaphas in the Gospel, Creon wants to act like a good head of state and bring the plague of doubles to an end. But he knows that he can only do this by cursing one of the two brothers and blessing the other, just as Isaac did in the story of the blessing of Jacob.

If Creon requires the Thebans to be unanimous in their execration of Polynices, it is because he realizes that this unanimity is the only means of endowing the scapegoat with the power of restructuring the community.

That is why Creon cannot put up with Antigone's behaviour. Antigone sets herself against the mythological falsehood; she declares that the doubles are identical and must be dealt with in exactly the same fashion. In effect, she is saying precisely the same thing as Christ, and, like Christ, she has to die: she too must be expelled from the community.

In one of her amazing insights, Simone Weil saw in Antigone the most perfect *figura Christi* of the ancient world. She drew particular attention to a beautiful line that Sophocles puts into the mouth of his heroine. This line, which states the truth about human community, is usually translated: 'I was not born to share hatred but love.' However, its literal meaning is: 'Not to hate together but to love together was I born.' The City of Man is founded on hating together, and whatever mutual love it enjoys rests on that foundation, which Antigone, like Christ, brings to light in order to repudiate.[68]

Creon can only repeat the old saw of every human culture: '*You cannot all the same treat friends as enemies.*' (A little earlier, however, he had asserted that there was no difference between the two brothers.) Antigone replies: 'Who can tell if the gods, below us, really wish for that? Is it for us to distinguish between good and evil by rewarding one and punishing the other according to our own lights?'

This line conveys implicitly what the Gospels make absolutely explicit: if the deity exists, it does not choose sides in the conflicts of doubles. There is no 'Gott mit uns' in Heaven. Sophocles's tragedy is very great. But in my opinion it cannot be put on the same level as the Judgement of Solomon. Antigone's protest arises in the context of the funeral rites that Creon denies Polyneices. It is not for a living child that she agrees to die (as does the harlot of the Book of Kings), but for a human being who is already dead. For this reason, the non-sacrificial message of *Antigone* is less spectacular than that of Kings. The Gospels clearly define what makes the tragic text somewhat inferior to the biblical texts when they say: *Leave the dead to bury their dead* (Matthew 8, 22).

It is certainly a great pity that Simone Weil never focused her interpretive genius on the great texts of the Old Testament. She was prevented from doing so by loyalty to her intellectual milieu. All her teachers, like the philosopher Alain, were hellenizing humanists and instilled in her the sacred horror *vis-à-vis* the Bible that characterizes modern humanism and anti-humanism as well, with a few slight exceptions.

J.-M. O.: Far from being an advance on sacrificial morality, the present violent repudiation of this morality is likely to drag us even further down. It is easy to understand why some people are afraid to jettison any form of sacrificial definition. Their fear is justified because such definitions enable certain original Christian values (values associated with the non-sacrificial definition) to filter through—though admittedly in a diluted form.

R. G.: So we do not propose to saddle sacrificial Christianity with the unreserved condemnation that at first seemed necessary in order to assert the radical incompatibility of the sacrificial and the non-sacrificial reading.

If we believed that we were justified in condemning sacrificial Christianity we would be repeating the very error to which sacrificial Christianity itself succumbed. We would be taking our stand on the Gospels and the non-sacrificial perspective they introduce, yet beginning all over again the abominable history of anti-semitism, directed this time at Christianity. We would be starting up the victimage mechanism once again, while relying on a text that, if it were really understood, would put that mechanism out of use once and for all.

A New Sacrificial Reading: The Semiotic Analysis

G. L.: Your reading of the Gospels is at variance with other recent readings that employ the semiotic method. Louis Marin gives some importance, in his treatment of the Passion story, to what he calls the 'semiotic of the traitor', with reference to Judas.[69]

This 'semiotic of the Passion' derives from Propp's work on the morphology of Russian folktales and the various studies based on his remarkable analyses. The folktales show that the hero is first the victim of the traitor but finally triumphs over him. He has his revenge, while the traitor receives the appropriate punishment.[70]

R. G.: If this schema were applicable to them the Gospels would have no claim to any real originality. There can be no doubt that the schema the semiotician claims to discover in the Gospels is very widespread, extending not merely throughout popular literature but through literature as a whole. If the Gospels can really be brought down to this, the true victim is not at all the one we thought him to be, and the text is based, in the final analysis, on the structuring potential derived from the concealed victim. The true victim would be this concealed one: not Christ, but Judas. If this is true, the text no longer has a claim to be the absolutely unique exception I have asserted it to be. We must either give up our thesis altogether or demonstrate that this semiotic interpretation does not allow us to reach the real significance of the text.

Even if we look at it from a purely quantitative point of view, the Judas theme does not appear to justify the place the semiotic thesis accords it in the story of the Passion. Judas's betrayal is episodic in character, as in the denial of Peter; the space devoted to the two incidents must be roughly the same. (I have not checked.) The betrayal is not indispensable to the Crucifixion. It has no particular concrete effect. Should we imagine that the writers were only impeded by their lack of literary expertise from developing a really good and convincing story of betrayal, such as we find on American television? This makes little sense. The text puts into Jesus' mouth unequivocal words that put an end to any thesis relying on conspiracy to account for the Passion: Jesus himself declares it to be more or less inconsequential:

> At that hour Jesus said to the crowds, 'Have you come out as against a robber, with swords and clubs to capture me? Day after day I sat in the temple teaching, and you did not seize me. But all this has taken place, that the scriptures of the prophets might be fulfilled.' Then all the disciplesforsook him and fled (Matthew 26, 55-56).

Notions like 'betrayal', 'conspiracy' and 'armed assault' are there in the text, but only so as to be set aside as meaningless. They are part of the mythic meanings that crystallize whenever there is a hint of any collective action involving a victim. The semiotic reading attaches far too much importance to them. The Gospels make us aware of the inadequacy of any kind of conspiracy theory, and in this respect, once again, they turn out to be 'deconstructive'—powerfully so—in their effect.

There is no special difficulty in understanding why the Gospels treat the pseudo-conspiracy of Judas and the ecclesiastical authorities in the way that they do. This conspiracy is presented as real but powerless. Jesus is the victim of a mimetic contagion that spreads to the whole community, and there can be no question of viewing him as the victim of one particularly evil individual, or even of several. The ways in which individuals behave are never of more than secondary importance, since everything culminates in the unanimous movement that is being formed against Jesus. It hardly matters, in the end, whether Pilate stands out for a moment against the collective involvement while others give in to it straightaway. The essential point is that no one stands out until the end. The jealousy of Judas is ultimately at one with the political attitude of Pilate and the naive snobbery of Peter, who betrays his master because he is ashamed of his provincial accent in the court of the High Priest. On the surface, motives appear to be individual, and conduct appears to fall into different patterns. But everything comes back in the end to the effect of mimesis, which works its power on everyone without exception—'the disciples forsook him and fled' (though this result turns out to be merely temporary for Peter and the ten other Apostles).

To prove beyond a doubt that in the Gospels we should not overemphasize the classic structure of betrayal, we can show that the final element in this structure is not to be found—the punishment of the traitor. The only difference between Judas and Peter resides, not in the betrayal, but in Judas's inability to come back to Jesus. Judas is not condemned by anyone; he commits suicide, despairing of himself and seeking to make the rupture definitive. The underlying factor here is the idea (a truly evangelical one) that men are never condemned by God: they condemn themselves by their despair. When he takes himself to be solely and uniquely responsible for the death of Jesus, Judas makes a mistake that is the exact opposite (though in the end the equivalent) of Peter's, when Peter states that even if all the other disciples are scandalized, he never will be. Basically, the same pride governs all people; they refuse to recognize that they are all equal in relation to the murder of Jesus, and therefore that they all take part in it in a more or less equivalent way—however much external factors may appear to differ.

What strikes me about the semiotic interpretation of Judas is how old-hat its 'demystification' turns out to be. No less conventional, and quite unjustifiable from my point of view, is the practice of defining the Kingdom of God in 'Utopian' terms. Here all the interpretations of nineteenth-century historical criticism return, despite the apparent opposition between semiology and historicism.

Obviously semiological research is still in its infancy. It offers no overall view and makes no effort to explain how a text that is, after all, very short, brings together the Passion and the Kingdom of God. I am afraid that if semiology ventures to take up this task, it will end in the impasse of historical criticism, as Albert Schweitzer described it in his essay (cf. p.196). I am afraid that despite the formidable 'technical' apparatus with which it is equipped, semiology is incapable of re-invigorating these problems. Once again, an air of 'scientificity' envelops in its prestige types of reading that remain grounded in the past.

The way in which the same old thing gets perpetuated despite the appearance of being different should not surprise us. The element that is used to pump new life into all attempts at gospel exegesis that neglect the founding murder can only be the sacrificial reading as it occurs in the Epistle to the Hebrews matter which concerns us; the device of using popular tales as a basis for comparison results in a particularly rustic type of sacrificial reading. The semiotics of the traitor cannot effectively engage the gospel text, which lacks the mythological structure people are so anxious to discover in it. By contrast, the semiotics of the traitor clarifies very effectively the particular version of this text given at certain junctures in the Middle Ages, since that version precisely falls back upon mythology and the sacrificial interpretation. Nowadays it is perpetuated in the Passion plays of Oberammergau and other places. There can be no doubt that in theatrical versions such as these, Judas plays a role important enough to satisfy the requirements of a 'semiotics of the traitor'. It is certainly interesting to show how, in popular circles during the Middle Ages, the Passion was brought down to the level of a folktale. But that belongs to the study of the sacrificial interpretation, and not to the study of the gospel text in itself. In fact, it only contributes to a particular type of sacrificial interpretation, since the readings deriving from the learned exegesis of the Middle Ages, though admittedly sacrificial, are less so and more complexly so than we might imagine from concentrating on the semiotics of the traitor.

So the recent attempts to give new life to old methods of exegesis end up like those of the less recent past; they are still sacrificial. They remain blind to the uniqueness of the Gospel's logic, which is a Logos of non-violence. Let us assume that there is no such Logos, and that in the last analysis the gospel text exists on the level of concealed victimage mechanisms and processes of self-justification, undertaken by a subject who was expert at hiding within the folds of the text. If we grant this, we cannot fail to see that the stratagems of this subject must be much more devious and subtle than the fairly coarse threads disengaged by semiotic analysis. They must exceed the old exercises in demystification pursued by Renan and his followers. And they must also go beyond the reductivist strategies pursued by Nietzsche in *The Anti-Christ* and Max Weber in *Antique Judaism*. Weber's thesis, which represented the Old Testament as the self-justification of a 'pariah people', was far from an attempt at justification; indeed, Weber was hardly favourable to the biblical text. But he was obliged to recognize the basic dynamics of the rehabilitation of the victim as being too powerful overall to be undermined by any contradictory episodic details. (Weber's thesis is applied only to the Old Testament, of course, but it could equally well be applied to the Gospels. In fact, this is where it is applied as early as Nietzsche's *Anti-Christ*.) Thus the semiotic analyses seem regressive to me, not only with regard to the non-sacrificial reading, but also with regard to the more advanced versions of the sacrificial reading, which are anxious to reassimilate this text to the general conditions that govern textuality.

The Sacrificial Reading and History

R. G.: Historical Christianity covers the texts with a veil of sacrifice. Or, to change the metaphor, it immolates them in the (albeit splendid) tomb of Western culture. By this reading, the Christian text is able to found something that in principle it ought never to have founded: a culture. Obviously this culture is not quite like those that preceded it, since it always contained the germs of the planetary society that has taken its place. But it was sufficiently similar to the others to perpetuate the great legal, mythical and sacrificial principles at the basis of every culture.

G. L.: What you say anticipates your answer to an objection that must have long troubled our readers. If the mechanism of the scapegoat is indeed at the foundation of every culture, and if by publicizing its secret the Gospels prevent the mechanism from working, then why, after the diffusion of the Gospels, do cultural forms continue to arise, flourish and pass away, as if nothing had happened? The most paradoxical case is Christian culture itself. This question, to judge by some of the evidence, already troubled the Christian community in the first century after Christ. Why does the world carry on in the same way as before? Why have the apocalyptic prophecies not been fulfilled?

R. G.: In modern times, when people have talked about a Christian vision of history they have not really been talking about a radically Christian appropriation of history, which could only be apocalyptic. Even if—perhaps especially if—a historian is a 'modern' Christian, he would be ashamed to take such old wives' tales, such idiotic old ramblings, seriously. What passes for a Christian vision nowadays, in enlightened European circles, is a notion of history that is both 'serious' and 'optimistic', replete with social progress and goodwill to all mankind.

J.-M. O.: The indefinite postponement of the earth-shaking events predicted in the New Testament has discredited the Christian point of view and even brought it into ridicule.

R. G.: Up to now we have confined ourselves to the meaning of the Gospels. We have not directly posed the question of their place in history. But we can understand the 'texts of persecution' in our world (as opposed to myths) and the resulting world crisis, only if we take into account the direct or indirect operation of the Gospels.

Most commentators, even those who are Christians, regard as entirely mythical the words that proclaim the Gospels' future influence on history. All the warnings against concentrating too much on the nearness of the end and on its precise date are taken as interpolations made to strengthen a popular faith that had been disturbed by the realization that the Christians were wrong about the end of the world.

There is no proof of this. Personally, I doubt very much that the text of Luke was modified by preoccupations of a modern, propagandistic nature. I think this kind of speculation, if made about any great religious text other than the Gospels, would rightly be regarded as cheaply anachronistic. If we questioned the good faith of Indian mysticism or Buddhist scripture in the manner that we do the Gospels, we would be suspected of an 'ethnocentric' bias. In our contemporary intellectual world, the Gospels alone are always fair game. Our effort to prove that we are free of ethnocentric bias may well be part of a new ethnocentrism that consists in Western thinkers immolating their own cultural and religious treasure on an altar of false renunciation, in hypocritical imitation of Jesus.

There is a clear distinction, particularly in Luke, between two related but distinct apocalyptic events—one Judaic and the other worldwide. The text is itself aware of the sacrificial *deferral* its own dissemination is likely to generate. If we take account of this awareness, we can see that there is a two-fold apocalyptic rationale, which has nothing to do with the cancellation or postponement of an earlier, more dramatic announcement but simply projects into the future a new pattern of deferral. It is easy to appreciate the need for this deferral as the Gospel is spread 'to the ends of the earth', where it will find a home among peoples who are necessarily regressive in their religious attitudes: thus the likelihood of new sacrificial readings being made is great among the Gentiles.

In our interpretation, divine intervention no longer violently changes the course of human history and suspends its ordinary laws of development. On the contrary, a text does disturb these laws, but only to the extent that it gradually reveals the state of sacrificial misapprehension protecting people from their own violence. Thus the treatment of history in the Gospels derives from the same basis in rationality as the rest of the text.

Far from invalidating the historical efficacy of the text (as described in the text itself), the course of history after the Gospels is more than compatible with the principle of deferral. How is it possible to miss the fact that the 'signs' are there, signifying to those who do not refuse to listen that 'the time is accomplished'? This structural notion of accomplishment does not necessarily imply that the world is at an end, but the possibility is among us. Indeed that is what the text says. No doubt there will always be opportunities for deferral, but there is no reason to be scandalized when believers do not see them and confuse their own vivid apprehension of the total process with the promise and threat of an immediate fulfilment.

We cannot escape the issue of a relationship with the real course of history. Indeed, we shall see that only by confronting the real course of history—which the gospel text claims to determine—can the astonishing coherence of the gospel logic be fully revealed in our time.

Paul and his companions begin the proclamation of the Gospel. The Jews reject it, but it succeeds remarkably throughout the whole Roman Empire. It reaches people who have not arrived at the same stage of religious evolution as the Jews—people who do not know the Law and the Prophets. The initial converts are joined by great segments of the population, then by the 'barbarian' world. This awe-inspiring spread of the Gospel could only have taken place with the terms of the sacrificial reading and was directly indebted to the reading.

On the level of history, the sacrificial reading is not an 'error', the result of accident or lack of insight. If we really understand the victimage mechanism and the role it has played for all of humanity, we can see that the sacrificial reading of the Christian text—however baffling and paradoxical in principle—was inevitable. It had on its side all the weight of an age-old, uninterrupted religious history, which among the multitudes of pagans had never been challenged by anything resembling the Old Testament.

We have already noted that the relationship of the Old Testament to the Gospels—in so far as concerns the revealing of the scapegoat—closely parallels the relationship of sacrificial Christianity to the Gospels. Let us apply this finding to the concrete historical circumstances of the diffusion of the Gospels and take into account the fact that the peoples who were evangelized had not been affected by the Old Testament. In these conditions, the role of historical Christianity becomes necessary within an eschatological process that is governed by the Gospels—a history directed towards revealing the universal truth of human violence. But the process requires an almost limitless patience: many centuries must elapse before the subversive and shattering truth contained in the Gospels can be understood world-wide.

The fact that in the synoptic Gospels Jesus claims to speak to the children of Israel alone does not prove that there is a pre-existent gospel layer that bears only on particularistic Judaic concerns. Speeches of this kind are governed by the historical (in Heideggerian terms (*geschichtlich* rather than *historisch*) character of the revelation—by the notion that Jesus can only present himself at *his hour*, which is both the most favourable and the last of all hours.

The apparent expulsion of certain peoples at this stage (or any stage) can only be temporary; it is a result of their lack of preparation. Unlike the Jews, they have not benefited from the long Exodus from the sacrificial system which is traced in the Old Testament. They have not been brought to the state of extreme receptivity, and so of urgency, that distinguishes the chosen people's relationship to the Kingdom of God, and accounts for the fact that they are, at least initially, the only ones to be threatened by the violence of the Apocalypse.

For other peoples, the decisive choice will have to be *deferred* until they will have 'caught up' and attained the point of social existence at which the preaching of the Kingdom becomes at once understandable and urgent.

G. L.: What will take the place of the Old Testament for these numberless peoples? For them what will play the propaedeutic role of the Old Testament?

R. G.: Each of these questions provides the other's answer. It is Christianity—in the sacrificial version, which is in religious terms very close to the Old Testament—that will educate the Gentiles. Christianity can only play this role to the extent that the sacrificial veil spread over its radical messages enables it to function once again as the founding element of a culture.

Science and Apocalypse

R. G.: The Gospels can serve as a foundation for a new culture, similar to all the previous cultures only as a result of a certain distortion of the original message. That point has been clearly brought out by Judaic scholars such as Joseph Klausner.[71]

Like every history within the sacrificial system, the course of historical Christianity consists in a gradual loosening of legal constraints in proportion to the declining efficacy of ritual mechanisms. We have argued that this development cannot simply be seen as decadence and decomposition. It is also incorrect to view the process as a liberating opening to a future of unlimited 'progress'. In both cases, the Christian text is interpreted as having already said its last word; it is there behind us, not in front of us.

It is easy to understand—if we note that Christians hold such attitudes—why for most intellectuals Christianity is just like all the other religions of the past, and why they feel nothing will be left of it at the conclusion of the present crisis. The idea that this crisis involves not the Christian text but only a particular reading of it—the sacrificial reading that was fated to dominate the initial stages of the Christian revelation—cannot become intelligible as long as a distinction between the sacrificial and the non-sacrificial reading is not made. The sacrificial reading is a protective envelope; beneath this envelope, which is finally crumbling to dust in our own time, is a living principle which has so far been concealed.

J.-M. O.: Even today this idea seems implausible. Hearing you propound it, people will think that, aiming to save Christianity from its inevitable decline, you have come up with a highly ingenious thesis designed to imbue the Christian text with a contemporary significance that it is incapable of recovering through its own resources.

R. G.: You are quite right. Everyone will say that I am myself undertaking the kind of 'repair job' that I have condemned various other doctrines for attempting. In spite of the remarkable examples of structural convergence that seem to suggest that the gospel logic is relevant to anthropology, there is no doubt that our readers will have been too schooled in the intellectual methods of modernity—accepting its notions of what is possible and what is impossible—for them to follow us into the territory where we are now trying to lead them.

To induce them to enter this unexplored territory, we must be able to offer them some even more striking examples of convergence between Scripture and history, some evidence more spectacular than anything we have offered yet. We need something conspicuous enough to be visible at all times and to all men. The 'signs of the times' mentioned in the Gospel—which humankind is reproached for not being able to read—must no longer have the least ambiguity, so that an inability to detect them can only come from an inexpressible desire not to see and not to hear the obvious.

J.-M. O.: The signs you speak of are all around us. In order not to recognize them and thus undo their signifying power, most of our contemporaries—both atheists and Christians—continue to hold tenaciously to the sacrificial reading. It sacralizes the Apocalypse and prevents us from discerning the objectively apocalyptic—which is to say, revelatory, as well as supremely violent—nature of our present circumstances.

R. G.: What the apocalyptic violence is first obliged to reveal—the only thing that it can directly reveal—is the purely human nature and the simultaneously destructive and cultural function of violence.

To understand that we are already living through this process of revelation, we have only think about our relationship, as members of a world community, to the terrifying armaments with which mankind has furnished itself since the end of the Second World War.

When people talk about the new methods of destruction, they speak of 'the bomb', as if there were only one and it belonged to everyone and no one—as if the whole world belonged to it. And the bomb does indeed seem like the prince of this world, enthroned above a host of priests and worshippers, who exist, so it would seem, only to do it service. Some of them bury the poisoned eggs of the idol beneath the earth; others deposit them at the bottom of the seas; yet others sprinkle the heavens with them, causing the stars of death to revolve endlessly above the teeming antheap. No slightest section of nature—now that science has cleansed it of all the ancient projections of the supernatural—has not been reinvested with the truth of violence. But this time we cannot pretend that the power for destruction is anything but human, even though it works in ways that parallel the workings of the sacred.

Humans have always found peace in the shadow of their idols—that is to say, of human violence in a sacralized form. This is still true, as humanity looks for peace under the shelter of the ultimate violence. In a world that is continually losing its sacred character, only the permanent threat of immediate and total destruction can prevent men from destroying one another. Once again, violence prevents violence from breaking out.

Never has violence so insolently asserted its dual role of 'poison' and 'remedy'. Now it is not the Dionysiac revellers of the ancient world with their human *pharmakos* or cannibals dressed in feathers who make this point: it is specialists in political science, such as Raymond Aron. To take their word for it—which we are unable to question—nuclear armaments alone maintain world peace. The specialists tell us without a blink that this violence alone can *protect* us. They are absolutely right. But they do not realize how oddly such statements sound amid a discourse that otherwise keeps on as if the types of humanism that inspired it (whether those of Marx, Montesquieu, Rousseau or anyone else) could still sound as convincing as they once did in this new—and very old—context. They dissect the situation with an expertise that is so level-headed and matter of fact—while keeping up their belief in the 'natural goodness' of man—that we must ask if cynicism has gained the upper hand, or if the experts are only naive and unaware.

However we look at it, the present threat resembles the forms of terror created by the sacred and requires the same type of precautions. We still must reckon with forms of 'pollution' and 'contamination', which can be scientifically detected and measured but are nonetheless reminiscent of their religious counterparts. And the only way of repelling the evil turns out still to be by way of the evil itself. Any renunciation of technology, pure and simple, seems to be impossible: the machine is so well set up that it would be more dangerous to stop than to go forward. The place to look for reassurance is in the very heart of the existing terror.

The hidden infrastructure of all religions and all cultures is in the process of declaring itself. This is the true god of humanity, whom we create with our own hands in order to contemplate him effectively—but henceforth no religion will succeed in dressing him up any longer. We did not notice his arrival because he no longer journeys on the outspread wings of the angels of darkness—because from now on he will always appear where no one expected him, in the statistics drawn up by scientists and in domains that have no connection whatsoever with the sacred.

A truly wonderful sense of the appropriate has guided the inventors of the most terrifying weapons to choose names that evoke ultimate violence in the most effective way: names taken from the direst divinities in Greek mythology, like Titan, Poseidon, and Saturn, the god who devoured his own children. We who sacrifice fabulous resources to fatten the most inhuman form of violence so that it will continue to protect us, and who pass our time in transmitting futile messages from a planet that is risking destruction to planets that are already dead—how can we have the extraordinary hypocrisy to pretend that we do not understand all those people who did such things long before us: those, for example, who made it their practice to throw a single child, or two at the most, into the furnace of a certain Moloch in order to ensure the safety of the others?

There is an inevitable connection between the strange peace that we are living through and the peace that specifically ritualistic religions managed to secure. Nevertheless, it would be wrong simply to equate these two phenomena. Their differences are even more important than their similarities.

If we say that mankind 'adores' his own destructive power, we are speaking in metaphors. The metaphor can, however, reveal something that is in no way an illusion. We cannot say that such an analogy is merely rhetorical or that we are dealing with a mere 'truth effect'. There is a lesson to be drawn from this analogy, and we cannot draw it if we yield to the dizzying effects of the cognitive nihilism that now is everywhere triumphant. There is a very good reason for that!

The lesson is far from simple. What impels us to behave in a fashion that is analogous to religious behaviour is not a terror that is sacred in the strict sense: it is a fear that is perfectly clear-sighted about the dangers of a nuclear duel for the human race. Peace at present rests upon a coldly scientific estimation of the uniformly disastrous and perhaps fatal consequences that the massive use of stockpiled weapons would have for all combatants.

We can already see the practical consequences of this state of affairs. Those who control the use of these monstrous weapons very carefully avoid having to draw upon them. For the first time in the history of 'great powers' we see potential adversaries who are genuinely desirous of avoiding any kind of action, or indeed any situation that might cause a major conflict. The notion of 'national honour' is disappearing from the vocabulary of diplomacy. Instead of deliberately inflaming disputes, people attempt to smooth them. Instead of crying out that there is 'provocation', they turn their heads and pretend not to see: they do not listen to the tub-thumping that has taken place in the past, and leave it to ideological fanatics.

G. L.: If you are saying that in the present situation there is something that could be compared to a first attempt at conforming to what the Gospels call the rule of the Kingdom, you run the risk of being seen as a naive partisan of science fiction. Your readers will not understand you, however much you have said about the rigorous and implacable character of this rule. In a world where violence has been truly revealed and the victimage mechanisms have ceased to function, humans are confronted with a dilemma that is extraordinarily simple: either they renounce violence, or the incalculable violence that they set off risks annihilating them all, 'as in the days of Noah'.

R. G.: That is beyond question. Obviously I do not claim that the decreasingly bellicose behaviour of our most powerful statesmen is motivated by the spirit of the Gospel. If there is something evangelical in the present situation, in the sense which we are now giving to that word, it is actually because the situation has nothing in common with the sly hypocrisy and dreadful condescension which so many people show when they dress up the Christian text to make it sweeter and more palatable—so they argue—to our period.

Threatened by the storm that they keep over their own heads, the nations now behave in a manner that, on the one hand, suggests the way in which men have always conducted themselves toward the idols of violence. On the other, their behaviour vividly reminds us that the Gospels demand the renunciation of all forms of violence.

So there can be no question of confusing what is taking place today with the coming of the Kingdom of God. If both contradictory implications of the nations' behaviour are genuinely to be found in the same set of historical facts, this is because that behaviour is ambiguous. The nations are not wise enough to abandon the power of creating mutual terror, nor are they mad enough to unleash irreversible destruction. So we must reckon with a complex situation that falls between these two positions, and all the forms of mankind's past and future behaviour can be discerned there. Either we are moving ineluctably toward non-violence, or we are about to disappear completely. But precisely because the present situation is an intermediary one, it allows mankind to avoid the enormous problems it now poses.[72]

The genuinely new element is that violence can no longer be relied upon to resolve the crisis. Violence no longer guarantees a firm base. For violence to be capable of carrying out its cyclical development and bringing back peace, there must be an ecological field that can absorb the damage done in the process. Nowadays, this field covers the entire planet, but even that has probably ceased to be enough. The environment can no longer absorb the violence humans can unleash.

In a purely mechanical way, journalists refer to this situation as 'apocalyptic', under the impression that it is very different from the one mentioned in the Gospels. That is because they still read the Gospels as describing a violence sent by God, specifically.

Our situation corresponds very closely to Gospel predictions for this world, which may not be as 'post-Christian' as it claims. So as not to notice the embarrassing relevance of our religious texts it becomes necessary to latch ever more despairingly on to the sacrificial reading—the reading that enables us to declare as God-given the violence predicted in the text. It is for this reason that atheists are even more determined than Christians to maintain the sacrificial interpretations.

G. L.: As in the past, the sacrificial interpretation prevents the violence from coming home to us.

R. G.: Curiously, the apocalyptic Christian sects also cling to the notion of a violence that comes from God. Our violence has already come home to us. The sacrificial interpretation rejects an increasingly accessible knowledge that is written in increasingly large characters into the history we are living through.

J.-M. O.: Today, nothing could be easier than to take the Christian, apocalyptic notion of history seriously. The difficult thing would be to treat these very striking texts as if they did not exist and to fail to see the remarkable convergences between their predictions and historical reality. Only the sacrificial reading could blind us to them. And this reading, though it still controls all other readings, hangs on by only a thread.

R. G.: A world that was swollen with pride and thought itself invulnerable could still believe with Renan, that the kingdom is 'Utopian'. But people who say nowadays that the gospel principle of non-reprisal is 'only masochism' fail to reflect on the constraints that weigh heavily upon us as a result of our excessive power for destruction.

J.-M. O.: You take for granted, I would imagine, that a radical desacralization, of the type indicated in the Gospels, was necessary before science and technology could invent our modern weapons. Only after the gods were driven out was it possible to steel oneself to treat all of nature as objects obeying *natural* laws.

R. G.: It is indeed worth underlining that essential point. In the world we have now entered, there is no longer any problem in articulating the various gospel themes, in particular those of the Kingdom and the Apocalypse—the celebrated enigma historical criticism has never managed to resolve. However, critics like Rudolf Bultmann, whose theories dominated German theology after the Second World War, still have attempted to 'demythologize' the Gospels. Bultmann simply cut out what could no longer be contained in the sacrificial interpretation and what could not yet be given a non-sacrificial reading. In consequence, he invited his readers to forget the theme of Apocalypse, referring to it as an old Jewish superstition that has nothing whatsoever to offer the modern mind. Indeed Bultmann, like Albert Schweitzer, always saw the Apocalypse in terms of the vengeance of God, a reading that has no basis in the Gospels themselves.[73]

For the first time, we have acquired the capacity to understand the text in most radical implications. This new-found ability comes to us because the sacrificial reading has ceased to cohere and contemporary history has entered upon a period of unprecedented crisis. We have before us a series of interconnected events that can only bring home to us—now on a world scale—the situation presented to us in the Gospels themselves as the historical pre-condition for the first announcement of the kingdom. This situation has returned at the conclusion of the diffusion made possible by the sacrificial reading, when all the peoples of the earth have become ready to receive the message.

J.-M. O.: It will be said that you are bringing back into circulation the terrors of the Apocalypse. . .

R. G.: As for the terrors of the Apocalypse, no one could do better in that respect nowadays than the daily newspaper. I am not saying that the end of the world is at hand. Obviously not: all the elements that I draw out in my analysis have something positive about them. The present situation does not at all imply that our predecessors were better or worse than we are. In effect, people's basic make-up has not changed in the slightest, and that is precisely what makes our situation so dangerous. What is being revealed has nothing new about it; violence has always been inherent in man. Yet at the same time the use of violence does not rest on an irresistible instinct. The proof of this lies in the fact that the ultimate violence has been at our disposal for a while, and, up to the present time at any rate, we have not yielded to the temptation to use it.

The world situation has to align itself with the announcement in the Gospels in order for us to understand, finally, what is involved, in the theme of Apocalypse. It is not a question of individual far-sightedness, but a set of pressing historical circumstances. The points of similarity are so striking that they must eventually overcome the increasingly tottering obstacles that our sacrificial habits of mind place in the way.

To say that we are objectively in an apocalyptic situation is in no sense to 'preach the end of the world'. It is to say that mankind has become, for the first time, capable of destroying itself, something that was unimaginable only two or three centuries ago. The whole planet now finds itself, with regard to violence, in a situation comparable to that of the most primitive groups of human beings, except that this time we are fully aware of it. We can no longer count on sacrificial resources based on false religions to keep this violence at bay. We are reaching a degree of self-awareness and responsibility that was never attained by those who lived before us.[74]

What is really frightening today is not the challenge of this new meaning, but the Kafkaesque rejection of all meaning. What is frightening is the conjunction of massive technical power and the spiritual surrender of nihilism. A panic-stricken refusal to glance, even furtively, in the only direction where meaning could still be found dominates our intellectual life.

All the voices of our culture conspire to reassure us by discrediting the Christian text and by avoiding it. Let us look at the state of that culture. It invented anthropology, the scientific study of myth, and the various forms of psychoanalysis. It has itself been periodically the victim of crises of an 'apocalyptic' kind. The last of these has been in progress for more than a third of a century; it is certainly the most severe, as well as the most agonizing, since it involves a number of very 'hard' scientific elements that are oddly combined with the most absurd superstitions and with elements of traditional religion.

Imagine some intelligent observers from another planet who have come to see how we carry on. They would see whole hosts of researchers devoting themselves to the study of social phenomena, interpreting the slightest reactions on the individual and collective scales. They would take note of the fact that our intellectuals have, for a century, been attaching an immense importance to a number of ancient Greek tales about a certain Oedipus and a certain Dionysus. They would be able to gauge the vast number of studies that have been devoted to these figures, and the almost religious respect that, since the sixteenth century, we have accorded, first to Greek culture, then to the whole of primitive culture.[75] They would be able to compare all this to a continually decreasing interest in the Judaeo-Christian tradition, whose texts make manifest—in a perfectly explicit form, which should be full of implications for the situation in which we find ourselves—a fully fashioned theory of the destruction of all things. Now, these particular texts are not from other peoples' religions, they are from our own religion. For good or ill, until now they have governed, and indeed may still govern, the impulse that is carrying us into the unknown. You might think that a society so concerned with observing and understanding itself would be capable of detaching at least a small battalion of the great army encamped in the shade of the Greek and primitive altars in order to verify if everything is as finally signed, sealed and delivered as it appears to be.

Nothing like this ever happens. Our thinking may not be based on the physical expulsion of violence and the truth that emerges from violence. But perhaps at present we are experiencing a kind of gigantic intellectual expulsion of the whole Judaeo-Christian tradition, which means, among other things, that any form of genuinely serious religious or cultural problematic is also expelled. The expulsion become more and more systematic in direct proportion to the increase in the intelligibility of the message—in proportion to the self-revelation of violence, in history and technology.

Clearly it is not the fault of the gospel text if the good news that we thought we had been relieved of comes back to us in such a formidable context. It is we who willed it so, we who developed the context. We wished for our house to be left to us. Well, so it has been (Luke 13, 35).

CHAPTER FOUR

The Logos of Heraclitus and the Logos of John

The Logos in Philosophy

J.-M. O.: I have always been intrigued by the way in which Christ is referred to as the Word, that is to say, in Greek, the *Logos*. Philosophers have always tended to see this as John's borrowing from Greek thought. Does not this idea blow a hole in the argument that you have just been developing?

R. G.: The word 'Logos' comes to be an essential philosophical term in the work of Heraclitus. It is a term that designates the actual object philosophical discourse is aiming at, over and beyond language as such. If such a discourse could come to completion, it would be identical to the Logos—that is to say, to the divine, rational and logical principle according to which the world is organized.

The word 'Logos' also appears in the Gospel of John. Its presence there, more than any other factor, has long led to this text being regarded as the most 'Greek' of the four Gospels. It is a term which designates Christ as the redeemer, in so far as he is closely identified with the creative work of God and with God himself.

The first centuries of Christianity betrayed a great deal of mistrust for Greek thought. The notion that Christianity could be translated into philosophical terms was only admitted very gradually. For many centuries, no one challenged the view that Christian thought was essentially concerned with the tasks of scriptural exegesis. In the Middle Ages, however, the proportion of attention devoted to the philosophy and exegesis gradually tended to reverse, in favour of philosophy. A passion for all things Greek and an avid pursuit of Greek knowledge occurred as the preoccupation with the *figura Christi* slowly declined. It is quite true, historically speaking, that you gradually turn away from the Bible as you move in the direction of philosophy.

When a 'Christian philosophy' comes into being, the two types of

Logos are brought together. That they are related to one another comes to seem more and more obvious. Clearly one cannot yet give priority to the Greek Logos; at the same time, one is well along the path that leads to this reversal. Greek philosophers can now be taken as precursors of Johannine thought, somewhat like the Jewish prophets. A new line of prophets can be sketched out within Greek culture. A modern theologian (quoted by Heidegger in his *Introduction to Metaphysics*) defines the relation between the two types of Logos in 'Christian philosophy' in the following terms: 'The real appearance of truth in the form of the God-man set the seal on the Greeks' philosophical insight concerning the rule of the logos over all existence. This confirmation and seal establish the classicism of Greek philosophy.'[76]

Modern rationalism is up in arms against this subordination of Greek thought to Christian revelation. The fact that the Greeks came first seems to prove that they and not the Christians discovered the Logos. So the Logos of John and Johannine thought in general is no more than a pale reflection of the only genuinely original thought, which is Greek. The New Testament is just the old jay of Judaism decked out with the feathers of the Greek peacock.

The rationalistic argument does not challenge the essential kinship between the two forms of Logos. Everything comes down to questions of precedence to mimetic rivalry. The ostensible aim is to re-establish what Christianity has upset with its vacuous claims. Healthy scholarship consists in acknowledging the originality of what came first. To sum up: Christian thinkers regard Greek philosophers as unconscious theologians. For post-Christians on the other hand, the very idea of a specifically Christian Logos is taken to be a shameless fabrication disguising a clumsy attempt to imitate philosophy.

Throughout Western thought, the two types of Logos have never been sufficiently *distinguished*. Christians and anti-Christians agree about the essential point: the word 'Logos' must always embody the same meaning.

The Two Types of Logos in Heidegger

J.-M. O.: Martin Heidegger wanted to break with this thousand-year-old tradition. He is the first to reject forcefully the idea that the two types of Logos are one and the same.

R. G.: As far as the Johannine Logos is concerned, Heidegger can only be distinguished in very minor respects from the other master thinkers of modern times. He is determined to discover in the Johannine Logos marks of a form of divine authoritarianism that seems to him characteristic of the Bible:

> Because in the Greek translation of the Old Testament (Septuagint) logos signifies the word, and what is more, the 'word' is the definite meaning of command and commandment; *hoi deka logoi* are the ten commandments of God (decalogue). Thus *logos* signifies the *keryx*, the *angelos*, the herald, the messenger who hands down commands and commandments.[77]

Here modern thought's most widespread cliché concerning the Old Testament is transposed to the Johannine Logos. Relations between God and man re-enact the Hegelian scheme of 'master' and 'slave'. This notion has been docilely accepted, even by those who claim to have 'liberated' themselves from Hegel. We find it in Marx, in Nietzsche and in Freud. People who have never read a single line of the Bible accept it unquestioningly. But this idea is quite wrong, even when it is limited to the Old Testament. In our own times, people take the liberty of extending it to the New Testament (which Hegel would never have done), giving only the most peremptory statements—like the one above—in justification.

So Heidegger merely extends the Hegelian interpretation of the Old Testament to the New Testament, in a simplified and cruder form. But he is much more interesting when he defines the Greek Logos. His essential contribution does not lie in an insistence on the notions of 'bringing together' and 'reassembling', which he shows to be present in the term Logos. He also states something much more important: the Logos brings together entities that are *opposites, and it does not do so without violence*. Heidegger recognizes that the Greek Logos is inseparably linked with violence.[78]

We must emphasize characteristics that Heidegger brings out if we are to distinguish between the Greek Logos and the Johannine Logos. That is what Heidegger proposes to do, and it seems to me a reasonable, indeed an essential aim. Heidegger allows himself the means to analyse the Greek side successfully when he defines the Heraclitean Logos—as the violence of the sacred, which keeps doubles in relative harmony and prevents them from destroying one another. By contrast, he is blind to the reality of the Johannine Logos. What stops him from analysing this side successfully is his concern to introduce violence not only into the Greek Logos—where it really has a place—but also into the Johannine Logos, which is thus represented as being the expression of a needlessly cruel and tyrannical deity.

Heidegger obviously means there to be a *difference* between the violence of the Greek Logos and the violence he attributes to the Johannine Logos. He sees the former as a violence committed by free men, while the second is a violence visited upon slaves. The Jewish Decalogue is simply an interiorized form of tyranny. In this respect, Heidegger is faithful to the whole tradition of German idealism, which represents Yahweh as an oriental despot—as he is faithful to the thought of Nietzsche, who takes this tendency to the extreme by defining the whole Judaeo-Christian phenomenon as the product of slavish thinking, devised for the benefit of slaves.

The illusion that there is difference within the heart of violence is the key to the sacrificial way of thinking. Heidegger fails to see that any form of violent mastery ends up in slavery because the model-obstacle comes into play, dominating thought in the same way that it dominates concrete relationships between people. He wishes to differentiate the two types of Logos, but by inserting violence into both of them, he deprives himself of the means for doing so! He is simply unable to dissolve the old association between the two types of Logos. Since the beginnings of medieval philosophy, they have been assimilated to one another; indeed this assimilation may be the best definition of European philosophy, since it allows philosophy to obscure the Christian text and give the sacrificial reading its full effect.

Heidegger differs from his predecessors only to the extent that he replaces the relationship of mutual tolerance between the two types of Logos with a relationship of antagonism. The warring doubles have been installed in the very heart of European thought—and it is a fact that, for Heidegger, the two types of Logos are indeed *doubles*. Heidegger claims to differentiate them, but in reality they are becoming increasingly undifferentiated. The more attempts are made to remedy this state of affairs, the more incurable it becomes. This confrontation of warring doubles is the philosophical translation of the present situation of Western thought. Precisely because Heidegger thinks he no longer reflects this confrontation, he reflects it especially clearly. If we define Western philosophy as the assimilation of the two types of

Logos, Heidegger undoubtedly belongs to its tradition; he is incapable of *concluding* the philosophical tradition because he cannot show the genuine difference between the Heraclitean Logos and the Johannine Logos.

What goes for Heidegger also goes for the other thinkers of modern times. His philosophy is not a fantasy. It serves its purpose. It may not bring about the separation it proposes, but it prepares for the decisive discrimination. It does genuinely presage the end of Western metaphysics which is its constant preoccupation.

What is Heidegger demonstrating when he declares that not without violence does the Heraclitean Logos keep opposites together? Unsuspectingly, he is talking about the scapegoat and the way in which it engenders the sacred. It is the violence of the sacred that inhibits the doubles from unleashing even greater violence. The Heraclitean Logos, in Heidegger's terms, is the Logos of all cultures to the extent that they are, and will always remain, founded upon unanimous violence.

If we look at Heidegger in the light of the scapegoat mechanism, we can see that the issue of the sacred invariably underlies his interpretation of the key terms in German and Greek, and especially his meditations on *Being*. Heidegger works back toward the sacred; he rediscovers certain elements relating to the many meanings of the sacred by examining the philosophical vocabulary. For this reason, he is particularly attracted to pre-Socratic philosophy, especially that of Heraclitus, the philosopher who is closest to the sacred.

It is this very relationship to the sacred, emerging in philosophical language, that makes Heidegger's text at once 'obscure' and fascinating. If we re-read him from our perspective, we can see that the 'paradoxes' that abound in his writings are always paradoxes of the sacred. Heidegger becomes crystal clear when we read him, not in a philosophical light but in the light not really of anthropology but of the 'meta-anthropology' we have been sketching out. Meta-anthropology does not satisfy me but it refers to what happens when the scapegoat mechanism is at last detected, and the multiplicity of meanings attached to the sacred is understood, not as a form of thought that mixes everything up together (as with Lévy-Bruhl and Lévi-Strauss) but as the original matrix of human thought—the cauldron in which not only our cultural institutions but all our modes of thought were forged, through a process of successive differentiation.

In so far as he remains a philosopher and, unwittingly, turns philosophy into the last, final refuge of the sacred, Heidegger is constrained within the limits of philosophy. To understand him better, we must read him, like the pre-Socratics before him, within the radical 'anthropological' perspective enabled by the revelation of the victimage mechanism.

J.-M. O.: Neither Heidegger nor any of his successors has been willing to trace philosophy back beyond the pre-Socratics into the territory of religion, where philosophy had not yet begun. You have chosen to open up this territory from an undefinable point of view, which seeks to throw light on philosophical thought, whereas philosophical light cannot uncover the victimage mechanism.

R. G.: Heidegger is like all the modern thinkers who make an enemy of sacrificial Christianity, which they invariably confuse with the Christian text as such. Heidegger, like all the rest, is really helping to produce the decisive break he talks about. But his work also operates as a powerful obstacle to this break. He is under the impression that he himself can accomplish what will indeed be accomplished—but in a spirit entirely foreign to that of his philosophy. There can be no real break, in fact, unless the Christian text is shown to be sovereign in all respects—unless it is taken as the sole interpreter of an historical process over which it already reigns in secret, despite or rather because of its exclusion.

Any real difference between the Greek Logos and the Christian Logos will have something to do with the question of violence. Either we have been talking nonsense, or the Johannine Logos has nothing whatsoever to do with the interpretation given by Heidegger when he uses the Ten Commandments to present it as a kind of downtrodden servant, whose only function is to transmit the orders of a dictatorial master. We have shown that the Old Testament as a whole counteracts the transferences brought about by the scapegoat and gradually relinquishes sacred violence. The Old Testament is, therefore, far from being dominated by sacred violence. It actually moves away from violence, although in its most primitive sections it still remains sufficiently wedded to violence for people to be able to brand it as violent without appearing totally implausible—exactly as Hegel does.

What appears to us to be Yahweh's violence is in fact the attempt of the entire Old Testament to bring to light the violent reciprocal action of doubles. As we have pointed out, this process reaches its climax in the Gospels. If we take this climax to coincide with the deity's absence, pure and simple, we are naively conceding that we can have no other god than violence. The Gospel of John states that God is love, and the synoptic Gospels make clear that God treats all warring brothers with an equal measure of benevolence. For the God of the Gospels, the categories that emerge from violence and return to it simply do not exist. When brother hates brother, neither one can expect this God to answer his call and come to his support.

The Son plays the role of intermediary between the Father and mankind, but he does not transmit the commands of an arbitrary despot. He is not in the least like a military herald, surrounded with pomp and announced by trumpeters. The Jewish prophets have no interest in the trappings of power and prestige. In fact, it is the Greeks and their spiritual descendants who, as lovers of theatre, greet the trumpets with applause. The Jews had no theatre.

G. L.: Surely the Father's non-intervention in the Gospels can be just as much a cause for complaint as the quite different attitude of the Yahweh of the Old Testament. People have only to learn of the one for them to cry out for the other, and vice versa. As the fable goes, the frogs are never content with their king.

R. G.: Yet this non-violence, which seems so inconsequential when attributed to a God who transcends human affairs, changes its character radically if we transpose it to this world—if mankind takes it as a model for interpersonal conduct.

If the Father is as the Son describes him, the Word of the Son (as we have just quoted it) is indeed the Word of the Father. It is not a gratuitous representation; it describes the very being of the Father. It invites us to become like the Father, by behaving as he behaves. The Word of the Father, which is identical with the Father, consists in telling mankind what the Father is, so that people may be able to imitate him: 'Love your enemies, pray for your persecutors; so shall you be sons of your Father.'

As an intermediary between the Father and mankind, Jesus transmits the father's Word to men. One can indeed argue that this amounts to a tyrannical command—more tyrannical than all the commands of the wicked Yahweh—since men have never yet managed to respond to it. But it would be wrong to see Jesus as the herald that Heidegger sees in him—as an occasional messenger, a mere transmission rod in an authoritarian and bureaucratic machine.

By persisting in behaving in due conformity with the Word Jesus proves that he is not a mere herald, despite the negative reception people give him. The relationship between Son and Father cannot be the terror-stricken subordination which Heidegger describes. It is a relationship of non-differentiated love.

Defining the Johannine Logos in Terms of the Victim

J.-M. O.: I would like to make two remarks here. First, you have distanced yourself from all that philosophers and psychoanalysts have made of the difference between the religion of the Father and the religion of the Son. Second, in stating that there is no difference between Father and Son, are you not risking the possibility that their relationship becomes a relationship of doubles?

R. G.: Like violence, love abolishes differences. A structural reading detects neither one nor the other; *a fortiori* it cannot see their radical incompatibility. This incompatibility is what we are trying to establish, and I can only refer you to the whole argument that has been traced up to this point, or alternatively to the Gospels, which speak of the inability of the wise to see what little children see.

If love and violence are incompatible, the definition of the Logos must take this into account. The difference between the Greek Logos and the Johannine Logos must be an obvious one, which gets concealed only in the tortuous complications of a type of thought that never succeeds in ridding itself of its own violence.

If this difference managed to escape philosophical attention up through Heidegger, that cannot be because it is genuinely difficult to locate. It is inconceivable that the Prologue to the Gospel of John could have 'forgotten' to stress this difference or failed to take it into account. The Johannine Logos must be specified in the prologue in an obvious and even striking way—even though no one has yet taken note of it, because they have not understood the role of violence in the Logos of human culture. If I have not been mistaken this far, the revelation of the scapegoat principle must be included in the very definition of the Logos: these few lines must reveal all that has been hidden, even though we may not be capable of assimilating that revelation.

Once the mechanism of the scapegoat is detected, the absolutely singular nature of the Johannine Logos becomes quite clear, and it can easily be differentiated from the Heraclitean Logos. As Heidegger puts the matter, *a world separates all of that from Heraclitus*—but it is not the world that the philosopher was thinking of.

No analysis is necessary. Seeing the striking difference is mere child's play, in the sense that only children can see the simple and essential aspect of things. As the Gospel tells us, the difference between violence and peace, which surpasses human understanding, is this:

In him [the Logos] was life;
and the life was the light of men.
And the light shineth in darkness,
and the darkness comprehended it not (John 1, 4-5 Authorized Version;
my italics)

He was in the world,
and the world was made through him,
yet the world knew him not.

He came to his own home,
and his own people received him not (John 1, 10-11; my italics)

The Johannine Logos is foreign to any kind of violence; it is therefore forever expelled, an absent Logos that never has had any direct, determining influence over human cultures. These cultures are based on the Heraclitean Logos, the Logos of expulsion, the Logos of violence, which, if it is not recognized, can provide the foundation of a culture. The Johannine Logos discloses the truth of violence by having itself expelled. First and foremost, John's Prologue undoubtedly refers to the Passion. But in a more general way, the misrecognition of the Logos and mankind's expulsion of it disclose one of the fundamental principles of human society.

In the space of a few lines, the essence of the matter is repeated three times. The Logos came into the world, yet the world knew him not, his own people received him not. Mankind did not understand him. In the two thousand years since they were written, these words have attracted innumerable commentaries. Read them, and you will see that the essential point always escapes the commentators: the role of expulsion in the definition of the Johannine Logos.

In effect, the attitude of philosophy and exegesis, both Christian and non-Christian, toward John's Prologue confirms the Prologue's literal meaning. Always we have the same misunderstanding and the same failures of recognition. There is not a single essential passage in the Gospels that does not reveal the founding victim or serve that revelation—starting with the text of the Passion.

Something common to all cultures—something inherent in the way the human mind functions—has always compelled us to misrecognize the true Logos. We have been led to believe that there is only one Logos, and that it is therefore of little importance whether that Logos is credited to the Greeks or the Jews. The same violence always manifests itself, first in the guise of religion, and then fragmented in the discourses of philosophy, aesthetics, psychology and so on.

These different forms of discourse are all equivalent to one another. To see this you only have to recognize that none of them succeeds in isolating the specificity of the Johannine Logos, which is to be an outcast. None of them can reveal the founding mechanism of the City of Man. In consequence, all the breaks that take place within them are of secondary importance. The main thing is their continuity, which has always prevented even Christian commentators from recognizing the absolute singularity of the Johannine Logos, even in the context where it becomes perfectly explicit.

Any attempt to appropriate the Johannine Logos must necessarily relapse into the mythic and philosophical Logos. The error on which the whole of Western thought is founded points clearly to the truth unique in this world: measured against the Greek Logos to which it has been inappropriately assimilated, the Johannine Logos will never successfully compete with it, it must always have itself expelled from a world that cannot be its own. This process can be identified with the sacrificial reading of Christianity. The 'mistake' is exactly the one made by the Jews, who believed that they could keep Yahweh in the Temple for ever, and shut their minds to the warnings of the prophets. Always the same 'error' perpetuates itself—the 'chosen people' maintains its self-sufficiency, perceiving very accurately the faults of others (the faults that will make others, in turn, heir to the promise), but not noticing, in its pride, that it commits the self-same faults.

The distinctiveness of the true Logos has never been noticed, since to miss it is exactly the same as being under the illusion of welcoming it, while participating in the process of its expulsion. People believe that they are making a place, an honoured place, for the Christian Logos in the Christian city. They think that they are finally giving it the earthly home it has never had. But in fact they are retrenching the Logos of myth.

Heidegger was the first thinker to draw rigorous consequences from the substitution of the Greek Logos for the Johannine Logos throughout Christian and post-Christian thought. The Logos which is expelled is impossible to find. Heidegger is absolutely right to state that there has never been any thought in the West but Greek thought, even when the labels were Christian. Christianity has no special existence in the domain of thought. Continuity with the Greek Logos has never been interrupted; when people began to think again in the Middle Ages, they started to think Greek all over again. In effect, Heidegger manages to trace the history of Western philosophy without making a single mention of Christianity. Heidegger makes the final gesture that disencumbers Western thought of all the pseudo-Christian residues that still clung to it; he separates the two types of Logos by showing that everything is Greek and nothing is Christian. He registers a definitive expulsion that had already been expressed in the sacrificial definition of Christianity.

However blinded he may be by his profound but discreet animosity to Judaism and Christianity, Heidegger, like any true thinker, participates in spite of himself in the immense process of the revelation. He is right to search for the antecedent of the Johannine Logos among the Jews rather than among the Greeks, locating it in the *Word of God* that plays so considerable a part in the Second Isaiah. Indeed that approach has become increasingly common among the best of biblical commentators, including W.F. Albright, especially in his *From Stone Age to Christianity*.[79]

J.-M. O.: This distinction between the two types of Logos is fundamental. What you are saying, basically, is that all the different forms of religion, philosophy and post-philosophy are in the business of multiplying distinctions so as to conceal, spirit away and even deny the existence of this particular distinction, which is the only really fundamental one. You are doing exactly the opposite. You are trying to demonstrate the emptiness of all the differences human beings respect, and you are seeking for one single distinction: the absolute distinction between the Logos of violence, which is not, and the Logos of love, which is.

R. G.: This revelation comes from the Logos itself. In Christianity, it is expelled once again by the sacrificial reading, which amounts to a return to the Logos of violence. All the same, the Logos is still in the process of revealing itself; if it tolerates being concealed yet another time, this is to put off for just a short while the fullness of its revelation.

The Logos of love puts up no resistance; it always allows itself to be expelled by the Logos of violence. But its expulsion is revealed in a more and more obvious fashion, and by the same process the Logos of violence is revealed as what can only exist by expelling the true Logos and feeding upon it in one way or another.

'In the Beginning. . .'

J.-M. O.: I don't think we can leave the Prologue to the Gospel of John without talking about the first sentence: 'In the beginning was the Word. . .' This sentence obviously recalls the first sentence of Genesis: 'In the beginning God created the heavens and the earth.'

R. G.: Some commentators take the view that the similarities with Genesis persist in the following verses with the themes of creation, light and darkness, which also occur in Genesis.[80] In the light of our analysis, this parallelism is especially important. The prologue to John shows the whole Bible being *recommenced* from the point of view of the Logos as victim—the very point of view we have been trying to make our own.

Throughout the Middle Ages, traditional interpretation taking its cue from particular passages in the Gospels and the Epistles of Paul, tried to read the Old Testament in the light of the New. The results became less and less interesting, and this type of interpretation was finally abandoned as being irrational and mystical. Medieval exegesis was not capable of gauging how right it was to see the great figures of the Old Testament as prefiguring and announcing Christ. Because the intuition could not be justified, subsequently it was rejected as groundless by modern rationalist research, whereas in reality—in spite of its limitations—it goes far beyond all that contemporary criticism has ever told us. A few present-day authors, like Paul Claudel and Father de Lubac, sensed the richness and power of this type of exegesis, but they did not manage to justify their intuitions in rational terms.[81] The religious intuition finds a systematic justification now that it coincides with the idea suggested by the Prologue to John: that, to clarify the whole Bible in the light of the New Testament and to re-read it in a genuinely Christological light, we must recognize the Word of truth as the true knowledge of the victim, continually eluded and rejected by mankind. As long as this recognition is delayed, it will be impossible to arrive at a genuine comprehension of the objective relationship between the two Testaments.

Really getting to grips with the relationship between the Creation story in Genesis and the Prologue to the Gospel of John involves us in reflecting upon the first great text of the Bible, that of Adam and Eve's expulsion from the Garden of Eden. This text appeals to some thinkers who believe that they can discover the Bible's essentially 'repressive' character in it. For a number of centuries, we have been treated to a flood of banal demystifications of this story, no less repetitive than the forty days of uninterrupted rain must have been for the passengers in Noah's ark.

All these demystifications fail to see that this text—just like the Prologue to the Gospel of John—establishes the relationship between God and humanity in terms of expulsion. The only difference is that *in the story of Adam and Eve, God manipulates and expels mankind* to secure the foundations of culture, whilst *in the Prologue to John it is mankind who expels God*.

The Genesis text already bears witness to the Old Testament's internal travail on the subject of victimization since, in determining the relationship between human and divine, it explicitly elevates expulsion—or what Lévi-Strauss would call 'radical elimination'—to a place of the first importance. In fact, Genesis is already 'structuralist'. But, just like structuralism and in consonance with all primitive myths, it still mistakes the *real direction* in which the expulsion occurs—what it leads to, and what it signifies. The Prologue to John reverses this meaning and direction. Nothing more is needed—and nothing less is needed—to shed *light* on all the myths. The gospel interpretation of the Old Testament can be summed up in this approach, and all the bases of our anthropology are there. This anthropology merely makes explicit the first sentence of the Prologue to John, in so far as that sentence is itself the repetition and translation of another sentence, the first in all the Bible. The same thing is being repeated, with just one crucial difference—the replacement the God that inflicts violence with the God that only suffers violence, the Logos that is expelled. There is never anything at issue but this, in all circumstances and in every kind of hermeneutics. When the consequences of this substitution finally come to fulfillment, there will be incalculable results.

Pascal writes somewhere that it is permissible to correct the Bible, but only by invoking the Bible's help. That is exactly what we are doing when we re-read Genesis and the whole of the Old Testament, and the whole of culture, in the light of these few lines from the Prologue to John. The immense labour that went into the inspired text of the Bible (which is also the onward march of humanity toward the discovery of its own truth) can all be summed up in this repetition of the first sentence of Genesis and the 'slight' rectification it carries out. Far from being condemned to live in absurdity and meaninglessness, unanimity is ready and waiting, in our own period, for astonishing discoveries whose meaning is proof against all the tools of modern criticism.

J.-M. O.: In the foregoing analyses, you seem to have been changing your position on historical Christianity. You categorically oppose the sacrificial reading of the Passion and the Redemption. But although you certainly do not arrive at the humanist reading that some of your critics believed to be foreshadowed in your earlier essays, you rediscover divine transcendence in exactly the same form as all types of Christian orthodoxy have always recognized it: the Father can only be reached through the Son as mediator.

The critics' misunderstandings are provoked—and they exist already, obviously, since all that you say here was sketched out in a discussion published in *Esprit* in November 1973—by the remarkable power of demystification that springs from placing the scapegoat at the centre of the analysis. The resulting type of thought *also* happens to be Christian—it is indeed necessarily and radically Christian—and from this point onwards, any form of radical demystification must take a Christian form. That is what no one—whether atheist, traditional Christian, conservative rationalist or progressive Christian—is yet ready to accept. All the classic oppositions of modern thought collapse when confronted with this challenge.

Love and Knowledge

J.-M. O.: This brings us back to what you said at the beginning of our discussion of the Scriptures. Love is the true demystifying power because it gives the victims back their humanity. . .

R. G.: As Anders Nygren clearly saw, there is a radical opposition between love in the Christian sense and the Greek concept of Eros—even if the term *agape* is not always used to express the Christian concept in the New Testament.[82] But love is certainly not a renunciation of any form of rationality or an abandonment to the forces of ignorance. Love is at one and the same time the divine being and the basis of any real knowledge. The New Testament contains what amounts to a genuine epistemology of love, the principle of which is clearly formulated in the first Epistle of John:

> He who loves his brother abides in the light, and in it there is no cause for stumbling. But he who hates his brother is in the darkness and walks in the darkness, and does not know where he is going, because the darkness has blinded his eyes. (1 John 2, 10-11)

These words have pursued us throughout our discussions. The love of which John speaks manages to escape the hateful illusions of the doubles. It alone can reveal the victimage processes that underlie the meanings of culture. There is no purely 'intellectual' process that can arrive at true knowledge because the very detachment of the person who contemplates the warring brothers from the heights of his wisdom is an illusion. Any and every form of human knowledge is illusory to the extent that it has failed to submit to the decisive test, which is the test of the warring brothers, as Nietzsche well showed. It may never confront that challenge and remain intact in its vanity and pride, but that will only result in sterility.

Love is the only true revelatory power because it escapes from, and strictly limits, the spirit of revenge and recrimination that still characterizes the revelation in our own world, a world in which we can turn that spirit into a weapon against our own doubles, as Nietzsche also showed. Only Christ's perfect love can achieve without violence the perfect revelation toward which we have been progressing—in spite of everything—by way of the dissensions and divisions that were predicted in the Gospels. The present expression of these dissensions is our increasing tendency to load responsibility for all these divisions upon the Gospels themselves. We can only agree among ourselves in attacking the Gospel, which by a wonderfully revealing symbolism is in the process of becoming our scapegoat. Human beings came together in the first societies of our planet simply to give birth to the truth of the Gospel, and now they are determined to deny that truth.

This will to deny the truth acquires a particular force of blindness and insight in Nietzsche's *The Anti-Christ*, which explicitly rejects the epistemology of love set out by the New Testament:

> Love is the state in which man sees things most of all as they are *not*. The illusion-creating force is there at its height, likewise the sweetening and *transforming* force. One endures more when in love than one otherwise would, one tolerates everything.[83]

G. L.: Nietzsche is quite coherent in his own terms, at least in this quotation. Choosing 'Dionysus instead of the Crucified', and not seeing the way in which collective violence is glossed over in the Greek myth, is obviously tantamount to rejecting the epistemology that the Epistle of John sets out.

R. G.: The idea that Christ brings with him the key to the Old Testament can be found throughout the Gospels, not only in the interpretations Jesus offers but also, significantly, in a number of scenes that occur after the Resurrection and are already (so it seems to me) dominated by the outpouring of truth—in other words, by the power of interpretation that is bestowed on humankind by the Passion of Christ.

In the Christian world, it is always a question of re-reading not from the end but from beyond this end; in the light of this beyond, former perspectives are shown to be false. Western culture as a whole, whether Christian or post-Christian, is under the illusion that it is moving further and further away from Christ, like the Emmaus disciples, while it retains a false, sacrificial conception of him. It is struggling to rid itself of Christ for good. But at the very point when it is under the impression of moving in quite a different direction, Christ is to be found beside it, as he has been for a long time, 'opening the Scriptures'.

All the grand theories of modern times, and all forms of thought in the human sciences and world of politics, have a bearing on the victimage processes and issue their own condemnations of these processes. But these condemnations are invariably selective; they are ranged against each other, with each way of thinking concerned to brandish its 'own' victims in the face of the others. Full of mistrust for the Christian texts, they perpetuate readings that maintain the same sacrificial point of view as historical Christianity, and they are recognizably products of the sacrificial system. All the same, taken as a whole these ways of thinking can only prepare for the revelation of the victimage process in all its breadth as the founding process of culture. They are all unconsciously working toward the vindication of the very texts that they claim to have put behind them.

We are told that scandal is the only worthwhile thing; we must think scandalously. Well, here at last is something which goes beyond the old scandals which have been heated up for the thousandth time—those pettifogging scandals associated with Sade and Nietzsche, which are just the old follies of the Romantics forcibly recycled. Here at last is a fine new scandal for the closing stages of the twentieth century, something that should cause real panic among moderns avid for new sensations. But we can bet that it will not take hold; people will try to conjure it away for as long as they possibly can.

It is extremely ironic that the huge task anthropology has set itself—one in opposition to the claims of the Judaeo-Christian tradition, and justifiably so, up to a point, because anthropologists have attacked the sacrificial interpretation of biblical texts rather than the texts themselves—has all of a sudden, at the moment it was nearing completion, met with a confirmation of those very claims that is as spectacular as it is unexpected.

Modern thought might make us reflect on all those people involved in moving deserts in the Second Isaiah: all those slaves—armed in our own day with splendid bulldozers—who have no notion of why they are levelling mountains and filling valleys with such bizarre and frenetic movements. They have scarcely heard speak of the great king who will pass in triumph along the road they are preparing for him.

I will quote from the text as it occurs in the Authorized Version of the Bible:

> The voice of him that crieth in the wilderness, Prepare ye the way of the LORD, make straight in the desert a highway for our God.

> Every valley shall be exalted, and every mountain and hill shall be made low: and the crooked shall be made straight, and the rough places plain:

> And the glory of the LORD shall be revealed, and all flesh shall see it together: for the mouth of the LORD hath spoken it.

The voice said, Cry. And he said, What shall I cry? All flesh is grass, and all the goodliness thereof is as the flower of the field:

The grass withereth, the flower fadeth: . . . but the word of our God shall stand for ever (Isaiah 40, 3-8).

BOOK III

INTERDIVIDUAL PSYCHOLOGY

TROILUS:
What is aught, but as 'tis valued?

HECTOR:
But value dwells not in particular will;
It holds his estimate and dignity
As well as therein 'tis precious of itself
As in the prizer: 'tis mad idolatry
To make the service greater than the god;
And the will dotes that is attributive
To what infectiously itself affects,
Without some image of th'affected merit.

WILLIAM SHAKESPEARE
Troilus and Cressida, II, ii, 52-60.

CHAPTER ONE

Mimetic Desire

Acquisitive Mimesis and Mimetic Desire

R. G.: Up to this point we have not breathed a word about what interests you particularly. We have hardly spoken the word 'desire'. We have only talked about the way in which the obstructive effects of mimesis are grafted on to the needs and appetites of animal life.

G. L.: The word 'desire' has attracted a great many different connatations in the modern world, and I can imagine that for this reason it was difficult for you to talk about it. I can also imagine, however, that your definition of desire will be based on the way in which mimesis cuts across the instinctual composition of animal life.

R. G.: Yes indeed. We must not allow human desire to have the rather too absolute degree of specificity with which psychoanalysis still endows it; this is inimical to any form of scientific treatment. It is evident among animals that the effects of mimesis are grafted on to needs and appetites, though these never reach the same pitch as with human beings. Desire is undoubtedly a distinctively human phenomenon that can only develop when a certain threshold of mimesis is transcended.

J.-M. O.: What holds for anthropology as a whole is necessarily the case for desire as well. On the one hand, we must refuse to allow the absolute distinctiveness of desire; on the other, we must also refuse to see man as an animal like all the others, as do the ethnologists and the behaviourists. Human desire is only relatively distinctive.

R. G.: This does not mean that we take the view of Hegel or Freud, whereby the threshold of hominization is crossed, and there appears a form of desire comparable to the one that we observe around and within ourselves. For there to be desire according to our definition, the effects of mimesis must interfere, not directly with animal instincts and appetites, but in a terrain that has already been fundamentally modified by the process of hominization: in other words, the mimetic effects and a wholsesale re-processing of symbols must develop in unison. All the elements of what we call normal psychology—and everything that constitutes us as human beings on the level that we call 'psychic', must result from the infinitely slow, but ultimately monumental work achieved by the disorganization and increasingly complex reorganization of mimetic functions. Our hypothesis makes it logical to imagine that the rigorous symmetry between the mimetic partners (which results in the paroxysm of rivalry that is in itself sterile and destructive but becomes fruitful to the extent that ritual retraces it in a spirit of fear and solidarity) must bring about two things among man's ancestors, little by little: the ability to look at the other person, the mimetic *double*, as an *alter ego* and the matching capacity to establish a *double* inside oneself, through processes like reflection and consciousness.

J.-M. O.: But this is not adequate to place what we call desire in a suitable context. Religious societies that are based on a rigid framework are capable of distributing the appetites and needs of individuals in divergent directions, thus they ward off the possibility of an uncontrolled interplay of mimetic effects. I would obviously not want to argue that the phenomenon we call desire does not exist in primitive societies. The definition of the term is in any case too vague to allow any such rigid categorizations. But undoubtedly desire is bubbling over and exceeding its boundaries in the modern world; for it to be capable of doing so, that obscure thing named desire must occur in a world in which barriers are pulled down and differences eradicated—something unlikely in religious societies.

Mimetic Desire and the Modern World

R. G.: All kinds of connotations relating to conflict, competition and subversion cluster around the term 'desire', and help to explain the amazing success—as well as failure—that both the word and the thing itself have experienced in the modern world. Some people equate the proliferation of desire with a loosening of the bonds of culture, which they deplore; they link it to the levelling of 'natural' hierarchies on a broad front, and the wreckage of all values worthy of respect. In the modern world, these enemies of desire are ranged against the friends of desire; the two camps periodically pass judgment on each other in the name of order against disorder, reaction against progress, the past against the future, and so on. In doing so, they oversimplify a very complicated state of affairs. In contrast to what the 'enemies' of desire are always telling us, our world shows itself to be quite capable of absorbing high doses of 'undifferentiation'. What would have acted as a deadly poison in other societies, giving rise to a crescendo of mimetic rivalry, can indeed produce terrifying convulsions within our own society. But up to now, these have proved to be merely temporary. The modern world has not only got over them; it has drawn from them new strength to flourish on an ever more 'modern' foundation: one that gets larger and larger, while developing its capacity to assimilate cultural elements and whole populations that had remained outside its sphere.

J.-M. O.: Everything that makes our world the most energetic and creative one that has ever been, in art, politics, modes of thought and, especially, science and technology—everything that contributed initially to the extraordinary pride of this world, its sense of invincible superiority, and that now contributes to its increasing sense of anguish—can be said to rest on the 'liberation' of mimetic desire.

R. G.: In the long run, the pessimism of 'reactionaries' never proves to be justified, but neither does the optimism of revolutionaries. The expansion of human potential that the latter expect from the final, complete liberation of desire never turns out to be the triumph that they expect. Either the liberated desire is channelled into competitive directions that, though enormously creative, are ultimately disappointing, or it simply ends up in sterile conflict and anarchic confusion, with a corresponding increase in the sense of anguish. There is a good reason for this.

Modern people still fondly imagine that their discomfort and unease is a product of the strait-jacket that religious taboos, cultural prohibitions and, in our day, even the legal forms of protection guaranteed by the judiciary system place upon desire. They think that once this confinement is over, desire will be able to blossom forth; its wonderful innocence will finally be able to bear fruit.

None of this comes true. To the extent that desire does away with the external obstacles that traditional society ingeniously established to keep it from spreading, the structural obstacle that coincides with the effects of mimesis—the living obstacle of the model that is automatically transformed into a rival—can very advantageously, or rather disadvantageously, take the place of the prohibition that no longer works. Men lose the kind of obstacle that is inert and passive, but at the same time beneficient and equal for all—the obstacle that for this reason could never really become humiliating or incapacitating. In place of this obstacle established by religious prohibition, they have to reckon increasingly with the kind of obstacle that is active, mobile and fierce—the model metamorphosed into a rival, interested in personally crossing them and well equipped to do so.

The more people think that they are realizing the Utopias dreamed up by their desire—in other words, the more they embrace ideologies of liberation—the more they will in fact be working to reinforce the competitive world that is stifling them. But they do not realize their mistake; and continue to systematically confuse the type of external obstacle represented by the prohibition and the internal obstacle formed by the mimetic partner. They are like the frogs who became discontented with the King Log sent to them by Jupiter and, by importuning the gods with their cries of protest, obtained more and more satisfaction. The best method of chastising mankind is to give people all that they want on all occasions.

At the very moment when the last prohibitions are being forgotten, there are still any number of intellectuals who continue to refer to them as if they were more and more crippling. Alternatively, they replace the myth of the prohibition with one that invokes an omnipresent and omniscient 'power' and can be seen as yet another mythic transposition of the strategies of mimesis. The greater part of Michel Foucault's work is erected on that false premise.

G. L.: You are going to get yourself branded as a dreadful reactionary again.

R. G.: That would not be at all fair. I do find it absurd that people should greet with a fanfare the liberation of a desire that is not being constrained by anyone. But I find it even more absurd to hear people calling for a return to constraints, which is impossible. From the moment cultural forms begin to dissolve, any attempt to reconstitute them artificially can only result in the most appalling tyranny.

I do not think that we should mince our words. We must refuse all the scapegoats that Freud and Freudianism have offered to us: the father, the law, etc. We must refuse the scapegoats that Marx offers: the bourgeoisie, the capitalists, etc. We must refuse the scapegoats that

Nietzsche offers: slave morality, the resentment of *others* and so on. All of modernism in its classic stage—with Marx, Nietzsche and Freud in the forefront—merely offers us scapegoats. But if individually every one of these thinkers is delaying the full revelation, their collective effect can only prepare for its coming; they prepare the way for the omnipresent victim, who has already been delayed from time immemorial by sacrificial processes that are now becoming exhausted, since they appear to be more and more transparent and less and less effective—and are proportionately more and more to be feared in the domains of politics and sociology. To make these processes effective once again, people are tempted to multiply the innocent victims, to kill all the enemies of the nation or the class, to stamp out what remains of religion or the family as the origins of all forms of 'repression', and to sing the praises of murder and madness as the only true forces of 'liberation'.

All modern thought is falsified by a mystique of transgression, which it falls back into even when it is trying to escape. For Lacan, desire is still a by-product of the law. Even the most daring thinkers nowadays do not dare to recognize that prohibition has a protective function with regard to the conflicts inevitably provoked by desire. They would be afraid that people might see them as 'reactionary'. In the currents of thought that have dominated us for a century, there is one tendency we must never forget: the fear of being regarded as naive or submissive, the desire to play at being the freest thinker—the most 'radical', etc. As long as you pander to this desire, you can make the modern intellectual say almost anything you like. This is the new way in which we are still 'keeping up with the Joneses'.

The Mimetic Crisis and the Dynamism of Desire

J.-M. O.: Desire is related to what happens in what is called 'ritual preparation' and all that it represents, in particular to the festivals and trials associated with initiation rites. Desire can, in fact, be defined in similar terms, as a process of mimesis involving undifferentiation; it is akin to the process of deepening conflict that issues in the mechanism of re-unification through the victim. Yet in our world, the processes of desire do not ever give rise to the collective crescendo that marks the ritual activities; at no stage are they concluded by an act of spontaneous expulsion.

R. G.: Desire forms part of a world that does not involve either the terrifying yet rapid epidemics that characterize primitive societies, or the cathartic peace that the rites of violence manage to bring about when such crises are not taking place. Desire is endemic rather than epidemic. As a state, it corresponds not so much to mimetic crises as they occur in primitive societies but to something at once similar and very different, which is linked to the lasting enfeeblement of founding violence within our own world. The Judaeo-Christian texts have produced a disintegration, whose effect has, however, been slowed down and moderated by the churches' sacrificial reading. The dynamism of desire thus takes the form of a mimetic crisis that has been enormously slowed down and lengthened, in the individual historical context.

Desire is what happens to human relationships when there is no longer any resolution through the victim, and consequently no form of polarization that is genuinely unanimous and can trigger such a resolution. But human relationships are mimetic nonetheless. We shall be able to discover, beneath the 'underground' (in the Dostoevskyan sense) and always deceptive form of individual symptoms, the dynamic style of the sacrificial crisis. In this instance, however, there can be no ritualistic or victimary resolution, and, if and when it becomes acute, the crisis ensues—what we call psychosis.

Desire is the mimetic crisis in itself; it is the acute mimetic rivalry with the other that occurs in all the circumstances we call 'private', ranging from eroticism to professional or intellectual ambition. The crisis can be stabilized at different levels according to the individuals concerned, but it always lacks the resources of catharsis and expulsion.

J.-M. O.: In other words, desire now flourishes within a society whose cathartic resources are vanishing—a society where the only mechanism that could renew these resources functions less and less effectively. Desire may not be a specifically modern invention, but it is in modern life that desire has blossomed; or, more exactly, it is as a modern phenomenon that desire has blossomed and it is in the light of this modernity that we re-read in terms of our own desire a whole range of ancient or non-Western phenomena, which are perhaps not yet wholly a product of it.

You postulate the existence of desire as a priori, in an almost deductive manner. Given that there exists a world—our own—in which the mechanisms of culture are exposed to the slow but inexorable subversion of a Judaeo-Christian element tempered by the sacrificial interpretation, the mimetic crisis must be lived out in this modified modern version, by each individual in his relationships with others. In fact, you allow yourself the luxury of defining desire before you describe it. People will accuse you of being too systematic and too speculative but you do this on purpose, in order that the definition may be clear. You want to show the capacity of your hypothesis to generate all the different forms of desire and all the symptoms of psychopathology, in so far as they are successive moments in a continuous process engendered by the original definition. As always, the only dynamic force necessary to explain the process derives from mimetic desire and mimetic rivalry.

R. G.: I believe that by proceeding in this deductive manner from a definition, we will discover—in an order of increasing seriousness and in forms that clearly demonstrate how and why they combine with each other, overlap each other and nest within each other—all the major symptoms that have been clumsily carved up by the discipline of psychopathology, in its chronic uncertainty over methods and perspectives.

Now, as before, I am mainly concerned with the hypothesis as a whole. This is the reason I have approached desire in the way you suggest, putting the hypothetical argument in the forefront—an approach that is admittedly paradoxical, since the hypothesis is grounded in primitive societies, and it is the gradual effacement of its hard core, the victimage mechanism, that will play the principal role in our analyses.

G. L.: If you can catch in the mimetic net some of the things that psychopathology has never really succeeded in grasping or understanding, you will indeed have shown that your hypothesis is relevant to all the human sciences.

R. G.: First, I must show that from the beginning the forms of misapprehension generated by mimetic interferences with human needs and appetites are governed by a process of aggravation and escalation. This process governs not only desire but our interpretation of desire, whether they be psychological, poetic, psychoanalytic or otherwise. It impels both individuals and communities toward ever more pathological forms of desire; these forms constitute new interpretations.

The Mimesis of Apprenticeship and the Mimesis of Rivalry

R. G.: Here, as in every case, we have to return to what one might call the primary mimeticism. This is a mimeticism which cannot fail to arouse conflicts. It is therefore disruptive and dangerous, but it is also indispensable to the cultural process. What is true for culture as a whole is also true for every individual member of it. No one can do without a highly developed mimetic capacity in acquiring cultural attitudes—in situating oneself correctly within one's own culture.

G. L.: Everything that we know under the titles of apprenticeship, education and initiation rests on this capacity for mimesis.

J.-M. O.: We have already made the point for animals; we know that the same is true of mankind. One proof lies in the fact that only with considerable difficulty can those who are deaf from birth learn their mother tongue.

R. G.: If there is nothing to direct it, the mimetic tendency will operate across all forms of human behaviour without distinction. The child is in no position to distinguish between non-acquisitive forms of behaviour—those that are good to imitate—and acquisitive forms, which give rise to rivalry. In fact there is no way of distinguishing on an objective basis, no way of making a systematic overall distinction, between forms of behaviour that are 'good' to imitate and those that are not.

Let us take a very simple example, if you like—that of the master and his disciples. The master is delighted to see more and more disciples around him, and delighted to see that he is being taken as a model. Yet if the imitation is too perfect, and the imitator threatens to surpass the model, the master will completely change his attitude and begin to display jealousy, mistrust and hostility. He will be tempted to do everything he can to discredit and discourage his disciple.

The disciple can only be blamed for being the best of all disciples. He admires and respects the model; if he had not done so, he would hardly have chosen him as model in the first place. So inevitably he lacks the necessary 'distance' to put what is happening to him 'in perspective'. He does not recognize the signs of rivalry in the behaviour of the model. It is all the more difficult for the disciple to do so because the model tries very hard to reinforce this blindness. The model tries his best to hide the real reasons for his hostility.

This is just one example of the inextricable *double bind* of imitation, which turns back against the imitator even though the model and the whole culture specifically encourage him to imitate.

In archaic societies, prohibitions are closely interlocked and the different compartments they establish determine the distribution of disposable objects between the members of the culture. We have the impression that if it were possible some cultures would dispense with individual choice altogether and so entirely eliminate the possibility of mimetic rivalry.

In contemporary society, the exact opposite increasingly takes place. No more taboos forbid one person to take what is reserved for another, and no more initiation rites prepare individuals in common, for the necessary trials of life. Modern education does not warn the child that the same type of imitative behaviour will be applauded and encouraged on one occasion, and discouraged on another, or that there is no way of telling what will happen by simply paying attention to the models themselves or to the objects to which desire is directed. Instead, modern education thinks it is able to resolve every problem by glorifying the natural spontaneity of desire, which is a purely mythological notion.

We cannot avoid at this point, a rather schematic argument. We must first present the situation in its universal dimensions. In so far as it pulls down all barriers to 'freedom' of desire, modern society is giving a concrete form to this universality; it is putting more and more individuals, from childhood on, in a situation that favours the mimetic *double bind*. How on earth is the child to know that his whole process of adaptation is governed by two contradictory and equally rigorous obligations, which cannot be discriminated objectively and which no one will ever mention? The absence of any guidance on the issue is demonstrated by the complete silence on the subject, however far you penetrate into the fastnesses of psychological and pedagogical theory.

For there to be a mimetic *double bind* in the full sense of the term, there must be a subject who is incapable of correctly interpreting the double imperative that comes from the other person: taken as model, imitate me; and as rival, do not imitate me.

Gregory Bateson's 'Double Bind'

G. L.: You make very frequent use of the expression *double bind*, which is borrowed from the theory of schizophrenia developed by Gregory Bateson. Clearly that does not mean that your hypothesis can be understood within the framework of communication theory.

R. G.: Bateson relates schizophrenia to a dual and contradictory message that one of the two parents—almost always the mother—communicates to the child. Some mothers, for example, speak the language of love and the most complete devotion, reaching out to their children on the level of discourse, but each time their children respond to these advances, they unconsciously behave antagonistically. They make themselves seem exceptionally cold, perhaps, for example, because the child puts them in mind of a man—his father—who has abandoned them. The child exposed to this contradictory alternation between warmth and frigidity will lose all faith in the capacity of language. In the long term, he will close himself off to all linguistic messages and exhibit other signs of schizophrenia.[84]

As far as the cultural sciences are concerned, information theory and in particular Bateson's notion of the double bind seem to offer a number of interesting elements. The first is that informational order comes into being on the basis of disorder, and is always capable of returning to disorder. Information theory allots disorder a place that Lévi-Strauss's structuralism and all that derives from it in the contemporary range of language studies are incapable of giving it. Edgar Morin has effectively pointed out this advantage.

A second, even more interesting point is the role played, in information theory, by the notion of *feedback*. Instead of being simply linear, in a classically deterministic manner, the cybernetic chain is circular. Event *a* gives rise to event *b*, which perhaps sets off any number of other events; but the last of them returns to *a* and has an effect on it. The cybernetic chain is fastened back on itself. The feedback is negative if every new stage develops in an opposite direction to the previous stages and, as a result, corrects for them in such a way as to keep the system in constant equilibrium. Feedback is positive, by contrast, if the successive stages develop in the same direction and become progressively greater; in that case, the system tends toward *runaway*, a kind of escalation which results in its complete disruption and destruction. These particular concepts are relevant to the study of ritualized equilibrium in human society, and the mimetic crisis can be seen as a kind of runaway.

In his book *Naven*, Gregory Bateson describes what I would call the mimetic crisis in terms of a cybernetic escalation. In the Naven ritual, he detects the elements of competition and the opposition of doubles, defining them as 'symmetrical schismogenesis'.[85] He notices that this tendency is abruptly discontinued and reversed in a terminal paroxysm, but he does not see the role played in the process of resolution by the specific mechanism of the victim. I think that if we analysed the Naven in the light of the mimetic process, we would have no difficulty in disentangling this connection with the victim.

It is very significant that research workers under Gregory Bateson's influence—Paul Watzlawick and his collaborators—responding particularly to Bateson's theory of psychosis, have arrived straightaway at the mechanisms for excluding the victim when they seek to develop, on the basis of information theory, a 'pragmatics' of human communication.[86] These researchers looked at very small groups, essentially the nuclear family. According to them, any tendency within these systems to become dysfunctional is immediately translated into an unconscious effort to re-establish the lost equilibrium. This works to the disadvantage of an individual member of the group, against whom the rest form a common front. It is this particular individual who exhibits mental disorder, which is precious to the group as a whole since it can be held responsible for everything that stops the group from functioning normally. So this particular reading of the situation, which is common to all the 'healthy' elements in the group, is capable of instating another type of equilibrium—one which is once again functional, however precarious it may be. In their book, *Pragmatics of Human Communication,* Watzalwick and his collaborators see the implications of their work reflected also in literature; they attempt an extremely interesting interpretation of an eminently sacrificial play, Edward Albee's *Who's Afraid of Virginia Woolf?* But they make no attempt to explore the vast cultural and religious context within which their research properly belongs.

J.-M. O.: This group from Palo Alto [Stanford University] is not concerned with the larger implications of the victimage mechanism and its specific role in founding all the systems of cultural communication that are based on the symbolizing faculty and on language.

R. G.: Because they limit themselves to the study of extremely small groups within modern society, they stay away from fundamental anthropology. In fact, Bateson's concept of the double bind and the basic postulates of communication theory, with its emphasis on equilibrium, prevent them from moving in this direction.

G. L.: Their notion of communication is much too narrow. It has a number of advantages over the psychoanalytic notion of desire, which does not succeed in ridding itself of irrationality. But it does not lead to the victimage mechanism, any more than does studying the behavioural patterns of animals—even when these are interpreted within the enlarged perspective of present-day ethology.

R. G.: All these perspectives are necessary. But they are all inadequate, and they remain irreconcilable. The only means of reconciling them and capitalizing on all their gains without suffering from their drawbacks is by applying the mimetic theory. Only this theory can function for animals as well as for humans; only it does away with a metaphysical rupture between the two realms, while avoiding any unwarranted confusion between them, since the mimetic process functions quite differently in each. Moreover, the mimetic process, without being foreign to language, is prior to language and goes beyond it in every respect; for this reason, the mimetic process makes it possible to universalize the principle of the double bind, to apply it to the whole process of mimetic appropriation, while introducing the principle of feedback and the threat of the runaway throughout the whole range of relationships between individuals.

Our research cannot reach the right definition of the problem if we do not see the need for counteracting the potentially destructive effects of the mimetic double bind. If we are willing to confront this apparently intractable situation, the road that leads to the victimage mechanism is open to us. Describing the problem in terms of entropy and negentropy is very attractive to modern minds, which have a penchant for thinking that metaphors taken from scientific disciplines can function as explanations, when they are simply another way of articulating the problem. The secret underlying cultural 'negentropy' is the victimage mechanism and the series of religious imperatives it engenders . . .

From Object Rivalry to Metaphysical Desire

R. G.: To untie the knot of desire, we have only to concede that everything begins in rivalry for the object. The object acquires the status of a disputed object and thus the envy that it arouses in all quarters, becomes more and more heated.

G. L.: Marxists will solemnly say that capitalism invented this escala-

tion. Marxists hold that the problems we are discussing have been resolved once and for all by Marx, just as Freudians think that they have
been resolved once and for all by Freud.

R. G.: As far as that goes, the real founders of capitalism, and also of
the Oedipus complex, are the monkeys. All that capitalism, or rather
the liberal society that allows capitalism to flourish, does, is to give mimetic phenomena a freer rein and to direct them into economic and
technological channels. For religious reasons that are far from simple,
capitalism is capable of doing away with the restraints that archaic
societies placed upon mimetic rivalry.

The value of an object grows in proportion to the resistance met with
in acquiring it. And the value of the model grows as the object's value
grows. Even if the model has no particular prestige at the outset, even if
all that 'prestige' implies—*praestigia*, spells and phantasmagoria—is
quite unknown to the subject, the very rivalry will be quite enough to
bring prestige into being.

The mechanical character of primary imitation makes it likely that
the subject will misinterpret the automatic aspect of his rivalry with the
model. When the subject interrogates himself about this relationship of
opposition, he will tend to endow it with meanings it does not possess.
Moreover, all explanations that claim to be scientific, including those
given by Freud, do the same. Freud imagines that the triangle of rivalry
conceals a secret of some kind, an 'oedipal' secret, whereas in fact it
only conceals the rivalry's mimetic character.

The object of desire is indeed forbidden. But it is not the 'law' that
forbids it, as Freud believes—it is the person who designates the object
to us as desirable by desiring it himself. The non-legal prohibition
brought about through rivalry has the greatest capacity to wound and
traumatize. This structure of rivalry is not a static configuration of elements. Instead the elements of the system react upon one another; the
prestige of the model, the resistance he puts up, the value of the object,
and the strength of the desire it arouses all reinforce each other, setting
up a process of positive feedback. Only in this context does it become
possible to understand what Freud calls 'ambivalence'—a pernicious
force that he identified but was unable to explain adequately.[87]

Legal prohibitions are addressed to everyone or to whole categories
of people, and they do not, as a general rule, suggest to us that we are
'inferior' as individuals. By contrast, the prohibition created by mi-

metic rivalry is invariably addressed to a particular individual, who tends to interpret it as hostile to himself.

Even if he holds himself to be persecuted, the subject will necessarily ask himself if the model has not got perfectly good reasons for denying him the object. An increasingly weighty part of himself will carry on imitating the model and, by virtue of this fact, will take the model's side, secretly justifying the hostile treatment he believes he is undergoing at the hands of the model and interpreting it as a special condemnation that he probably deserves.

Once he has entered upon this vicious circle, the subject rapidly begins to credit himself with a radical inadequacy that the model has brought to light, which justifies the model's attitude toward him. The model, being closely identified with the object he jealously keeps for himself, possesses—so it would seem—a self-sufficiency and omniscience that the subject can only dream of acquiring. The object is now more desired than ever. Since the model obstinately bars access to it, the possession of this object must make all the difference between the self-sufficiency of the model and the imitator's lack of sufficiency, the model's fullness of being and the imitator's nothingness.

This process of transfiguration does not correspond to anything real, and yet it transforms the object into something that appears superabundantly real. Thus it could be described as metaphysical in character. We might well decide to use the word 'desire' only in circumstances where the misunderstood mechanism of mimetic rivalry has imbued what was previously just an appetite or a need with this metaphysical dimension. Here we have no alternative but to use philosophical language, because philosophy stands in the same relation to the primitive sacralizing features of violence as 'metaphysical' desire does to the mimetic frenzy induced by the gods of violence. This is why modern eroticism and the literature that deals with it tend—beyond a certain level of intensity—to reach back to the vocabulary of the sacred. All the great lyrical metaphors derive, whether directly or indirectly, from sacred violence. But literary criticism, though it registers the fact, does not investigate it in earnest. Literary criticism is generally more interested in reviving the old 'frisson' that metaphors of this kind communicate than in genuine understanding.

By invoking the notion of metaphysical desire, I am not in any way giving in to metaphysics. To understand this notion, we have only to look at the kinship between the mimetic structure we have discussed and the part played by notions such as honour or prestige in certain types of rivalry that are regulated by society: duels, sporting competitions, etc. These notions are in fact created by the rivalry; they have no tangible reality whatsoever. Yet the very fact that there is a rivalry involving them makes them appear to be more real than any real object. To whatever small degree these notions go beyond the invariably ritualized framework that gives them their appearance of being finite—within a world stabilized by victimage mechanisms—they will escape measures of objective control. They truly become 'infinite', 'absolute'. At this moment, in the primitive world, everything collapses back into the mimetic frenzy, the death struggle and, yet again, the victimage mechanism. In our own world, we end up with an 'infinite' measure of desire—with what I have called ontological or metaphysical desire.

The 'metaphysical' threshold or, if we put it a different way, the point at which we reach desire properly speaking, is the threshold of the unreal. It can also be seen as the threshold of psychopathology. Yet we should insist upon the continuity, even the identity, between such a level of desire and everything that passes as completely normal because it is defined in terms sanctioned by society, such as the love of risk, thirst for the infinite, stirrings of the poetic soul, *amour fou*, and so on.

J.-M. O.: You are always referring to a subject who never gets the upper hand in his struggles with his rival. But the opposite can happen. What happens if the subject successfully gains possession of the object?

R. G.: For victory to change anything in the fate of the subject, it must come about *before* the gap has started to widen between all that possession can offer in the way of pleasure, satisfaction, enjoyment, and so on, and the increasingly metaphysical aspirations that are brought into being by the misconceptions of rivalry.

If the gap is too wide, possession will be such a disabusing experience that the subject will put all the blame for it upon the object, not to mention the model. He will never blame desire as such, or the mimetic character of desire. Object and model are both rejected with disdain. But the subject sets off in search of a new model and a new object that will not let him down so easily. From this point, desire seeks only to find a resistance that it is incapable of overcoming.

To sum up, victory only speeds up the subject's degeneration. The pursuit of failure becomes ever more expert and knowledgeable, without being able to recognize itself as the pursuit of failure.

J. -M. O.: In effect, whether he succeeds or fails, the subject always courts failure. Rather than conclude that desire itself is a cul-de-sac, he can always find pretexts for coming to more favourable conclusions and giving desire one last chance. He is always ready to condemn the objects he has once possessed and the desires he has already experienced—the idols of yesteryear—at the very moment when a new idol or a new object comes over the horizon. But fashion works like this, as well. The person obsessed by fashion is always ready to give up everything, himself included, so as not to have to give up fashion—so as to keep a way open for his desire.

So long as you have not triumphed over all the obstacles, there is still one possibility—which admittedly gets slimmer and slimmer, but never quite disappears—that behind the last rampart, guarded by the last dragon, lies the treasure that has been sought for everywhere, just waiting for us.

R. G.: Desire has its own logic, and it is a logic of gambling. Once past a certain level of bad luck, the luckless player does not give up; as the odds get worse, he plays for higher stakes. Likewise, the subject will always manage to track down the obstacle that cannot be surmounted—which is perhaps nothing more than the world's massive indifference to him, in the end—and he will destroy himself against it.

J.-M. O.: People always refer to Pascal's famous wager about the existence of God as if it were the only one of its kind. What you have been saying amounts to what Pascal perceives when he theorizes about *divertissement*. Desire is also a kind of wager, but it is always a losing wager. Betting on the existence of God is therefore betting on a God radically other than the God of desire, a non-violent and benevolent, rather than a violent and perpetually frustrating, divinity.

CHAPTER TWO

Desire without Object

Doubles and Interdividuality

J.-M.O.: It seems to me that the difficulty many readers have in understanding your theory comes from the fact that they do not see an important point. This is that the difference between subject and model can only exist in a first stage, which can be real, no doubt, but is more frequently a theoretical one, only necessary for didactic purposes.

R.G.: Mimetism is indeed the contagion which spreads throughout human relationships, and in principle it spares no one. If the model himself becomes more interested in the object that he designates to his imitator as a result of the latter's imitations, then he himself falls victim to his contagion. In fact, he imitates his own desire, through the intermediary of the disciple. The disciple thus becomes model to his own model, and the model, reciprocally, becomes disciple of his own disciple. In the last resort, there are no genuine differences left between the two, or, to put it more precisely, between their desires; it is not satisfactory to think merely in terms of differences being exchanged, displaced and diverted. These vanishing differences are nothing more than interruptions in reciprocity, and they always involve an element of the arbitrary, since they are rooted in the victimage mechanisms and in mimetic rivalry; they dissolve in the face of violence, which makes everything return to the pure state of reciprocity. In rivalry, everyone occupies all the positions, one after another and then simultaneously, and there are no longer any distinct positions.

Everything that one of the partners to violence experiences, thinks about, or carries into action at a given moment, will sooner or later become observable in the other partner. In the last analysis, there is nothing that can be said of any one partner that must not be said about all partners without exception. There is no longer any way of differentiating the partners from one another. This is what I call the relationship of *doubles*.

G.L.: Only you present doubles as real individuals, dominated by a reciprocal violence beyond their comprehension, which becomes more and more identical on both sides, not merely at the stages of positive imitation we have already covered, but at the stages of negative imitation and actual physical violence. Traditionally, the term 'double' has been used in a different sense to mean a weak reflection, an image in the mirror, a ghost. Hoffmann and other Romantic authors employ it in this sense, and Freud, Rank and other psychoanalysts remain faithful to that usage when they detect, in some patients, what they call a hallucinatory double.

R.G.: I believe that it is possible to refer the hallucinatory double back to the real doubles I talk about. Physical violence is the perfect accomplishment of the conflictual mimetic relationship, and it is completely reciprocal. Everyone imitates the other's violence and returns it 'with interest'. Uninvolved spectators see this unmistakably. In order to understand it, we have only to view the relationship as Punch and Judy, bashing each other over the head.

In so far as they remain pure spectacle, doubles are the basis for all forms of action in the theatre, irrespective of whether they are comic or tragic.

Once the symmetry of the mimetic relationship really takes hold, it must be eliminated. The reciprocal violence transforms every model into an anti-model; although the imitators now differ from the model rather than resembling him, the reciprocity is still maintained, precisely because everyone is trying to break away from it in the same way. The desire is always the same, even when it no longer involves belief in the transcendent status of the model.

J.-M.O.: What you have said applies to contemporary life in its most grandiose as well as its most insignificant aspects. For instance, in intellectual life fashion becomes all-powerful exactly at the point when everyone agrees to differ. People all try to differ in the same way, and in no time at all they find their singularities to be identical; giving up a fashion becomes just as fashionable as taking it up in the first place. This is why everyone is opposed to fashions; everyone is always deserting the reigning fashion in order to imitate what has not yet been imitated, what everybody is only beginning to imitate. If our gurus follow each other more and more rapidly and the very essence of intellectual life seem endangered, this is because fashion, like everything else, escalates. As soon as everyone begins to understand its workings better and better, fashion accelerates, and giving up fashion is no longer a pipe-dream; fashion itself ends up by going out of fashion. In this area, *haute couture* is in advance of theory. *Haute couture* was the first to realize that it no longer existed, as one of my friends, himself a *grand couturier*, shrewdly observed.

R.G.: It is not a feature of ancient writers only, but of modern writers as well, that when they become really great, they tend to focus upon doubles. They reach the crucial point that critical theory never reaches, stuck as it is with its linguistic prejudices at the zero point of difference, being neither the philosophical object nor the philosophical subject, but merely mimetic rivalry.

Take Proust for example. You can find texts by him which interpret the deep-seated misapprehensions of desire with a comic flair reminiscent of Charlie Chaplin. And yet the misapprehensions are the same as desire in its most lyrical expression, as it operates within all of the characters, beginning with the narrator himself. These key Proustian texts make the point that we are always dealing with the same structure—in other words, that desire is not really as interesting as it would like to make out. Far from being limitless in their possibilities, the surprises sprung by desire are always the same, always predictable and calculable. They only succeed in surprising desire itself, which is invariably caught in its own game and works against its own interest. No strategy can ever bring desire what it seeks, but desire never abandons strategy. If the will to absorb and assimilate never succeeds in overcoming the difference of the other, the will to differ—which is basically the same thing—never succeeds in conjuring away sameness and reciprocity. That is what is being demonstrated in the 'stroll along the boardwalk' taken by the holiday-makers at Balbec:

> All these people . . . pretending not to see, so as to let it be thought that they were not interested in them, but covertly eyeing, for fear of running into them, the people who were walking beside or coming towards them, did in fact bump into them, became entangled with them, because each was mutually the object of the same secret attention veiled beneath the same apparent disdain.[88]

G.L.: To defend your point of view about doubles, you must take issue with the psychoanalytic doctrine that the experience of the double, by those who are seriously ill, is inconsistent and out of touch with reality.

R.G.: Despite the hallucinatory aspects, we should not call such experiences entirely *hallucinations*, because that would imply they have no basis in human relations. These terms refer to the 'inexplicable' collision of two individuals who are seeking reciprocally to avoid one other and the continual re-enactment of this collision.

Doubles, in short, display the reciprocity of mimetic relationships. Since the subject aims only for difference—since he refuses to admit to any reciprocity—reciprocity triumphs, thanks to the very strategies to which each partner resorts, strategies that are always counterproductive precisely because all partners resort to them more or less simultaneously. This denied reciprocity 'haunts' the subject—it is the ghost of the real structure Proust and other greater writers have detected, which most people manage to exorcize in their immediate understanding of themselves. As regards others, they are just as perceptive as we always are when we are uninvolved in a conflict. This perceptiveness invariably lets us down when we become involved, but it is real enough most of the time to convince us we that we are still objective and detached at the times when in fact we are not.

When mimetic rivalry has 'undifferentiated' all relationships, not the double but difference is a hallucination. The hallucinatory reading of doubles is the last trick desire plays in order not to recognize, in the fact that the mimetic partners are identical, its own final failure—or deplorable success. If the madman sees double, it is because he is too close to the truth. 'Normal' people can still function inside the myth of difference, not because the difference is true, but because they have not pushed the mimetic process to the acceleration and intensification that make reciprocity visible. The quickening exchange of differential positions ends all distinctness. Everyone occupies all positions simultaneously, and where difference proliferates—in the form of monstrous nightmares—it tends to cancel itself out.

The sick person asks the doctor to vouch for the fact that he would be made to abandon difference for identity. He asks science to take note of the monsters and the doubles; but he does not want it to see them as the scrambling and final abolition of the mythic differences of culture. Instead, he wants it to see them as supplementary differences within a pattern of experience that is nothing but a tissue of differences—in other words, a text, or as we would say nowadays, an intertextuality. He is still a post-structuralist.

In short, desire relieves its subject of an intolerable knowledge. The subject cannot integrate doubles into his differential scheme; he cannot assimilate them to his logic; he is forced to drive himself out of the path of 'reason', in company with his doubles; he chooses, in short, to sacrifice his experience and his reason in preference to abandoning his desire. He asks the doctor to give a social sanction to this sacrifice by providing the diagnosis of madness.

G.L.: Medicine has always gone along with this. Doctors, unlike novelists, have never regarded doubles as anything but illusory games with mirrors, or strange, 'archaic' memories. Freud himself was caught in this trap. All the supposed experts reject doubles as meaningless, even though they regard them as extremely serious symptoms.

R.G.: Because the doctor refrains from contradicting the patient's views, psychopathology perpetuates, in effect, the point of view of desire itself. The sick person is the first to proclaim himself mad, or to behave in a way that convinces us he is, and he must be well aware what card he is turning up. Like contemporary philosophy, psychopathology bases its point of view in difference and cannot tolerate the identity of the doubles. Everything still rests on the principles inherited from Romantic individualism.

J.-M.O.: You are saying that 'desire' does this and that. . . . Would you not agree that you are tending to give desire a false identity?

R.G.: If desire is the same for all of us, and if it is the key to the system of relationships, there is no reason not to make it the real 'subject' of the structure—a subject that comes back to mimesis in the end. I avoid saying 'desiring subject' so as not to give the impression of relapsing into a psychology of the subject.

Rather like an insect that falls into the crumbling trap its rival has dug for it, with the grains of sand that it tries to grasp giving way as it tries to move its feet—desire counts on differences to *get up the slope*. But the differences are obliterated precisely because of its efforts, and it falls back once again on the doubles.

The mimetic aspect of this process set off by desire becomes more and more self-revelatory. It reaches such a pitch that even the observers who are most determined not to see anything end up by recognizing its existence. Then they begin to talk about schizophrenic histrionics—but they do so as if they were discussing a phenomenon that had no antecedents and no intelligible connections with anything whatsoever, especially not with the phenomenon of doubles.

G.L.: The fact is that the more aggravated the symptoms become, the more desire becomes a caricature of itself—and the more the phenomena we are considering become transparent to our analysis. In the light of these phenomena, it will become all the more easy to rethink the entire process.

R.G.: In effect, desire is responsible for its own evolution. Desire tends to become a caricature of itself, or, to put it another way, to cause all the symptoms to become more and more aggravated. In contrast to what Freud thinks in his constant preoccupation with the 'unconscious', desire knows itself better than any form of psychiatry does. What is more, it gets better and better informed because it observes, at every stage, what is happening to it. This knowledge governs the aggravation of symptoms. Desire is always using for its own ends the knowledge it has acquired of itself; it places the truth in the service of its own untruth, so to speak, and it is always becoming better equipped to reject everything that surrenders to its embrace. It always does its best, at both the individual and the collective levels, to generate the double binds in which it gets caught, seeking always to entrap itself in the cul-de-sac that is its very *raison d'être*.

The idea of the demon who bears light is more far-reaching than any notion in psychoanalysis. Desire bears light, but puts that light in the service of its own darkness. The role played by desire in all the great creations of modern culture—in art and literature—is explained by this feature, which it shares with Lucifer.

J.-M.O.: In the first place, as we have seen, the mimetic rivals quarrel over an object, and the value of the object increases by virtue of the greedy rivalry it inspires. This becomes detached from the object and comes to rest upon the obstacle that the adversaries constitute for one another. Each wishes to prevent the other from incarnating the irresistible violence he wishes to incarnate himself. If you ask the adversaries why they are fighting, they will put forward notions like prestige. Each is concerned with acquiring the prestige that threatens to devolve upon the other and so with becoming the magical power—analogous to the

Polynesian *mana* and the Greek *kudos*—that circulates among combatants under the form of violence.[89]

R.G.: Fighting over prestige is literally fighting over nothing. In the absence of any concrete object, the 'nothing' of prestige appears to be everything—not only from an adversary's point of view, but in the eyes of all. Even before the adversaries are reconciled by the violent expulsion—supposing that they ever are—they participate in a vision that can be described as the vision of metaphysical violence.

This description does not hold only for the duels of Homeric heroes or for rituals in which people attempt to assimilate the sacred violence by devouring the victim. Escalating violence, the violence of reciprocal exchange, remains in the symptoms in psychiatry that come forward as alternation. Only in the light of this exchange can the desire whose relationships appear in these symptoms be made fully intelligible.

Symptoms of Alternation

R.G.: In the world of doubles, with its deep-rooted rivalries, there can be no neutral relationships. There are only those who dominate and those who are dominated. Since the meaning of the relationship rests neither on brute force nor on any form of external constraint, it can never achieve stability; it is played and replayed in terms of relationships that the onlooker could well believe to be without any significance. Each time he dominates or thinks he is dominating his rival, the subject believes himself to be at the centre of a perceptual field; when his rival has the upper hand, the situation reverses. More and more often, and for longer and longer, this rival does or seems to carry the day. So there is an inbuilt tendency for depression increasingly to overtake the initial mimetic euphoria.

Seen against the comings and goings of the violence that both separates and unites them, the two partners come to be, by turns, the one and only god, who sees everything converge on him and kneel before him, and the puny, speechless, trembling creature at the feet of this god, who has mysteriously taken up residence with the other person, the rival and model for desire.

This relationship puts us in mind of a swing, where one of those playing is always at the highest point when the other is at the lowest, and the reverse. Psychiatrists do not know what causes this alternation because they only see a single person playing. To make the sick person go down to the abyss, you must have a second player who is proceeding upward to the summit and vice versa.

J.-M.O.: But psychiatrists will reply that if there was a second person playing they would notice his presence. You never see two severe cases of manic-depressive illness regulating each other reciprocally in the manner that you have described.

R.G.: Psychiatry regards the sick person as a kind of monad. Even when he insists upon the importance of relationships with the other, the psychologist does not attach sufficient weight to their foundational character. Obviously, the role of the other can become an imaginary one. But it has not always been so, and, even if it is imaginary, it is still decisive at every moment in determining the violent swings that are registered by the subject. For example, the various thymic symptoms are simply the subject's reaction to the exchange of violent behaviour, to the ups and downs of a struggle that goes back to some real mimetic rivalry. We do not see this oscillating violence, but it is real for the patient, who reads victory and defeat in signs that are more and more inaccessible to an outsider.

G.L.: Psychiatry is quite willing to talk delirium with those who are ill. But she likes to think of herself as healthy with those who are in good health. You must not disturb those in good health by suggesting that there is no more than a tiny difference in degree between them and the sick—nothing, perhaps, but a rather more robust sensibility, a less finely tuned intelligence for all that goes on in human relationships, especially in our modern world, which lacks the stabilizing forces of tradition.

R.G.: We ought to examine what goes on in the sectors of modern life where feverish competition and the pangs of promotion by merit flourish within a context of relative leisure, which favours reciprocal observation: business circles, obviously, and especially intellectual circles, where the talk is always of others, by people who pay scant attention to themselves.

In these circles, a kind of cyclothymia is fed by signs that are not at all illusory and meaningless, even if the most remarkable divergences can arise in their interpretation. Those whose professional future and reputation hang upon signs of this kind are obsessed by them. We might call this obsession objective, like the thymic alternation that accompanies it. It is hard not to be pleased at something that depresses your rival, and not to be depressed at something that pleases him.

Everything that brings me up brings down my competitors; everything that brings them up brings me down. In a society where the place of individuals is not determined in advance and hierarchies have been obliterated, people are endlessly preoccupied with making a destiny for themselves, with 'imposing' themselves on others, 'distinguishing' themselves from the common herd—in a word, with 'making a career'.

As we have pointed out, only our society can unleash mimetic desire in a number of different domains without having to dread an irreversible escalation in the system, the runaway defined by cybernetics. It is because of this unprecedented capacity to promote competition within limits that always remain socially, if not individually acceptable that we have all the amazing achievements of the modern world—its inventive genius, and so on. The price for all of this is perhaps not invariably the aggravation beyond all bounds, but certainly the democratization and vulgarization, of what we call neuroses, which are always linked, in my view, to the reinforcement of mimetic competition and the 'metaphysical' aspect of the related tensions.

The 'manic-depressive' is possessed with a huge metaphysical ambition. But this metaphysical ambition does not form something apart. It can vary according to the individual case, but it is the paradoxical result of the obliteration of differences and the unleashing of mimetic desire in its specifically modern form. All these factors hang together.

In a world where individuals are no longer defined by the place they occupy by virtue of their birth or some other stable and arbitrary factor, the spirit of competition can never be appeased once and for all. Indeed it gets increasingly inflamed; everything rests upon comparisons that are necessarily unstable and insecure, since there are no longer any fixed points of reference. The manic-depressive has a particularly acute awareness of the state of radical dependence that people occupy *vis-à-vis* one another, and the lack of certainty that results. As he sees that everything around him consists of *images, imitation* and *admiration* (*image* and *imitate* derive from the same Latin root), he passionately desires the admiration of others. He wishes for all mimetic desires to be polarized around himself, and he lives through the inevitable lack of certainty—the mimetic character of what develops—with a tragic intensity. The smallest sign of acceptance or rejection, of esteem or disdain, plunges him into dark despair of superhuman ecstasy. Sometimes he sees himself perched on the top of the pyramid of being—sometimes, by contrast the pyramid is inverted and, as he is still situated at the point, he is in the most humiliating position of all, blotted out by the entire universe.

For this experience to reach the clinical stage, the individual terrain must be particularly favourable. But, in a slightly milder form, the ordeal is that of most intellectuals. The manic-depressive is never wholly out of touch with human relationships, particularly in the world in which we live. The sick person is not completely justified in carrying to an extreme, as he does, everything capable of affecting his relationships with others. But neither is he completely unjustified, since the mimetic and contagious nature of these relationships, and their tendency to 'snowball', in either are in no way products of the imagination. For him, moderation is no longer possible, and in effect it is becoming less and less possible in a society that becomes increasingly destructured and so is increasingly threatened by the uncontrollable oscillations of mimetism.

J.-M.O.: Frankly psychotic symptoms may well be linked to organic factors. But that is not at all embarrassing, so it seems to me, from your point of view. If these organic factors are absent, the process of mimetic escalation will never go beyond a certain threshold. Also they may temporarily be neutralized by certain chemical products.

Some people believe that the proportion of severe psychotic cases hardly varies from society to society: the organic factor would explain that. But this factor can be envisaged in a way that does not invalidate what you are saying in the least. It may weaken or render ineffective the forms of defence—also organic—raised against the aggravating effects of mimetism.

R.G.: It is hard to believe that the mimetic context does not play a central role in determining the particular susceptibility of certain professions to the psychopathological states we are describing; I refer to the various activities and vocations that depend most directly on the judgements of others in their most brutal and arbitrary, and least subtle, forms. I am thinking of those who are in direct contact with the crowd and live off its favours, like politicians, actors, playwrights, writers and so on.

The person who pays attention, of necessity, to collective reactions knows by experience that nothing in this area can ever be taken at face value; turn-arounds can take place quite suddenly and unpredictably. The man of the theatre can see the 'flop' of a *première* be transformed next morning into a raging success, and vice versa, without there being any ascertainable cause for the change. How is it possible to make a hard and fast distinction between a manic-depressive tendency and the emotions registered by someone whose existence largely depends on the arbitrary decisions that arise from mimetic contagion?

Desire is far too well informed that scapegoats and divinities are near at hand when individuals and societies are in the process of becoming destructured. To judge from Nietzsche and Dostoevsky, we might well feel that psychosis always threatens when an individual's intuition of these matters exceeds a particular threshold. We have only to read *Ecce Homo* in the light of what has just been said to understand that Nietzsche is in the process of tipping over into psychosis.

J.-M.O.: If the signs of incipient psychosis can be detected in the works of Nietzsche, it is possible to note in Dostoevsky, by contrast, the moment at which the writer overcomes the threat and produces his first real work of genius, the first work that is to reveal and not merely reflect mimetic desire and its paradoxes: *Notes from Underground*.

The oscillatory movements associated with cyclothymia flourish in our society behind a whole range of cultural phenomena that people would not think of associating with them. For example, just think of all those manuals that claim to teach the secret of success in love, business, etc. What they reveal is always a strategy for relating to the other person. The one secret—the ideal recipe that is repeated over and over again—is that all you require for success is to give the impression that you have it already.

Nothing could be more depressing for the reader than this cold comfort. He is already more than convinced that everything depends, in the encounters awaiting him, on the impression that is given and received. Equally, he is more than convinced that these two sides of the impression will give rise to a struggle: each person will try to prove to the other that he already possesses the stake, which in reality must be reconquered all the time by being snatched away from the other—this stake being the radiating certainty of one's own superiority.

R.G.: It would seem to me that the cyclic tendency must be statistically more frequent in our world, and that there is a special affinity between it and our time. It is striking that, since the end of the eighteenth century, literature and thought have been defined by great psychotic minds, who interpret what is happening among us in essential ways that are generally ignored by their contemporaries. Posterity, by contrast, puts these essential matters on a pedestal, making an ideology of them—in other words, a sacrificial substitute—whose major ingredient is, of course, a high indignation directed against the incapacity of the contemporaries to recognize the genius who had done them the honour of speaking to them.

To sum up: the manic-depressive embodies the two opposing faces of the sacred, which are interiorized and lived through interminably in an alternating pattern. I believe this is what Nietzsche is alluding to, on the threshold of madness, when his long-standing opposition between Dionysus and Christ completely disappears. Instead of writing Dionysus *against* the Crucified, he writes Dionysus *and* the Crucified. What Nietzsche never detected in his researches, what he was unable to make his own on the level of knowledge—the identity of God and the scapegoat—he was able to realize in his madness. Wishing to be God, he became the victim, his own, primarily: he experienced the destiny of the scapegoat.

A good many primitive societies attest this relationship between madness and the sacred. They see in the madman the two faces of God's violence and in consequence they treat him simultaneously as an 'infection', a source of pollution, which must be kept at bay, and as a possible source of blessings, a being to be venerated.

In the *Birth of Tragedy* and in his work on Greek religion, despite all his intuitions, Nietzsche never uncovered the real significance of the Dionysiac *mania*. But even a relatively ignorant ancient Greek, on reading this book, would have been able to predict that the author would go mad. You cannot espouse Dionysus, in the way that Nietzsche does, outside any form of ritual, without exposing yourself to the unrestrained release of the *mania*.

How does it come about that our sciences still cannot measure up to the most humble religious insight?

The Disappearance of the Object and Psychotic Structure

J.-M.O.: What strikes me about all you have been saying is that there is no longer any object. Everything comes down to the relationships between the mimetic rivals, each of which is model and disciple to the other. The fact that the object disappears must, I imagine, be an aspect of desire's tendency to become a caricature of itself and proclaim in its own terms its own truth—the ascendancy of the mimetic model over the object. From the outset, desire interferes with the way in which the instincts are ordered and directed toward objects. By the stage of psychosis, the object is no longer there at all; all that remains is the mimetic double-bind, the obsessive concern with the model-obstacle. Madness is particularly human in so far as it carries to an extreme the very tendency that is furthest removed from the animal part of man—a form of mimetic behaviour so intense that it can take over from the instinctual arrangements.

R.G.: Freud was well aware of this dynamic force driving man to madness and death, but he could only cope by inventing a 'death instinct' in order to provide an explanation. We must return to this urge to postulate an instinct. Desire itself leads to madness and death if there is no victimage mechanism to guide it back to 'reason' or to engender this 'reason'. Mimetic desire can account for it all more directly and efficiently. Thanks to it, we can come back to Edgar Morin's excellent formula: *Homo sapiens demens.*[90] The mysterious link between madness and reason takes on a concrete form.

At his own expense, the subject manages to release the logic of mimetic desire. Desire becomes detached from the object, bit by bit, and attaches itself to the model. This development is accompanied by a marked aggravation of the symptoms—for behaving normally is not a matter of escaping from mimetic desire (no one can do that) but of not giving in to it to the extent of losing sight of the object entirely and only being concerned with the model. Being rational—functioning properly—is a matter of having objects and being busy with them; being mad is a matter of letting oneself be taken over completely by the mimetic models, and so fulfilling the calling of desire. It is a matter of pushing to final conclusions what distinguishes desire—only very relatively of course—from animal life and of abandoning oneself to a fascination with the model, to the extent that it resists and does violence to the subject.

How do you, as psychiatrists, see psychosis from the perspective that I have sketched out?

G.L.: We are not very good at providing the right vocabulary because we are working—how could it be otherwise?—within a culture, a period, and an 'order' that are necessarily post-sacrificial. Yet when we talk, even from the moment that we exist, the founding sacrifice has already taken place.

Our weakness is conveyed by the fact that we are obliged to call everything that existed previously—that is to say, everything that belongs to the pre-sacrificial period—by pejorative and negative names: non-culture, disorder, and so on.

J.-M.O.: This pre-sacrificial period is not in any sense 'destructured'. It does not correspond to a dissolution of the structures of culture as we know them, let alone to a complete absence of structure. On the contrary, we know now that the disorder of the pre-cultural and pre-sacrificial stage possesses its own structure, which is exactly defined and is based, paradoxically, on the principle of absolute symmetry.

It is this mimetic symmetry—which generates disorder and violence, and is in a perpetual disequilibrium—that is stabilized by the scapegoat mechanism: the zero hour of culture and the zero degree of structure.

The culture produced by this differentiating mechanism will possess a structure based upon asymmetry and difference. And, this asymmetry and the differences associated with it form what we call the cultural order.

That is how 'order' comes out of 'disorder'. But we know now that both are structured and that one is not a destructured form of the other. Overall, one well-determined structure gives way to another through a previously misunderstood mechanism, that of the scapegoat.

G.L.: What we have just been saying about order and disorder also applies to logic and confusion. 'Confusion' is structured symmetrically and organized with a view to lack of difference. Logic, on the other hand, is structured asymmetrically and depends on difference.

We can appreciate that 'consciousness' comes out of differentiation. But we can also see that the 'unconscious' has the same point of origin; both, to the extent that they belong to a post-sacrificial and cultural space-time, are structured through difference—both are 'structured as a language'. This point appears even clearer if we reflect that the pre-sacrificial period is one of symmetry, undifferentiated violence and inarticulate cries.

The claim that we can define psychosis equally well by calling it the 'destructuring of consciousness' and the 'emergence of the unconscious' thus comes to seem mistaken on both counts. If consciousness is destructured, what is the structure of the form of disorder we refer to as psychosis? No one seems capable of giving a clear reply to this question.

If psychosis is the 'emergence of the unconscious', then we must agree with Henri Ey that there must logically be a dissolution of consciousness before that emergence can take place. It is even less easy to understand how the unconscious—which we now know to be structured within the cultural order, just like consciousness—could become incomprehensible from the very moment that it emerges and speaks for itself, even though the people who claim to explain psychosis in this way also say that the unconscious is structured as a language.

J.-M.O.: So how can we come to terms with the structure of psychosis, on the one hand, and psychotic structure, on the other, and with the relationships between them? We can hardly imagine, after all, that the two are only related to each other coincidentally.

Psychosis cannot be understood as a kind of externalization of the unconscious. This explanation is too bound up with metaphysics and Romanticism—different aspects of the psyche are telescoped together, and ghosts emerge from behind the curtain. . . . If we abandon this reliance on philosophical panaceas and establish that the psychotic structure is a structure of symmetry, a structure of doubles, which implies a return to the pre-sacrificial, undifferentiated state of mimesis, then we come to understand the following points:

(1) the structure of psychosis is constituted, bit by bit, by the psychotic structure that 'sees' it as a possible outcome, that is to say, a possible way of reintroducing difference;
(2) the time experienced by the psychotic is no longer the time of 'other people', and this is why the psychotic lives in a world that is totally 'foreign';
(3) 'normal' people see the psychotic structure as a form of destructuring.

In fact, the only form of difference that they cannot accept, or even imagine, is the one upon which their culture and their reason are founded: the difference between the pre-sacrificial order and the cultural order, the difference in nature between a structure founded on symmetry and undifferentiation, and one founded on asymmetry and differentiation. Pyschiatrists continue to lend their support to this distinction without ever understanding it; they keep on thinking of psychosis as a form of loss, as a falling out of cultural structure.

Psychoanalysts, for their part, see one essential thing; they recognize a dynamic element in the formation of psychosis. But they are prisoners of their own philosophical concepts, which oblige them to hypostatize the unconscious and reify as essential causal mechanisms what are simply functional ones.

As for the anti-psychiatrists, they can see very well that 'madness' has its own truth. They see it as a caricature of reason, and so it is, in a certain sense, in the way a caricature can reveal the essential qualities of the model. But they have no understanding of the structure of psychosis, or of the reasons why it has no operational force. They see it as being powerless and think that they can restore its value by weakening the repressive cultural order. What the anti-psychiatrists manage to see, consequently, is no more than a commonplace: that reason and madness are incompatible, that the structure of the double and the structure of difference do not go together. They are unable to explain why these structures are incompatible or to explain their existence. So they keep themselves happy by taking over-simplified 'political' attitudes—in effect, by deliberately choosing one structure over another, without the least awareness of what they are doing.

The anti-psychiatrists also fall into the trap that chronology lays for cultural time. They tell themselves that madness—the double structure—is in advance of reason—the structure of difference. In that respect they are victims of the same illusion as the psychoanalysts who see madness as a form of regression, and so judge it to be retarded by comparison with reason.

In effect, our most essential discovery is precisely the zero hour of culture, which is also the hour of sacrifice—the founding sacrifice. This zero hour absolutely and radically separates the structures of the cultural order and those of the disorder of undifferentiated violence, while transforming the one into the other. So if these two structures are engendered mutually—like the two sisters mentioned to Oedipus by the Sphinx—it makes no more sense to talk of one being in advance of the other than it does to talk of one being behind the other.

G.L.: So we are managing to get away from the myths, and that includes the myth of mental illness. On the basis of your way of thinking, we can observe the gradual emergence of the working mechanisms through which the psychotic structure—and, at a later stage, the structure of the psychosis—are brought into being, without having to rely on mythic hypotheses or to produce rabbits out of a hat.

We can see how the exacerbation of mimesis—its progressive development—culminates in a *relationship of doubles* with the other. This other can take on a singular form, as it did with Wagner, Hölderlin and Schiller. Or it can be multiple and plural, as with the cases of psychosis in our hospitals.

From a working mechanism that is both simple and basic, we therefore get the creation of order no less than disorder, differential structure no less than undifferentiated structure, reason no less than madness. That is what makes our human condition so unusual and so precarious.

J.-M.O.: Psychotic structure is the relationship of doubles, in conditions where mimesis becomes exacerbated—where the dysthymic inversions take place faster and faster, like the frames of cinematography.

The structure of psychosis—delirium—is the mythic story constructed by one or other of the protagonists in the relationship of doubles in order to latch on to the cultural order and to try to explain himself, though without getting any closer to understanding his situation.

G.L.: 'The splitting of the Ego'—Freud's *'Spaltung'*—is the mythic reading carried out on the mythic speech that the patient manifests to the psychoanalyst. The patient speaks to the psychoanalyst about his double relationship with his *mimetic rivals*. This is quite obviously a real relationship, but the subject of delirium cannot admit it as such; thus it has to be expressed mythically in terms of doubleness and hallucination. The psychoanalyst, who reads the myth on its literal level, gives it a further mythic dimension under the pseudo-scientific label of the 'splitting of the Ego', which sustains and even encourages it.

J.-M.O.: The contribution of the mimetic thesis to psychology and psychopathology seems to us to consist in demonstrating the complete continuity between the two domains, on the level of the mechanism that gives rise to both. At the same time, it enables us to detect the zero hour, or the zero degree of structure, which introduces between them the most radical discontinuity.

It is through the hypothetical mechanism of mimetic resolution that we can pass from animal to man, from child to adult, and explain the processes of apprenticeship and culture. We can also unmask the structure of reason and difference, and provide an intelligible genesis of the diachronic dimension. Through the aid of this mechanism, we can take account of violence and disorder, together with the structure of undifferentiation and madness.

Between madness and reason, between violence and peace, between undifferentiation and culture, there is only a *grading of intensity* in the mechanism of conflictual mimesis. All are continuous on the level of the mechanism that lies at their base.

Furthermore, you explain the radical inversion triggered off by the sacrificial crisis. The scapegoat mechanism allows passage from one structure to the other, and marks their absolute discontinuity, while confirming their continuity where the founding mechanism is concerned.

G.L.: So the cycle continues, as the Hindus rightly saw. The self-same mechanism serves to pass from violence to peace, and from peace to violence—or from reason to madness and from madness to reason. Every possible point in the scale between the two structures can generate actual phenomena, including the point of neurosis, even though the two structures are so radically different. Surely one can see why psychiatrists like ourselves have shown interest in such a brilliant revelation? Here at last we can find a way of understanding why one can go into psychosis and come out of it again, that one can be sunk in psychosis for ever or at momentary intervals. This was inexplicable as long as people held fast to the myth of a rigid, hypostatized psychotic structure, or even a predetermined structure.

So we now understand how there can be psychotic moments in the evolution of a neurotic structure. The mechanisms by which reason is created and destroyed are becoming visible.

Now it is our job to rid ourselves vigilantly of the old mythic habits and rethink all psychopathology in the light of our new principles—though the risk is that we may be blinded by their very simplicity.

Hypnosis and Possession

R.G.: As you say, the psychotic structure is characterized by two things: the disappearance of the object and the relationship of doubles.

And yet in hypnosis and possession there is no object involved, though nobody thinks of using the term 'psychosis'. How do you see these states?

J.-M.O.: I have thought a great deal about this, and I obviously have no satisfactory, hard and fast answer to give. I think that in the first place we can safely state the following: psychotic structure is a structure of doubles, and in consequence it belongs to pre-sacrificial 'time'—that is to say, the time of the mimetic crisis, the 'time' when disorder is structured symmetrically within an overall lack of differentiation. The subject cannot see any difference in the other. It is because this difference is lost that the other becomes his double, and he becomes a madman.

Hypnosis and possession, by contrast, are situated in a post-sacrificial 'time', a structure that is symmetrical and differential. The subject under hypnosis never loses sight of the difference between himself and the hypnotizer, the god who is possessing him.

So there is a fundamental structural distinction between psychosis on the one hand, and possession and hypnosis on the other.

This leads me to one preliminary remark. Psychologically, the processes of mimesis involve modifications in the state of consciousness. In the process that leads from the sacrificial crisis to its paroxysm, the participants' state of consciousness has been 'destructured'. It would be unthinkable for the scapegoat to be assassinated if everyone kept full awareness. This point is confirmed by the various rituals that attempt to reproduce changes in the state of awareness of those taking part, so that the end result will be violent unanimity. Moreover, this approach strengthens our thesis in so far as the murder of the victim calms everything down; it unknots the relationships of doubles, brings back full consciousness and lucidity, and so founds, or refounds, culture. By his death, the victim establishes difference; he delivers the men who have killed him from the psychotic structure and, by this act, restructures their consciousness.

R.G.: And yet we are told by all observers that cults of possession also bring about significant modifications in the state of consciousness.

J.-M.O.: Indeed so. We must, however, stress the following points: people in a state of possession are never psychotic, and the phenomena of possession have always been discussed in relation to hypnotic trances. That cannot be entirely arbitrary.

I think we must resolutely class states of ritualized possession within a 'time' that is post-sacrificial, in a structure of differences. Nevertheless, these states of possession are accompanied by modifications in states of consciousness, which are clearly brought about by the mimetic mechanisms. On the one hand, the subject is prepared for possession by monotonous dances and incessantly repeated sound rhythms. That is obviously reminiscent of how a hypnotic trance is induced. What strikes me most is the *repetition of the same,* on a musical and gestural level, as a means of modifying the state of consciousness. On the other hand, there characteristically appears in the man under possession a perfect imitation of his model: this can be a divine, archetypal or cultural model, or even a living model—say, one chosen from among the French officers by an Algerian trooper.

At this point, two processes can be observed: the acquisitive mimesis plus the engenderment of conflict through mimesis; and a peaceful mimesis, in the 'appearance' of a model who has never formed an obstacle and engenders no such conflict. Both are exacerbated by the state of possession and both can modify the state of consciousness. For psychiatrists and psychologists like us, this seems to me to be very important: the mimetic mechanisms that you are discovering can be subjected to experimental verification and observation; what is more, they can change the structure of the psychic apparatus, or the psychosomatic apparatus, if we wish to think of it in those particular terms.

R.G.: You talk about ritualized states of possession. But there are also quite different states of possession, for example, those that concern exorcists.

J.-M.O.: Certainly. One of the best examples of this type of possession is the 'Devils of Loudun', admirably described by Aldous Huxley.[91] I personally believe that ritualized possession—by which I mean cults of possession and possession by 'devils'—comprises two very different phenomena. Although I cannot go much further into the matter today, I would simply like to emphasize that:

—in cults of possession men and women often come forward in an apparent state of possession. These people are immediately detected by the priests of the cult and considered to be hysterics. I became aware of that with the help of my friend Dr Charles Pidoux, who has spent years studying the problems of possession firsthand and knows them better than anyone else;[92]

—people have always diagnosed cases of possession by 'devils'—for example, the Devils of Loudun—as hysteria (though I am uncomfortable with this word).

R.G.: What meaning are you giving to the word 'hysteria'?

J.-M.O.: Because of its origin (i.e., in referring to the uterus), the term 'hysteria' has never been a good one. Now it is worse than ever. It has been so over-used that it now means both everything and nothing. When people talk about 'collective hysteria' in cases of ritual possession, in my view they say nothing at all.

I think we are dealing with hysterical phenomena in cases of 'pathological' possession, which our culture associates with 'devils'—if we take 'hysteria' to mean something midway between psychosis and ritual possession.

It shares with ritual possession the fact that the difference between the subject under possession and the being possessing him is never lost. The hysterics of Loudun, for example, never lost sight of the difference between themselves and Urbain Grandier. But hysteria has in common with psychosis the fact that the mimetic model is perceived as an antagonist. In fact, he is perceived as an enemy and a source of pollution, as an aggressor capable of rape, and so on.

I believe that this shows why any exaggeration of aggressive and antagonistic tendencies can turn into psychosis, as when the exorcist does not succeed in expelling the devil or cannot achieve a resolution by sacrifice, by victimizing of the other, as happened with Urbain Grandier. Perhaps we can also appreciate how the hysterical structure—when it is unable to move toward either one of these extremes—can attempt to put an end to its crisis by expelling or victimizing an organ or a limb, thus making it a scapegoat.

It is not hard to understand why all the authors who have dealt with hysteria have emphasized catharsis as the basic cure for hysterical neurosis.

R.G.: Hysteria has been linked with hypnosis for a very long time. You yourself have done a lot of work on the problem. How do you see the relationship between hypnosis and what we have been discussing?

J.-M.O.: The very close but also rather mysterious links between hypnosis, hysteria and possession have often been noted by the authors who have looked into these phenomena over the centuries.[93] However,

it seems to me that the emphasis has always been placed either on modifications in the state of consciousness and their links with sleep and
para-hypnotic states, or on the critical and spectacular phenomena that
come about in all these states.

From the perspective that you propose, these neuro-physiological
phenomena are secondary to the interdividual psychological processes
that register the effects of exacerbated mimesis. Hypnosis seems to me
to be a caricature of interdividual psychological mechanisms. Like any
caricature, it is capable of revealing some of the essential aspects of its
model. In the process of hypnosis, what you call the mediator, or the
model, is there in front of the subject. And he lets it be known directly
what he requires of the subject, what he wishes the subject to do: he
presents him with his *desire*—directly, firmly and unambiguously. This
peremptory way of revealing desire is what Bernheim calls the model's
suggestion.

From then on, if the subject acts in conformity with this desire, he
enters a state of peaceful mimesis—mimesis without any element of
rivalry since the model invites the subject to copy the model's desire,
and this desire does not bear upon any object that belongs to the model.
It most frequently involves a form of conduct that is banal and natural:
sleep. Bernheim took note of the fact that when the suggestion is to
sleep, the subject actually goes to sleep!

So we can initially define hypnosis as a *precipitate of mimetic desire*. (I
take the word 'precipitate' in its chemical meaning.) In hypnosis the
interdividual process results in a physiological precipitation. We have
to show that hypnosis is a concrete, empirical precipitation of mimetic
desire—a phenomenon that brings in its wake physiological as well as
psychophysiological modifications (measurable by an electro-
encephalogram as well as by the subject's state of consciousness). We
have to show that the manifestations of hypnosis demonstrate experimentally, up to a point, the reality of the mimetic processes.

What I have said about hypnosis will enable us, I believe, to bring to
light the essential difference between your point of view and that of
Hegel. In Hegel the subject experiences desire *for* the other's desire;
desire for recognition. This Hegelian desire is only one particular
instance—what I would call a 'complication', in the medical sense of the
term—of the interdividual mimetic desire you define as desire *according*
to the other's desire. Hypnosis can be taken as an empirical verification
of your point of view.

Yet the 'complication' noted by Hegel is never very far away. Pierre Janet entitles Chapter XII of his book *Névroses et idées fixes*[94] 'Somnambulistic influence and the need for direction'. The need for direction, the need for a leader, is desire according to the other's desire—it is the subject's capacity, even necessity, to enter into a state of hypnosis. By contrast, in the somnambulistic experience the game of rivalry is introduced little by little into the interdividual relationship of hypnotizer and hypnotized. In fact Janet was well aware that the further you go away from a hypnotic trance, the more the situation tends to become inverted. Once again, mimetic rivalry gnaws away at all the structures, the game of the model-obstacle starts up; the subject's desire contradicts the desire expressed by the model—the permitted desire, or what I would call the model's wish—and directs itself toward the model himself, toward what he 'has' and so on, as what he has acquires an ontological status, toward what he 'is', his 'being'. Nietzschean 'ressentiment' appears at the same time as what Janet calls the 'somnambulistic passions—at the point when, for certain authors, the subject is "possessed" by his hypnotizer'.

R.G.: Hypnotic phenomena were at the centre of all pre-psychoanalytic and psychoanalytic controversies at the end of the nineteenth century and the beginning of the twentieth.

J.-M.O.: Yes, indeed. Today, your theory seems capable of reconciling Charcot, Bernheim, Janet and Freud. Charcot held that hypnosis was a pathological phenomenon, confined to hysterics and therefore exceptional in its occurrence. Bernheim argued that it was, on the contrary, a normal, general process—that there was in fact no hypnosis but only suggestion. Finally, Freud considered hypnosis to be a pathological phenomenon that was at once neurotic and general. He had absorbed half of the views of each of his masters into his own.[95] It seems to me that each was observing mimetic desire at work; but each was seeing it at a different stage in its development.

R.G.: I can now see better what you mean by a 'precipitate'. In effect, all the phenomena of mimetic desire are there, in a caricatural form. This would account for the fact that hypnosis never really produces a cure, and that it always has to be begun over again.

J.-M.O.: Yes, of course. I am not quite as pessimistic as you about the therapeutic effects of hypnosis, but I would make the point that—as

Henri Faure has conclusively demonstrated—hypnosis is much more effective therapeutically with children than with adults. The child's aptitude for good mimesis, peaceful mimesis—for taking a model who is not at the same time an obstacle—seems to explain this phenomenon. Everything that you will be saying presently about the *skandalon* follows the same line of argument, as far as I can see.[96]

The adult—the floating subject, whose desire is always fluctuating, who cannot tell which model to adopt—is able to derive some profit from a relationship with a special kind of mediator, the hypnotist, who gains ascendancy by using his technical ability and imposes himself as the model. In that situation, it is possible for the best—as well as the worst—results to arise.

R.G.: The hypnotist's technique, which you have just mentioned, most often involves making the subject stare at a shining object and asking him to concentrate his attention on this object.

J.-M.O.: Yes, indeed. I regard this as particularly illuminating. In fact, all the authors on the topic, especially Pierre Janet—have noticed that hypnosis is accompanied by a 'contraction of the field of consciousness' and that suggestion can only be effective with a subject whose attention remains undistracted.

In the writings of many of those authors, we keep finding terms like 'fascination' and 'capturing the look'. This seems very evocative of the model's ascendancy over the subject. The techniques of hypnosis simply try to reproduce, as faithfully as possible, the conditions of the subject's fixation on the model—the conditions that allow the desire of the subject to be modelled on the desire of the other.

That is why hypnosis can be practised on the stage—where the mimetic game is shown to the public in an explicit and experimental way. The theatre of Shakespeare (to take one example) offers the spectacle of mimesis at work in the course of a more elaborate set of circumstances.

All the paradoxes of the sacred can be found in hypnosis. It can give rise to laughter in the theatre, like any form of caricature. It can equally well be very dangerous, when it is manipulated by criminals. And of course it can be beneficial and curative when it is employed in medicine.

R.G.: What you say about the theatre, and about Shakespeare in particular, is of very great interest to me, as you can imagine.

J.-M.O.: Indeed I can. I do not think that you have much difficulty in showing that the theatre of Shakespeare, like all other forms of theatre, exhibits the functioning of mimesis and all the complicated steps of mimetic desire.

A particular phenomenon often found in the theatre can be related very closely to hypnosis: the lover's passion. As it develops, the passion contracts the field of consciousness and concentrates the subject's whole attention upon the object of desire. The element of theatre begins at the point, precisely, where that object makes its appearance. In this case, the fascination is no longer fixed upon the model, but upon the object of desire. The triangle of relationships appears in filigree and the rivals can make their entry. Theatre comes into being as a transfigured and symbolic expression of mimetic desire, which reaches beyond the spontaneous and caricatural expressions offered by possession and hypnosis.

These kinships must be emphasized. Moreover, it seems to me that in certain cultures there develop forms which are midway between theatre and possession, and clearly underline the continuity of the whole phenomenon. If a young man is in love with a girl, it is promptly said that he has been possessed by her.

We must emphasize that the passion of love involves a contraction of the field of consciousness to a single object, and other objects are simply not seen—just as the subject under hypnosis sees only the brilliant object the hypnotist puts before him. The hypnotist in fact says to his subject, 'You can hear nothing but my voice now'. Thus mimetic desire is the loss of relativity, the model as an absolute. And of course, it is also the restriction of liberty.

R.G.: On the therapeutic side, how would you explain that the different authors who have worked on hypnosis early in their careers—I am thinking of Freud in particular—have turned away from it later?

J.-M.O.: As we said previously, hypnosis is the caricature of mimetic desire—at once its simplest and strongest manifestation. If the hypnotic relationship contains in embryo all the possibilities of interdividual relationships—if it concentrates in essence all the potentialities of mimesis—then hypnosis will lie at the source of almost all the psychological and psychopathological intuitions of these authors. Clearly each researcher who works on the phenomenon is bound to note some of its aspects and exploit them at the expense of others.

A case in point is Freud's discovery that unconscious processes can be brought to light under hypnosis. Freud concentrates on these processes and develops psychoanalysis. Yet even within his theory the concept of *transference* plays still a fundamental role. Transference is identical with the fluid of the magnetizers, from Mesmer and Puysegur to the charlatans of the present. Both are essentially the same as mimesis and mimetic desire.

Schultz tells us that the individual under hypnosis experiences a certain number of physiological changes—as regards weight, heat and so on—and these can trigger a sort of self-generated training. Bernheim argues that because the individual under hypnosis is more sensitive to suggestion, it is possible to alleviate his symptoms or even to make them disappear altogether. Charcot claims that the individual under hypnosis relives traumatic events from an earlier period and that his memory is over-stimulated. But, as Janet puts it, the individual can also be programmed in a state of hypnosis as if he were a computer—he can be ordered under hypnosis to do an action at a later stage, and the order will remain in the unconscious until the moment for it to make its appearance on the level of consciousness.

Hypnosis therefore makes time problematic. The subject under hypnosis *takes leave* of time, and the proof is that he has no memory of the time during which he was hypnotized—a case of partial amnesia. Janet was in the habit of defining somnambulism as a form of conduct that eludes memorization. Out of all this evidence, I would suggest that the most important point is that the concept of the unconscious in Freud as well as in Janet originates with hypnosis and therefore with the interdividual mimetic relationship.

I believe that two directions of research emerge from the consideration of hypnosis. The first deals with shamanistic, psychosomatic, surgical and medical phenomena; here your theories can be applied to the mechanisms of obtaining a cure. The second is the application of interdividual psychology to the phenomena of hypnosis itself—including suggestion, possession and the problem of time and loss of memory—all the aspects of memory, in fact. Memory is indeed a gigantic machine for repeating itself in time and ought to provide a whole range of illustrations for mimesis.

This is a very broad picture that we are brushing in. It is also a quick and schematic one, which will have to be elaborated and illustrated with texts and cases of clinical practice.

R.G.: All the same, the fact that you keep such a central place for hypnosis among the various psychological and psychopathological processes is an interesting one, whose consequences could be fruitful.

J.-M.O.: The phenomena of hypnosis and possession do in fact seem to me to illustrate the hypothesis of mimesis and the sacred in an exemplary way. In particular, they demonstrate the *paradoxes* that you are constantly bringing to light—involving violence, the sacred, mimesis and desire. This paradoxical aspect, which ordains that the same psychological or psychosocial impulse can have quite contradictory and diametrically opposed results, did not escape the Ancients in their wisdom; only yesterday you drew my attention to what Aesop said about language.

The problem of choosing at every moment between two contrary potentialities gives rise, on the interdividual level, to the whole range of psychological and psychopathological problems. On the philosophical level, this choice is none other than the problem of free will, but that is another story.

CHAPTER THREE

Mimesis and Sexuality

What is known as 'Masochism'

G.L.: The way in which you define metaphysical desire—desire properly speaking—already takes for granted an area that psychiatrists have always viewed as being pathological and looked over for symptoms. You show, for example, that there is no such thing as a straight search for failure. The subject knows by experience that disillusionment awaits him on the other side of any obstacle that can too easily be overcome. So he sets out to find the insurmountable obstacle, the unbeatable rival, and the ungraspable object. Desire seeks ever for success. But it will have nothing to do with easy successes; like Nietzsche, it is only interested in lost causes.

R.G.: For an observer who is unaware of the context, this type of search seems to originate in a preference for failure. The label *masochism* implies a direct aim for what is initially no more than the consequence of desire—an inevitable one, perhaps, but never, at this stage cultivated in its own right. We must therefore do without this label, since it muddies the exceptional clarity of the phenomenon. To talk about masochism—as I have done myself in the past—is to neglect the fact that, long before the arrival of psychiatrists, desire has been asking questions about itself and coming up with answers. Unfortunately the only hypothesis it has been unwilling to accept, with an obstinacy that deserved a better cause, has been the mimetic hypothesis, which is both the simplest and the only truthful one. If rivals and obstacles are coming up before us all the time, this is because we are imitating their desires. Precisely because desire rejects this commonsensical truth, which, if desire was really willing to face up to it, would induce desire to recognize its own absurdity and give the whole thing up, desire must launch itself into a range of interpretations that, though never contrary to logic, become more and more subtle, contrived and unbelievable in order to justify the perpetuation of its own existence.

Desire refuses to understand why the model changes into an obstacle, but it sees clearly that this change always takes place. A phenomenon as reliable as this really must be taken into account. Instead of taking account of it in the only reasonable way, desire launches itself head first into the only escape route it can find. Through a process of reasoning that is false but logically impeccable, it puts its stake—as we said before—on the least likely probability. It does not extend the results of its previous failures to all the desires that are possible and imaginable, but decides to restrict their scope only to previous experiences—those concerned with the objects that are most accessible, the rivals that are least difficult to deal with, and everything that can make life easy and agreeable, everything that still enables us to 'function' as the modern term so appropriately puts it. It decides that the only objects worthy of being desired are those that do not allow themselves to be possessed; the only people who are qualified to guide us in the choice of our desires are the rivals who prove invincible and the enemies who cannot be disposed of.

After changing its models into obstacles, mimetic desire in effect changes obstacles into models. Since it is observing itself, it takes note of the transformation that has occurred, and not wishing to treat what it has just learned in the only way that makes sense, it treats it in the only other possible way: it makes what was initially no more than the result of its past desires, the pre-condition of any future desire.

Henceforth desire always hastens to wound itself on the sharpest of reefs and the most redoubtable of defences. How can observers possibly not believe in the existence of something that they call *masochism*? But of course they are quite wrong to do so. Desire aims to achieve shattering triumphs and pleasures that cannot be described. That is why it cannot hope to find them in ordinary experiences and relationships that can be brought under control. Desire will increasingly interpret the humiliation that it is made to suffer and the disdain that is is made to undergo in terms of the absolute superiority of the model—the mark of a blessed self-sufficiency that must necessarily be impenetrable to its own inadequacy.

J.-M.O.: If I follow you correctly, the subject becomes weighed down by failure and devalued in his own eyes, and at the same time the surrounding world becomes enigmatic. Desire can easily see that appearances cannot be trusted. It lives more and more in a world of signs and indices. Failure is not sought for its own sake but in so far as it signifies quite a different thing—the success of another, obviously, and only this other is of interest to me, since I can take him as model; I can enrol in his school and finally obtain from him the secret of the success that has always eluded me. This secret must be in the possession of the other, since he knows so well how to make me fail, how to reduce me to nothingness, how to bring out my own inadequacy when confronted with his unalterable being.

In the course of a long journey across a desert, the thirsty traveller will be cheered considerably by the unexpected presence of animals, however unpleasant and dangerous they may be. He sees it as a sign that water is not far away; soon, no doubt, he will be able to quench his thirst. It would be ridiculous to draw the conclusion that this unfortunate person takes pleasure in snake-bites and insect-stings—that his 'morbid masochism' draws an enjoyment from them that would be unintelligible to normal beings like ourselves.

Yet that is what is done by those who believe in masochism and stick this obfuscatory label on forms of conduct that are easy to interpret in the light of the mimetic hypothesis.

Theatrical 'Sado-Masochism'

G.L.: All you have said about the pseudo-masochistic structure of mimetic desire seems to be controverted by the existence of a much more spectacular, even theatrical, form of masochism on the basis of which the theory of masochism was set up. I am thinking of the masochistic *mise-en-scène* as Sacher-Masoch describes it. In this interpretation, masochists are people who ask their sexual partners to make them undergo all kinds of insults and humiliations—whipping, spitting and so on—with the aim of reaching sexual fulfilment.

R.G.: This is only an apparent contradiction. In order to come to terms with it, we have only to concede what we have already conceded—that desire, just like psychiatry but well in advance of it, observes what is happening but does not interpret it correctly. The false conclusions become the foundations of further desires. Far from being unconscious in Freud's sense and only appearing in its true form in our dreams, desire not only observes but never stops thinking about the meaning of its observations. *Desire is always reflection on desire*. From the basis of this reflection, it takes its direction and, from time to time, modifies its own structures. Desire is a strategist and it alters its aim, if I can put it like that, as a function of what it has learned about itself. These successive modifications always move in the direction of an aggravation of the symptoms, since, as I have said already, the knowledge that has been acquired by former desires always puts itself in the service of new and 'improved' ones. If we grant the primordial error of desire— its inability to recognize that it is founded on the *double bind*—we can see that desire gains nothing by getting to know itself better and better. On the contrary the more this knowledge is extended and deepened, the more capable the subject becomes of causing his own unhappiness, since he carries to a further stage the consequences of the founding contradiction—the more he tightens the *double bind*.

Desire has always got there already before psychiatry, and fallen into the traps that psychiatry, taking its cue from desire, then proceeds to fall into. Psychiatry is a discipline that insists in falling into these traps; it gives a very precise but prudent description, which will 'call a spade a spade' yet refrain from interpreting anything in a matter that would be at a variance with desire itself. Psychiatry does not come to terms with the element of implicit reflection that causes desire to develop—it fails to recognize in desire what it ought to recognize: a strategy that is always determined by the most recent observations, but always arrives at the same decisions in the light of the same data, which come up again and again in the same order. Psychiatry does not see the dynamic flow of this strategy. It thinks it sees clearly distinguished symptoms like objects laid side by side on a table.

Desire is the first to think up all the errors to which professional observation later succumbs, making them the principle of its pseudo-knowledge. Everyone has suspicions about the accuracy of this knowledge, but no one, until now, has really taken note of the unsettling simplicity of the force that distorts it in the first place. From the point this motive force is identified, there can no longer be any room for doubt. The continuity and coherence of the process are such that our incentive to develop the hypothesis further is constantly reinforced. We shall see that by being integrated in this dynamic process, all the symptoms usually given static and fixed descriptions will become intelligible moments of the process.

Everyone recognizes the highly theatrical character of the type of eroticism known as masochistic. This is a case of a *mise-en-scène*. The subject attempts to reproduce in his sexual life a particular type of relationship that arouses him intensely and therefore procures pleasure. The type of relationship involved is something the subject understands or thinks that he understands. Relationships concerned with violence and persecution are involved; but these are not necessarily associated with sexual pleasure. Why are they there at all?

To understand this, it is necessary to abandon the notion that there are inscrutable instincts and impulses of a specifically masochistic kind and return to the train of reasoning suggested a few moments ago—the reasoning that helped us abandon the illusion that the masochistic label makes any sense. People all around us repeat the familiar syllables *masochism*, as if the word were self-explanatory, something obvious and unproblematic, adding up to a concept that perfectly coincided with the phenomena under investigation.

The 'masochistic' subject wants to reproduce the relationship of inferiority, contempt and persecution that he believes he has—or he really does have—with his mimetic model. So it is necessary for the subject in question to have reached a stage at which the model interests him solely as a rival, with the opposition and violence of that rival already coming out into the foreground. The opposition and the violence are not there in their own right, only for the sake of all that they promise or appear to promise to the imitator of that model. Far from aspiring toward suffering and subjection, this imitator in fact aspires to the virtually divine sovereignty that the cruelty of the model suggests to be near at hand.

The only thing that theatrical masochism contributes to this structure derives from the element of sexual pleasure itself, which has hitherto remained fixed upon the instinctual object. In such masochism, sexual pleasure detaches itself from the object, either partially or completely, in order to fix itself upon the real or imagined insults that the model and rival inflicts.

This process has nothing incomprehensible about it. Let us grant that the value of the object can be measured by the level of resistance that the model puts up. It is perfectly understandable that then desire will tend to set a higher and higher value on violence itself, that it will fetishize violence and make of it the obligatory seasoning for all the pleasures that it can still have with the object, or even—at a still more advanced level—with the model itself, which becomes the beloved persecutor. Once the structure of mimetic rivalry begins to influence sexuality, there is no reason at all why it should stop short on such a promising road, and erotic pleasure is quite capable of detaching itself entirely from the object so as to attach itself to the rival alone.

If we do not appreciate that masochism belongs to the structure of mimetism, and if we take it to be a separate phenomenon that derives from a 'drive' or an 'instinct' more or less independent of all the other 'drives' or 'instincts', then this is because we attach too much importance to the purely sexual aspects of the overall phenomenon to be deciphered. In order to achieve pleasure, the subject has to reproduce the whole structure of his desire, as he reads it himself. He can no longer dispense with the real or assumed violence of the rival, since this is an integral part of that structure. This fact, which becomes perfectly intelligible through our reading, has always made such an impression on observers that they have set it apart from all the rest; they have taken it out of its original context and turned it into an absolute so that it becomes meaningless. Like the pseudo-masochists themselves, its deluded interpreters fetishize violence.

On reflection, we can see that the first scientific observers to look at this kind of phenomenon nearly always committed this kind of error. By directing itself toward the obstacle to the exclusion of everything else, the specifically sexual element emphasizes that obstacle to such a degree that the observer can no longer see anything else and so takes the obstacle as being the original *object* of desire and pleasure.

J.-M.O.: To say that masochism is *theatre* is to say that it is *imitating* an action or situation that is more or less real. Masochism 'properly speaking', or in Freud's terms 'secondary masochism', is therefore mimetic in the second degree; it is the mimetic representation of the subject's mimetic relationships with the most violent of models, that is to say, with the most insurmountable of obstacles. This progression is very similar to the one that takes place when the idols of violence are engendered originally, in real collective violence.

G.L.: We have to dispense completely with labels, like 'masochism' that suggest specific essences. All that we are ever dealing with is a particular moment in the mimetic process.

R.G.: We must indeed reverse the tendency of classic psychiatry, which tries hard to separate out its false essences from the basis of the phenomena that it considers to be *the most clearly differentiated*—such as 'masochism properly speaking'.

When Freud terms theatrical masochism 'secondary'—opposing it to a primary masochism that would find its way into essential aspects of the life of the psyche—he is on the right path but he is unable to follow it to the end. He keeps the inscrutable term 'masochism' to apply to the 'primary' process and he is incapable of making the necessary radical critique of the concept itself, which would result in its complete 'deconstruction'.

What Freud terms 'primary masochism' is in fact none other than conflictual mimesis—after the point when it sees in the most insuperable rival its model for the most stunning success. Let us repeat the point. The subject has repeatedly observed the disillusionment that he experiences when he defeats his own rival and remains the unchallenged and secure possessor of the object. To counteract such disillusionment, this subject will henceforth place all his faith in an impenetrable obstacle. The only type of model that can still generate excitement is the one who cannot be defeated, the one who will always defeat his disciple.

Secondary masochism is simply the theatrical representation of this phenomenon, which draws sexual pleasure in its wake. The subject makes the model and rival play a triumphant role without ever ceasing to mime his own failure in the model's presence. The violence whose object he wishes to be witnesses at each moment the presence of the desirable.

R.G.: The proof that we are dealing with a *model* here and that it is always a matter of *being with him*, *becoming* like him, can be found in the fact that primary masochism can also result in another form of theatre, which is symmetrical from the outset: sadism.

In the *mise-en-scène* he creates of his relationships with the model, in secondary masochism the subject plays his own role—the role of the victim. In sadism, he plays the role of the model and persecutor. Here, the subject imitates not the desire of the model, but the model himself, in what now forms the major criterion for selecting this model: his violent opposition to all conceivable aspirations of a normal human being.

What we have said suggests that in so far as the mimetic process comes to a conclusion, the model of desire is transformed increasingly into an ontological model. The more the value of the object increases, the more this object comes to appear linked to an ontological superiority—a possession of the object which no one even thinks of claiming from him. So the subject places all his faith in the impenetrable obstacle; he no longer searches for the traces of the being which is capable of freeing him from his failure, except in the one which invariably causes him to fail.

J.-M.O.: From that point onwards, desire is going to attach itself more and more to the violence which surrounds and protects the supremely desirable object.

Secondary masochism is simply the theatrical representation of this phenomenon, which draws sexual pleasure in its wake. The subject makes the model and rival play his triumphant role without ever ceasing to mime his own failure in the model's presence. The violence whose object he wishes to be is a witness at each moment to the presence of the desirable.

R.G.: The proof that we are dealing with a model here and that it is always a matter of being like him, becoming like him, can be found in the fact that primary masochism can also result in another form of theatre—which is absolutely parallel on the structural level: this is of course sadism.

In the *mise-en-scène* which he creates of his relationships with the model, the subject can play his own role—the role of the victim—and this is the so-called secondary masochism. He can also play the role of the model and persecutor, and this is what is known as sadism. In this case the subject is no longer imitating the desire of the model, but the model himself, in respect of what forms from that point onwards the major criterion for his choice: the model's violent opposition to all that the subject could still take as a desirable object.

What we have just said suggests that, in so far as the mimetic process comes to a conclusion, the model of desire is transformed increasingly into an ontological model. The more the value of the object increases, the more this object comes to appear as being linked to a superiority in being—a superiority that, in the final analysis, is that of the model itself. To sum up: once again desire tends to relinquish the object and become fixated on the model itself. The sexual appetite may become included in this general drift; that has happened when the subject cannot become excited unless the real or supposed atmosphere of its relationship with the 'ferocious' model is theatrically reconstituted, so that it can assume the part of the persecutor in a fake theatre of cruelty.

It is important at every stage to stress the continuity and rigour of what we have been saying—all of which is invariably fragmented in the classic interpretations. The more desire becomes attached to the resistance of the model, the more this resistance increases as a result of being imitated and therefore resisted, and the more desire becomes oriented toward a violence exchanged between the two subjects, mimetically. If these subjects rival each other in violence, this is because the greatest violence—which always passes for being the glorious monopoly of the triumphant rival—is now confused with the plenitude of *being* that the subject lacks.

J.-M.O.: Since this imitation is pushed to the point of actual *simulation* and can no longer be ignored by the observers who failed to notice it before, psychopathologists call up a specialized vocabulary—'sadism' and 'masochism'—to persuade themselves that imitation is not characteristic of desire in all its manifestations.

R.G.: The process that makes desire more and more metaphysical and the process that makes it more and more 'masochistic' are one and the same, since the metaphysical element is already inseparable from violence. The word 'metaphysical' itself is a substitute for the old notion of the sacred, which never gets as far as religion in the proper sense, except in the metaphors of great writers, which are effective precisely to the extent that they evoke the religious element without drawing too much attention to it.

To invite brutal treatment from a love partner who plays the role of the model, or conversely to treat the partner brutally—making him submit to the ill-usage one believes oneself to suffer at the model's hands—is always to seek to become a god mimetically. The subject increasingly aims at the model in preference to the object it initially designated, which formed the point of departure for the whole process. If the object has not been designated in the first place, the model would never have been transformed into an obstacle and a persecutor. Most observers would see this structure as being masochistic or sadistic only from the stage when the interplay of mimetic interferences comes to affect the sexual appetite itself: when, if the rival is absent, pleasure is diminished or impossible. Pleasure ordinarily comes to a halt, falls under *interdict*, when confronted with violence done to the subject. But instead of avoiding this violence, the subject can become fixated on it, as a result of a mimetic behaviour that takes the violence more and more as its object. We can verify that at this juncture.

To understand this process, it is necessary to reject everything that is taken for granted about sadism and masochism. Mimetic behaviour of a more or less theatrical kind is not something secondary, in the service of libidinal impulses that are specifically sadistic or masochistic. The very opposite is true. Mimetism is the motive force, and the specifically sexual appetite is taken in tow. The interplay of model and obstacle may or may not affect the sexual appetite enough to attract an observer's attention and bring the labels 'sadism' and 'masochism' to his lips. Alas, he only becomes deaf and blind to the impeccable continuity in the whole process.

Homosexuality

R.G.: If we recognize that the sexual appetite can be affected by the interplay of mimetic interferences, we have no reason to stop at 'sadism' and 'masochism' in our critique of false psychiatric labels. Let us grant that the subject can no longer obtain sexual satisfaction without involving the violence of the model or a simulation of that violence—and that the instinctual structures we have inherited from the animals, in the sexual domain, can allow themselves to be inflected by the mimetic game. We then have to ask ourselves if these cases of interference are not likely to have a still more decisive effect and give rise to at least some of the forms of homosexuality.

We have already come a large part of the way. In effect, we have already talked about homosexuality, at least indirectly since the model and rival, in the sexual domain, is an individual of the *same* sex, for the very reason that the object is heterosexual. All sexual rivalry is thus structurally homosexual. What we call homosexuality is, in this case, the total subordination of the sexual appetite to the effects of a mimetic game that concentrates all the subject's powers of attention or absorption upon the individual who is responsible for the *double bind*—the model as rival, the rival as model.

To make this genesis even more apparent, we must mention a curious fact that has been noted by the ethologists. It happens that, among certain types of monkey, a male who recognizes himself to have been beaten by a rival and so renounces the female disputed between them, puts himself in a position (so we are told) of 'homosexual availability' towards his victor. This is a gesture of submission, of course, but, in the context of a mimetism that intensifies in the transition from animal to man, it seems to mean something more. It does suggest to me the genesis I have just put forward. If there is no 'genuine' homosexuality among animals, that is because, with them, mimetism is not intense enough to have a lasting effect on the sexual appetite of the defeated rival. Yet it is already sufficiently intense, when the mimetic rivalries reach paroxysm, to produce something like an adumbration to this effect.[98]

If I am right, we ought to be able to find, in forms of ritual, the missing link between the vague sketch given by the animal world and homosexuality in the proper sense of the term. In fact, ritualized homosexuality is a fairly frequent phenomenon. It takes place at the paroxysm of the mimetic crisis and can be found in cultures that apparently allot no place to homosexuality outside the context of these religious rites. A comparison between the animal phenomenon, ritualized homosexuality and modern homosexuality cannot fail to signal that mimetism brings in the sexuality and not the other way round!

Ritualized homosexuality must be compared with a certain form of ritualized cannibalism practised in various cultures, where (as with homosexuality) cannibalism does not exist at ordinary times. In both cases, so it seems to me, the instinctual appetite, whether it be for food or sex, becomes detached from the object that human beings quarrel about and becomes fixated on the person or persons who are quarrelling. As always, desire tends to be inflected toward the mimetic model. In cannibalism, the rivalry must originally be over food. Within the alimentary context, the growing obsession that the model creates can be translated into an irresistible tendency to see him as something good to eat. Within the sexual context, the same obsession is translated into an irresistible tendency to see him as a possible object for sexual intercourse.[99]

G.L.: If we bring together these three phenomena—the animals' preliminary version, ritualized homosexuality, and then the deritualized form—the similarities and differences suggest successive stages in a single continuous process. This genesis of homosexuality properly speaking corresponds point by point to the notion of the transition from animal to human that results from our analyses. So we have reason to see the sequence which has been traced here as a further confirmation of our general hypothesis.

J.-M.O.: I can support your demonstration by bringing in the case, which I have had occasion to observe recently, of a young man—engaged to a young lady in the most traditional fashion—who fell in love with a man older than himself, taking him first of all (by his own avowal) as a model, then as a master and finally as a lover. The lover himself, although 'exclusively homosexual', was to tell me later that he was not at all interested in my patient to start with, but had only become attracted to him as a result of the presence of his fiancée and the triangular situation created on the occasion of a dinner party. When the patient became jealous of his lover, and left his fiancée for him, the lover completely lost interest in him. When I asked him about his reasons for this about-face, he told me: 'Take my word for it—homosexuality is wanting to be what the other is.'

R.G.: One of the advantages of this genesis by rivalry is that it occurs in an absolutely symmetrical way in both sexes. In other words, any form of sexual rivalry is homosexual in structure, with women as well as with men—at least for as long as the object remains heterosexual, that is to say, remains the object prescribed by the instinctual structures inherited from animal life. We must jettison the far too absolute concept of sexual difference which obliges Freud, for example, to misread the obvious symmetry between certain forms of homosexual behaviour in both sexes and to create a host of different types of instinct—specifically heterosexual and homosexual drives—in order to explain everything that moves more and more obviously nowadays toward blurring and even obliterating differences.

There is a whole imbroglio here of a distinctly mythological character. To put Freud right, we must not just change our vocabulary, as Lacan has done, for example, substituting the French word *pulsion*, 'drive', for instinct in translating the German term *Trieb*. We must eliminate not just the false difference between masculine and feminine types of homosexuality, but also the false difference between homosexual and heterosexual eroticism.

Homosexuality corresponds to an 'advanced' stage of mimetic desire, but this stage can also correspond to a form of heterosexuality in which the partners play the roles of model and rival, as well as that of object, for one another. The metamorphosis of the heterosexual object into a rival brings about effects very similar to the metamorphosis of the rival into an object. This is the parallelism that Proust recognizes when he states that you can transcribe a homosexual experience into heterosexual terms without in any way betraying the truth of one desire or the other. Quite clearly, Proust is more correct than those people who for reasons of attraction or repulsion wish to make homosexuality into a kind of essence, and thereby fetishize it.

Mimetic Latency and Rivalry

R.G.: Mimetic desire always succeeds in creating more and more undifferentiation. It is hardly necessary to go into all the different aspects of the process. The great writers have described it much better than we could ever do. They alone are capable of seeing that the sexual side of the matter is far from being primary and must be subordinated to mimetism, which succeeds in obliterating difference all the more successfully as it seeks it more greedily. Contrary to what is stated by the theory of narcissism, desire never aspires to something that resembles it; it is always searching for something that it imagines to be most irreducibly *other*. If, in homosexuality, desire paradoxically seeks it in the same sex, this is just another example of the paradoxical outcome that characterizes mimetic desire from one end of its course to another: the more desire seeks what is different, the more it stumbles upon the same.

J.-M.O.: The whole analysis you have just provided bears on phenomena that Freud also describes and analyses. According to Freud, there exist both overt and 'latent' homosexuality. The latter is 'repressed' and makes a good partner for 'masochism' and 'pathological jealousy'. Freud draws up this clinical report for Dostoevsky. He connects 'latent' or 'repressed' homosexuality—*verdrängte Homosexualität*—and what he describes as 'excessive tenderness for the rival in love', *sonderbar zärtlichen Verhalten gegen Liebesrivalen.*[100]

R.G.: Dostoevsky's case is by no means unique, but it is very important from our point of view for a number of reasons. The only one that concerns us for the moment is that Dostoevsky was never one of Freud's clients. Freud gets to know him through documents that are all available to us—his novels, his letters, everything that he wrote himself and everything that has been written about him, his temperament, the events of his life, etc. We are therefore on exactly the same footing as Freud, and no one can wave in front of us, as a red flag, the famous doctor-patient relationship, which makes the psychoanalyst privy to information to which an amateur like me has no access.

We must not engage in sterile polemics. Instead, we must begin by paying tribute to the quality of Freud's observation. Morbid jealousy, masochism, excessive tenderness for the rival in love—all these observations are admirable. All of this is worth three hundred tedious works on the philosophy of Dostoevsky. But it is admirable—I do not deny the irony here—as impressionistic description and, if I may say so, as the type of insight that would be disdainfully labelled 'literary' by psychoanalysts. If you look closely at the concepts Freud employs to describe the structure of 'Dostoevskyan psychology' (a structure that is common to literary works and interdividual relations, despite those who defined the work of art as 'pure fabrication'), you will notice that all of them basically say the same thing. You can bring all of them back to the same mimetic process. But Freud himself fails to see the utter redundancy of the three levels; he is under the impression that he is talking of three somewhat different things. We must criticize this false difference.

What is meant by jealousy, and why should it be qualified as morbid? It is the element of *repetition* that makes jealousy morbid. Every time the subject falls in love, a third party also gets into the picture—a rival who, for the most part, angers him greatly and is cursed by him, but nonetheless awakes in him the strange sentiment of 'excessive tenderness'.

If the masochism, the morbid jealousy, and the latent homosexuality constantly appear together, it is crucial to observe good scientific practice and ask if these three phenomena could not be assimilated to one another.

How does the subject actually manage always to have at his disposal—when he is inclining towards a sexual object—a rival who makes life hard for him, who is generally more fortunate than he is, and who nearly always runs off with the girl?

The only conceivable answer to this is that the last to show up in the triangular arrangement, the actual *third party*, is not the one we thought him to be. Even though he swears by all the gods that his desire for the object preceded the appearance of the rival—even if he arranges things chronologically so as to seem to have reason on his side—the subject should not be believed. The real third party is the subject himself, and if his desire always takes a triangular form, it is because it is the carbon copy of a pre-existing desire, his rival's desire.

If the subject desires a particular woman rather than another one, this is because of the flattering attentions of which she is the object. And the more flattering these attentions turns out to be, the more successfully will they enhance the sexual object in the eyes of the subject, in so far as they come from a greater expert in the area—an individual who passes for being unbeatable on the erotic level.

The masochism that Freud talks about, in this case, is the irresistible propensity to get bogged down in inextricable situations and to bring failure after failure upon oneself in one's sexual life. How is it possible to ensure that one fails in sexual terms without ever expressly wishing it, and without noticing that one is working towards one's own failure? The only really effective recipe is the one I am setting out here: it consists in considering the seduction of women as a function of the criteria I call 'mimetic'. The accredited Don Juans are, of necessity, much the most fearsome of rivals, much the most likely to inflict on the aspiring seducer the many reverses that he is doing his utmost to attract— without it being in any way necessary to explain the mechanism of his behaviour by bringing in some incomprehensible masochistic drive.

Nor is it any more necessary to invoke the notion of *latent* or *repressed homosexuality* in order to explain his ambivalent attitude toward the rival. The rival diverts toward himself a good proportion of the attention that the subject, as a good heterosexual, ought to keep for the object. This attention is necessarily 'ambivalent', since it comprises both the exasperation provoked by the obstacle and, the admiration and even exasperation provoked by the Don Juan's prowess.

Latent homosexuality has no more existence as a separate entity than masochism or morbid jealousy do. The theory of latent homosexuality presupposes an intrinsic homosexual force, crouching somewhere in the subject's body or in his 'unconscious' and only waiting for the subject's 'resistances' to collapse before it shows itself in the full light of day.

J.-M.O.: The best way of defining your position on masochism, morbid jealousy and 'latent' homosexuality, which is identical with the *sonderbare Zärtlichkeit*, excessive tenderness for an erotic rival— phenomena that Freud recognizes as being linked but fails to perceive as a unity—is perhaps to use more directly the work Freud believes himself to be criticizing when it is in fact criticizing him: the work of Dostoevsky.

R.G.: What makes Freud's observations about 'excessive tenderness' particularly striking is that he had evidently never even read the work in which this tenderness (mingled with its opposite, of course) is deployed in the most spectacular manner: *The Eternal Husband*. The only allusion that might involve this work would be to the outstanding intelligence shown by Dostoevsky, in Freud's view, when he describes situations that can only be clarified by invoking the notion of repressed homosexuality. I will quote the passage in question, not only because of this possible connection but because it contains the essentials of Freud's thesis on Dostoevsky. I give it in the original German because it is apparently impossible (or so the French say) not to falsify Freud's thought if you quote it in a foreign translation, as I did in *Violence and the Sacred*:

> Eine stark bisexuelle Anlage wird so zu einer der Bedingungen oder Bekräftigungen der Neurose. Eine solche ist für Dostojewski sicherlich anzunehmen und zeigt sich in existenzmöglicher Form (latente Homosexualität) in der Bedeutung von Männerfreundschaften für sein Leben, in seinem sonderbar zärtlichen Verhalten gegen Liebesrivalen und in seinem ausgezeichneten Verständnis für Situationen, die sich nur durch verdrängte Homosexualität erklären, wie viele Beispiele aus seinen Novellen zeigen.

> Thus a strong innate bisexual disposition becomes one of the preconditions or reinforcements of neurosis. Such a disposition must certainly be assumed in Dostoevsky, and it shows itself in a viable form (as latent homosexuality) in the important part played by male friendships in his life, in his strangely tender attitude towards rivals in love and in his remarkable understanding of situations which are explicable only by repressed homosexuality, as many examples from his novels show.[101]

In fact, Dostoevsky does give proof of a quite outstanding intelligence in his *Eternal Husband*. I have already spoken of this work in *Deceit, Desire and the Novel*. If I come back to it today, this is because it particularly clarifies both the basic structure of mimetic relationships and the mechanism through which they are repeated—everything that Freud himself did not manage to elucidate, everything that makes his reading of Dostoevsky in terms of latent homosexuality and abnormal Oedipal relationships distinctly inferior to the implicit thesis that comes out of the literary work, a thesis that coincides with the one I am expounding.

Let me begin by reproducing a résumé of the novel:

Veltchaninov, a rich bachelor, is a Don Juan in his maturity who is beginning to be overtaken by boredom and tiredness. For a number of days he has been obsessed by the fleeting appearances of a man who is both mysterious and familiar, disturbing and rather grotesque. The identity of this character is soon revealed. It is a certain Pavel Pavlovich Troussotsky whose wife—a former mistress of Veltchaninov—has only just died. Pavel Pavlovich has left his province to join the lovers of his dead wife at St Petersburg. One of them dies in his turn and Pavel Pavolovich follows the funeral procession, in deep mourning. There remains Veltchaninov whom he plies with the most bizarre attentions and wears out with his assiduity. The deceived husband has the most strange things to say about the past. He makes a visit to his rival in the middle of the night, drinks his health, kisses him on the mouth, and cleverly torments him with the help of a sad young girl about whom we never get to know whether he is her father.

The wife is dead and the lover remains. There is no longer any object, but the model and rival, Veltchaninov, still exerts an insuperable attraction. This model-rival is an ideal narrator because he is at the centre of the action, and yet he hardly takes any part in it. He describes the events with all the more care as he is not always able to interpret them and is afraid of neglecting some important detail.

Pavel Pavlovich is thinking of a second marriage. Once again, this victim of fascination pays a visit to the lover of his first wife; he asks him to help choose a present for the newly chosen one; he begs him to accompany him to her house. Veltchaninov demurs but Pavel Pavlovich insists, entreats him, and ends up having his way.

The two 'friends' are very well received at the young girl's house. Veltchaninov talks well, and plays the piano. His worldly-wise air is a great success: the whole family gathers around him, including the young girl whom Pavel Pavlovich already considers as his fiancée. The disregarded claimant makes hopeless attempts to appear seductive. No one takes him seriously. He contemplates this new disaster, trembling with anguish and desire. . . . A few years later, Veltchaninov once again meets Pavel Pavlovich in a railway station. The eternal husband is not alone; a charming woman, his wife, is accompanying him, together with a dashing young officer.[102]

In Dostoevsky's description, the subject does not choose a model once and for all, and the model does not designate an object for him once and for all. For the designated object to retain the value that comes to it from the model, it is necessary for him to continue to value it by not ceasing to desire it. If Troussotsky is stupid enough to take Veltchaninov to his fiancée's home, this is not so that this hated rival can make a conquest of her, but so that he will desire her, and—by so doing—register and ratify the choice that Troussotsky had made of her. Because Veltchaninov has triumphed over him, Troussotsky surrounds him with a halo of 'Don Juanesque' prestige, which he dreams of having himself, but which, by virtue of his constant failures, tends more and more to take refuge with his rival.

Of course there is a hint of homosexuality in this affair, which Dostoevsky himself underlines when he shows Troussotsky kissing his rival on the mouth. But we should not let some mythic and obscure notion of latency blind us to the operation of mimetic rivalry—the primary and the only truly intelligible explanation for these features on the genetic level.

G.L.: Troussotsky's dream is not to make love to Veltchaninov but to take a spectacular revenge on him by snatching his fiancée away from the burning passion that will make her godlike because it comes from the god of love, and finally to become a god himself, as he possesses the godlike object.

R.G.: Sexuality is indeed controlled by rivalry. The more the subject believes himself to be fighting on his own behalf, in mimetic rivalry, the more he is in fact surrendering to the victorious rival. Only the rival has authority in desire; only he can confer upon the subject the seal of the infinitely desirable by desiring it himself. So the subject always makes this rival play an active part as an intermediary, literally that of a 'mediator' between himself and the object. The human subject does not really know what to desire, in the last resort. He is quite incapable on his own of fixing his desire on one object and, on his own, of desiring that object consistently and relentlessly. That is why he is given over to the paradoxes of mimetic desire. If we look at Troussotsky's behaviour, we can easily see why 'morbid jealousy', 'latent' homosexuality and 'masochism' must always arise *together*.

The supposed masochist is rather like a general who has already lost a battle and who is so humiliated by defeat that he has no wish to engage in combat from that point except with the aim of making up for this one defeat. So he tries to recreate the same conditions, or conditions that are even more unfavourable, in his subsequent campaigns. It is not a question of losing yet again, but of winning the only battle that is really worth the trouble—the battle he has already lost. So he puts all his efforts into encountering his old antagonists once again and reproducing the circumstances of his earlier defeat. The triumph he is aiming for can no longer be imagined outside the framework of this defeat and everything that goes with it. No victory is likely, therefore to follow the first defeat, only a series of new defeats, which might lead superficial observers to conclude that defeat is the real purpose of these endless manoeuvres.

If we put this particular game—which is simply one particular modality of mimetic absorption—within the domain of amorous rivalry, it becomes clear that the player is always trying to reproduce conditions that are likely to generate more and more jealousy, and more and more 'masochism'. He need only allow himself to be fascinated by the most formidable of rivals. Then the conditions that favour the displacement of a properly sexual interest in the direction of the rival will be met. To gather all the symptoms into the unity that is suggested by their conjunction, the accent must be placed, not on sexuality as such, as Freud places it, but on the mimetism of rivalry. Only this mimetism can make sense of the conjunction, for it has only to become aggravated for all the 'symptoms' to appear together. They are indissociable, and their diversity is a mere illusion; believing in this diversity shows how incapable we are of bringing everything back to its unique source in mimetic rivalry.

As long as the rivalry bears only on a heterosexual object, there is no true homosexuality. Does that mean homosexuality is 'latent'? Freud is so quick to talk about latency that he opens the way to a false kind of perceptiveness, where you only have to note the smallest signs of jealousy to be able to invoke homosexuality. To judge from amateur psychoanalysts, rivals always in the last resort want to sleep with one another, never with the woman over whom they apparently quarrel.

So sexual rivalry is always a mask for a different rivalry. Only by crediting the reality of this other rivalry, by recognizing its mimetic character, can we understand its real link with the homosexual element.

It is crucial that rivalries be seen as *real*, whether or not they are sexual. They must be obsessional and intense in order to succeed in displacing the sexual appetite, on occasion, and allowing it to polarize upon the rival. Either this unhooking takes place, or it does not. Where it does take place, that must be at a very early age. With Dostoevsky, it clearly does not take place. No unavowed homosexual repression prevents Dostoevsky from sleeping with his rivals; he has not the least inclination to do so. In his case, the sexual appetite remains fixated upon the female object. Freud's article on Dostoevsky would be a better one if it were about Shakespeare!

G.L.: You are probably aware that you are imprudently exposing yourself to the accusation of latent homosexuality, repression, resistance and over-compensation?

R.G.: I have been radically demystified quite a few times already, but I am still an impenitent sinner. Instead of subordinating rivalry to a form of concealed homosexuality meant to produce it like a shadow, we should subordinate homosexuality to the rivalry that *can* produce it but, no less frequently, does not produce it, even where it becomes obsessional, as in Dostoevsky.

Freud's mistake, as usual, consists in taking as the sole motor and basis of a psychic process a sexual appetite that the obsession with the rival does not always succeed in displacing, however strong it may be.

The close relationship between sexual rivalry and homosexuality does not in any way mean that all forms of sexual rivalry are the product of latent homosexuality. The very concept of latency seems to me a mythological one. But it is easy to understand why it captivates the observer in a society where the intense disapproval to which homosexuality was always subjected is in the process of ebbing away. If any form of sexual rivalry with a rival of the same sex implies automatically that there is latent homosexuality, then why should we not talk of latent heterosexuality in relation to a homosexual who is jealous of a rival of the other sex?

There can be no question of doing so, because the theme of latency is linked to a form of moral terrorism; it only comes into play to the extent that the 'latency' works in favour of the most scandalous of sexual desires—the one most opposed to the system of prohibitions now in the process of collapsing. 'Latency' caters to the demystificatory itch by giving it a constant opportunity for relief that does not require any great expenditure of grey matter. From the moment latency is mentioned, the slightest exception taken to it will land you automatically in the camp of the latent, of those who do not dare be homosexual but probably would be, if they were less 'bourgeois'.

The burning certainty that there are always naive people to demystify, traitors to confound, infidels to ward off—victims to persecute, if it comes down to it—is what cements the union of the faithful around the great guru of universal demystification.

What a pity this triumphal progress of latency did not yet exist in the time of Bouvard and Pécuchet. Flaubert would surely have launched these two good fellows on this highly promising track. He loved nothing more than the truly modern forms of gullibility, the ones to which we succumb with the illusion of transcending gullibility once and for all. The contempt that he shows for 'phallic symbol'—which had already begun its career in his day—did not stop the garden variety of demystification from spreading everywhere in the fields of culture like a kind of indestructible crabgrass. We are always upbraiding each other for the brevity of our intellectual fads—but the phallic symbolism already seemed ridiculous to Flaubert and it has hardly started to go out of fashion. Let me read the passage. Without the proper names, no one would believe that this is a text more than a hundred years old!

> . . . towers, pyramids, candles, signposts and even trees had the meaning of a phallus, and for Bouvard and Pécuchet everything became a phallus. They gathered in the traces of carriages, the legs of chairs, the bolts from cellar-doors and chemists' pestles. When people had seen them, they asked:
> —What do you think that is like? Then they revealed the mystery, and, if people protested, they shrugged their shoulders in pity.[103]

G.L.: Throughout the psychiatric and psychoanalytic tradition, and for Freud in particular, homosexuality passes as a 'perversion'. This perversion is supposed to originate with a homosexual drive, that is to say, a specific type of instinct.

R.G.: I would repeat once again that homosexuality, in literary works, is often the eroticizing of mimetic rivalry. The desire bearing on the object of the rivalry—an object that need not even be sexual—is displaced toward the rival. Since the rival need not necessarily be of the same sex—the object itself being not necessarily sexual—this eroticizing of rivalry can also take the form of heterosexuality.

In my opinion, there is no structural difference between the type of homosexuality and the type of heterosexuality that we are discussing at this point. Proust is correct, in his dispute with Gide, to reject the notion of homosexual *difference* postulated by the latter.

The theory of instincts or *pulsions*, is uninteresting because it is non-functional. It prevents the exploitation of phenomenological analogues. It actually reinforces the tendency of psychiatrists to imagine that there are separate essences on every occasion when they come across an observation that only seems to be new because they are incapable of recognizing a new effect produced by the same 'cause', or a slightly modified perspective on a phenomenon observed already.

Obviously I am not denying that there may be other forms of homosexuality than the one we have described. I have no basis for making a judgement on this issue. I say only that if Freud postulated a latent homosexuality in the cases that concern us here, particularly that of Dostoevsky, it is because he did not uncover the forms of mimetic rivalry that Dostoevsky uncovered in his novels, even if Dostoevsky did not come up with a full conceptual definition of them.

The mimetic hypothesis seems superior to me because it completely dispenses with what in Freud is a supplementary postulate—the idea that there is a specific drive rooted somewhere in the body or whatever. The mimetic hypothesis succeeds in integrating at least one type of homosexuality within the overall process we have been sketching out. The process itself reveals once again how remarkably apt it is for organizing and making sense of very different types of phenomena. Not only does Freud gain absolutely nothing by postulating 'drives', he actually prevents his disciples from perceiving that the stunning simplicity of the mimetic solution is not 'simplistic' at all, since it single-handedly generates a great variety of complex phenomena.

The End of Platonism in Psychology

R.G.: It would be possible to show that in Freud's time pansexualism was an inevitable approach; it offered the most accessible way of solving problems since it introduced elements of differentiation observers could not yet do without. For a long time it has been difficult to imagine that some of these differentiations within the psyche could have their roots in something less differentiated, even in what is the source of all lack of differentiation: mimesis.

J.-M.O.: Basically, we are doing with the labels, categories and classifications of psychiatry what we have already done with the various institutional and ethnological classifications. In all these spheres, we have shown that the human mind looks for difference, and has a tendency to hypostatize it improperly—not because the mind is incapable of thinking through the kind of process which we have identified, but because that is a difficult task, one that only becomes possible (paradoxically enough) in the aftermath of the period in which synchronic structuralism was the rage.

R.G.: Structuralism is not exclusively the establishment of separate synchronic moments; already it suggests and prepares for their *transformation*. By thinking of structures as mimetic transformations of one another, we begin to come upon a few scraps of genuine diachrony. Starting from these, it becomes possible to develop a hypothesis about how any structure was generated and developed.

G.L.: Freud placed a great deal of weight on the continuity or identity of structure between homosexuality and paranoia, that is to say, persecution mania. How do you see the matter?

R.G.: The person who persecutes is, as a rule (within our 'psychopathological' context of course), the model and rival. It goes without saying that all forms of substitution and transference of a sacrificial kind—are possible. So it is clear that we are still very close to everything that we have been talking about and will continue to talk about. I am not merely incompetent on the clinical level; I distrust on principle any form of classification. For me, to isolate illnesses from one another is, by definition, to extract them arbitrarily from the continuing process of which they are merely separate stages. Of course, this does not alter the fact that patients can become stabilized on a long-term basis, at a particular level.

It is undoubtedly true that the paranoiac can perceive, as we do, the homosexual character of the structure in which rivalry occurs. But, as often as not, he has no sense of responsibility for his 'homosexuality', which in a sense comes upon him from the outside, and he has no wish to assume responsibility for it. Paranoia involves the disappearance of the object and the persistence of rivalry in its pure state.

If we are less and less able to understand desire in its more advanced stages, this is because desire tends to forget the earlier stages and use their consequences as a basis; it transforms them into a point of departure. Once you have grasped the fact that the spring of the whole process is mimesis, you are able, not only to reconstitute all the stages in their logical continuity, but it becomes obvious that the final goal only seems obscure to us because of its excessive intelligibility. Madness involves only the model and caricatural imitation of the model. It is simply megalomaniac identification, persecution, and so on. The obscure part of madness is one that we create by our blindness to the caricaturally mimetic nature of its desire, because our own desire would be revealed as only a more moderate version of the same thing.

Here again there is obviously a parallel between the approach of madness and the approach of a reason that must expel its own caricature as madness in order not to understand itself too well. Beyond a certain threshold, the madman is also unable to tolerate what he is succumbing to. He does not want to know any more about it, and he takes steps to expel himself—if we can put it like that—to unhook his own mind, by methods that are even more brutal than ours, with the aim of closing himself to any awareness of the processes for which he still serves as victim.

J.-M.O.: Desire becomes detached from the object and attaches itself to the model that is taken as an obstacle. All the phenomena you have described or pointed out come back to this single principle and can invariably be deduced from it in an almost priori fashion. It is through failure to appreciate this point that we are prone to see at every stage disconnected symptoms of separate illnesses and heterogeneous collections of phenomena. In reality, there is only the mimetic process, directed toward its own form of truth—which, however, always tends to become arrested at a more or less advanced stage according to the particular individual.

To sum up, there is psychosis when there is no longer any possibility of making an objective discrimination between doubles; but, from the perspective of the psychotic himself, this indiscriminateness is the totality of his being, which oscillates dizzily between himself and his double.

R.G.: The mimetic process does not, in our world, unfold in the light of day, in crises that involve the whole community and attain a level of

paroxysm and near-frenzy so that the victimage mechanisms can be unleashed. On the contrary, it dominates relationships between individuals in a subterranean fashion, employing forms that possess
sufficient permanence to appear to both partners in the guise of well-
differentiated and individualized traits of what was first called 'character' and later was reinterpreted as 'symptoms'.

The sacrificial crisis that is gaining momentum in our own time
brings about the disappearance of any character psychology. The transition to the notion of psychopathological symptom must be understood as an effect of this acceleration. If we look at Freud's terminology,
we can see that this transition is not yet with him, as is attested by expressions like 'pathological jealousy', 'neurotic envy' and 'envious
neurosis'. Bear in mind that these expressions denote an *intermediate*
stage. At the present moment, there is an increasing tendency—as a
result of this same process of evolution—for the notion of symptom to
wither away in turn and become empty of any substantial meaning.

By a parallel process, the concept of a 'madman' has been giving way
to notions like 'psychosis' which are no more precise but express modifications of the being rather than that being in itself. For the moment,
psychotic phenomena are still kept separate from neurotic phenomena.
But the goal of psychopathology henceforth will be to articulate the former in relation to the latter, and to conceive of a single approach in
terms of which delirium and reason can be interpreted and made intelligible on a mutual basis.

J.-M.O.: Suppose that desire and its psychopathological manifestations can be interpreted according to the mimetic perspective you
have opened up, and suppose that we can detect on this particular level
a process that parallels the one we postulated as underlying primitive
societies, but unfolds according to its own modalities, which are deter-
mind by the gradual withdrawal of the victimage mechanisms and the
protection that they offer. In that case, we would understand how it is
that the development of the psychopathological symptom and the place
it holds in psychiatry have kept pace closely with the stages of desacralization that govern our culture as a whole. In other words, the contemporary crisis of psychopathology and psychiatry would be the same
crisis as the one all the sacrificial institutions are undergoing.

R.G.: The processes and mechanisms you are talking about, in my
view, are one and the same. It is not a question of scrubbing out the old

classifications but of deconstructing the ones that distinguish between 'genus' and 'species', as botany and zoology have tended to do. We can show that Freudian psychoanalysis has been a stage in this process of evolution, but the increasingly rapid retreat of notions like 'being' and the 'sacred' has diminished its therapeutic value. Psychiatry is at an even more advanced stage of disintegration, and anti-psychiatry has already come into being.

Instincts, drives, fetishized sexuality, 'characters' or 'symptoms'—all are just false essences we are attempting to deconstruct—they are merely Platonic ideas that are in the process of disappearing.

CHAPTER FOUR

Psychoanalytic Mythology

Freud's Platonism and the Use of the Oedipal Archetype

J.-M. O.: We must spend some time on what Freud called the Oedipus complex. There can be no doubt that Freud thought up the Oedipus complex as a way of accounting for a situation involving triangular rivalries: the woman, the lover and the rival. The example from Dostoevsky is just one among many. Freud immediately attributes to the Oedipus complex the fact that this writer's life and work constantly involve triangular relationships in which the rival becomes the object of morbid hostility as well as of unusual tenderness, Freud's *sonderbare Zärtlichkeit*.

G. L.: Freud invents the Oedipus complex as a way of explaining all these triangles, of explaining why this ambivalence repeats itself in so many cases of rivalry. According to the complex, in its authentically Freudian form, the triangle reproduces the familial triangle. The loved woman always takes the place of the mother, and the rival that of the father. The ambivalence depends upon the complex feelings that the subject has for his father, who is both a rival and a father.

What connection is there between mimetic desire and the Oedipus complex? Can mimetic desire and the Oedipus complex coincide with one another—all the time, or on certain occasions? At the very least, are they compatible with one another?

R. G.: Mimetic desire and the Oedipus complex are incompatible for two main reasons. (1) For Freud, the desire for the mother as object is an intrinsic one; there can be no question of it being based on something else, let alone another form of desire. This intrinsic nature of the desire for the mother, combined with the intrinsic element of narcissism, provide Freud's definition of the *humanity* of human desire, what makes it specifically different:

Wir sagen, der Mensch habe zwei ursprüngliche Sexualobjekte: sich selbst und das pflegende Weib, . . .

We say that a human being has originally two sexual objects—himself and the woman who nurses him—

If desire for the *pflegende Weib* ('nurturing female') is original, natural and spontaneous, it cannot be derived or copied from anything else at all. (2) For Freud, the father certainly serves, from the son's point of view, as a model for identification, both before and after the Oedipus complex. But this model for identification is never a model for desire. Freud never though identification with the father could involve desire; indeed he never thought through the relationship between desire and identification. He states expressly that desire for the mother grows independently from identification with the father, and the father appears first of all as the rival and the personification of the law.[105]

Mimetic desire does not appear anywhere in Freud. He makes no reference to it, even in connection with the Oedipus complex, but it is not difficult to see that the two notions are mutually exclusive. The Oedipus complex is what Freud invented to explain triangular rivalries, when he failed to discover the remarkable possibilities of the principle of imitation, precisely in connection with issues of desire and rivalry.

G. L.: Are you ruling out the possibility that the father serves as a mimetic model?

R. G.: Not in the least. Not only do I not rule out this possibility, but I take it as a normal phenomenon, in the sense in which Freud considers identification.with the father to be normal, though it has nothing to do with the Oedipus complex. It is normal for the father to serve as a model to his son, but it is not normal for the father to become a model for his son in the area of sexual desire; it is not normal for the father to become a model in domains where imitation will give rise to rivalry. In other words, in normal family circumstances, the father serves as a model for apprenticeship and not for sexual desire.

G. L.: That means that for you the family, like all forms of social institution—in principle, at any rate—furnishes the child with models and prohibitions that avert certain forms of rivalry and alleviate others. Thus it prepares and strengthens him for a world in which imitation and rivalry are not as well canalized and restrained as they are in the normally functional family.

R. G.: The family does not play the same *necessary* role as it does for Freud in the pathology of desire. The pathology of desire does not have its basis in the family. It is mimetic. Of course, that does not mean that the family cannot become pathological. It not only can become so, but very often does in the conditions of our world. The more pathological the family becomes, the further it deviates from what it is when it functions normally. Relationships within the family then become similar to what they are outside the family; they become characterized either by total indifference or by the type of morbid attention that accompanies mimetic desire wherever it flourishes, within the family or outside it.

G. L.: If the Oedipus complex is absolutely incapable of accounting for what Freud wants it to account for, we still have to explain how it is that the idea has been so extraordinarily successful. The tendency to explain all forms of rivalry by the Oedipus complex has become as ingrained as Aristotelianism was in the university circles of the fifteenth century. Yet once you realize the superior effectiveness of the mimetic principle—its simplicity, its intelligibility—you cannot fail to wonder about the reason for its belated appearance and for the incredible vogue that the Oedipus complex has enjoyed and continues to enjoy.

R. G.: It is important to bear in mind that Freud was (as he himself claimed) the first person to take a systematic approach to phenomena that had been the unique preserve of the great writers up to his time. He not only observes a whole range of phenomena, but he also provides them with their first more or less 'technical' vocabulary, up to a point the only one that we have ever had. So it is hardly surprising that Freudian notions, despite their inadequacy, should have gained an extraordinary grip on people's minds. But I think that there are also other, more fundamental reasons for the success of the Oedipus complex and narcissism, the twin pillars of psychoanalytic doctrine. These are linked to a range of ideas and habits that have always been a feature of our thought and stand in need, once again, of mimetic analysis. Basically, we have to do the same work on what I would not hesitate to call Freud's Platonism (a very individual kind of Platonism, it must be said) as we have already done in too hasty a fashion on the pseudo-scientific classifications of ethnology. Focusing the Oedipus complex, I think we shall be able to push this task a little bit further.

Freud did not base the Oedipus complex on observations of children; he took as his material the triangular relationships he observed among mental patients and in famous works like the one by Dostoevsky. Any scientific mind would try to look for a unitary explanation to deal with the frequency and the obsessive character of these triangular relationships. Obviously I agree with Freud about the importance of these relationships, and I do not share the opinion of Deleuze and Guattari, that the triangles only began to proliferate when Freud invented the famous complex. I cannot accept that these triangular relationships, in our world, are no more than an imitation of Freud, even I am willing to acknowledge that this type of mimicry too, plays a role in contemporary life.[106]

To understand how Freud arrived at the Oedipus complex, one must try to retrace his approach—one must reconstruct what he thought when he found himself before all these triangular relationships. The Western researcher's first idea—his almost automatic reaction in the circumstances—is that there must be an archetypal triangle somewhere of which all the other triangles are reproductions.

Once you have set out on this road, which is the high road of human thought, you end up with the family triangle. Since there can be no question, for modern materialists, of setting the archetypal triangle outside this world, in some eternal, intelligible kingdom of ideas, such as Jung, up to a point, imagined, the Platonic idea has to be brought down into this world. Obviously the family triangle is the only possible candidate for the archetypal role, given these circumstances.

For a triangle to be able to play this role, it must possess the stability, the universality and the chronological precedence that will enable it (at least on the surface) to serve as an origin and a foundation stone. It must have all the requisite qualities that allow it to serve as the model for all the later triangular relationships. Only the family triangle possesses these indispensable attributes. There can be no individual existence that does not begin with it, in principle at any rate; only this triangle has a legal existence and a sociological weight that make it adequate for the role Freud intends it to play.

Only the family triangle can fit Freud's bill. No other type of triangle order can possibly replace it. It seems to have been put there, on the threshold of life, to play the particular role that Freud wants it to play. Why should we be surprised at the enormous prestige that the Oedipus complex, in one form or another, has exerted ever since on the modern mind.

Yet its ascendancy is quite illusory. The Oedipal scheme cannot generate all the possible triangular configurations that structure the erotic relationships of the mentally ill or, indeed, the plots of literary works, be they comic or tragic, plays or novels.

How do you reproduce a Triangle?

R. G.: If you reflect on the archetypal family triangle, you will see that with Freud as with Plato the transition from essence to appearance, or from the family archetype to the actual situation of triangular rivalry, can only take place through the mediation of mimesis, or imitation. To pass from the child's Oedipus complex to the adult's erotic rivalries, the individual dedicated to triangular relationships must imitate in one way or other the original triangle of his family relationships.

In other words, we are both very close to our mimetic relationship and very far from it. To understand this closeness and distance, we must ask psychoanalysts the following questions. Patients are familiar with the experience of obsessive rivalry; they even seem incapable of doing without it. But how, precisely, do they reproduce in their everyday lives—especially in their erotic undertakings—their childhood relationships with their parents? How do you go about copying the family triangle? Since imitation must be involved, what must be imitated to give the desired result—to provide a rival who makes us just as jealous as (in Freud's view) we originally were of our fathers? What method makes it possible continually to recreate this situation?

No doubt psychoanalysts will reply that this is a secret of the unconscious. Being specialists of the unconscious, psychoanalysts should certainly have an idea of the procedures to which their patients resort—or their knowledge is not all that it claims to be. After all, the situation I am describing is commonplace—nothing more banal can be thought of. The possible answers are not unlimited in number, and those who cultivate pathological rivalries must surely possess some recipes for reproducing them—recipes that cannot all be passed over in silence. What has the psychoanalyst to say to us on this matter?

Nothing at all. Freud is, as usual, honest enough to admit it. In *Beyond the Pleasure Principle* he concedes that the repetition of what causes ever more suffering poses an insoluble problem if all behaviour stems from the 'pleasure principle'. In order to resolve this mystery, Freud must postulate a further drive—the death instinct, so prized by contemporary French psychoanalysis.

Not only the *why* of repetition poses a problem, but also its *how*. If we look at Oedipal relationships, we can conclude (as we did a few moments ago) that the only link between them is the extrinsic factor of the law. Desire for the moment develops quite independently from identification with the father. Interference only arises by virtue of an almost accidental rivalry, brought about, not by creative imitation of the father, but by the fact that the mother is the father's wife and belongs legally to him.

How can the father serve as a model for 'identification', and thus for this particular desire, given that he incarnates the law—that is to say, an obstacle having nothing to do with desire? The father is an obstacle without ever having been a model for the only relationship that really counts—the desire that generates rivalry.

If you look at Freud's writings on 'identification', the Oedipus complex and the 'super-ego' (as I have done in *Violence and the Sacred*), you will notice that all Freud's formulations return in different ways to the same basic inability to recognize that the principle of the model and that of the obstacle are one and the same—and that this identity has nothing paternal about it. The real principle is and must be a mimetic one. But to notice it, you must do away with the standard definitions of imitation, which evacuate its potential for rivalry. Freud circled around this secret all his life without ever coming to terms with its deceptive simplicity. That is why he falls back on mythological concepts. These concepts are examples of false differentiation and reflect once again his incapacity to detect that the fundamental mechanism of human conflict resides in a mimesis that precedes representation and exists on the level of animal appetite. This origin does not, of course, prevent mimesis from eventually becoming extremely elaborate and including in its operation the most refined forms of representation.

G. L.: How can the 'Oedipal' relationship be reproduced? How is it possible to discover simultaneously the person whom Freud sees as a substitute for the mother, and beside her, the person whom Freud sees as a substitute for the father—the rival who is to obsess us?

R. G.: The only possible answer is the one we have given—the mimetic solution. The only infallible way of producing triangular rivalry consists in imitating a pre-existing desire—in never desiring any woman except when she is designated by the desire of another. To desire through the mediation of a model is to desire through the mediation of a rival—and to put oneself in the power of that rival. Without a doubt, this is how the kind of *ambivalence* that Freud observes came into being! At the same time, the explanation nicely eliminates the need for a separate 'death instinct', because, in the absence of the victimage mechanism, it cannot lead anywhere but to more and more destruction and death.

So the only way of resolving the problem of mimetic reproduction is through mimetic desire itself—which means, in the final analysis, our concept of acquisitive mimesis, which is quite distinct from the Oedipus complex and is not even specifically human, since it can be found in the animal kingdom.

There is no way of accepting this solution without rejecting the archetypal system of the Oedipus complex, which *it formally excludes*. The indispensable *rival* can be secured only when the subject imitates the desire of a *model*, through an automatic mechanism that the subject, possessed by his mimetic urge, cannot see. The triangle of rivalry is always around precisely because the rivalry is never Oedipal in the Freudian sense. If the subject truly inherited his desire from his own past, he could not so readily adopt the desire of another model and so make up the third tip of the triangle, rather than the first one, as the archetypal conception in its implicit solipsism would have us believe.

The problem of repetition can only be resolved in the light of a mimetic desire that cannot, by definition, coincide with the Oedipus complex. It is even less likely to coincide with it in so far as it provides a principle of rivalry and conflictual behaviour in the *present* and not in the *past*—one that is much more dynamic than rivalry with the father. It accounts for the repetition of symptoms and for their intensification, which is completely unintelligible in the psychoanalytic scheme.

Either you bring rivalry into being through mimetic desire and get rid of the false hypothesis of the Oedipus complex, or you remain faithful to the Oedipus complex and come up against the insoluble problem of repetition. The Oedipal relationships are inert. Neither Freud nor anyone else will ever be able to think them through in such a way that they react on one another to provide a positive *feedback* and inveigle the subject into the ever more disastrous impasse of an increasing obsessional rivalry. For this impasse to develop, the rivals must be carefully chosen precisely as a function of their *invincibility*—which is to say, their capacity for preventing us from reaching the objects they designate to us.

This role of model and rival has nothing paternal about it. We need not hesitate to state that Oedipus is only a later version of the age-old mythology that nowadays has become a basic resource for a society that believes itself to be enlightened but in actuality simply projects upon institutions that are in the process of breaking down (as is the rule in any form of sacrificial crisis) the mimetic difficulties provoked by that very breakdown. Who believes in the repressive father any more?

If the modern family in the West and the patriarchal system that preceded it are at the origin of the said difficulties, this is not because they have been as repressive and constraining as people make out; on the contrary, it is because they have been considerably less repressive than most human cultural institutions, and so they are as direct predecessors of the increasingly aggravated state of undifferentiation that marks our present situation.

Mimesis and Representation

R. G.: With Freud as with our own mimetic scheme, the Oedipal subject has his eyes fixed upon a model. Since this model is not a desire, all Freud's efforts to provide a satisfactory mechanism for the reproduction of triangles at the unconscious level invariably end up metaphors drawn from typographical reproduction: seals, matrices, imprints, inscriptions, *Wunderblocke* and so on. This is a great treat for the fanatics of *écriture* and evidently presupposes a concealed problematic of representation and the sign, even if there is no indication that this problematic is truly relevant. To resolve this issue and really leave behind Platonic 'metaphysics', we must not draw away from the Platonic concept of mimesis as if it were carrying the plague. Instead, we must look the plague in the face.

What is missing in Freud is exactly what is missing in Plato—an understanding that the mimetic is itself a desire and is therefore the real 'unconscious' (supposing that there is still any point in keeping such a term). Non-representational mimesis is perfectly capable—uniquely capable—of giving rise to all the forms of triangular rivalry.

The subject indeed has his eyes fixed upon a model, but this model is not a triangle, a geometrical figure, a mother or a father. It is no family group whatsoever, but a desire that the imitator has no need to *represent* and is even incapable of representing.

Freud never resolved the problem of reproduction because he never discovered mimetic desire. According to Freud, the subject has only himself to draw upon. He is restricted to one tip of the triangle; he must find a first partner whom he will mistake for his mother and a third whom he will mistake for his father. If he is really searching for his mother in the object and his father in the rival, what miracle makes it possible for him to re-generate the appropriate structure of desire and rivalry every time?

To be aware of Freud's error, we have only to note that Dostoevsky managed to resolve the problem of reproducing the triangle within his works and that he invites us to observe this resolution. Father Karamazov is certainly a mimetic model for two of his sons, but this is precisely because he no longer has anything of the father in him.

If the imitator is led to interpret the interference effects of mimesis in a way that favours his rival over himself, then two consequences follow. First, the subject who still associates the most desirable object and the most prestigious model with the most implacable form of opposition, can only desire henceforth within a context of 'morbid jealousy', 'masochism' and 'latent homosexuality'. Second, the subject will find it easy to recreate once again the structure that incorporates all these 'symptoms' in the event that an earlier one comes apart.

J.-M. O.: If the subject chances to gain a triumph, the object remaining in his hands would no longer be given value by the momentous desire of a victorious rival and would thus be devalued on the spot. The unhappy subject would then go off in quest of a truly godlike model—a model who would not let the object be taken from him so easily.

R. G.: At the stage illustrated by Dostoevsky, the object and the model are both necessary, but they only have value in terms of their mutual relationship. In fact, it is neither the woman nor the rival that the subject desires, but the couple as such. This alone seems to be capable of realizing the autonomy the subject dreams of—a kind of blessed *narcissism for two*, from which the subject feels himself to be excluded. Likewise in Racine's *Phèdre* the heroine's desire becomes aggravated when she learns that her beloved has a beloved and the two young people seem to desire one another. Of course, this is also the theme of Rousseau's *Nouvelle Héloise*.

So it can easily be explained why, in a number of Dostoevsky's early works, the subject actively tries to bring the woman he loves and his rival together; he hopes that the couple will give him recognition and find a little place for him as a third party in their paradise of intimacy.

This theme, as it occurs in Dostoevsky, reveals the undecidable element in the situations created by mimetic rivalry. The subject has no wish to triumph completely over the rival; he has no wish for the rival to triumph completely over him. In the first event, the object would fall to him, but it would have lost all value. In the second event, the object would attain an infinite value, but it would be forever outside his reach.

However painful it may be, the triangular relationship is less painful than a decision that would end it in one way or the other. That is precisely why it has a tendency to perpetuate itself and to reproduce itself if it has collapsed. Rivalry is intolerable, but the absence of rivalry is even more intolerable. It brings the subject up against nothingness. That is why the subject makes every effort to persevere or to begin again, often relying on the undisclosed complicity of partners who are aiming for similar goals.

J.-M. O.: That is where the real *ambivalence* comes in, where real *doubles* are involved.

R. G.: Because Freud is a Platonist, all the psychoanalytic heresies are platonic heresies. In Jung, the element of rivalry is totally expelled, and nothing is left except a Platonian mystic contemplation of the archetypes. In Melanie Klein, by contrast, there is nothing but conflict; but fundamentally this conflict has no real existence because it is fixed and given an almost other worldly status by a notion of the first relationships with the mother. In Deleuze and Guattari, not the Oedipus complex itself but the text of psychoanalytic theory—Freud's Oedipus text—multiplies rival triangles, as a result of the universal tendency to simulate that it incites.

All the problems of Platonism return in psychoanalysis. As it is impossible to constrain dynamic processes within a system of archetypes, Freud finds it necessary to create more and more essences, rather like structuralism, which takes more and more synchronic 'cuts' because of its own incapacity to conceive of any genuinely diachronic mechanism.

Freud not only retains the essences of his predecessors, like masochism, sadism and even 'jealousy', 'envy' and so forth, but he is also forced to double up the essences that he has just invented; he has two kinds of masochism, two kinds of Oedipus complex, in a vain attempt to reconcile the eternal and immutable features of his psychoanalytic limbo with the real movement of the earth.

The Double Genesis of Oedipus

G. L.: In this connection, one particularly interesting feature is the distinction between a normal and an abnormal Oedipus. It seems to me that this is where we can see most clearly that Freud's observations really bear upon the process of mimetism, though they are unable to take account of this within the Oedipal theory.

R. G.: Freud uses the term 'ambivalence', as we have noted, to describe the contradictory feelings the model inspires when he becomes a rival. He connects the negative side of this ambivalence, hostility, with rivalry with the father, and the positive side, admiration, with what he describes as the 'normal affection' that the son feels for the father.

This 'normal affection' seems to Freud an adequate explanation for cases of 'normal' and 'ordinary' ambivalence. But Freud also tells us that there are 'abnormal' types of ambivalence—extraordinary cases when the contradictory feelings are pushed to the pitch of hatred and veneration. Freud connects these abnormal cases with a variant form of the Oedipus complex that he calls the abnormal Oedipus.

This abnormal ambivalence results, Freud tells us, when the small child undergoing the Oedipus complex is not satisfied with feeling for his father the complex feelings of a rival and a 'good son', endowed with 'normal affection for the father who has begotten him'. Besides these 'normal' feelings, the small child can also entertain a passive homosexual desire for the father—a wish to be desired by the father as a homosexual object! What obviously strikes Freud in the increasing rivalry is a growing fascination with the rival. This growing fascination, as we have seen, both can and must derive from the mimetic process itself. Because Freud does not see this possibility, he concludes that he is dealing with a new factor which is strictly homosexual—a separate form of homosexuality that could not be anticipated among the more 'normal' and 'ordinary' forms of ambivalence. As always, Freud tends to hypostatize homosexuality and make it into a kind of essence. Because he is obliged to fit all of this into his Oedipal archetype, where the rival is invariably the father, he is also compelled to think up this new story, one that strikes me as particularly outlandish in the context of the 'normal affection' that immediately precedes it. But, of course, it is not more outlandish than a good many of the elements that make up the two Oedipal structures—parricide, incest, and a libido fixated on the mother are all supposed to co-exist:

(1) with the 'normal affection' of a normal son for his normal father, and

(2) with a homosexual desire for the father.

G. L.: This notion of the son's homosexual desire has no basis whatsoever, we must remember, in any observation of children. How could you object to Freud's proceeding in this way, since everything is held to take place in our mysterious 'unconscious'?

R. G.: The unconscious has a very broad back in psychoanalysis, but this homosexual desire of the small infant for his father is quite a heavy weight, even for the broadest of backs. We could easily grant Freud this particular desire if it only kept company with the desires for incest and parricide, since it would then be playing its part very appropriately in the horror movie of the birth of the Oedipus complex. But for it to pick up just where the 'affection' of a normal son for his normal father leaves off—this ploy makes my jaw drop with admiration.

G. L.: You could say that it is the straw that breaks the back of this particular camel—which was far too docile in putting up with all these loads.

R. G.: This is the second head of the two-headed Oedipal calf. The monstrous sacrificial beast needs one head to account for 'normal' ambivalence. But it needs a second one to take care of the even greater ambivalence in 'sick' people like Dostoevsky.

Freud turns to two separate explanations in order to account for a single unified process. And he is fully aware of the unitary character of the process, since he has no wish to do away with his single Oedipal matrix, even where it seems fantastic.

J.-M. O.: To sum up: once you have missed the process of mimetic rivalry, you are forced to revert to an archetypal vision, and once you are trapped in this vision, you really have to come up with something like the Oedipus complex. Since there is no mimetic *feedback* to account for the increasing ambivalence, you can only see it as a kind of ready-made homosexuality. Because this homosexuality forms part of a phenomenological whole that you are honour-bound to explain in terms of the family archetype, you must also find a place for it within the archetype. You therefore must fix it on the father, since all cases of rivalry necessarily must relate to the father. It is very clear how Freud, beginning with such presuppositions, was led both by the rigour and by the limitations of his observations to explain things in the bizarre way that he did.

R. G.: There is nothing in the edifice set up by Freud whose presence cannot be accounted for by the desire to interpret the phenomena that we have explained by the mimetic principle alone. Freud attempts to account not only for the 'ever-increasing affection for the rival' but also for the 'ever–increasing hostility toward that same rival'. Since the two aspects of ambivalence, within the Oedipal scheme, are incapable of reacting upon and aggravating one another, Freud has to complicate his story with the supposition that the son's passive homosexual desire increases his terror of his father, specifically of being castrated by his father. All the consequences that flow from an aggravation of mimetic rivalry are there, but Freud is obliged to think up the most far-fetched tales in order to confine them within his Oedipal schema. He fails in the attempt. Even if he were to think up a third and a fourth type of Oedipus, he would be unable to contain all the nuances within his interpretation, since he is incapable of conceiving of the process as a process. His Platonism bars the way, and the double genesis of the Oedipus complex stands in relation to the system of mimetic *feedback* rather as a lobster's clumsy claw stands in relation to the suppleness and dexterity of a monkey's arm or a human arm and hand. You can find more and more articulations, but you will never end up with anything but a crustacean.

Freud does not see that his system of fixed positions makes it impossible for him to think through what he calls ambivalence, in particular, ambivalence that is increasingly exacerbated. For the negative side (hostility) not merely to coexist with, but to increase in proportion to, the positive side (veneration), the antagonism must feed on mimetism while mimetism, conversely, intensifies the antagonism. No pattern deriving from the past—no Oedipal matrix—is capable of accounting for this process.

Why Bisexuality?

R.G.: Any observer who does not detect the dynamism of rivalry is obliged to see homosexuality as a thing in itself, whose opacity blocks his view. Freud's disciples will not admit this. Rather, they discreetly slide under the carpet everything that embarrasses them in Freud's thought, or, if they are real fanatics, they latch on to the unbelievable aspects of his theory all the more obstinately precisely because they are unbelievable. They make such tenets the test of true faith, the dividing line between the heretics and the orthodox. There can be no room for discussion: Freud's thought has become so sacred that there can be no question of reconstituting its genesis or questioning even its weirdest features.

And yet Freud's procedure can be reconstituted quite easily if we start from the mimetic principle. By doing so, we arrive at a more hesitant and changeable Freud than the Freud for whom the veneration of the psychoanalytic movement has prepared us. If we look carefully at the texts where the different origins of the Oedipus complex are formulated, we can see that some of the ideas could only have arisen as a result of Freud's own dissatisfaction on re-reading his previous analyses. He must have felt dissatisfied with their excessive rigidity and fixity, and yet he was powerless to eradicate these faults.

J.-M. O.: You can certainly detect that in some of his revisions and nuances, Freud is trying hard to reinstate a continuity within the process under observation, but that this continuity is necessarily broken by the very conceptual scheme to which he remains wedded.

R. G.: What Freud calls the fundamental bisexuality of human beings usually comes up in the text after the references to homosexuality, as if he were trying to find a corrective for the excessive tilt produced by this term, attempting to attenuate the sharp division between heterosexuality and homosexuality.

The notion of bisexuality is only there, in the last analysis, as a means of toning down the rather too absolute cleavage between heterosexuality and homosexuality. It is not a genius's unfathomable insight into the *fundamentale Bisexualität* of life in its entirety, but the shrewdness of a psychologist who sees he is not doing justice to the unity and continuity of what he really observes: neurotic processes of rivalry, jealousy, and envy. Freud is too shrewd not to be secretly perturbed by the inability of the Oedipal schema to account for this continuity, even when it is doubled into the normal and the abnormal Oedipus.

Freud can easily see that the arbitrary injection of 'latent homosexuality' into the structure is not very satisfactory from the viewpoint of theoretical consistency. Because he either will not or cannot let go of the fundamental principles of his thought—that is to say, the Oedipal schema and the notion of pansexualism—he attempts to scramble a difference that is too clear-cut on the instinctual level by taking refuge in the notion of *bisexuelle Anlage*. He invents an instinct that is heterosexual and homosexual at once, with a view to correcting the absolute distinction between the two types of Oedipus. By contrast with Lévi-Strauss, who holds that any process of thought consists in 'passing from continuous quantity to discrete quantity'—and by contrast with Bergson, who holds just the opposite—Freud attempts to reconcile these two types of thinking because he needs both. He needs synchronic stability *and* diachronic dynamism: like all genuinely first-rate thinkers, he looks for a means to reconcile the stability of structure with the fluidity of structuring and de-structuring processes.

He is not able to achieve his objective. Indeed, no one could without making use of the notion of mimesis, which pivots on the scapegoat mechanism. Speaking of bisexuality amounts to leaving everything in a state of dissolution and undifferentiation, when it is important to do the exact opposite—and show how rivalry gives rise to undifferentiation. Once again, mimetic rivalry is lost in the shuffle.

The role of bisexuality in forcing continuity accounts for the fact that it is invoked almost ritually by Freud's disciples, along with the latent homosexuality that it invariably claims to be 'going beyond'. The former is always invoked *after* the latter, just as Tiresias always comes on after Oedipus to put him right and tell him the score in the psychoanalytic stakes that bear his name. Any spectacle of sexual rivalry always gives rise to the same kind of commentary, whose elements succeed one another in an immutable order. First comes Bouvard, the sagacious observer, who diagnoses latent homosexuality, and then follows Pécuchet, a man of even more profound sagacity, who makes the pitch for a basic bisexuality.

What made Claire Brétécher a successful comic, in the cartoon strip entitled *Les Frustrés*, is the fact that she drew our attention to the way in which sequences of this kind are invariably set up. In this case, 'frustration' results from psychoanalytic thinking itself, which always impels us to describe the same circular processes and imprisons us in absolute repetitiousness without even having the unifying and pacifying capacities that the rites underlying the ancient form of community undoubtedly possessed.

We must be under no illusion that psychoanalysis will ever muster any resources very different from the one we have been describing. What has changed is not the content of psychoanalysis, but the intellectual operation employed to bring it out. With Freud there is a life and movement to the thinking that constantly takes it in new directions, whereas today the psychoanalytic themes have reached a caricatural stage of vain repetition, and their limitations are plain to see.

G.L.: We perhaps ought to explain that by criticizing Freud's notion of 'bisexuality' we are not just carrying out a rearguard action in favour of sexual difference. I hope that the reader will appreciate the spirit in which the criticism is made.

R.G.: I hope so too. The same people carry on about bisexuality at one moment and about sexual difference at the next.

J.-M.O.: Your attitude toward Freud himself is rather nuanced. You see him as an observer of the highest order, but none of the conceptual *results* that you find in his work seems to be worth keeping. The real interest of the theses connected with the Oedipus complex needs to be revised. Your type of analysis enables you to reject them yet discover a kind of genetic and indirect justification for them, in so far as they reflect certain aspects of the mimetic process and even serve to reveal them, though partially and inadequately, since the revelation is falsified by the fundamental prejudices that dominated Freud's thought. Of course you are not the first person to criticize Freud's pansexualism and his theory of instincts, but you do so from a perspective that is neither too dependent on Freud, like that of the deconstructionists, nor so distant from him, like that of Sartre and Merleau-Ponty, that it makes close contact with the text impossible.

Narcissism: Freud's Desire

J.-M. O.: We must examine another of Freud's concepts in connection with the mimetic process, and this is narcissism. Of course we ought to try to look at the whole range of Freudian concepts in the light of the mimetic principle. But we have no time to do so. We must focus on narcissism, however, because Freud credits it with some effects that you would relate to mimetism.

Narcissism, Freud writes, occurs when the subject takes himself as an object. And the subject, up to a certain point, is always taking himself as an object. This implies that a primary, basic narcissism affects all individuals. That is why Freud states that man has two original sexual objects—himself and the woman who took care of him in his childhood. Thus there are two poles in desire: the maternal object and the unique type of object that I am for myself.

R. G.: The radical distinction between our 'interdividual psychology' and Freudian psychoanalysis lies in the fact that in Freud these two poles, though simultaneously present, are partly independent, and one always dominates the other. According to the mimetic process, it is for the benefit of everything that we would call Ego that the subject submits to the model and obstacle, making itself more and more a slave to the other. From the mimetic perspective, the two poles cannot be inversely proportionate as they are with Freud. The mimetic process implies that 'narcissism' and submission to the other can only exacerbate one another. The more narcissistic you become—or the more 'egoistic', as it used to be said—the more you become morbidly 'object-directed' or 'altruistic'. Here I am merely redefining the mimetic paradox that is the foundation of our anthropology and our psychology.

For Freud, narcissism is not incompatible with object choice, but the more narcissism there is, the weaker object choice becomes. Besides, the choice tends to be oriented toward an individual who 'resembles' the subject. To sum up: the highly narcissistic individual is really centred on himself. Freud's example *par excellence* of this intense form of narcissism, where object choice is weakened, is the woman—or rather, a certain type of woman whom he considers to be *the most purely feminine: 'dem häufigsten, wahrscheinlich reinsten und echtesten Typus des Weibes'.*[107]

Freud in effect distinguishes between two types of desire. Object-directed desire, which is principally masculine, tends to be accompanied by an over-estimation of the sexual object and implies a 'libidinal impoverishment' of the Ego—*'eine Verarmung des Ichs an Libido'*. Narcissistic desire, which is principally feminine, involves objects in an accessory way but does not really 'value' them, since the libido is bestowed not on the other but on the Ego, which therefore recovers all its 'libidinal energy' and does not suffer 'impoverishment'.

Freud goes on to say—and it is an important point—that this type of feminine narcissism is most often found in attractive women. At puberty, he argues, such women do not partially renounce childhood narcissism, but a recrudescence takes place, at the very moment when the 'latency' of the female sexual organs comes to an end.

Freud repeats several times that these women are attractive, but he also makes the point that they hold a particular fascination for men, not only because of their beauty, but also (as he puts it) in view of some 'interesting psychological constellations'—*infolge interessanter psychologischer Konstellationen*. The lines that follow are so remarkable that I will read them out *in extenso*, providing a translation:

> Es erscheint nämlich deutlich erkennbar, dass der Narzissmus einer Person eine grosse Anziehung auf diejenigen anderen entfaltet, welche sich des vollen Ausmasses ihres eigenen Narzissmus begeben haben und sich in der Werbung um die Objektliebe befinden; der Reiz des Kindes beruht zum guten Teil auf dessen Narzissmus, seiner Selbstgenügsamkeit und Unzugänglichkeit, ebenso der Reiz gewisser Tiere, die sich um uns nicht zu kümmern scheinen, wie der Katzen und grossen Raubtiere, ja selbst der grosse Verbrecher und der Humorist zwingen in der poetischen Darstellung unser Interesse durch die narzisstische Konsequenz, mit welcher sie alles ihr Ich Verkleinernde von ihm fernzuhalten wissen. Es ist so, als beneideten wir sie um die Erhaltung eines seligen psychischen Zustandes, einer unangreifbaren Libidoposition, die wir selbst seither aufgegeben haben.

For it seems very evident that another person's narcissism has a great attraction for those who have renounced part of their own narcissism and are on the search of object-love. The charm of a child lies to a great extent in his narcissism, his self-contentment and inaccessibility, just as does the charm of certain animals which seem not to concern themselves about us, such as cats and the large beasts of prey. Indeed even great criminals and humorists, as they are represented in literature, compel our interest by the narcissistic consistency with which they manage to keep from their ego anything that would diminish it.

It is as if we envied them for maintaining a blissful state of mind—an unassailable libidinal position which we ourselves have since abandoned.[108]

This passage deserves further examination. From the mimetic perspective, we can hardly take its explicit content seriously but that makes it all the more suggestive. It both conceals and reveals something Freud talks about yet does not talk about—his own mimetic desire. So we must submit this text to a kind of 'psychoanalysis', a 'mimetic analysis'. Freud betrays not only the inadequacy of narcissism as a concept, but the reason for this inadequacy, which lies in his partial blindness to his own desire.

Freud thinks he is describing a type of woman that is objectively real and indeed typical; this is the *eternal feminine*. She is beautiful; she is cold; she has no need to give herself; she occupies an impregnable libidinal position. She seeks to attract masculine desire and she succeeds perfectly in doing so. But this is less the result of her beauty than of her *indifference*, which is both terribly irritating and exciting for the male.

At no point does Freud admit that he might be dealing not with an essence but with a *strategy*, by which he himself has been taken in. This strategy bears a classic name, and it is called coquetry. In Molière's *Le Misanthrope*, Célimène acknowledges the strategic character of coquetry; she cynically tells Arsinoë that she might well turn into a prude on the day she is no longer beautiful. Prudishness is also a strategy. Indeed, misanthropy—which is very like it—is akin to an intellectual prudishness, which Nietzsche would call *ressentiment*: that is to say, the *defensive* strategy of the losers, of those who speak against desire because they are unsuccessful in their attempts to attract it and capitalize on it.

The coquette knows a lot more about desire than Freud does. She knows very well that desire attracts desire. So, in order be desired, one must convince others that one desires oneself. That is how Freud defines narcissistic desire, as a desire of the self for the self. If the narcissistic woman excites desire, this is because, when she pretends to desire herself and suggests to Freud a kind of circular desire that never gets outside itself, she offers an irresistible temptation to the mimetic desire of others. Freud misinterprets as an objective description the trap into which he has fallen. What he calls the self-sufficiency of the coquette, her blessed psychological state and her impregnable libidinal position, is in effect the metaphysical transformation of the condition of the model and rival, which we outlined earlier.

The coquette seeks to be desired because she needs masculine desires, directed at her, to feed her coquetry and enable her to play her role as a coquette. She has no more self-sufficiency than the man who desires her, but the success of her strategy allows her to keep up the appearance of it, since it offers her a form of desire she can copy. If the desire directed toward her is precious to her, this is because it nourishes her self-sufficiency, which would fall to pieces if she were wholly deprived of admiration. To sum up: in just the same way as the admirer caught in the trap of coquetry imitates the desire that he really believes to be narcissistic, so the flame of coquetry can only burn on the combustible material provided by the desires of others.

The coquette is all the more exciting, and her mimetic seduction is all the stronger, if she attracts the desires of many. This is why Molière makes Célimène the centre of a salon where her admirers crowd around her—a real Versailles of coquetry!

After desire becomes metaphysical, it only succeeds in exerting its transfiguring power upon obstacles. In them it can recognize a form of self-sufficiency that is the counterpart to its own insufficiency. Desire turns into a very humiliating, painful and disagreeable experience. It can easily be understood that everyone wants to avoid this experience, and the best way of avoiding it is by imposing it on others. Nothing is more apt to divert us from others and turn us back on ourselves, reassuring us about ourselves, than the spectacle of others taking us for their object of desire, thus conferring upon us the blessed self-sufficiency of which they deprive themselves.

The strategy of desire (and that does not mean only sexual desire) consists in setting up the dazzling illusion of a self-sufficiency that we shall believe in a little ourselves if we succeed in convincing the other person of it. In a world that is utterly devoid of objective criteria, desires are devoted entirely to mimetism; everyone has to try to convert to his own benefit mimetism that is still seeking a point to fix on which it will always find by reference to other desires. So each person must feign the most impressive narcissism, must advertise as subtly as he can the desire that he experiences for himself, so that he can compel others to imitate this appetizing desire.

We must beware of all labels here, in particular those that we ourselves are obliged to draw on, like coquetry. We must take care not to limit the substance of what I have been saying to a single area—that of sexuality—any more than to a single sex, the feminine. We must also have some reservations about the term 'strategy', which implies rather too much lucidity and an untenable, clear-cut division between the mask and the real face behind it. We must think everything through as a function of the struggle of doubles, which is at the same time a form of reciprocal support and collaboration, contributing to the blossoming of mimetism and the illusions that accompany it.

In the light of the mimetic principle, despite the weaknesses in the language of psychology (whichever system is used), we can now appreciate the inadequacy of the Freudian critique as it applies to the phenomena described in *Zur Einführung des Narzissmus* (*Introduction to Narcissism*). Freud is determined to maintain the distinction between: (1) the *object-directed desire*, which impoverishes the libido and only exists in men who are 'truly men'—those who have given up a part of their libido, this is to say a part of their narcissism, and (2) *narcissistic desire*, which bears essentially on oneself and, if it has an object, uses that object solely to enrich its own libido. The latter type of desire seeks only to be desired by men, and men are only too willing to place their own libidinal riches at the feet of this treasure of libido that refuses to become impoverished.

Freud tells us that object-directed desire prefers to attach itself to a narcissistic woman, but we must go further and see in that point the essence of what Freud calls 'object-direction'. He will not admit that, far from forming an odd but rather secondary feature of object-directed desire, the fascination aroused in him by *what appears to him as narcissistic* is in fact all there is to this type of desire.

Object-directed desire clearly feels impoverished from the outset and continues to impoverish itself, but this does not stop it from cherishing as a dream the kind of richness that the narcissistic being keeps for itself and appears capable of protecting. On the contrary, it dreams of not having to waste its desire on objects, of not impoverishing itself; it dreams of the riches of narcissism—indeed, desire never dreams of anything else.

J.-M. O.: To sum it up: object-directed desire is lacking in 'narcissism'. How could it not be so, since it has foregone a part of its narcissism, in order to direct its desire toward objects? How could we fail to notice that the narcissistic being is the object *par excellence* of desire—or at least the way in which any desirable object looks to the desiring subject, since the subject tends to over-value it and credit it with a richness that it does not possess. Since Freud holds that the only riches are those of the libido and that all being is libidinal, his own terminology lets him down. You only have to follow through the logic of his metaphors to see the distinction between the object-directed being and the narcissistic being dissolve into thin air.

R. G.: Object-directed desire in fact desires narcissistic libido because it is a mimetic desire like all the others; it copies the desire of a libido that gives the appearance of desiring itself—this is what desire is all about. In the last analysis, object-desire does the same thing as the narcissistic libido, but unsuccessfully. Narcissistic libido also does the same thing as all the others, after cleverly putting itself forward as a model. The narcissistic libido feeds on the desire that it directs toward itself, but quickly enough this food comes to seem a delusion. The very fact that others' desires are directed to it causes them to become devalued and lose their identity.

What polarizes these two types of desire and fixes upon one particular double can only be the result of clever manoeuvring and does not imply any essential difference. We learn this from all the manuals that point us toward success in love, in business and in social life. In our world duplicity is covered with a veneer of morality. Manuals like these actually know a good deal more than Freud about the workings of desire, not because their authors are more observant, but because since his time things have developed in the direction of an increasingly relentless and crass mimetic rivalry. What is really unsavoury is how strategic duplicity has been vulgarized. Its text-books are available at the lowest possible prices, claiming to provide everyone with a solution to his many problems.

If we look more closely at the position Freud takes, it will confirm what we have just been saying.

Clearly Freud counts himself among the serious folk—heroes of conscience and morality, defenders of the categorical imperative—who have given up a part of their narcissism in their high-mindedness but feel all the more attracted to coquettes, however *incongruous* this attraction may appear to be. If you are the inventor of psychoanalysis, the great modern master of not taking things at face value, you should not let an incongruity of these proportions go unexamined it seems to me. Something here deserves a bit of attention. The sentence that follows is even more odd. It means more or less: it all happens as if we were experiencing envy. *Es ist also*: it is as if. But why does Freud say *as if*? Why does he not simply say: we do in fact experience envy for the self-sufficiency, the impregnable libidinal position? He does not deny the point but he wills it to be not entirely true. He means to persist with the myth that narcissism is given up more or less *voluntarily*, as a result of an essentially ethical decision—rather like the 'maturity' that comes at such a high price in American psychoanalysis, or the 'engagement' of Sartre, which is both an assertion of freedom and a sentence of unhappiness.

G. L.: But Freud never says explicitly that renouncing infantile narcissism is purely voluntary. That would really be hard to accept.

R. G.: Let us try to imagine how Freud, in his more lucid moments, might have reacted to our reading of his text. No, he does not say that renouncing narcissism is voluntary, but all the words he uses—beginning with 'renounce' itself—seem to suggest that this is how it is.

So what status, from the psychoanalytic point of view, should we give to this *incongruous* form of attraction, almost amounting to envy, which we wise men, we true adults, cannot help experiencing in the face of the 'intact narcissism' of the pretty coquette?

If Freud shows us this envy as if it were not entirely true, this is because he is unwilling to recognize the supposedly intact narcissism of the other as the real lost object of desire. He admittedly shows us the situation as an interesting oddity, *eine interessante psychologische Konstellation*, but he goes no further. He is ready to react with the interest of an enlightened amateur, but he sees no reason why he should be led to reconsider the basic positions of his system, for example, the distinction between narcissistic desire and object-directed desire. He just sees the situation as an inconsequential oddity and points it out to us; he invites us to contemplate it for a moment before moving on to something else, as good scholars—or even tourists of the libido! The Guide Michelin of psychoanalysis would make this a curiosity worth one, or at the most two stars: worth a detour but not a whole trip.

J.-M. O.: While he half admits what is going on, Freud is always concerned to defend himself against the attraction of this intact narcissism, which seems real to him precisely because he cannot stop desiring it. He fails to see that what he calls over-estimation of the object in object-directed desire is one and the same thing as what he describes under the label of intact narcissism.

R. G.: Freud is much too fascinated with the coquette's winning ways to detect that a *game* is being played—as Shakespeare, Molière and Marivaux could see. He takes the phantom for true being. He fails to see that, far from *incongruous* for the being whose desire (as he puts it) is object-directed, the choice of intact narcissism is absolutely imperative since it is 'narcissism' and nothing else that desire always needs. No one has ever voluntarily renounced the blessed autonomy, the impregnable libidinal position, etc.—everything that Freud refers to under the label 'narcissism'. We have no difficulty in recognizing in all this the mirage produced by the model and obstacle when it resists our imitation; it is the metaphysical ghost that is invariably conjured up—manifested by the model and obstacle—for the benefit of a desire that becomes increasingly fascinated by it, since desire always returns to bump and bruise itself against it.

Let us accept that the equivocations and hesitations in Freud's text—in particular his *Es ist also*, his 'as if'—have a bearing on the decisive points of his analysis. In consequence, we have only to get rid of these minor untruths to be able to see that there is really only one single, mimetic desire where Freud posits two desires and two separate poles—the narcissistic and the object-directed (that is to say, the Oedipal). Freud is moving in this direction, but he cannot get to the end of his own logic because he still believes in the mythical transfigurations of mimetic desire, in which he himself has indulged. He cannot get behind the manoeuvres of the coquette and observe that she has exactly the same desire as he does—turned in a slightly different direction, perhaps, but that does not change anything essential.

Once this point is taken, the text gets simpler. The definition of narcissism and the definition of object-directed desire always imply one another reciprocally: narcissism is what object-directed desire really desires, and object-directed desire is what narcissism does not desire—what, by virtue of the fact that it is not desired, feels itself to be 'impoverished' in relation to the colossal richness of narcissism.

The intact narcissism of the other is the indescribable paradise where the beings that we desire appear to live—and it is because of this that we desire them. They give us the impression that no obstacle exists for them and that they are never in need of anything. This impression that they are never in need of anything is exactly the same as the impression that they have no need of us. Their plenitude is taken for granted. With nothing to desire outside themselves, they draw all desires toward themselves like magnets and compel all men of *duty*, like Freud, to desire them, if only a little. In fact, desire really must be disturbing Freud's vision quite a lot for him to believe in the reality of the *Selbstgenügsamkeit* that the coquette appears to enjoy after the *Pubertätsentwicklung* of her *weiblichen Sexualorgane*. This self-sufficiency is not an earthly thing; it is the last glimmering of the sacred.

Belief in the intact narcissism of the other is the phantasm of desire *par excellence*. Freud views his discovery of narcissism as analogous to the discovery of a chemical element. But an examination of his demonstration that this psychic entity really exists reveals an illusion based on an uncritical acceptance of the narcissistic phantasm, on Freud's own desire. At one extreme, his narcissism consists in falling into the snare of coquetry, while at the other extreme it is supposed to be deeply rooted in biological realities; it is one with individual self-apprehension. 'Primary' narcissism ensures that any form of life instinctively searches for what it needs and avoids what is harmful to it. To put it in a nutshell, Freud confuses the most delusory blandishments of metaphysical desire with the basic life force. We really must stress the element of mere fantasy in this amalgamation, since it is no more than an amalgam in this first essay on the subject.

Object-directed desire dreams of an intact narcissism because it dreams of the absolute and indestructible being who does violence to everything around it but suffers none itself. That is why, in Freud's terms, narcissism is libido itself—which is the same thing as energy and power, *energeia* and *dunamis* in the Greek. The functioning of the system resembles Polynesian *mana*. Intact narcissism is the greatest possible accumulation of libido in a stable form—a reservoir that is full to the top. If everything gravitates around the chief, or strong man, in the world of the Polynesians, that is because he possesses more *mana* than the others. And if he already possesses more of it, he will manage to get still more, since every desire converges upon him. Less strong *manas* are attracted by his and come to increase its bulk, while they themselves get thinner and thinner.

G. L.: You could also say that Freud's system of narcissistic libido tends to work in the same way as capitalism. The richer you are, the easier it is to conduct increasingly lucrative financial operations without really putting your capital at risk. Poor old object-directed desire clusters around intact narcissism and gets poorer and poorer in the process. To sum up: money is only lent to the wealthy, and desire always pursues desire, just as money pursues money.

R. G.: Metaphors taken from economics and finance are as pertinent here as the great themes of the sacred, but we must not conclude that they have any priority, any more than we must conclude that libido or even the sacred has an absolute priority. Behind all of this, you always have mimetic desire. The priority belongs to it, irrespective of the many cultural contents with which it can be vested—but only as long as it has not been fully unleashed and is still regulated, at least up to a point, by mechanisms derived from the scapegoat. These vestiges of ritual make it possible for the game to operate by blinding us a little to the fact that it has no anchor in the real. The difference between what Freud saw and what we are capable of seeing today results not from our greater perceptiveness but from the far greater rootlessness that has developed in the half-century separating us from the last stages of Freud's work.

The moralistic tone of the essay on narcissism is worth emphasizing. Intact narcissism is presented as infantile, egoistic, perverse and inferior in all respects to object-directed desire, which all the same grovels abjectly at its feet. Object-directed desire is the desire of the man who is truly a man and who gives up his childhood illusions in order to launch himself on the austere but noble path of great achievements for the sake of his family and his culture. It is object-directed desire which—with a little bit of sublimation, naturally—succeeds in inventing psychoanalysis.

What Freud gives away here, on the sexual level, is the fact that his erotically charged rivalry is directed toward the other sex. Women appear both as obstacles and as rivals. As a result, the text takes on an anti-feminine character despite Freud's explicit denials.

We have it from Freud himself, I believe, that he broke off sexual relations with his wife at a very early age. *Zur Einführung des Narzissmus* shows him admitting quite ingenuously that a particular type of woman has always fascinated him. This always makes me think of the wayward innocence of the old bearded professor in the film *The Blue Angel*: a close-up of Marlene Dietrich's long legs, sheathed in black stockings. . .

At the time when he was writing on narcissism, Freud had a number of vivacious female disciples, like Hélène Deutsch and Lou Andreas-Salomé. When they failed to turn up at his seminar, he would write them letters that were ambiguous, to say the least. They, in turn, were attracted by the genius in him, the founder of psychoanalysis.[109]

J.-M. O.: Narcissism is in fact the final manifestation of the idol worshipped by the Romantics. It gives its own mythological character away when it turns uncritically to the narcissus myth and interprets it as a myth of solipsism, while in reality the image behind the mirror (as in the story of the nymph Echo) conceals the mimetic model and the struggle between doubles.

R. G.: What gives the text on narcissism its particular charm and makes it seem so lively in its observations and so youthful in its impact is the fact that beliefs from another age and an almost naive faith in the distinctiveness of the female sex are still very present in it. But there is also a darker side to the essay, which is linked to the welling up of Freud's Puritanism. Narcissism is condemned because of the resentment invariably inspired by the mimetic model and obstacle—a resentment that plays a much greater part in our own intellectual world than it ever did in Freud's work.

Anything that puts itself forward as a form of 'demystification' nowadays has become the principal business of *avant-garde* researchers, their passionate calling, their only *raison d'être* after the advent of nihilism. If we think about this a little, we can see how the interpretation called for by this demystificatory urge is to be sketched out from the mimetic point of view. We have here a form of desire that frustrates the great *avant-garde* researcher that Freud was, and projects around itself, from his perspective, the metaphysical mirage of self-sufficiency that he ascribes to intact narcissism.

Metaphysical desire experiences a violent rancour toward the object that it desires—an object that insolently refuses access. A time will come when this most advanced mimetic desire realizes that it is the victim of an illusion. But this will be no more than an intellectual awareness, an abstract form of disillusionment that will not liberate its victims from the traps still being laid by desire the strategist, who exploits every appearance of indifference, whether real or imaginary.

Desire must convince itself that the other's self-sufficiency is just a superficial deception, something that has no right to exist. In order to do this, it will commit itself increasingly to the task of convincing the other that this is really so—of disenchanting and demystifying him, or, in other words, of persuading him that he has no reason to believe in his own happiness. If the other has not lost all confidence in the world and in human beings, this must be because he is not perceptive enough (or too ill-informed) to notice how pointless and desperate everything is, including ourselves. The other is a victim of mystification and he must be demystified, at all costs.

G. L.: If we take a broad view of modern literature and theory, we can see that present-day thinkers are invariably obsessed by the people whom they are trying to demystify—people who still to some extent rely on the sacrificial mechanisms that keep all the values in place.

R. G.: There is no way of branding this activity of demystification as intrinsically 'good' or 'bad'. What we have is mimetic desire itself, gnawing away at the last vestiges of the sacrificial system inveigling everything outside its grasp into the mad whirl of doubles. The more aggravated mimetic desire becomes, the more it allows itself to be fascinated by ontological illusions, from which it has ceased to draw any benefit. That is why anything that seems to be endowed with the least stability, everything that escapes or appears to escape the structure of doubles, stirs up resentment and gives our intellectuals the demystificatory itch on which their analyses of desire are inevitably dependent.

G. L.: That is what finally comes about at the end of a 'successful psychoanalysis'. The patient and the analyst have reached the same point of mutual disillusionment when they call it quits. There is no longer any transference involved, and the best sign of a 'completed analysis' is the patient's lack of gratitude.

R. G.: Desire has given up the illusions of ontology and substance that it had in the past, but not so much that it is no longer haunted by them. The very idea that some people could still entertain these illusions is impossible to bear. The desire to 'enlighten' or 'demystify' is a way of assuring oneself that the illusions of the past are nowhere to be found and ensuring that everyone has an equal share in the universal deprivation. By aiming for this equality in misery, demystificatory desire aligns itself with a number of revolutionary movements that also end up being uniformly oppressive—movements that may well owe their very existence to this radicalization of mimetic rivalry, since they appear simultaneously with it.

J.-M. O.: This is the stage when the subject suffers for his increasing awareness of the mechanisms of culture. This awareness has not yet reached the point where he can look fairly and squarely at the *envy* inspired in him by everything that remains intact in the sacrificial order—everything that, by virtue of the fact, still gives the appearance of being at one with nature, possessing a superior life force and enmeshed in the most basic biological processes.

R. G.: The more I think of the *Inkongruenz* that Freud sees as residing in the choice of the woman with intact narcissism as the preferred object for object-directed desire, the more I appreciate why Freud had to present this choice as he did, and dismiss as inconsequential its incongruous aspect. For Freud the 'true' object choice always involves some 'maternal' aspect, since the object preceding all others is the mother—or, what comes to the same thing, the *pflegende Weib*, the woman who first attends to the child. What could be less maternal, less *pflegend*—than the woman with intact narcissism? The coquette is as little *pflegend* as she can possibly be. She makes fun of everyone, particularly of the man who behaves towards her like a slave and pays her the undeserved homage of his desire.

There is a contradiction here between what the Freudian conception of the mother calls for and what desire actually wants. Desire as it appears in the essay on narcissism is not in the least preoccupied with motherly and nurturing qualities. On the contrary, it invariably goes off in search of a mirage that will increase its lack rather than remedy it. Desire will little by little make any form of satisfaction or even communication with the loved person quite impossible—desire proceeds in the direction of dissociation, decomposition and death.

I think that Freud must have noticed the contradiction: men capable of an object choice ought to orient themselves toward beings who are no less capable of object choice—of devotion, that is to say—than themselves. If such were the case, then everything would be for the best in the best of possible Oedipal worlds. But here comes a strange little devil who pushes us in the very opposite direction to the one indicated by Freud and posted by his Theban police at every crossroads. Freud's observation is too acute for him not to notice this gigantic *Inkongruenz* and his honesty is too great for him not to inform us of what he notices. There is certainly sometimes incongruous—according to the dictionary, something that does not quite fit the situation Freud envisages, something that does not conform, in other words, to psychoanalytic theory. The *Inkongruenz* stands out in the text on narcissism and tests our powers of intelligence and observation. Let us bear in mind that scientific research always has to be on the look-out for the element that can only be defined in terms of its *incongruousness*, within whatever theory or domain it happens to crop up. A critique is not effective until it succeeds in integrating the *Incongruenz* of the earlier theory into some new theory and makes it disappear within the context of the new theory, so that it can be explained by the regular application of the methodological principles that govern the new theory.

I feel that it is possible to do just that in looking at psychoanalytic theory from the mimetic perspective. In the light of the mimetic principle, the seductive powers of the coquette no longer create an *In-kongruenz*; they are a banal application of the general rule. In the light of the mimetic theory, the Freudian distinction between Oedipal and object-directed desire on the one hand, narcissistic regression on the other, simply does not hold up; it is rooted in Freud's particularly strong tendency to segregate 'worthy desires' from 'unworthy' ones and to activate victimage mechanisms that psychoanalysis cannot criticize because it is wedded to them—because they remain fundamental to it in the sense in which victimage mechanisms remain fundamental to any kind of mythology.

J.-M. O.: If we were living under a genuinely scientific regime in the human sciences, a radical critique would be welcome. If it is not—if psychoanalysis takes the view that any attempt to open its fundamental principles to examination is a kind of sacrilege—then we can be sure that we are still dealing with remnants of the sacred.

R. G.: It is particularly striking to observe, within the Freudian mythology, the return to Greek mythology, which is a genuine mythology where violence is paramount. Psychoanalysis is like all the modern pseudo-sciences in believing that the way to combat the sacred is by attacking the Judaeo-Christian tradition with all the force that one can muster. This struggle is not based on entirely false premises; the sacrificial elements in the traditional interpretation of the Judaeo-Christian scriptures justify this mistake to some extent. Yet all the mechanism of delusion is still around when people believe that complete liberation from the sacred can be achieved only by wrenching themselves definitively away from the Judaeo-Christian text.

The reason Freud has to return uncritically to mythology is hardly different, in essence, from all the other reasons that have kept humanity within the grip of mythology—and these come down to an inability to detect the mechanisms of mimesis. Freud's thought does not add up to a doctrine. It opens up in our mythological delusions (for which we are made to suffer) some gaps that are then immediately papered over by other mythological delusions. We should hardly be surprised to see Freud placing radical examples of deconstruction beside his most old-fashioned returns to mythology. These two aspects come together in a particularly obvious way in texts like the essay on the 'uncanny', *Das Unheimlich*. We would need a lot of time to give a close reading to all that Freud writes about the *double*, in this essay in particular. There is real insight here, as usual. Freud comes to the conclusion that the problem of doubles and that of repetition are linked, and he even makes an allusion in this connection (so it would seem) to Nietzsche's *Eternal Recurrence*—a relevant connection, indeed! But his whole argument remains trapped within a basic inability to recognize the structure of doubles all around him, in everything that he is talking about. Following from Rank, Freud talks of the double as a phenomenon linked to a long-vanished mythological past and to what he terms 'primary narcissism'. What he sees is essentially an image, a ghost, and not a genuine other, a mimetic adversary.[110] He does not succeed in escaping from the constraints of mythical thought, and this is what is made very clear, as you pointed out a moment ago, by his reading of the narcissus myth.

The Metaphors of Desire

R. G.: If we look at the metaphors for 'intact narcissism', we see that all of them tend in the same direction. They involve the diminishment or absence of self-awareness, or its not yet being present, which amounts to the same thing.

Freud compares what he calls the *Reiz* of intact narcissism—what gives it its piquancy, its stimulating, provocative, irritating quality—to the *Reiz* of the small child whose needs are satisfied and that of the wild beast with a sleek, well-groomed coat. He also refers to the master criminal and the humorist, both of whom he sees as having particularly well protected egos.

It seems to me that these metaphors dehumanize their objects. They start by feminizing (in a sense that, for Freud, is pejorative) and they carry on by infantilizing and bestializing the object. Then they identify it with the kind of violence that causes expulsion, the violence of crime or of laughter.

These metaphors have nothing specifically Freudian about them. They would not be 'good' in the literary sense if they were entirely 'original'. Indeed they can be found in all great writers concerned with desire. They occur in descriptions of the objects that are desired and of the process whereby these objects are transfigured by desire, giving rise to what Freud calls *over-estimation*—though he does not notice that his own text forms an excellent example. If Freud had been a bit more self-aware, he would not have believed so firmly in the objective reality of what he calls narcissism.

J.-M. O.: I doubt if these metaphors are the monopoly of writers. They seem to me to be universal and it ought to be possible to find them in very diverse languages and cultures. To take one example: an Arab expression, once used on the elegant beaches of Beirut, describes the behaviour of a young fellow walking along the shore and showing his physique to best advantage, apparently indifferent to all the attention he was getting, as 'acting the *tiger*'. This expression is just another variant of the metaphor Freud was using.

R. G.: These particular metaphors do not depend on the whim, or the talent, of the person using them. They can be found in the symbolism attaching to African kings, in medieval heraldry and in the whole linguistic apparatus which refers to the traditional experience of the sacred.

Thanks to these metaphors, it is easy to see the contradictory way in which the subject conceives of the object of his desire. Narcissism is blessed self-sufficiency; it is therefore awareness of self, since without that awareness, self-sufficiency would be unable to experience itself and know itself as blessed. And yet it cannot fail to be significant that Freud can only describe this blessed awareness through recourse to beings that, though alive, are defective in self awareness—the wild beast and the small child.

However, your Lebanese expression makes me think of a text by Proust that is simply a massive extension of it. I would like to look at this text with you for a while and show you that it contains all the metaphors from Freud's text on narcissism, cleverly arranged around the object of desire, which Proust also presents in terms of its inaccessible self-sufficiency. The difference between Proust and Freud does not reside in the specifically literary element in the two texts. Freud is just as 'literary' as Proust. There is, however, a difference, and it lies in the fact that Proust knows perfectly well that he is speaking of his own desire and of nothing else; he has no notion of engaging in science. Precisely because he has no illusions on this score he has to be credited as being a better psychoanalyst than Freud. Proust underlines the mimetic unity of all the desires that Freud attempts to distribute between the fallacious categories of object-directed and narcissistic desire. He knows that there is only one kind of desire and that it is the same for everyone, even if it bears on different objects—even if it can appear in less intensified forms than his own.

I select this text because in it I can find all that I am looking for in a very short space, but it is by no means exceptional. It forms part of the basic sub-text of desire throughout the whole of *A la recherche du temps perdu*, and tens or even hundreds of similar examples could easily be provided:

> . . . I saw five or six young girls as different in appearance and manner from all the people one was accustomed to see at Balbec as would have been a flock of gulls arriving from God knows where and performing with measured tread upon the sands—the dawdlers flapping their wings to catch up with the rest—a parade the purpose of which seems as obscure to the human bathers whom they do not appear to see as it is clearly determined in their own birdish minds.[111]

We begin, as you see, with an animal metaphor whose function Proust explains in the process of developing it. The movements of the seagulls seem inscrutable to the bathers; and the seagulls, for their part, appear not to see the bathers. Between the desirable and the person who desires there is no possibility of communication.

The group of girls gives the narrator a sense of not belonging to the crowd that surrounds it. But the crowd does not exclude the little band; the little band excludes the crowd. The whole description aims to establish a mirage of extraordinary self-sufficiency:

> . . . the interplay of their eyes, animated with self-assurance and the spirit of comradeship and lit up from one moment to the next either by the interest or the insolent indifference which shone from each of them according to whether her glance was directed at her friends or at passers-by, together with the consciousness of knowing one another intimately enough always to go about together in an exclusive 'gang', established between their independent and separate bodies, as they slowly advanced, an invisible but harmonious bond, like a single warm shadow, a single atmosphere, making of them a whole as homogeneous in its parts as it was different from the crowd through which their procession gradually wound (p.851).

The closed character of the little band—what we might be tempted to call its 'metaphysical closure'—seems so real that it becomes almost visible to the onlooker. It has a tendency to materialize, rather like the line of prohibition within a culture that is still strongly religious.

The girls present an impression of great youthfulness, and at the same time of strength, agility and trickery. Their eyes are described to us as 'insolent'. For the narrator, they form an obstacle that is fascinating precisely because it is impenetrable. For the girls, on the other hand, there are no obstacles at all. In their play they are capable of crossing any obstacle in their path; everything parts to allow them free passage:

> Just as if, within their little band, which progressed along the esplanade like a luminous comet, they had decided that the surrounding crowd was composed of beings of another race not even whose sufferings could awaken in them any sense of fellowship, they appeared not to see them, forced those who had stopped to talk to step aside, as though from the path of a machine which has been set going by itself and which could not be expected to avoid pedestrians; and if some terrified or furious old gentleman whose existence they did not even acknowledge and whose contact they spurned took precipitate and ludicrous flight, they merely looked at one another and laughed. They had, for whatever did not form part of their group, no affectation of contempt; their genuine contempt was sufficient. But they could not set eyes on an obstacle without amusing themselves by clearing it, either in a running jump or with both feet together . . . (pp.848-49)

Here psychoanalysis would accentuate the sexual symbolism—it would talk about the masochism of a desire that is blatantly always trying to get itself under the feet of the cruellest and most sincerely contemptuous member of the gang. But psychoanalysis would not be capable of seeing that the absolute unity of this structure resides in a mimetic game that is being played out on the ultimate level of expulsion. The desiring subject always sees himself in the position of one who has been or is about to be expelled; he takes the place of the victim, not by refusing violence—not in the way in which that place is occupied by those who speak in the Old and New Testament—but *because he desires it*. Psychoanalysis would speak of masochism here because it has no notion of the meaning of this desire, which is not a desire to be expelled but a desire to be with those who are doing the expelling, to find a way into the little band and form part of the 'gang'.

Like Freud's narcissism, the little band incarnates both absolute and diminished—almost vanished—awareness. His animal imagery can be related to the 'sporting' and 'anti-intellectual' side of the young girls, which allows the narrator, Marcel, to come to the conclusion that he belongs to the 'antipathetic type', the sickly, slight, and intellectual type, which they are absolutely determined to avoid:

> It was not perhaps mere chance in life that, in forming this group of friends, had chosen them all so beautiful; perhaps these girls (whose demeanour was enough to reveal their bold, hard and frivolous natures), extremely aware of everything that was ludicrous or ugly, incapable of yielding to an intellectual or moral attraction, had naturally felt a certain repulsion for all those among the companions of their own age in whom a pensive or sensitive disposition was betrayed by shyness, awkwardness, constraint, by what they would regard as antipathetic, and from such had held aloof . . . (p.848)

This last passage states once again that the girls have a characteristic that already featured in the earlier quotations: they are prone to making fun of people in a cruel way. They are always laughing at everything that is outside themselves. This tendency enables us to appreciate why Freud credits the humorist with a high level of narcissism. He views the profession of the humorist as a kind of licence to make fun of the public at their expense—as a means of expelling the public. In fact, the very opposite happens. If the humorist behaved like the little band, he would not make his public laugh at all. The little band is in no way laughable from the narrator's point of view. It fascinates and terrifies him, but it is certainly no laughing matter. To make other people laugh, as a rule you have to make them laugh at your expense. Obviously Proust is right here, just as Baudelaire is when he discusses laughter.[112] To take part in the type of laughter mentioned here—to put yourself on the side of those who are laughing—you must associate with the violence contained in their laughter and not become the underdog. To make other people laugh, you must occupy—voluntarily or involuntarily—the position of the victim . . .

J.-M. O.: Here we have found in Proust yet another of the metaphors for intact pseudo-narcissism. You are surely not going to tell me that we can also find the metaphor of the 'master criminal' there, are you?

R. G.: Not exactly. But Marcel does credit these 'little girls' with an irresistible tendency to behave delinquently. This tendency is an integral part of their fascination. The young girls are not criminals, but there is no law regulating their behaviour, any more than there is for the agile and cunning beasts whom they resemble. Let us look closely at the text; we have already got as far as the 'blue jeans' and see-through négligés of the present day:

> . . . this girl must have parents of high position who valued their self-esteem so far above the visitors to Balbec and the sartorial elegance of their own children that it was a matter of the utmost indifference to them that their daughter should stroll on the front dressed in a kit which humbler people would have considered too modest. . . . In any event, none of my suppositions embraced the possibility of their being virtuous. At first sight—in the way in which they looked at one another and laughed, in the insistent stare of the one with the matt complexion—I had grasped that they were not. Besides, my grandmother had always watched over me with a delicacy too tremulous for me not to believe that the sum total of the things one ought not to do is indivisible and that girls who are lacking in respect for their elders would not suddenly be stopped short by scruples at the prospect of pleasures more tempting than that of jumping over an octogenarian (p.850).

What proves the essential contradiction inherent in desire is the fact that one of the young girls seems to notice Marcel—and immediately loses, in his eyes, her share of the prestige that all the others continue to enjoy because they pay him no attention whatsoever. Marcel straight away comes up with the idea that he might be able to make the acquaintance of the most accessible of the girls, and that she might serve as a go-between to reach the most inaccessible of them—who are the only ones that really interest him, though they would obviously cease to do so if he actually got close to them:

> And in the same way could I not rejoice at having seen this dark girl look at me (which made me hope that it would be easier for me to get to know her first), for she would introduce me to the pitiless one who had jumped over the old man's head, to the cruel one who had said 'I

feel sorry for the poor old boy,' to all these girls in turn of whom she enjoyed the prestige of being the inseparable companion? (p.853)

At the very end of the description, we have the final proof of our argument, with the introduction of a religious theme. The model and obstacle is sacralized through the mediation of a historical and aesthetic metaphor, which the superficial reader might well believe to be purely anecdotal. In fact, as always Proust does not write anything without explaining to us why he is writing it, and in the few lines that follow he sums up the essential significance of the whole passage. What constitutes desire is the apparently complete incompatibility between the subject who desires and the desired object—which of course in this case is not an object at all (the point hardly needs emphasis) but the model and obstacle itself. Proustian homosexuality has no object in the proper sense of the term. It is always directed at the model, and this model is selected because it is out of reach—because it is both obstacle and rival, in effect, before it ever becomes a model. It exists in a kind of religious-infernal transcendence, which only appears to be real as long as it withholds itself from the subject:

> And yet the supposition that I might some day be the friend of one or other of these girls, that these eyes, whose incomprehensible gaze struck me from time to time and played unwittingly upon me like an effect of sunlight on a wall, might ever, by some miraculous alchemy, allow the idea of my existence, some affection for my person, to interpenetrate their ineffable particles, that I myself might some day take my place among them in the evolution of their course by the sea's edge—that supposition appeared to me to contain within it a contradiction as insoluble as if, standing before some Attic frieze or a fresco representing a procession, I had believed it possible for me, the spectator, to take my place, beloved of them, among the divine participants (p.853).

So we find in Proust all the metaphors from Freud's text on narcissism, or variations on them: the child, the animal, the criminal and the humorist. Not only are these metaphors explained much more insightfully than by Freud, but Proust is fully aware—as I never tire of repeating—that the self-sufficiency his desire wreathes around the little band is in no way real. It has nothing whatsoever to do with some notion of 'regression to intact narcissism at the time of puberty'. Proust does not pontificate about what might have been happening to the *Sexualorgane* of all these young girls at this stage. Once Marcel has made their acquaintance, their transcendence and self-sufficiency quickly evaporate. The narrator's desire for Albertine is only reawakened to the extent that she appears to have been unfaithful and so sets his string of 'pathological jealousy' vibrating, through an almost mechanical reflex which no longer involves any real element of transfiguration. This is pure hell, and the description of it is not embellished in the slightest.

J.-M. O.: Fortunately for *A la recherche du temps perdu*, Proust was not contaminated by the psychoanalytic delusion about 'narcissism'. If he had believed in the reality of narcissism, he would have remained at the mercy of the illusions created by desire, he would have been incapable of describing it in the powerful way that he does. He would have been blocked at the level of Freud's *Zur Einführung des Narzissmus*.

R. G.: I have no wish to 'go in for paradoxes' and make literary criticism even more *précieux* than it already is when I say that Proust's *superior knowledge* must be firmly stated. Proust goes further than Freud in his analysis of desire. He never makes the mistake of supposing that, besides object-directed desire—which causes an impoverishment of the libido—there exists a narcissistic desire that is directed toward *the same* and not toward absolute otherness, aiming at what most resembles the narcissistic subject himself. Proust knows every well that there is no desire except desire for absolute difference and that the subject always lacks this difference absolutely:

And no doubt the fact we had, these girls and I, not one habit—as we had not one idea—in common must make it more difficult for me to make friends with them and to win their regard. But perhaps, also, it was thanks to those differences, to my consciousness that not a single element that I knew or possessed entered into the composition of the nature and actions of these girls, that satiety had been succeeded in me by a thirst—akin to that with which a parched land burns—for a life which my soul, because it had never until now received one drop of it, would absorb all the more greedily, in long draughts, with a more perfect imbibition (p.852).

J.-M. O.: According to the classic Freudian perspective, the desire
we are dealing with here should be a pre-eminently narcissistic desire
because it is a homosexual desire. In homosexuality, as we mentioned
on a previous day, the element of seduction relies (as it must always do)
on the semblance of absolute otherness that the potential partner
affords; this semblance derives, of course, from the fact that the partner
is in the position of a model and rival, rather than an object. It is just the
same, as you have said, with rivalry in heterosexuality. That is why
Proust is right to have no scruples about changing the sex of his characters. If we ponder the description he puts before us, we realize that
elements that might have seemed slightly implausible when he wrote
the novel have become very much less so because of the decreasing difference between masculine and feminine behaviour. That has the
consequence, among others, of increasing conformity with the undifferentiating logic of mimetic desire. It does not prevent the doubles,
however, from misunderstanding this process of undifferentiation and
taking each other as examples of absolute difference.

R. G.: The mythic character of narcissism has made it possible for the
term to become universally accepted—to degenerate over a short period
of time into the most banal, everyday concept, like so many other psychoanalytic notions. Yet it is quite wrong, in my view, for people to
accuse the 'vulgar herd' of disfiguring and oversimplifying the psy-
choanalytical concepts that the Viennese Master has bequeathed to us.
If we look at the way the word 'narcissism' is used in the society around
us—particularly in the United States—we can see that it is exactly as
Freud understood it, judging by the text which after all cannot be suppressed: *Zur Einführung des Narzissmus.*

G. L.: Narcissism can always be brought in by anyone who wants to
smuggle the prestige of a psychoanalytic diagnosis into the frustrating
experiences we undergo as a result of the indifference of other people,
and into the desire this indifference succeeds in polarizing. There is no
narcissism that does not involve the other. No one ever really thinks: I
am narcissism intact. Of course a lot of people say it, or imply it, but
that is all part of the mimetic game—of the endless strategy that characterizes interdividual relationships in our world. We are always best at
this strategy when we are still hoodwinked by it. But at the same time,
as far as I can tell, we are never completely hoodwinked, unless delirium takes over.

R. G.: We are quite ready to accuse others of 'narcissism', in particular those whom we desire, with the aim of reassuring ourselves and relating their indifference, not to the very minor interest that we hold in their eyes or even perhaps in absolute terms (a piercing fear always at the edge of any exercise in amateur psychoanalysis), but to a kind of weakness that afflicts others. We credit them with an excessive and pathological concentration on themselves—with a kind of illness that makes them more sick than we are and consequently incapable of breaking out of their over-protected ego and meeting us half-way as they should. Accusing the desirable object of narcissism is equivalent, nowadays, to accusing a woman of egoism and coquetry at the time of Freud. If Freud has changed our vocabulary, this is not because he made a genuinely new contribution in this field, but for the exactly opposite reason. He was happy to refurbish the old tales thought up by desire and to give them new currency within the culture, so that for at least a few years people could have a sense of saying and seeing things that no one had taken note of before.

Our earlier statement that the will to demystify is a product of desire does not apply to Proust's desire. Rather, Proust's desire shows us a variant of this desire, indeed, an inverted form of it. What fascinates his narrator is not the stability conferred upon the model by his unbroken links with the delusions arising from sacrifice, but the very opposite. The narrator credits the desirable object with a degree of demystification that is more radical than his own—an insolent cynicism about all the forms of value that he still respects, and a capacity to manipulate expertly and imperturbably all the types of prestige attaching to violence. The chief point is that desire never aims at anything but difference and that difference always fascinates it, in whatever form, even in what remains wedded to the past or what has progressed much further in the disintegration of all differences that mimesis brings about. What is more, precisely this fascination with what is 'low', and undifferentiated—these symbols are being used relatively—dominates the whole development.

J.-M. O.: It is essential to recognize that Freud both reifies and standardizes positions that exist only as a function of each other—in the last analysis, only, as a function of the mimetic attachment to the obstacle. If we are capable, nowadays, of seeing the falsehood of the notion of narcissism that Freud offers in *Zur Einführung des Narzissmus*, then this is because mimetism has reached a higher pitch in the society around us and clarifies certain issues for us.

What impoverishes the ego is the very desire to be that ego—the desire for the kind of narcissism that is never ours but can be seen radiating from the other to whom we enslave ourselves. We need such things as the present-day fetishism of difference (which has replaced the failed Ego fetishism) in order to feed the engine of undifferentiation and the decreasing sense of concrete difference that is bringing our history toward its inevitable fulfilment.

R. G.: Let us return for the last time to the two texts we have been comparing, by Freud and Proust. It is easy to see that Proust's superiority over Freud derives from his much greater lucidity about his own desire, but this lucidity is tinged with ambiguity in so far as it cannot be completely separated from the historical progress of mimetic desire as such. The darker side of Viennese frivolity in the Belle Epoque is shifting, in Proust, to the darker shades of the First World War and after.

CHAPTER FIVE

Beyond Scandal

Proust's Conversion

R. G.: The one of Proust's works that best illustrates Freud's notion of narcissism is not *A la recherche du temps perdu* but the first sketch for it, *Jean Santeuil*. The novelist never published this work, because he realized that he had not arrived at a true understanding of his desire.[113]

By comparison with *A la recherche*, *Jean Santeuil* is a middling work, though it is distinctly superior to some of the literary pieces from which Freud draws examples in his writings. Although the hero, Jean Santeuil, uses the word 'I', he seem to be a case of what Freud describes as 'intact narcissism'. If you examine this character, you will quickly come to the conclusion that, by comparison with *A la recherche*, he is obviously living a perpetual lie. Even if the lie is not to be detected, it is hardly less untruthful for being lived out with such 'sincerity'.

Jean Santeuil is tremendously interested in himself and in the effect he produces on other people. This is always the finest possible effect, apart from a few snobbish and disagreeable characters who become green with envy at his worldly success. Jean Santeuil goes in for desire—an experience such a brilliant young man would not wish to do without—but his desire never escapes beyond the charmed circle of which he forms the centre. The young woman with whom he falls in love belongs to the same milieu as he does; she has the same refined tastes and the same ideals and aspirations.

Jean frequents the most aristocratic of milieus, but this is not because of snobbery since he hates all snobs. He is naturally attracted to people whose intellectual and aesthetic ideas and preferences he can share; people whom he resembles all too closely, in effect, not to have a spontaneous sympathy for them.

Clearly, at the centre of *Jean Santeuil* exists an ego that functions according to the laws of Freudian narcissism, particularly the type of narcissism credited to the artist. The individual ego is put forward as the true origin of any kind of spiritual and poetic richness: it transfigures everything by communicating a fleeting beauty that derives only from itself and belongs to itself alone.

Jean Santeuil is like a working model of the theory of narcissism. This should not surprise us: the novel is entirely consistent with the dominant aesthetic at the time Proust was writing, that is, in the first years of the twentieth century. Here we have the Romantic and Symbolist aesthetic at its most banal, celebrating the ego's superiority over the world and making that ego the origin and foundation of all poetry; the poet indulges in a kind of noble and generous error when he commits himself to beings and things that are outside of him. In reality, everything resides in the transfiguring power of his ego, which is the only true being, the only divinity worth adoring. When the poet becomes disillusioned with the world, he comes back to this ego, and it consoles him for all his suffering.

We find this dominant aesthetic in Freud's not very original description of 'the artistic temperament'. Like many people of his time, Freud is inclined to take at face value what a large number of artists (though not the best) have been repeating about themselves and their 'temperaments' ever since the beginning of the nineteenth century. He is inclined to take too seriously what he might call the narcissistic self-advertisement of these 'artistic temperaments'. Freud legitimates this stand; he gives it a negative connotation only in his high-minded renunciation of intact narcissism. At no point does he suspect that the narcissistic stand might be an aspect of the strategies with whose aid mimetic desire contrives to conceal the fascination exerted upon artists by their potential public. To lay claim, as the artistic temperament does, to an ego of inexhaustible richness is to invite others to make it the object of their desire; by implication, the ego is too self-sufficient to desire them itself, too confident of incarnating the 'beautiful totality' that has no need of anything else, the *Selbstgenügsamkeit* of Freudian narcissism.

G. L.: We have seen that Freud does not really feel at ease with the genuinely great literary works. In the middle of his essay on Dostoevsky, to take one example, he turns his back on his author and devotes the remaining pages to a story by Stephan Zweig, which is not up to the level of *The Eternal Husband*, even, indeed especially, in the respect that most concerns Freud.[114]

R. G.: If you compare Proust's two novels with *Zur Einführung des Narzissmus*, you can easily see why *Jean Santeuil*, the lesser achievement of the two, would suit Freud's purpose better than Proust's work of genius. As a psychoanalyst he would be able to find banal ideas there about the artistic temperament and narcissistic desire, which the early Proust still holds in common with him. By contrast, the late Proust— the Proust of *A la recherche*—repeats these banalities only in a few purely theoretical pronouncements about desire. Separated from the novel's actual substance, these theoretical reflections never succeed, with Proust as with so many other writers, in doing justice to what the novelist is really doing in his actual practice; it is this actual practice that relates to what we call interdividual psychology. The most stringent and savage critique of *Jean Santeuil* need not be made by us. Proust himself makes it in *A la recherche:* for example, the 'artistic temperament' of Jean Santeuil can be rediscovered in the character Legrandin, with his cravat that trails in the wind, his commonplaces on nature and the ideal, and the liking for solitude on which he preens himself. Actually he is an appalling snob, who is anguished that he has not been received by the aristocrats living round about, and will put up with any platitudes or humiliations to worm his way into the favour of the meanest country squire.[115]

Marcel Proust is very much aware, it seems to me, of making Legrandin speak in the style he himself used at the time of *Jean Santeuil*. I find it ironic that some critics greeted the publication of *Jean Santeuil* by acclaiming a Proust who was much more 'healthy', 'natural' and 'spontaneous' than the Proust of *A la recherche*: a Proust with whom everyone, or almost everyone, could identify.

A comparative study would reveal very quickly that all the attitudes presented in *Jean Santeuil* as the truth of the hero, the authentic expression of his 'narcissistic' subjectivity, can be reclassified in *A la recherche* among the various strategies of desire in its confrontations with symmetrical studies. The mediocrity of *Jean Santeuil* arises from the fact that the work still reflects back the image of himself that Proust, as a man and a writer, wanted to convey to others. By contrast, *A la recherche* exposes this image and concentrates upon the why and wherefore of this strategy.

In the interval between *Jean Santeuil* and *A la recherche*, there must have been a complete revolution in the way in which Proust regarded himself and his desire. In fact, Proust speaks of just such a revolution in the last volume of his great novel, *Le Temps retrouvé*, which purports to describe an experience of the type necessary to account for the difference between the two works. To this experience Proust attributes his capacity to write *A la recherche du temps perdu*.

J.-M.O.: In *Deceit, Desire and the Novel*, you make the point that Proust gives a much more explicit account than the great novelists before him of the necessary pre-condition for any work that is to reveal mimetic desire. This is an experience of the type that he attributes to the narrator of *A la recherche*, and attributes to himself in his more directly autobiographical texts, not to mention some of his letters. You stated that this experience is placed as a general rule in the closing stages of the work. The hero is made to reflect the novelist's earlier blindness about his own mimetic desire; at the end of his course, which often turns out to be at the moment of death, he discovers the vanity of this desire. In other words, he goes through the experience that enabled the novelist to write, not another *Jean Santeuil*, but an *A la recherche du temps perdu*. You point out that this symbolism is always a symbolism of religious conversion.[116] Yet even those who have reacted favourably to your analyses in the book have found it very hard to accept this statement. They look upon it as a tendency to fall back into religious sentimentalism, which means to say, into the very illusions you have been condemning.

R. G.: I think there is no problem in showing that the unchallenged superiority of *A la recherche* in the domain of desire and its capacity to communicate the lived experience of desire to us—which also means conveying the anguish that accompanies the experience—depend upon modifications in structure that can easily be identified when the work is compared with *Jean Santeuil*.

In both works, to take an example, we have scenes at the theatre. Although they may seem to be quite different in tone, style and even content, they can easily be shown, under careful examination, to have close parallels with one another. In the light of these close parallels, we can show what kind of upheaval has taken place between the writing of the two works. It is connected with the structural position of desire itself as it affects the narrator in each of the two novels.

In *Jean Santeuil*, the hero himself occupies a place in the box; he is the sole focus of everyone's attention, the object of flattery and even adulation by all the most highly placed characters. An ex-King of Portugal is so friendly that he even rearranges Jean's tie for him. The vulgarity of the episode makes you think of present-day advertising. Use such and such a beauty product, and you will stimulate irresistible passion on all sides; crowds of admirers of both sexes will find it impossible to stay away from you. To make his triumph complete, the hero's enemies—the equivalent in *Jean Santeuil* to the Verdurin couple in *A la recherche*—witness it from afar; mingling with the faceless crowd in the stalls, they are mortified by the sight of this amazing event.

In *A la recherche*, it is the narrator who is lost in the crowd and gazes avidly at the almost unearthly spectacle of the box full of aristocrats. Nowhere in the novel is there an equivalent to the theatre scene in *Jean Santeuil*; at no point is it possible to detect this circular economy of a desire that feeds on itself, one might even say ingurgitates itself, but in the process never suffers the slightest diminishment, corresponding exactly to the Freudian definition of intact narcissism.

Or rather, it is possible. The phenomenon can certainly be found, but only in so far as it is the supreme mirage of desire. The blessed state of autonomy that Freud speaks of, the impregnable libidinal position, is once again involved with the metaphysical transcendence of the model and obstacle, which is figured symbolically by the circularity and closure of the box. In the superior artistry of *A la recherche*, all of this is reserved for the model and obstacle alone, in other words, only for others, to the extent that they are transfigured by desire. In the setting of Balbec, this role is given to the little band; in the theatrical setting, it is provisionally reserved for the aristocrats of the Faubourg St Germain, as long as they remain reluctant to receive the narrator and so form a fascinating obstacle for him. Once the narrator succeeds in getting himself invited to the Guermantes', and the obstacle thus ceases to work for him in this way, his desire completely evaporates.[117]

To make things a bit easier, I have taken a rather extreme example and simplified it as I presented it. But this only serves to bring out more clearly the nature of the structural change that has taken place between the two novels. Even though desire desperately seeks to see itself in the glorious situation of Jean Santeuil, it basically occupies the depressive position, not because it is persecuted by others or by society, but because it works all that up for itself, by projecting upon the most resistant of obstacles, such as contempt or mere indifference, the mirage of the self-sufficiency that it will devote all its efforts to overcoming.

The early Proust imagines that this self-sufficiency does exist somewhere, and that sooner or later he will be able to possess it. He dreams continually of the moment of this conquest and represents it to himself as if it had already taken place. Desire sells the skin of the sacrificial bear before it is in the bag!

Sacrifice and Psychotherapy

R. G.: The late Proust knows that narcissism has no existence *in itself*; he knows that to represent desire in a convincing manner, you must represent it from outside the Guermantes' box, unable to gain access. Desire should not attempt to make us believe that it is in control of the situation. The only situations that concern it are those in which it is dominated. Here I must repeat that this is not a matter of an objective situation, but of the interpretation that desire gives its situation. (This interpretation, in turn, tends to make the situation objectively real.)

Of course, it is not too difficult to recognize the accuracy of what I am saying in the abstract, which means to apply it to other people. It is a good deal harder to seek out the areas in which each of us operates a little bit like Jean Santeuil, to demystify our own feelings and not merely those of others, and to detect what is hidden behind our very passion for demystification.

Reaching this particular stage, in however partial and limited a fashion, is no simple matter. And it is certainly not something reserved exclusively for great writers. I have the sense that it may be even less common with writers than with other people. I make no concessions to the fetishizing of the literary work. I would just say that the people who have this experience are few in number, to judge by the way the world works. If writers do in fact have it more frequently than they appear to, then perhaps they have it too late, as a general rule, for them to be able to draw any benefit from it on the purely literary level. Sometimes such an experience does not open upon a higher form of literature but purely and simply deters the writer from literary activity. It can usually be linked to the trials that desire obliges us to suffer, but however harsh these trials may be, there is no guarantee that a writer will experience the 'fall' necessary to turn him into a great writer.

G. L.: Argue that such a form of experience really exists and is similar to what has always been called religious experience, and most of our contemporaries will see red. Something makes the very thought of it intolerable—something that must be bound up with the almost universal hostility toward Judaeo-Christian ideas.

R. G.: I can well understand this hostility, not simply because the type of experience in question can be dressed up in the most provocative way, but also because the principle of structural displacement I have just described can come up in the most widely differing circumstances and occur on many different levels. What rouses the modern conscience against any form of initiation or conversion is a refusal to allow any distinctions—they are now considered *hypocritical*, in the gospel sense—between legitimate and illegitimate violence. This refusal is in itself quite reasonable and commendable, but it is sacrificial all the same because it takes no account of history. At the present moment, sacrifice is being sacrificed; culture in its entirety, especially our own culture, historic Christianity, is playing the role of the scapegoat. We attempt to wash our hands of any complicity with the violence that lies at our origins, and this very attempt perpetuates the complicity. We all say: 'If we had lived in the time of our forefathers, we would not have joined ourselves with them to spill the blood of the artists and philosophers.'

Now the sacrifice will be kept going in the very gestures that claim to abolish it, in people's burning indignation about everything that still expels, oppresses and persecutes, especially if this scandal takes place very close to them and is perpetuated *in the name of the Judaeo-Christian*. The dynamic content of the Judaeo-Christian revelation is being brought to a conclusion. But frequently this conclusion implies a spirit of hatred and violence that is itself an aberration. The proof of this lies in the fact that the Judaeo-Christian text is misunderstood; people try to erase it completely from our memories and take pleasure in the idea that by now the process is more or less complete.

In reality, no purely intellectual process and no experience of a purely philosophical nature can secure the individual the slightest victory over mimetic desire and its victimage delusions. Intellection can achieve only displacement and substitution, though these may give individuals the sense of having achieved such a victory. For there to be even the slightest degree of progress, the victimage delusion must be vanquished on the most intimate level of experience; and this triumph, if it is not to remain a dead letter, must succeed in collapsing, or at the very least shaking to their foundations, all the things that are based upon our interdividual oppositions—consequently, everything that we can call our 'ego', our 'personality', our 'temperament', and so on. Because of this, great works are few and far between. Although they are all secretly related to one another, at least in literature and the 'human sciences', they require time before they can be accepted. This time is necessary to exhaust the various mythologies dominant at the moment of their creation. Everything that they appear to get wrong, everything that their contemporaries see as the immortal acquisition of the most recent wave of demystification, must come to an end before they can be appreciated.

The other experience, the conversion experience of the truly great writer, however strictly determined as to content, always retains the form of the great religious experiences. These can be shown to be all alike, whatever religion provides their framework. This experience can be picked up in the sacrificial framework of primitive religious institutions, where it forms what we refer to as initiation. It is always a question of breaking out of mimetic desire with its perpetual states of crisis, a question of escaping from the violence of doubles and the exasperating illusion of subjective difference in order to reach (through a kind of identification with the deity, particularly with his power of intercession) an ordered world defined in terms of a lesser violence, even if that is a sacrificial violence. This kind of experience can be found in the great oriental religions. But there the aim is to allow the individual to escape completely from the world and its cycles of violence by an absolute renunciation of all worldly concerns, a kind of living death.

J.-M.O.: If I understand you properly, today there can be no real knowledge of mimetic desire and its victimage mechanisms without shattering what in each of us is still structured or is always trying to restructure itself in accordance with this desire and these mechanisms. That means that the awareness we have sought from the beginning of these discussions is only truly accessible through an experience similar to what has traditionally been called religious *conversion*, though there may be no reason to avoid describing it in rational terms at the same time.

R.G.: This is perhaps less strange than it seems. Even in the investigation of nature, which does not put the same barriers in the way of developing awareness as humans do, the great minds who have effected the most decisive intellectual breakthroughs have always apparently passed from one mental universe to another—something that sub-sequent observers, who cannot understand how and why it happens, regularly describe as 'mystical'.

The most remarkable thing is that even in our world, where the Judaeo-Christian text has disclosed the mechanisms underlying all forms of cultural order, the process of conversion is similar in form and symbolism to that of all previous religions. But in our world it will have ever more radical consequences for knowledge, starting with an investigation of nature and later spreading to culture.

J.-M.O.: There is a paradox here. In a world that is secretly governed by the gospel revolution and reflects the extraordinarily concrete character of this revolution, as well as the desacralization it brings about and the way in which it brings to light the most hidden mechanisms of human culture, the type of experience you describe may indeed reproduce the immemorial process of religious conversion, but for the first time it need not rely on divine agency, as can be seen by the great works of literature that reflect it.

Such reliance will seem all the more unnecessary because there are already quite enough concrete results—both literary (like Proust) and non-literary—so that reference to any transcendence besides that of the knowledge being acquired will appear superfluous or even antithetical to the truth embodied in that knowledge.

G. L.: You are suggesting in that the complete break between the sacrificial gods and the non-sacrificial God—the Father who has been made known to us only through Christ—in no way excludes a continuity between the sacrificial religions and this universal renunciation of violence to which all humanity is called. This continuity, however, is part of the human perspective, not the divine.

R. G.: There is an absolute separation between the only true deity and all the deities of violence, who have been radically demystified by the Gospels alone. But this should not prevent us from recognizing in the religions of violence, which are always in search of peace, anyway, the methods that initially helped humanity to leave the animal state behind and then to elevate itself to unprecedented possibilities, though they are combined with the most extreme dangers.

At each of these stages, especially at the more advanced stages like our own, humankind could choose a path different from that of violence and rejection, and could reach the god of non-violence. But the choice of violence is of no ultimate consequence; whether humanity wishes to or not, it always moves in the same direction, toward the same goal.

It is one of the most profound mysteries that a measure of continuity should link the Logos of violence with the Johannine Logos, for the benefit of mankind. But, far from contradicting the complete separation between the one Logos and the other, this continuity is only possible as a result of the separation.

Beyond the Pleasure Principle
and Structural Psychoanalysis

G. L.: Before we speak of the death instinct, I would like to ask about the points of contact between your viewpoint and that of Jacques Lacan.

R. G.: I think that both of you have already made the essential points, in your remarks on psychosis. The issue that structuralism will never be able to work out, and Lacan is a structuralist, is the reciprocal dependence between the differential principle and the undifferentiated symmetries in the relationship between doubles, the 'zero degree' of structure. It is impossible to articulate these matters without taking into account the victimage mechanism. The distinction between object choice and narcissism in the work of Freud displays his inability to disengage the mechanism of structuration. The same inability can be found in Lacan, and there is the same over-absolute separation between the *symbolic* structurations deriving from the reinterpretation of the Oedipus complex and the 'dual' relationships that derive from a reinterpretation of narcissism—Lacan's mirror stage and his whole notion of the imaginary. The inability to think through how these concepts are reciprocally dependent is brought out in the static character of the system, as with Lévi-Strauss, and by the lack of any temporal dimension. This inability becomes all too evident when psychosis is defined as the 'foreclosure' of the symbolic, pure and simple.[118]

We are only too aware that, if in psychosis the symbolic dimension is progressively withheld as a stabilizing factor, this is because it gradually becomes the very *stake* of the mimetic rivalry. So you cannot simply treat this dimension as if it did not exist in psychosis. The Lacanian definition fails to explain why, for over a century, the great discoveries in the field of culture and its symbolic dimension have been made by individuals who have themselves frequently ended up by tipping over into psychosis, or being threatened by it. It is hard to see how that could be so if we accept a thesis that treats psychosis as a lack in the stabilizing element, pure and simple. In reality, the psychotic goes furthest in objectifying what people have never been able to objectify, since he strives, in his 'metaphysical hubris', to incarnate this stabilizing element within himself. It is precisely because he cannot succeed in this attempt yet will not give up, that he sees the element as incarnated by the other, the double. Hölderlin sees the god of poetry take the form of Schiller. Nietzsche cannot help seeing Wagner as the 'true' incarnation of Dionysus. If we look carefully at the intellectual struggles taking place around us, we can see that this is always the point at issue. With Lacanian theory, in particular, the game invariably means watching other people's failure to achieve the symbolic dimension and savouring Lacan's exquisite paradoxes on the subject of the 'symbolic'. To the non-initiated, they look like incomprehensible puns, and they become enormously enjoyable for the initiate as a result.

G. L.: There is, or there seems to be, a Lacanian initiation process, and like all initiations it sets up a hierarchy of knowledge. The discovery of the scapegoat mechanism is not an initiation. There is never any question of our having discovered it; it can only be rediscovery. Similarly, no credit attaches to us for having done this; history does the job for us.

J.-M.O.: With Lacan, the distinction between object choice and narcissism comes to the fore to explain conflicts of doubles and related phenomena whose symmetry he can see more clearly than Freud did, although he fails to draw the radical conclusions for structuralism and psychoanalysis that follow as a matter of course. Instead of relating this symmetry to reciprocal mimetism, Lacan sees it as what he calls the 'capture by the imaginary', because he is entrenched in the postulate he defines as the 'mirror stage'.

R. G.: The whole imagery of mirrors and the imaginary rests (as does the Freudian thesis) on the myth of Narcissus, who looks at himself in the mirror of the pool and allows himself to be captivated by his own image, as he was captivated by the sound of his own voice in the Echo episode. We know exactly how to deal with themes like this. These metaphors always conceal doubles; in endowing them with an explanatory value, you are still working along the lines of mythology. The mirror stage is a naive resurgence of mythology.

Lacan falls into the error that is shared by the whole psychoanalytic school when he writes about capture by the imaginary—a desire that is not inscribed within the system of cultural differences and so could not be a desire for difference, but necessarily bears on something like the same, the identical, the image of one's own ego, etc. In opposition, we can cite Proust's text, which describes all desire, even at its most 'narcissistic', as a thirst for the greatest possible difference. All of the great works of literature will readily testify against a conception that minimizes the role of violence and conflict in individual or collective orders and disorders.

One of the most crucial texts for this psychoanalytic school is *Beyond the Pleasure Principle*. To support the thesis of the entry into language and the symbolic dimension, Lacan isolates the passage about the small child who amuses himself by making a reel on a thread appear and disappear, representing, in Freud's reading, the mother who is at one time absent and at another present. Lacan readily claims that this story is of major importance for the Saussurian reading of Freud: he sees it as the child's apprenticeship to the signifier. In a note, Freud shows us the child playing at *Fort/Da* with his own image in a mirror. In these few lines, you have all you need to give rise to Lacan's two most important theses.

I believe that *Beyond the Pleasure Principle* is one of Freud's most essential texts. What strikes me in this text is that the *Fort/Da* game is presented from a perspective that is both mimetic and sacrificial, and this is a point worth emphasizing. Freud converts the moment when the child throws the reel away from him into a veritable sacrificial expulsion, whose motive originates in an impulse of revenge directed toward the mother, because she happens to absent herself:

> Das Wegwerfen des Gegenstandes, so dass er fort ist, könnte die Befriedigung eines im Leben unterdrückten Racheimpulses gegen die Mutter sein, weil sie vom Kinde fortgegangen ist.

> Throwing away the object so that it was 'gone' might satisfy an impulse of the child's, which was suppressed in his actual life, to revenge himself on his mother for going away from him.[119]

According to Freud's explanation, the child stages, in his games, all his most unpleasant experiences, and he thus converts them into pleasant experiences because he succeeds in gaining mastery over them. Freud has already placed on record that, in the case under observation, the subject did not allow himself to express any emotion when his mother went away from him. Freud tells us that this is not an untypical case. He writes that other children have been known to express their feelings of hostility by throwing away objects in the place of the individuals toward whom their feelings are really directed.

Wir wissen auch von anderen Kindern, dass sie ähnliche feindselige Regungen durch das Wegschleudern von Gegenständen an Stelle der Personen auszudrücken vermögen . . .

Man sieht, dass die Kinder alles im Spiele wiederholen, was ihnen im Leben grossen Eindruck gemacht hat, dass sie dabei die Stärke des Eindruckes abreagieren und sich sozusagen zu Herren der Situation machen. Aber anderseits ist es klar genug, dass all ihr Spielen unter dem Einfluss des Wunsches steht, der diese ihre Zeit dominiert, des Wunsches: gross zu sein und so tun zu können wie die Grossen (pp.14-15).

We know of other children who like to express similar hostile impulses by throwing away objects instead of persons . . .

It is clear that in their play children repeat everything that has made a great impression on them in real life, and that in doing so they abreact the strength of the impression and, as one might put it, make themselves master of the situation. But on the other hand it is obvious that all their play is influenced by a wish that dominates them the whole time—the wish to be grown-up and able to do what grown-up people do (pp.16-17).

One of the most painful scenes, which children repeatedly play at, is, according to Freud, a surgical operation. Creating such a mimetic *mise-en-scène* gives pleasure because the child is able to distribute the roles among his playmates in such a way as to get back at the person who stands in for the author of the disagreeable experience: 'and so he revenges himself on the person of this substitute' (p.15).

In fact, Freud is bringing up the whole question of ritual behaviour, but he does so in a kind of chiaroscuro, not going beyond the level of the individual. This is confirmed in the same paragraph by a reference to the art of drama and its mimesis; tragedy exposes adult spectators to the most disagreeable impressions, but they become a source of pleasure. Here we return to Aristotelian *catharsis* and the ritual expulsions it involves:

> Schliessen wir noch die Mahnungen an, dass das künstlerische Spielen und Nachahmen der Erwachsenen, das zum Unterschied vom Verhalten des Kindes auf die Person des Zuschauers zielt, diesem die schmerzlichsten Eindrücke zum Beispiel in der Tragödie nicht erspart und doch von ihm als hoher Genuss empfunden werden kann (p.15).

> Finally, a reminder may be added that artistic play and artistic imitation carried out by adults, which, unlike children's, are aimed at an audience, do not spare the spectators (for instance, in tragedy) the most painful experiences and can yet be felt by them as highly enjoyable (p.17).

This is an extraordinary passage. For, mentioned in the same breath as the appearance of language and sign systems, we get not just the coldly intellectual games of structuralism, but a thirst for 'revenge' that becomes 'constructive' in its cultural context because it can be spent upon a *Stellvertreter*, a sacrificial substitute. The whole process takes place within a framework that makes the passage much more profound than the Oedipus-complex problematic.

It is important to look closely at everything in these few pages that bears on the question of imitation and the imitative: *Nachamung, nachähmlich*. There is a lot of material here, despite a certain reticence Freud seems to show and despite a tendency (which contemporary structuralism will greatly magnify) to keep the theme of sacrifice in the background.

Freud understands (or so it seems) that the *Fort/Da* amounts only to the imitative reprise of a game initiated by adults. If the mother can easily tell that the 'o-o-o-o-o' of the child signifies *fort*, it is because she has acted as a *model* to the child; in fact, it was she who taught the child this game. Freud goes on to say that it makes no essential difference, *for the affective value of the game*, where it is invented in all its details by the child or whether he takes it up as a result of a suggestion from somewhere else.

Für die affektive Einschätzung dieses Spieles ist es natürlich gleich-
gültig, ob das Kind es selbst erfunden oder sich infolge einer An-
regung zu eigen gemacht hatte (p. 13).

It is of course a matter of indifference from the point of view of judging the effective nature of the game whether the child invented it
himself or took it over on some outside suggestion (p. 15).

Obviously, such a question cannot be unimportant for us. The issue is
whether the process by which symbolism arises is the result of imitation. No great ingenuity is required to see that imitation, together
with substitution, does play a crucial role in all the stages of the virtually ritualistic exercise Freud is describing. The substitution is not primary but secondary, for it is in itself no more than the imitation of a
substitution that is inherent in all victimage processes and in all violent
impulses which tend irresistibly to pass from object to object. Our conclusion is that even if Freud does not actually uncover the scapegoat
mechanism, he comes very close to it in this text when he states that
there is a reciprocal affinity between revenge and the 'constructive' processes of substitution.

Freud understands so well the importance of imitation in the entire
process that he feels he must account for the absence of any explicit
thoughts on the subject. There is no need, he suggests, to assume that a
special imitative instinct provide the motive for the *Fort/da* game:

Aus diesen Erörterungen geht immerhin hervor, dass die Annahme
eines besonderen Nachahmungsstriebes als Motiv des Spielens
überflüssig ist (p. 15).

Nevertheless, it emerges from this discussion that there is no need to
assume the existence of a special imitative instinct in order to provide
a motive for play (p. 17).

Here particular emphasis is placed on the word *besonderen* ('special'),
and Freud would not dream of denying imitation any role. If Freud had
dwelt on the matter a bit longer, he might have realized that pure *invention* is not feasible: either the child is imitating a form of behaviour
which has already acquired symbolic form from the adults, or the spirit
of violence and revenge prompts the symbolization by suggesting ways
of combating the state of powerlessness when no real revenge can be

taken through substitutes. In neither case is imitation 'superfluous'.

Freud never succeeds in fully distinguishing these two sorts of imitation from one another. Both of them crop up again in the following sentence, which refers to the imitative arts of the human race and in particular to the one most closely associated with revenge, tragedy. The whole process is shown as being an adult form of *Nachahmen*, almost exactly like the child's *Nachahmen*: 'Schliessen wir noch die Mahnungen an, dass das künstlerische Spielen und Nachahmen der Erwachsenen . . .' (p.15); 'Finally, a reminder may be added that the artistic play and artistic imitation carried out by adults . . .' (p.17).

The structuralist reading helps to bring out some of Freud's intuitions, but only in so far as they fit in with the principle of a static differential order. The issue is not uninteresting, but this gain is accomplished at the expense of something far more crucial which, though present in Freud's texts, fails to reach full formulation. This is, of course, the mimetic game, which incorporates not only the most elementary forms of imitation but also the paradox of doubles and a hint of the scapegoat mechanism. Everything in Freud that relates to this essential point—both in the text we are reading and in those already considered, on the double genesis of Oedipus for example, and *Zur Einführung des Narzissmus*—is passed over in complete silence by the structuralist interpretation—in fact, it is sacrificed to the all-powerful principle of a differential structural order that is 'always already' given.

We might conclude that two paths opened up after Freud and continued beyond him. One was concerned with maintaining the sacred character of difference, but could only do so on the level of language; the other took its bearings from all the aspects of Freud's work that tend to undermine and secretly subvert this principle of difference. The first is still definable within the context of psychoanalytic practice and, at best, draws attention to everything touching on the issue of linguistic differences in Freud's text; it sacralizes language on the level of *wordplay* and, in a number of ways, in its relationship with Freud recalls the difference between Molière and Marivaux.

The second path consists in focusing on acquisitive mimesis, that is to say, in discovering the conflictual nature of imitation. If the principle is pursued to its final conclusion, it will inevitably lead to the shattering of the great Freudian myths of Oedipus and Narcissus. It is therefore impossible to keep the issue within the psychoanalytic context. This path is so radical that those who follow it are left with no decisive reason to give Freud any precedence over the various other modern masters of suspicion. All of them are moving, we can see, in the direction of the scapegoat mechanism and the gospel revelation, but they do so in reverse, so to speak. They invariably turn their backs on the goals at the very moment when they come closest to it. I wish we had more time for some of the others, especially Nietzsche and Antonin Artaud.

Obviously, these two paths have had to be taken one after the other, beginning with the first for people to realize that only the second is really productive. It is capable of incorporating what is valid in the first, but the converse does not hold.

J.-M. O.: To demonstrate the close links between all your readings and show that they work on all levels, it is worth pointing out the close parallel between the mistakes that Lévi-Strauss makes in his reading of the Ojibwa and Tikopia myths in *Totemism Today* and Lacan's mistake in the reading of the *Fort/Da*. Just as Lévi-Strauss sees an 'immaculate conception' of human thought in the 'radical elimination' and 'negative connotation' of the 'eliminated fragment', so psychoanalytic structuralism emphasizes the purely logical aspect of the *Fort/Da* process without noticing that Freud himself sees the spirit of vengeance and sacrificial catharsis as being inextricably caught up in the process. Yet again, Freud opens up a direction that structuralism temporarily closes off again. But this closure is not entirely pointless; structuralism performs a kind of synchronic analysis that enables us to take up the important way forward with new vigour.

The Death Instinct and Modern Culture

J.-M. O.: From what you have just been saying, I come to the following conclusions: (1) Unlike Freud, you see desire as totally divorced from pleasure. In a certain sense, desire has pleasure in tow. (2) You want to discover a genetic mechanism by which the various psychological 'complexes' were produced. And you also explain the mechanism by which these 'complexes' or combinations of circumstances are repeated and become more and more serious. (3) If I follow you correctly, you ought by now to be in a position to 'deconstruct' the famous 'death instinct'.

R. G.: Yes, we must turn at this point to what interests Freud most in *Beyond the Pleasure Principle*—the problem of repetition. Freud distinguishes two types of repetition. One of these we have already touched on—it is related to the *Fort/Da* mechanism, the ritual game designed to guarantee mastery over an unpleasant experience. This initial group comprises traumatic neuroses, and it can be characterized using the Freudian model of imprinting, though with a die stamp that loses ink with each application and thus produces a less and less clear impression. With traumatic neurosis, this loss of definition goes hand in hand with a growing mastery over the experience that caused the trauma.

Freud quite honestly admits that nothing in psychoanalysis explains the second type of repetition. This type of repetition is an escalation that brings more and more suffering, and it is liable to appear in 'normal' individuals, who show no symptoms and come across simply as passive victims. For such repetition, Freud must invent the death instinct, based on the tendency of living beings to revert to a completely inert state. Nothing could be more revealing than the way in which Freud brings up this insoluble problem of worsening repetition that can only end in death. The subject is unable to do what his psychoanalyst wants: he cannot discover in his present experience a fragment of his early childhood—his own individual version of the Oedipus myth, in other words—and convince himself on this basis that the psychoanalyst's conclusions are correct. He is intent on repeating the experience; he even wants to involve the psychoanalyst in the process. Instead of an effective psychoanalysis, what results is a 'transference neurosis'.

Here the psychoanalyst is entirely at a loss. With what types of patient does he reach this impasse? To judge from a later passage, it can be almost anyone, for in a few lines, Freud describes the effects of mimetic desire—obviously without identifying them as such because he does not understand the principle at work, but in such a way that it is impossible not to recognize the dynamic system that we have been discussing over the last few days. This system completely bypasses the categories of psychoanalysis, as Freud concedes with his usual honesty:

What psychoanalysis reveals in the transference phenomena of neurotics can also be observed in the lives of some normal people. The impression they give is of being pursued by a malignant fate or possessed by some 'daemonic' power; but psychoanalysis has always taken the view that their fate is for the most part arranged by themselves and determined by early infantile influences. The compulsion which is here in evidence differs in no way from the compulsion to repeat which we have found in neurotics, even though the people we are now considering have never shown any signs of dealing with a neurotic conflict by producing symptoms. Thus we have come across people all of whose human relationships have the same outcome: such as the benefactor who is abandoned in anger after a time by each of his protégés, however much they may otherwise differ from one another, and who thus seems doomed to taste all the bitterness of ingratitude; or the man whose friendships all end in betrayal by his friends; *or the man who time after time in the course of his life raises someone else into a position of great private or public authority and then, after a certain interval, himself upsets that authority and replaces him by a new one*; or, again, the lover each of whose love affairs with a woman passes through the same phases and reaches the same conclusion. This 'perpetual recurrence of the same thing' causes us no astonishment when it relates to *active* behaviour on the part of the person concerned and when we can discern in him an essential character-trait which always remains the same and which is compelled to find expression in a repetition of the same experiences. We are much more impressed by cases where the subject appears to have a *passive* experience, over which he has no influence, but in which he meets with a repetition of the same fatality. [Italics added][120]

Freud uses the death instinct to cope with the confession of incapacity freely given here, and his honesty is admirable. In fact, the whole passage is remarkably to our purpose. The lines that I have italicized come as close to the mimetic process as it is possible to do without managing to disclose it completely. All of the phenomena described by Freud, including those found outside the quotation we have given, can be reduced to the process defined in the italicized lines, that is to say, to the process of mimetic rivalry, with the model first metamorphosing into an idol and then turning into an obstacle and a hateful persecutor, which reinforces his sacred status. Freud himself recognizes that the Oedipus complex cannot make sense of these phenomena, despite their kinship with the phenomena that he associates with this complex; it is precisely because Freud does not refer to Oedipus here that he comes so close to us. Freud quite clearly recognizes that it is impossible to discover the origins of this type of repetition by searching for it in the patient's childhood.

If Freud had discovered a single explanatory principle to cover both the phenomena he associates with Oedipus and the phenomena described here, he would certainly have adopted it. He could hardly have been satisfied with giving two opposing explanations for data that are not at all dissimilar as symptoms. Freud himself describes as speculative the pseudo-scientific phantasmagoria that led him to postulate his 'death instinct'. He formulates this hypothesis for lack of anything more credible.

When we spoke of the double genesis of Oedipus, we showed that the Oedipus complex cannot conceivably account for any forms of reproduction or repetition, and that, if only for this reason, the Oedipal hypothesis must be rejected. If we look at the two types of repetition that are described as distinct and incompatible in *Beyond the Pleasure Principle*, we can see that Freud has written the text from beginning to end bearing this inadequacy of Oedipus in mind, even if he retains, in a purely nominal way, an area within which Oedipus continues to function as an explanation. Clearly, Freud is a long way from explicitly acknowledging the possibility we are trying to set out, and he has no hope of doing so because he cannot identify the principle of mimetic rivalry. All the same, in *Beyond the Pleasure Principle* he submits his own postulates to an implicit criticism that acquires a crucial significance in the light of the mimetic hypothesis.

The mimetic principle makes repetition intelligible and even necessary; it retraces the style of the repetition as well as its tendency to deteriorate, even into madness and death—in other words, a tendency toward a goal that must appear, to a spectator unable to spot the mimetic game, as its direct existential aim. In postulating his death instinct, Freud once again does what we have seen him do at every stage in his analysis, or in other words, at every level of the mimetic process: he is perceptive enough to recognize that the 'compulsion to repeat' is directed towards death on every occasion when it does not carry a ritualistic or para-ritualistic meaning; but once again he is not perceptive enough to discern the principle that could provide a unified and satisfactorily explanation for all the phenomena. He therefore concludes that death is the *goal* of the desire, but he has no real explanation and therefore must resort to the expedient of invoking another 'instinct' or 'drive'.

The proof that the death instinct is merely a fantasy can be found in the fact that it is no more capable than the Oedipus complex of supplying the impetus to repetition featured in the *Eternal Husband*. The repetition of a prior situation must indeed result from *imitation*—but not of the full situation, as Freud imagines in the case of Oedipus, but of a particular element in the situation, the desire of the other, of the idolized and hated obstacle/model.

Just as it is not possible to 'reproduce' a triangle by using the Oedipal triangle as a model, [121] so it is not possible to reproduce the same triangle or any other disastrous situation by assuming the existence of a 'death instinct'. If there really was a death instinct, it would have to be expressed via the imitation of an imitable element in the repeated scene. The only other way would be for the death instinct to prevail upon the patient to throw himself out of the window or under the wheels of a vehicle. Freud is obviously not talking about suicide, and we must assume that the death instinct, like the Oedipus complex, operates indirectly and through the mediation of the *Nachahmung* (imitation) that is omnipresent in the text until we reach the death instinct 'properly speaking', when imitation disappears, in a kind of pseudo-scientific phantasmagoria.

In each case, all we need do to account for the bad repetition is to conceive of the *Nachahmung*, the imitation, in a non-Platonic mode. That resolves all the difficulties and integrates all the genuine observations of Freud in a satisfactory manner.

Let me once again restate the mechanism of mimetic repetition. The subject who is not able to decide for himself on the object that he should desire relies upon the desire of another person. And he automatically transforms the model desire into a desire that opposes and frustrates his own. Because he does not understand the automatic character of the rivalry, the imitator soon converts the very fact of being opposed, frustrated and rejected into the major stimulant of his desire. In one way or another, he proceeds to inject more and more violence into his desire. To identify this tendency is to recognize that, in the last resort, desire tends towards death, both the death of the model and obstacle (murder) and the death of the subject himself (self-destruction and suicide). This dynamic of mimetic desire does not operate only in those who are 'sick', in those who push the mimetic process too far to be able to function normally; it is also, as Freud acknowledged, a feature of the people we call 'normal'.

G. L.: Giving yourself over to the mimetic obstacle is like wandering among the tombs. It is committing yourself to death.

R. G.: This tendency is at work in some of the main aspects of contemporary culture, much more obviously than in Freud's time. It is concretized in a particularly spectacular manner in nuclear rivalry. In a notable essay, Michel Serres has demonstrated that the modern practice of science and technology is centred upon death; everything is organized for the benefit of death and leads toward death.[122]

Everything converges on death, including the types of thought that draw attention to this convergence, such as the thought of Freud or that of the ethologists, who also believe that they can detect something resembling an instinct, or the theory that the whole universe is evolving toward entropy.

If what threatens us is the result of an instinct, and if every embodiment of our history is simply a particular aspect of an inexorable scientific law, then there is nothing to do but abandon ourselves to the movement that carries us along with it; we are caught up in a destiny that we have no hope of mastering.

To come up with another new instinct, which is independent of all the others and rounds them off (as Freud does) is to ignore the fact that the dynamism of mimetic desire has always been oriented towards madness and death. Freud does not notice that the metaphors he uses in the text on narcissism—metaphors that, if you remember, reveal his own desire by comparing the desired object with infants, animals and criminals—are already well launched on the path that leads desire toward nothingness.[123] To prefer the object that seems to be endowed with what Freud calls intact narcissism is to take the mimetic obstacle for the most vital thing of all, while in reality it leads us toward suffering and failure. This preference is indistinguishable from what Freud elsewhere calls 'masochism' and what he calls the 'death instinct' in *Beyond the Pleasure Principle*. He does not see that in all these cases the same 'drive' is being discussed. The seductive effect that intact narcissism has on the unfortunate object-directed desire can be interpreted just as well through the death instinct as through the pleasure principle. It is certainly a surplus of life or pleasure that makes the pretty coquette glitter in the eyes of Freud and awaken his desire. But she always brings him just the opposite. Invariably, subject-directed desire ends up with 'libidinal impoverishment', with a diminishment of vital force.

Freud introduces distinctions where there should be unity because he does not see that his pleasure principle and his death principle are two partial and imperfectly understood effects of one and the same cause, which is mimetic desire. Mimetic desire thinks that it always chooses the most life-affirming path, whereas in actuality it turns increasingly toward the obstacle—toward sterility and death. Only what seems implacably indifferent or hostile, only the doors that fail to open when we knock, can awaken this desire. That is why mimetic desire knocks in the places where there is no one to open and tends to mistake the thickest of walls for doors.

We should try to situate these texts by Freud and Proust within the general drift of contemporary culture and literature. In the metaphorical realm in particular, they both reflect a very general tendency whose overall significance is perfectly clear; it concerns the mounting obsession with, and in consequence the 'hardening' of, the mimetic obstacle. 'Blessed self-sufficiency', which is in the last analysis the quality possessed by the deity, tends to be located more and more in forms of existence that are as far removed from us as possible, even to the inorganic world, in the impenetrable substance of the hardest of materials, like metal or stone. Desire finds a final outlet in the icy void of the spaces of science fiction—in the black holes discussed by astronomers, which are so frighteningly dense that over a broader and broader range all matter is sucked into them, increasing their power of attraction.

J.-M. O.: This is still the seductive force of 'intact narcissism', or of Polynesian *mana*. But the form it adopts grows more and more inhuman all the time.

R. G.: It is also the kind of cultural discourse that dominates what is now called post-modernism. We can look forward, I suppose, to a post-post-modernism that will rehash the same thing once again in an even more obvious and repetitive fashion. All members of the post-modern family file in behind the hearse that leads the way to the places described by the prophet Jeremiah, the desert generated by idolatrous desire. Here is the prophet, giving his definition of mimetic desire and what it results in:

Thus says the LORD: 'Cursed is the man who trusts in man and makes flesh his arms, whose heart turns away from the LORD. He is like a shrub in the desert, and shall not see any good come. He shall dwell in the parched places of the wilderness, in an uninhabited salt land' (Jeremiah 17, 5-6).

The Skandalon

J.-M. O.: We have now returned to the Judaeo-Christian scriptures. Perhaps the moment has come to look at them in the light of psychology and desire. In our previous discussions, we talked about their powers of revelation in the context of anthropology. No doubt these powers also exist in the domain of psychology. But it should be possible to make the issue more concrete by singling out the ideas and processes in scripture that match your exposition.

R. G.: I believe that the Gospels are no less effective in dealing with psychological matters than with any others. To show that interdividual psychology is also present in the Gospels, I shall concentrate in particular on the use of the word *skandalon*, which is rarely mentioned by the commentators.

Skandalon is usually translated as 'scandal', 'obstacle', 'stumbling block', or 'snare' lying in wait. The word, with its derivative *skandalizo* ('to cause scandal') comes from the root *skadzo*, which means 'I limp'.[124] A whole group of texts in the Gospels centres on the notion of scandal, and in others it makes a significant appearance. Bring all these usages together, and you will reach a definite conclusion, even though the texts are quite heterogeneous.

In the Gospels, the *skandalon* is never a material object. It is always someone else, or it is myself to the extent that I am alienated from other people. If most translators were not so anxious to jettison the word *skandalon* for terms which they consider more intelligible, we would have a better chance of seeing that the scandal invariably involves an obsessional obstacle, raised up by mimetic desire with all its empty ambitions and ridiculous antagonisms. It is not an obstacle that just happens to be there and merely has to be got out of the way; it is the model exerting its special form of temptation, causing attraction to the extent that it is an obstacle and forming an obstacle to the extent that it can attract. The *skandalon* is the obstacle/model of mimetic rivalry; it is the model in so far as he works counter to the undertakings of the disciple and so becomes an inexhaustible source of morbid fascination. This is exactly opposite to how love in the Christian sense works:

> He who loves his brother abides in the light, and in it there is no cause for stumbling [*skandalon*]. But he who hates his brother is in

the darkness and walks in the darkness, and does not know where he is going, because the darkness has blinded his eyes (1 John 2, 10-11).

Children are particularly vulnerable to mimetic interference. The child's confident act of imitation always runs the risk of coming up against the desires of adults, in which case his models will be transformed into fascinating obstacles. As a consequence, to the extent that in his naivety he is exposed to impressions from the adult world, the child is more easily and lastingly scandalized. The adult who scandalizes the child runs the risk of imprisoning him forever within the increasingly narrow circle of the model and the mimetic obstacle, the process of mutual destruction we have so often described. This process is directly opposed to the process of opening up, of welcoming others, which is life-giving:

> 'Whoever receives one such child in my name receives me; but whoever causes one of these little ones who believe in me to [be scandalized], it would be better for him to have a great millstone fastened round his neck and to be drowned in the depth of the sea. Woe to the world for [scandals]! For it is necessary that [scandal] comes, but woe to the man by whom the [scandal] comes!
>
> And if your hand or foot [are a scandal for you], cut it off and throw it away; it is better for you to enter life maimed or lame than with two hands or two feet to be thrown into the eternal fire. And if your eye [is a scandal for you], pluck it out and throw it away; it is better for you to enter life with one eye than with two eyes to be thrown into the hell of fire' (Matthew 18, 5-9).

The millstone, which is turned by asses, is a symbol of repetition. This passage contains the very best of psychoanalysis, while avoiding the main pitfall of psychoanalysis, which is to embrace scandal: to assume that the individual being is rooted in scandal, according to an absurd and mythic thesis that presents parricidal and incestuous desire as the condition for the development of any form of consciousness.

The second part of the text that has just been quoted is a *locus classicus* for humanist indignation. Some have actually said that Christ is recommending self-mutilation in order to avoid succumbing to what can only be the 'sin of the flesh'.

People try to find the key to these texts in the Freudian castration complex and in a whole load of pretentious nonsense that does not in the least clarify the real meaning of a term like *skandalon*. What the text states, is that physical wholeness is of little account compared with the ravages scandal can bring about—a point that should be obvious to us by now.

The fact that hell and Satan are both associated with scandal is a further proof that the latter can be equated with the mimetic process as a whole. Satan is not only the prince and the principle of every worldly order, he is also the principle of all disorder—the very principle of scandal, in other words. He is always placing himself in our path as an obstacle, in the mimetic and the gospel senses of the term.

Nothing could be more illuminating, in this connection, than the denunciation of Simon Peter when he is scandalized by Christ's first announcement of his future passion:

> And Peter took him and began to rebuke him, saying, 'God forbid, Lord! This shall never happen to you.' But he turned and said to Peter, 'Get behind me, Satan! You are a hindrance to me; for you are not on the side of God, but of men' (Matthew 16, 22-23).

The Greek says *skandalon ei emou*, and the Vulgate *scandalum es mihi—You are a scandal to me*. In this passage, there is a perfect integration between the physical reality of the obstacle and its mimetic significance. From the human point of view, rather than the divine, the Passion can only be a scandal. That is why Christ thinks it necessary to give his disciples warning, in all four Gospels. He warns them a great many times, but without the slightest effect. 'I have said all this to keep you from scandal' (John 16,1).

If Jesus runs the risk of being scandalized by Peter, this is because Peter himself is in a state of scandal. Scandal is a relationship that has equally bad consequences for the person who provokes it and for the person who submits to it. Scandal is always a relationship of doubles, and the distinction between the person provoking the scandal and the person undergoing it will always tend to vanish; the passive object of scandal becomes an agent of it and contributes to its diffusion. That is why Christ says, 'woe to the man by whom scandal comes', for his responsibility can extend to many people.

There is an element of idolatry and scandal in the type of ascendancy that Jesus holds over his disciples before the Resurrection. That is why they never appreciate what the real issues are. They still credit Jesus with the worldly prestige of a great chief, a 'leader of men' or a 'master thinker'.

The disciples see Jesus as being invulnerable—they see him as master of a superior form of power. They are his followers so that they can take part in this invulnerability—so that they can become godlike according to the logic of violence. So it is inevitable that they be scandalized. The issue is raised again a little later when Jesus announces for a second time that he is going to his death and will be a cause of scandal to his friends. Once again, Peter protests: 'If everyone is scandalized because of you, I will never be.' Then Christ foretells that Peter will betray him three times—Peter will be unable to resist the new form of violent mimetic contagion that will arise when public opinion turns completely against Jesus. To imagine oneself immune to scandal is to claim the self-sufficiency of the god of violence and so to expose oneself to imminent disaster.

The fact that these words attributed to Christ name Peter as Satan can be seen as a further proof that Satan is the mimetic model and obstacle *par excellence*. All the traditional imagery associated with Satan suggests that he is the master of all mimetic tricks. In the Gospels we find two types of text: one of them, like the previous quotation, entirely 'deconstructs' Satan by equating him with the mimetic principle, and placing him 'on the side of men', whereas the other shows him playing a personal role but incorporates the same basic data. This is the case with Christ's Temptation in the Desert. In spite of the supernatural context, Satan still appears as the mimetic obstacle and model—the violent principle underlying all forms of earthly domination and all forms of idolatry, who tries to divert toward himself the adoration that is strictly due to God alone.

> Again, the devil took him to a very high mountain, and showed him all the kingdoms of the world and the glory of them; and he said to him, 'All these will I give you, if you will fall down and worship me.' Then Jesus said to him, 'Begone, Satan! for it is written,
> "You shall worship the Lord your God
> and him only shall you serve." ' (Matthew 4, 8-10)

J.-M. O.: The Gospels are written in Greek, but we have to look in the Old Testament rather than in Greek culture for the antecedents of the word *skandalon*, as with the word *Logos* and, indeed, all the central notions of the Gospels. *Skandalon* first occurs as the translation, in the Greek Septuagint Bible, of a Hebrew term meaning the same thing: 'obstacle', 'snare', 'stumbling block'.

R. G.: In the Old Testament the term can be used to refer to material obstacles, like those that could be placed in such a way as to hold up the passage of an army. In a very strange verse from Leviticus, the Jews are forbidden to put the Hebrew equivalent of a *skandalon* beneath the feet of a blind person:

> You shall not curse the deaf or put a stumbling block before the blind, but you shall fear your God: I am the Lord (Leviticus 19,14).

This sentence occurs in the middle of a series of prescriptions that govern behaviour to one's neighbour and are intended to keep people on good terms within the community. It is just before the sentence 'you shall love your neighbour as yourself' (Leviticus 19,18).

In the Pleiade edition of the Old Testament, a footnote suggests that the point about the deaf and the blind is that the faithful must not 'take advantage of the disabilities of their neighbours'. A footnote in the Jerusalem Bible offers the following commentary on the prescription about behaviour to the deaf: 'He cannot respond by cursing you in turn.'[125] In other words, he is incapable of reprisal. But oddly enough, all the surrounding prescriptions are trying to avoid anything that might give rise to reprisals and set off a process of vengeance without end:

> You shall not go up and down as a slanderer among your people, and you shall not stand forth against the life of your neighbour: I am the Lord. You shall not hate your brother in your heart, but you shall reason with your neighbour, lest you bear sin because of him. You shall not take vengeance or bear any grudge against the sons of your own people, but you shall love your neighbour as yourself (Leviticus 19, 16-18).

The text lists cases of violence against people who are capable of responding and spreading violence within the community just as much as the cases of violence against those who are unable to respond, and in particular those who are disabled in some way and so (as we have seen) find violence polarizing upon them when it searches for an outlet. This is a rejection of anything that bears any resemblance to the Greek *pharmakos* and the other rites involving *human* scapegoats. If you forbid violence against those who are capable of reprisals, then you naturally increase the probability that violent measures will be taken against those who are incapable of such action—who run a high risk, as a result, of becoming scapegoats. It is very much in the spirit of the Old Testament to detect the relationship between the two types of violence and the way in which they connect with one another, and to refuse them all together. But this refusal commits the community to the road of superhuman conduct; it means replacing all the negative and formal prescriptions, in the final analysis, with the frightening principle 'you shall love your neighbour as yourself'. The passage closes with this formula. We are back on the same territory as the Ojibwa and Tikopia myths, but there is a striking difference in how the disabled are treated![126]

The stumbling block is implicitly associated with the disabled person and with the scapegoat. And the quintessential scandal, in the Old Testament, is idolatry, which means the scapegoat given sacred status in the form of a solid and material object—the obstacle made divine. Idolatry is the quintessential stumbling block, the snare that always lies in wait for the Jewish people; it sums up everything that tends to turn the people away from the path Yahweh has prepared for them.

The paradox is an amazing one, but it can certainly be explained. God tries to free mankind from the obstacle and the tendency to sacralize the obstacle. And yet he appears as the very person who sows the obstacles and distributes snares under the feet of his faithful people. The scandal arises here from God's refusal of sacrificial worship:

Your burnt offerings are not acceptable,
nor your sacrifices pleasing to me.
Therefore thus says the Lord:
'Behold, I will lay before this people
stumbling blocks against which they shall stumble;
fathers and sons together,
neighbour and friend shall perish' (Jeremiah 6, 20-21).

There is more than enough in this passage to rouse the well-meaning apostles of contemporary humanism and provoke their heartfelt sympathy with the unfortunate Jews, who are always obsessed (so we are told) with the cruellest of all sacralized 'fathers'.

The God of the Bible is also the Rock of Ages, offering a refuge that never fails, and (for those who hold fast to idolatry) the quintessential obstacle, since he strips the idolaters of the altars that are their support and maintain the precarious equilibrium of their communities. So he appears to be the one responsible for the crisis taking place in the two kingdoms. In the eyes of the prophets, he is untying the balanced arrangements in which difference is rooted, without allowing a true solidarity to take the place of the old order; this is the true cause of the decadence and later the fall of the two kingdoms, much more so than external enemies, who finally just finish off the internal disintegration of a people that has come gradually apart on the obstacle that each person represents for the other:

> And he will become a sanctuary, and a stone of offence, and a rock of stumbling to both houses of Israel, a trap and a snare to the inhabitants of Jerusalem. And many shall stumble thereon; they shall fall and be broken; they shall be snared and taken (Isaiah 8, 14-15).

In quite a number of passages, the mode of functioning of the obstacle that fascinates, and is both human and divine, seems like that of a grinding machine, a mill that is supposed to be working under Yahweh's supervision but obviously relates to the interferences created by mimesis and the relationships between individuals.

The Prophets never completely succeed in disentangling the law that serves to separate the various potential antagonists from the principle of mimetic desire, which first gnaws away at the law and later becomes more and more conflictual as it escapes constraint. Although they are able to reveal the mimetic game with more and more clarity, they tend to involve God in every stage of the process, to see him first as the one who sets up the law and later as the one who gradually withdraws it and leads humanity into temptation, while putting forward a higher morality for their consideration. Humanity succumbs to the temptation, but cannot understand the higher morality. So the same God comes to punish humanity by 'overturning their wickedness upon themselves', which means by abandoning them to reciprocal violence.

Modern thinkers are equally incapable of recognizing the fundamentally inert and protective character of the law. This misunderstanding, together with the constant confusion between the law and the mimetic obstacle, succeed in perpetuating the Old Testament's inability to detect the strictly human character of the mimetic process and the violent escalation that derives from it.

It is the same with all the contemporary thinkers who have turned to the subject of desire. From Hegel to Freud, from Heidegger to Sartre, not to mention all the varieties of neo-Freudian, Reichian, Lacanian and Marcusian thought, and the other variants of psychopathology with their rigid forms of classification—modern thinking on desire has kept to an essentially 'Old Testament' pattern when trying to cope with the purely mimetic genesis of forms of order and disorder that correspond to the 'New Testament' notion of the *skandalon*. There are still survivals of idolatry and violence, which can be detected in the way the concepts of law, transgression and language are dealt with, as well as in the notion, which has never been completely abandoned, that Yahweh claims, 'Vengeance is mine'. As a result, all these forms of modern thought are rigid in their anti-theism; they obstinately persist in reading the gospel text from a sacrificial perspective—in other words, they still give an Old Testament reading of the New Testament. It is always the same story. No one is capable of undertaking a deconstruction of the principle of sacralized difference and taking it to its final conclusion.

It is not God who places fascinating obstacles before the feet of his faithful servants, and no law could take his place in this role, as the accepted wisdom of our culture would fondly have it. The texts from Leviticus that we have been reading are a good deal more important than those that recommend not eating kids in the milk of their mothers, and yet no one refers to them. Why is this? No doubt because they clearly demonstrate that the law is far from being an obstacle and a temptation for humankind; on the contrary, it is the first attempt to eliminate obstacles and foresee the circumstances of human violence.

It is fathers and sons, neighbours and friends, who become obstacles for one another. The Old Testament gets very close to this truth, but it does not finally make it clear; it does not really make this truth its own. Its concept of the deity therefore still contains vestiges of sacralized violence, as does the sacrificial version of Christianity. Violence is still laid at the door of the divine victim and has not yet become the responsibility of the *generation* that will hear the gospel message.

As the barriers between people start to disappear, mimetic antagonisms multiply. People become for each other the stumbling block that the Old Testament shows Yahweh placing before their feet. Modern thought becomes increasingly ridiculous in its attempt to equate this stumbling block with a law whose effectiveness is on the wane. The system that the Gospel sets before us involves the suppression of any form of scapegoat, whether from God or from the law, and the recognition that a world with fewer and fewer fixed and institutionalized barriers will afford more and more opportunities for people to be fascinating obstacles for each other—for them to be a cause of reciprocal scandal to one another.

Woe unto the world because of the scandals! It is necessary for scandals to occur, but woe unto the man by whom scandal occurs! If humanity will not transform the Kingdom of violence into the Kingdom of God without suffering or danger, then there will inevitably be scandals. The historical process is inevitable, but it is human rather than divine. Scandal always arrives through humans, and it always affects other humans: this circular process is that of doubles and of all the expressions of mimetic desire that we have been discussing over the past few days.

There is one important way of coming to terms with the close kinship between the sacrificial error, as it is perpetuated in religious exegesis, and the error involved in types of thought that attempt to escape from 'Christianity' by scapegoating the sacrificial reading after confusing it, however, with the text. (That scapegoating is, of course, just another way of perpetuating the sacrificial process.) This is by turning our attention to the way in which religious Puritanism, from Origen to our contemporaries, has given an exclusively sexual interpretation to the notion of scandal. This exclusive insistence on the sexual corresponds very closely to the tendency in psychoanalysis to read sexuality into everything; in fact, psychoanalysis is fetishizing the mimetic obstacle by interpreting it in a much too unilaterally sexual fashion. It is only the latest version of the mimetic process.

Following the notion of the obstacle throughout its historical evolution is tantamount to following the Bible's immense attempt to disengage itself from the myths of sacrifice and end up with the gospel revelation. If we fail to understand the meaning of the *skandalon* in the New Testament, this is not because of the notion itself, which is not obscure in the least, but because our own ways of thinking, unlike those of the Gospels, are still mythological and sacrificial. We fail to appreciate the purely mimetic and structural concept that the Gospels put forward because our thinking is still at a less advanced stage. We think we can dissect a stronger type of thinking using as a tool a weaker type—rather like trying to cut a diamond using a softer stone:

> Behold, I am laying in Zion for a foundation
> a stone, a tested stone,
> a precious cornerstone, of a sure foundation:
> He who believes will not be in haste.
> And I will make justice the line,
> And righteousness the plummet; (Isaiah 28, 16-17)

J.-M. O.: The traditional Christian perspective, which is always far too influenced by philosophy, always runs the risk of viewing the transition from the Old to the New Testament as one of 'idealization' and 'spiritualization'. We can easily see, by examining the *skandalon*, that the transition ought to be interpreted quite differently.

The movement from the Old to the New Testament does not dematerialize the obstacle, turning it into a metaphysical phantom. Exactly the opposite is true. In the Old Testament, the obstacle is both too much of a thing and too much of a metaphysical entity. In the Gospels, the obstacle is the other as an object of metaphysical fascination—the mimetic model and rival.

R. G.: That is why this notion of the *skandalon* is so extremely important. It is completely rooted in the Old Testament, and this fact compels us to remember the basic sacrificial structure of the interference caused by fascination—whose omission from modern thinking about desire is the essential reason for the inadequacy of that thinking. Yet the gospel notion of the *skandalon* gets rid of everything 'thing-like' and 'reified' in the Old Testament notion, as well as dispensing with its sacralized character. The *skandalon* avoids the reefs on which philosophical thought has always run aground, from the Greeks up to our own time: empiricism and positivism, on the one hand, and on the other, the tendency to subjectivize, idealize, and derealize everything.

The Gospels tell us that Christ must not be sought in false extremes and false oppositions generated by the competitive bidding of the doubles. When it arrives, the revelation will be an overwhelming one:

> So, if they say to you, 'Lo, he is in the wilderness,' do not go out; if

they say, 'Lo, he is in the inner rooms,' do not believe it. For as the lightning comes from the east and shines as far as the west, so will be the coming of the Son of man. Wherever the body is, there the eagles will be gathered together (Matthew 24, 26-28).

Even in its accepted modern meaning, which converts scandal into a mere matter of representation, the notion of the scandalous cannot be defined univocally. Scandal always implies a mutual reinforcement between desire and indignation through a process of *feedback* in the interplay of mimetic interferences. The scandalous would not be scandalous if it did not form an irresistible and impossible example, offering itself for imitation, as both model and anti-model at the same time.

This means that the implications of the scandalous are identical with the implications of a notion like Nietzsche's 'resentment' in so far as it fits the conditions of the mimetic interplay. But the *skandalon* accentuates the model/disciple relationship and *interdividual* psychology, rather than the individual psychology that in Nietzsche is still required by the (sacrificial and victimary) distinction between a 'good' desire (the 'will to power') and a 'bad' one ('resentment').[127]

The indignation caused by scandal is invariably a feverish desire to differentiate between the guilty and the innocent, to allot responsibilities, to unmask the guilty secret without fear or favour and to distribute punishment. The person who is scandalized wants to bring the affair out into the open; he has a burning desire to see the scandal in the clear light of day and pillory the guilty party. This eager and morbid curiosity is closely akin to the passion for demystification on which we previously touched. Scandal always calls for demystification, and demystification—far from putting an end to scandal propagates and universalizes it. Present-day culture is caught up in this process. There must be scandal to demystify and the demystification reinforces the scandal it claims to combat. The more passions rise, the more the difference between those on opposite sides tends to be abolished.

In fact, we have the very process of a mimetic crisis, reaching a level of unprecedented paradox. The scandal is really violence and the violent knowledge attaching to violence, which take on more explicit and bloody forms than ever before, in large-scale persecution and in large parts of the planet burdened with the most grotesque types of oppression. Yet the scandal is also often present in subtle and concealed forms, even in the language of non-violence and in the concern for those who are suffering.

If we look at the Gospels we can see that even where no mention is made of the *skandalon*, we are still dealing with the same interdividual relationships; invariably the texts condemn the game of scandal and of reciprocal demystification, with a perfect aptness:

> Judge not, that you be not judged. For with the judgement you pronounce you will be judged, and the measure you give will be the measure you get. Why do you see the speck that is in your brother's eye, but do not notice the log that is in your own eye? Or how can you say to your brother, 'Let me take the speck out of your eye,' when there is the log in your own eye? You hypocrite, first take the log out of your own eye, and then you will see clearly to take the speck out of your brother's eye (Matthew 7, 1-5).

The speck is a hasty judgement that my brother is guilty of, with regard to another person. Hypocrisy is always involved when someone thinks he can spare himself by denouncing someone else.

No mere chance places the log in the eye that is quick to spot the speck. The critic really is good at spotting that kind of thing. The speck is certainly there, but the critic fails to see that his own act of condemnation reproduces the structural features of the act deserving condemnation, in a form that is emphasized by the very inability of the perspicacious critique to see its own failings. At each level in this spiral, the person offering a judgement believes that he is exempt from the judgement that he passes. He believes himself to be invariably on the other side of an 'epistemological cut', which cannot be crossed, to be safe within a 'type of logic' or a 'metalanguage' that will shelter him from the circularity he detects so cheerfully at all the levels spiralling beneath him.

In the gospel metaphor, the speck/log series remains open; nothing comes in to interrupt the circularity of the judgement. There is no place from which truth can speak, except the one from which Christ himself speaks—that of the perfectly innocent and non-violent victim, which he alone can occupy.

In the Epistle to the Romans, another expression conveys the same idea of symmetry between doubles, with judgement constantly seeking to render account to the other but never succeeding. Here we have just the right commentary on the speck and the log:

> Therefore you have no excuse, O man, whoever you are, when you

judge another; for in passing judgement upon him you condemn
yourself, because you, the judge, are doing the very same things
(Romans 2, 1).

It is easy to see why Christ puts his disciples on guard against the *skandalon* that he himself might be, from their human point of view. He is
depriving humankind of the last sacrificial crutches and he bows out
whenever they want to substitute him for what he is depriving them of,
by making him into a chief or a legislator. He is destroying what is left
of the mythic and ritual forms that moderate scandal, but this seems to
be a mere waste of time, since he will destroy himself in the ultimate
scandal: the Cross.

What, according to Paul, *scandalizes* believers and passes for *nonsense*
in the eyes of unbelievers is the fact that the Cross can be presented as a
victory. They fail to understand what this victory could possibly consist
in. If we return to the 'parable of the vineyard' and the commentaries
that have been devoted to it, we can see that the *skandalon* figures there
in a very significant place.

The commentators have no idea why, after this parable that reveals
the founding murder, Christ presents himself as the author of this revelation and as the person who will overturn the whole order of human
culture, by occupying the position of the founding victim in a visible
and explicit way. In Luke's text, this first addition, which already
seems disconcerting and superfluous to many people, is followed by an
allusion to scandal that seems even more inappropriate and is said to be
the result of 'verbal (or metonymic) contamination'. In other words,
they say the symbolism of the corner*stone* summons up the *stone* of scandal, but this connection has no rhyme or reason. This is the passage
under discussion:

> . . . But he looked at them and said, 'What then is this that is writ-
> ten: "The very stone which the builders rejected has become the
> head of the corner"? Every one who falls on that stone will be broken
> to pieces; but when it falls on any one it will crush him.' (Luke 20,
> 17-18)

As usual, a number of commentators wring their hands about the nastiness of this passage, which supposedly does harm to the gospel
message, especially since it occurs in Luke, the most kindly of the evan-

gelists. They console themselves with the thought that the threatening phrase does not really belong in the text, but has slipped in purely as a result of verbal association.

There is more than a mere matter of words here. If by now we still fail to understand the point, we really do have eyes and see not, ears and hear not. The quintessential scandal is the fact that the founding victim has finally been revealed as such and that Christ has a role to play in this revelation. That is what the psalm quoted by Christ is telling us. The entire edifice of culture rests on the cornerstone that is the stone the builders rejected. Christ is that stone in visible form. That is why there can be no victim who is not Christ, and no one can come to the aid of a victim without coming to the aid of Christ. Mankind's failure of intelligence and belief depends upon an inability to recognize the role played by the founding victim at the most basic level of anthropology.

For proof that the connection between the cornerstone and the stone of the *skandalon* is not fortuitous, we have only to look into the Old Testament, where it is already made there, albeit in a less explicit way. The connection is also made in another New Testament text, the first Epistle of Peter:

> To you therefore who believe, he is precious, but for those who do not believe, 'The very stone which the builders rejected has become the head of the corner,' and 'A stone that will make men stumble, a rock *that will make them fall*'; for they stumble because they disobey the word, as they were destined to do (I Peter 2, 7-8; italics mine).

The Cross is the supreme scandal not because on it divine majesty succumbs to the most inglorious punishment—quite similar things are found in most religions—but because the Gospels are making a much more radical revelation. They are unveiling the founding mechanism of all worldly prestige, all forms of sacredness and all forms of cultural meaning. The workings of the Gospels are almost the same, so it would seem, as workings of all earlier religions. That is why all our thinkers concur that there is no difference between them. But in fact this resemblance is only half of the story. Another operation is taking place below the surface, and it has no precedent. It discredits and deconstructs all the gods of violence, since it reveals the true God, who has not the slightest violence in him. Since the time of the Gospels, mankind as a whole has always failed to comprehend this mystery, and it does so still. So no empty threat or gratuitous nastiness is involved in the text's saying exactly what has always been happening and what will continue to happen, despite the fact that present-day circumstances combine to make the revelation ever more plain. For us, as for those who first heard the Gospel, the stone rejected by the builders has become the permanent stumbling block. By refusing to listen to what is being said to us, we are creating a fearsome destiny for ourselves. And there is no one, except ourselves, who can be held responsible.

Christ plays this role for all who remain scandalized by the wisdom embodied in the text. His role, though understandable, is paradoxical, since he offers not the slightest hold to any form of rivalry or mimetic interference. There is no acquisitive desire in him. As a consequence, any will that is really turned toward Jesus will not meet with the slightest of obstacles. His yoke is easy and his burden is light. With him, we run no risk of getting caught up in the evil opposition between doubles.

The Gospels and the New Testament do not preach a morality of spontaneous action. They do not claim that humans must get rid of imitation; they recommend imitating the sole model who never runs the danger—if we really imitate in the way that children imitate—of being transformed into a fascinating rival:

> He who says he abides in him ought to walk in the same way in which he walked (1 John 2, 6).

On one side are the prisoners of violent imitation, which always leads to a dead end, and on the other are the adherents of non-violent imitation, who will meet with no obstacle. As we have seen, the victims of mimetic desire knock at all the doors that are firmly closed and search only where nothing is to be found. On one side is the bet that is always lost, since it seeks being where only death resides, and on the other is the road to the Kingdom, which may seem arid but in reality is the only fruitful one. In all truth, it is an easy one, since the very real barriers that await us are nothing compared with the obstacles raised up by metaphysical desire:

> Ask, and it will be given you; seek, and you will find; knock, and it will be opened to you. For every one who asks receives, and he who seeks finds, and to him who knocks it will be opened (Matthew 7, 7-8).

Following Christ means giving up mimetic desire. The outcome predicted here will come to pass. If you look carefully at the text of the Gospels, you will see that throughout runs the theme of the obstacle that is dreaded by the faithful but is removed at the last moment—when all hope seems to be lost. The most striking case is that of the women on the morning of the Resurrection. They think only of corpses, embalming and tombs. They fret about the heavy stone that seals off the tomb and will prevent them from reaching the goal of all their efforts—the dead body of Jesus. Behind the obstacles, there are only dead bodies; every obstacle is a kind of tomb. When they finally arrive, nothing that they were expecting is to be found; there is no obstacle and no dead body any more:

> And when the sabbath was past, Mary Magdalene, and Mary the mother of James, and Salome, bought spices, so that they might go and anoint him. And very early on the first day of the week they went to the tomb when the sun had risen. And they were saying to one another, 'Who will roll away the stone for us from the door of the tomb?' And looking up, they saw that the stone was rolled back—it was very large (Mark 16, 1-4).

TO CONCLUDE . . .

G. L.: You must expect people to ask: 'Where are you speaking from?' The aim of this question is to show that within language there is no privileged stance from which absolute truth can be discovered.

R. G.: I agree that no such stance exists. That is why the Word that states itself to be absolutely true never speaks except from the position of a victim in the process of being expelled. There is no human explanation for his presence among us.

If you need proof that this is no mere rhetorical formula, you only have to consider that for two thousand years this Word has been misunderstood, despite the enormous amount of publicity it has received. Today this misunderstanding is dissipating, for the major historical reasons that we have been discussing—the process takes place for all of humankind *at the same time*.

Within the exclusively ethnological context of our initial discussions, the notion of the founding victim simply appeared to be a remarkably coherent hypothesis governing the human sciences. My answer to the question 'Where are you speaking from?' would therefore be 'I do not know and I do not care. Compare your findings with mine.' But unfortunately the people who ask have no interest in concrete findings. They talk a lot about texts, but they rarely make the texts themselves talk. If we knew where we are speaking from, we would not need hypotheses; we would be on firm ground at all times. The attitude behind your question seems to me conducive to intellectual stagnation.

Within the context of the gospel revelation, the situation is obviously different. I can no longer believe that I am the first to have entertained what I just called *my* hypothesis. I could only rediscover it, within a historical process where previous attempts to systematize anthropology and desire also have a place. I can see quite clearly that everything is governed, in the final analysis, by the gospel text itself; all we are doing is to go beyond the sacrificial reading that is inevitable at the first stage, thanks to the mimetic crisis that our own history has become, and the new perspective that it opens for us.

Our own ability to detect the scapegoat mechanism is wholly determined by the detection that has already taken place within the gospel text. We have reason to think that there are still extremely important aspects we do not yet see, but these will eventually be made clear. And the detection now taking place has no need to rely on a privileged relationship to the text or even a particularly outstanding capacity for interpretation. The intermediary is history, which was indirectly set off on its course by the gospel text; thanks to the steady disintegration of sacrificial Christianity, the authentic reading of the gospel text comes more and more into prominence. Under the pressure of circumstances that we ourselves have brought about, we are being irresistibly compelled to correct the mistakes of the sacrificial reading. Because we initially refused to take seriously the text's warnings about violence, it is only logical that our improved understanding should coincide with the modern threat of a violence that knows no limits. This limitless violence appears for the first time as purely human rather than divine in origin.

All the data of fundamental anthropology as it relates to the Judaeo-Christian scriptures are from now on at humanity's disposal. All the texts to be brought into relation to one another—the texts of the Gospel, or ethnology and of history. Just one last push has to be given, and everything will tip over on to the non-sacrificial side. This final push comes as a follow-up to all the critical thought of the nineteenth and twentieth centuries.

If you want proof that we are in the same historical succession as all the people we have mentioned, you have only to observe that we treat them in the same polemical spirit and with the same unceremonious lack of fairness as they treated their predecessors. Like them, we are motivated by the worldly ambition to refute and replace the dominant modes of thought. The only advantage that we have is that we happen to be at a more advanced stage in the same historical process, which is accelerating and leading toward an increasing revelation of the truth.

J.-M. O.: You will not satisfy your interlocutors by answering the question 'Where are you speaking from?' in this way. You are taking for granted a notion of history that structuralism and the succeeding movements would not accept. All that people will see is an undercover regression to some kind of Hegelianism.

R. G.: I am afraid so. And yet this notion of history does not oblige us to modify what we have said about the hypothesis and its scientific status. Our hypothesis has this scientific status because it is not directly accessible to empirical or phenomenological intuition. The attitude to philosophy that still dominates the various methodologies of the human sciences cannot accommodate a hypothesis of this kind. Everything is still subject to the ideal of a mastery that arises immediately and intuitively, from direct contact with the data—this is perhaps one aspect of what we nowadays refer to as the 'metaphysics of presence'. Yet a discipline can only become genuinely scientific by giving up this ideal of direct, unmediated mastery and looking at the data with sufficient detachment to be able to ask whether the principle that would really enable them to be brought within a system cannot be directly observed from within that system.

The scientific spirit is, in effect, a rather crafty kind of *humilitas*, which agrees to depart from the data and to look far afield for what it has not discovered near at hand. But for the philosophical spirit, moving away from the data in this way is to abandon the only conceivable form of knowledge—the knowledge that seizes upon its object straight away, without intermediaries. A departure that rules out one kind of certainty (in fact, a deceptive one) paves the way for the only kind of *verification* in which science is interested. If the hypothesis is sufficiently removed from the data to remain separate, it will become possible to engineer confrontations that would have been impossible at an earlier stage; only these can tell us if the hypothesis holds up or not.

G. L.: In *The Savage Mind*, Lévi-Strauss makes a number of observations about scientific thought but has nothing to say about the notion of a hypothesis. He defines scientific thought in terms of the thought of the engineer.[128] In actuality, real scientific thought arises from pure research and the formulation of hypotheses, on the basis of which some applications become possible. The engineer only works on the level of application.

R. G.: When Michel Foucault criticizes the human sciences in *The Order of Things*, he relies on the notion of an *empirico-transcendental doublet*.[129] This comes down to saying that man is both the object and the subject of knowledge. Foucault is making a philosophical critique of the philosophical methodologies in the human sciences. He is using the old argument that the eye cannot observe itself, and so on. You have to pay for every *insight* with some form of *blindness*, etc. Science has no truck with this argument. It takes no account of the possibility—which though it has never yet been realized in the human sciences, is in no way unthinkable—of a hypothetical knowledge in the sense in which Darwin's thesis is hypothetical.

Obviously it is not possible to state in advance that a satisfactory hypothesis can be found, or even that it exists. If we have set out on the search, this is because the data of religion and ethnology *appear* to be accessible to systematization. No one can say that they are, *until they have effectively been systematized.*

The scientific spirit is pure expectancy. If you want proof that it is still absent in the human sciences, you have only to consider that no one, or hardly anyone, asks 'Does it work?' when discussing my hypothesis. They bring forward dogmatic and theoretical objections. For the most part, people are still prisoners of the 'metaphysics of presence'.

J.-M. O.: And yet this metaphysics will have to be overthrown, if I follow your train of reasoning, for your hypothesis to reach the stage of formulation—as indeed it is doing in this work. As long as philosophy retains its power, any form of thought based on hypothesis remains inconceivable. For the human sciences to reach the scientific stage, they must become hypothetical, and they cannot become hypothetical as long as the philosophical methodologies continue to nurture illusions.

R. G.: These illusions about the effectiveness of ready-made methodologies will disappear at the same time as the illusions of metaphysics and philosophy disappear. As I have pointed out already, I do believe that philosophy has used up its resources. In effect, this event, if it is an event, took place long ago. The crisis of philosophy is the crisis of all forms of cultural difference, but its effects have been *deferred* for a long time, and the philosophers who also speak of philosophy as being exhausted state simultaneously that no form of thought is possible outside philosophy. I believe, on the contrary, that the end of philosophy brings with it a new possibility of scientific thinking within the human domain; at the same time, however strange this may seem, it brings with it a return to religious faith. The Christian text returns in a completely new light—not at all buttressed by some existing science that would be exterior to it, but as identical with the knowledge of man that is surfacing in the world today.

The Christian text is this knowledge. But this text also explains why so far it has not been, or has been only to a limited degree. It explains that its own action has been delayed, as a result of readings of its message—readings that it foretells, as it foretells all the effects of *difference* deriving from this reading. There is no contradiction in (1) offering the scapegoat hypothesis as a scientific hypothesis and (2) stating simultaneously that this hypothesis has come to the fore in the course of a history governed by the Christian text in which the hypothesis figures in its original formulation—it was perfectly explicit at this original stage, even though it was never detected, paradoxically, by that text's innumerable readers.

G. L.: Clearly, people will say that you are getting embroiled in the most irrational kind of metaphysics. I have no doubt you will reply that your complete hypothesis is a means of clarifying not merely the texts of religious ethnology but also the text of the contemporary Western world; in particular it explains why the 'text of persecution' appears in this world, and what its consequences are.

R. G.: In modern research, everything must take second place to the findings. We should not convert into a stifling ideology a number of methodological principles that have been imposed by a particular state of knowledge and ought not form a barrier to further progress.

Today's epigonal thinkers are all the more ready to stress these methodological taboos because they belong to the rearguard of the movement that they have joined and can only conceive of any threat to it as a regression to the past, in which they are still caught up. They interpret the historical moment they have witnessed in far too absolute a way and fail to see that a new breakthrough—perhaps made possible by the one they have too single-mindedly adopted—is abruptly bringing back into the field of theory everything that their own schema seemed to have eliminated for good. To take one example, people have believed for some time (in France, at any rate) that any form of evolutionary perspective had been more or less eliminated from the human sciences by the synchronic basis of structuralism. In a few years' time, there will be no more talk about that.

For about two centuries, the only vigorous bodies of thought have been critical and destructive ones. In my view, the positive common denominator of their efforts was a struggle (though they have never taken it to a conclusion) against mythological thinking; the witness to this has been, first and foremost, what we refer to as the 'text of persecution'.[130] These bodies of thought cannot be dissociated from the dominant role played in our world by the Judaeo-Christian texts. They all point toward the revelation of the founding mechanism; they all tend unconsciously to retrieve what has already been laid down in the text and make it explicit. Again, all of this takes place through the mediating role of mimetic desire and the sacrificial impulse. These bodies of thought denounce specific forms of persecution, but they do so to the benefit of other forms, which remain unseen and continue to exist or even get worse.

It is the same with the private discourses of delirium and psychosis as it is with the discourses of politics and sociology; meaning is deconstructed, but this process is inseparable from the one of putting on show certain kinds of victim (rather than all of them) in a way that is still effectively unilateral and revengeful. The notion that the victimage process is a universal one remains hidden from view.

What marks our various forms of discourse—even those that appear the most playful and benevolent, or those that like to think of themselves as hardly significant at all—is their radically polemical character. The victims are always there, and everyone is always sharpening his weapon for use against his neighbour in a desperate attempt to win himself somewhere—even if only in an indefinite, Utopian future—a plot of innocence that he can inhabit on his own, or in the company of a regenerate human race. The paradox is strange but quite logical. Sacrifice is the stake in the struggle between doubles, with everyone accusing everyone else of giving in to it, everyone trying to settle his own account with sacrifice by a final sacrifice that would expel evil for good. 'The law and the prophets were until John; since then the good news of the kingdom of God is preached, and everyone enters it violently' (Luke 16, 16).

All of this had to happen, since humanity has no wish to give up sacrifice by common agreement, simultaneously and unanimously. But these bodies of thought have done their negative work. They have *analysed*, dismembered and devoured the sacrificial forms that were in existence, and now they have nothing to get their teeth into. Their only course is to go for one another—so from now on, they are as dead as their victims. They are just like the parasites that die for want of food on the carcasses of the animals that they have slaughtered.

This failure has finally become visible. In our world, judgements manage to come full circle and inevitably turn against their authors in the end: 'You shall not judge, O man, for when you judge another, you are doing the very same thing.' A blatant example is staring us in the face, but only the most courageous of our intellectuals have started to come to terms with it.[131] Legions of intellectuals, whole generations, have devoted themselves to exposing the (often quite genuine) complicity of their contemporaries with one form of totalitarian oppression. But they are now shown to have been in complicity with another, which constitutes the perfect 'enemy twin' of the first, so that the symmetry of *doubles* once again dominates our recent history.

This spectacle almost makes us conclude that critical thinking is never anything more than an attempt at personal justification, and that it must be given up, because it only serves to set people at each other's throats. We are running away from universality. We hope to find refuge in some sort of intellectual regionalism, and perhaps give up thought altogether.

G. L.: The failure of modernity is only prolonged and intensified by the huge wave of scepticism that has taken its place.

R. G.: People tell us that there is no language worthy of our adherence apart from the deadly equations of science, on the one hand, and on the other a form of speech that acknowledges its own futility and ascetically denies itself the universal dimension. As for the unprecedented events that we are witnessing—the grouping of the whole of mankind into a single society, which proceeds apace—there is nothing to be said, nothing definite or even relevant. None of this is of any interest at all. We must bow down before systems of the infinitely large and the infinitely small because they can prove that their power is explosive. But there is no place for any thinking on the human scale. No one takes the trouble to reflect uncompromisingly about the enigma of a historical situation that is without precedent: the death of all cultures.

Condemning humanity to nonsense and nothingness at the very moment when they have achieved the means of annihilating everything in a blink of the eye, entrusting the future of the human habitat to individuals who now have nothing to guide them but their desires and their 'death instincts'—all of this is not a reassuring prospect, and it speaks volumes about the incapacity of modern science and ideology to master the forces that they have placed in our hands.

This complete scepticism, this nihilism with regard to knowledge is often put across just as dogmatically as the various dogmatisms that preceded it. Nowadays people disclaim any certain knowledge and any authority, but with a more assured and authoritarian tone than ever before.

We are getting away from one form of Puritanism, only to fall into another. It is now a matter not of depriving mankind of sexuality, but of something we need even more—meaning. Man cannot live on bread and sexuality. Present-day thought is the worst form of castration, since it is the castration of the signified. People are always on the look-out to catch their neighbours red-handed in believing something or other. We struggled against the Puritanism of our parents only to fall into a form of Puritanism far worse than theirs—a Puritanism of meaning that kills all that it touches. This Puritanism desiccates every text and spreads the most deadening boredom even in the newest situations.

J.-M. O.: But we cannot regain contact with meaning if we rely on the fallacious base that persists from the past. The critical thinking that we have absorbed is opposed to dead meaning, and so, to an even greater extent, are the historic catastrophes of the twentieth century: the failure of ideologies, the great massacres by totalitarian states, and the uneasy peace of the present, which is founded upon the terror spread on all sides by the atom bomb. All of this means that we must abandon not only the illusions of Rousseau and Marx, but anything else of the kind that anyone could come up with.

R. G.: It is important for us to rediscover something in which we can believe; but there must be no cheating, either with the conditions that are forced upon us by the terrible world in which we live or in terms of those that dictate that the most rigorous research must do without any form of ethnocentrism, or even any form of anthropocentrism.

What kind of thought can satisfy these necessary conditions? It cannot derive from the masters of the nineteenth century: Hegel, Marx, Nietzsche and Freud. Nor can it return to Christianity as we find it today, whether in the directly sacrificial version or in the 'progressive' version, which thinks it has done away with sacrifice but remains more than ever in its thrall because it has sacrificed a large part of the text to an ideal, without noticing—irony of ironies!—that this text is the only way of attaining it. Sacrificial Christianity still believes in divine thunderbolts, while its progressive *double* completely stifles the apocalyptic dimension and so deprives itself of the most valuable card that it has in its hands, under the flimsy pretext that the first priority is to *reassure* people. It is better to say nothing, in my view, of the people who take the Judaeo-Christian scriptures to be a corpse, and attempt to slow down the process of corruption by giving it massive injections of structuralized Freudo-Marxist chloroform.

We are attempting to accept the constraints of the time in which we live. We are going further than our predecessors in our rejection of anthropocentrism, since our anthropology is rooted in the animal kingdom. We have followed through all the forms of critical thought deriving from the nineteenth and twentieth centuries, and by pushing them even further in the direction of excessive modern iconoclasm, we have come out not simply with a particular mode of the victimage principle, but with a recognition of the principle in itself—as the only truly central and universal principle. The thesis of the founding victim is the logical culmination of the great atheistic bodies of thought of the nineteenth century. It completely deconstructs the sacredness of violence, together with all its philosophical and psychoanalytic substitutes.

Within the same line of argument, the Judaeo-Christian text comes to the fore again. As long as the founding victim remains hidden from view, it appears to be more and more similar to all of the others. But then it suddenly comes to seem radically different because the revelation of the founding victim was first achieved in this text, and we have been incapable of recognizing or assimilating it, as the text itself predicted.

People who stand for a radical intertextual approach would reach exactly the same result if they followed their cherished principle to its conclusion and included ethnological texts, religious texts and texts of persecution in their analysis. They would then see clearly that everything becomes systematic in terms of the scapegoat mechanism, but that at this point a new, unique and hitherto undetected difference comes to the fore—between texts reflecting misapprehensions of the victimage principle, which are all mythic or derived from mythology, and the Judaeo-Christian scriptures, which alone bring these misapprehensions to light.

Obviously, the revelation that they bring about cannot be dissociated from the dynamic, anti-sacrificial current running all through the Judaeo-Christian scriptures. We were able to detect a series of stages in the Bible that invariably pointed toward the attenuation and later elimination of the practice of sacrifice. Sacrifice must therefore appear in the light in which the great biblical thinker, Moses Maimonides, placed it in his youth: not as an eternal institution that God genuinely wished to found, but as a temporary crutch made necessary by the weakness of humankind. Sacrifice is an imperfect means, which humanity must do without.[132]

This remarkable thesis is just one testimony among many of the non-sacrificial inspiration that has always been preserved in medieval and modern Judaism. I am bound to mention at this point a Talmudic principle that is often quoted by commentators drawing inspiration from Judaism, like Emmanuel Levinas and André Neher, and is always described as 'well-known'. According to this principle, any accused person whose judges combine unanimity against him ought to be released straight away. Unanimity in accusation is in itself a cause for suspicion! It suggests that the accused is innocent.[133]

As a result of our analysis, not only the Old Testament but all the religions of mankind appear as intermediate stages between animal life and the crisis of the present day, when we must place our bets either on the total disappearance of the human race or on our arriving at forms of freedom and awareness that we can hardly imagine, swaddled as we are in myths that now have become, paradoxically, myths of demystification. We think we can bring these myths to a positive conclusion through our own means, but they are actually leading us straight to destruction, now that there are no more Others to demystify, now that naive confidence in science and humanism have given way to the terrifying presence of a violence that is completely unmasked.

From the perspective of humanity, there is thus a continuity between past and present experience. Every great crisis has always been a matter of driving violence out of the community, but the religions and humanisms of former times have never made it possible for violence to be expelled without claiming its own share—at the expense of the victim, of the human element that remains outside of all human societies. Today we can envisage something that is both very similar and very different. It is still a matter of rejecting violence and reconciling people with one another, but now there is no violence and no 'outside'. That is why the continuity between all religions, from a human perspective, in no way obviates the fact that there is no contact, no complicity and no compatibility whatsoever between the Logos that has now been finally superseded—the Logos of sacrificial violence—and the Logos that is itself always sacrificed and increases its pressure on us from day to day.

That is the most remarkable thing about it, so it seems to me. On the one hand, there is a complete cleavage, and on the other there is a continuity which is capable of reconciling us with the past of all humankind —not to mention the present, the site of our own culture, which does not deserve either the excessive praise once heaped upon it or the bitter condemnation directed against it today. Surely it is extraordinary that the most radical perspective on our cultural history should finally turn out to be the only tolerant and favourable one—the one that is as far removed as possible from the absurd scorched earth policy Western intellectuals have practised for more than a century? I see this as being the height of good fortune and, in a sense, the height of humour as well.

Traditional Christian thinkers could proclaim the cleavage between Christianity and everything else, but they were incapable of demonstrating it. Anti-Christian thinkers can note the continuity but they are unable to come to terms with its true nature. Among our contemporaries, only Paul Ricoeur, particularly in his fine work *La Symbolique du mal*, is willing to argue with determination that both positions are necessary.

The non-sacrificial reading of the Judaeo-Christian scriptures and the thinking that takes the scapegoat as its basis are capable of coming to terms with the apocalyptic dimension of present times without relapsing into frightened hysteria about the 'end of the world'. They make us see that the present crisis is not an absurd dead-end into which we have been pitched by a scientific error in calculation. Interpreting the present in this way is not an attempt to force outdated meanings on mankind's new situation, nor is it a desperate attempt to stop new meanings from coming across; there is simply no need for frivolous expedients of this kind. We have carved out such a strange destiny for ourselves so that we can bring to light both what has always determined human culture and what is now the only path open to us—one that reconciles without excluding anyone and no longer has any dealings with violence.

In the light of the non-sacrificial reading, the crisis of the present day does not become in any way less threatening. But it does take on some hope for the future—which means a genuinely human significance. A new kind of humanity is in the process of gestation; it will be both very similar to and very different from the one featured in the dreams of our Utopian thinkers, now in their very last stages. We are now absolutely unable to understand and for a long time we shall still understand only very inadequately, the basis of mankind's suffering and the way of setting mankind free. But we can already see that there is no point in condemning one another or maligning our past.

J.-M. O.: What strikes me particularly is the way in which the mimetic and victimary hypothesis always ends up by rejecting the twin forms of extremism; its own radicalism frees it from the false oppositions present-day thinking cannot slough off. Where desire is concerned—to take one example—it liberates us from the mystic terror, the purely maleficent form of sacralization, that dominated centuries of Puritanism and was then followed by a beneficent sacralization, first in Surrealism and a certain direction of Freudianism, and in our own day with a whole host of epigonal movements so devoid of real creativity that they seem more pathetic than dangerously misleading.

R. G.: What is important above all is to realize that there are no *recipes*; there is no *pharmakon* any more, not even a Marxist or a psychoanalytic one. Recipes are not what we need, nor do we need to be reassured—our need is to escape from meaninglessness. However large a part of 'sound and fury signifying nothing' there may be in public and private suffering, in the anguish of mental patients, in the deprivations of the poor and in the rivalries of politics, these things are not lacking in significance, if only because at each moment they are open to the ironic reversal of the judgement against the judge that recalls the implacable functioning of the gospel law in our world. We must learn to love this justice, which we both carry out and fall victim to. The peace that passes human understanding can only arise on the other side of this passion for 'justice and judgement', which still possesses us but which we are less and less likely to confuse with the totality of being.

I hold that truth is not an empty word, or a mere 'effect' as people say nowadays. I hold that everything capable of diverting us from madness and death, from now on, is inextricably linked with this truth. But I do not know how to speak about these matters. I can only approach texts and institutions, and relating them to one another seems to me to throw light in every direction. I am not embarrassed to admit that an ethical and religious dimension exists for me, but it is the result of my thinking rather than an external preconception that determined my research. I have always believed that if I managed to communicate what some of my reading meant to me, the conclusions I was forced to reach would force themselves on other people as well.

I began to breathe more freely when I discovered that literary and ethnological critiques are inadequate—even if they are not totally worthless—when confronted with the literary and cultural texts they claim to dominate. This was before I came to the Judaeo-Christian scriptures. I never even imagined that those texts were there for the purpose of passive enjoyment, in the same way as we look at a beautiful landscape. I always cherished the hope that meaning and life were one. Present-day thought is leading us in the direction of the valley of death, and it is cataloguing the dry bones one by one. All of us are in this valley but it is up to us to resuscitate meaning by relating all the texts to one another without exception, rather than stopping at just a few of them. All issues of 'psychological health' seem to me to take second place to a much greater issue—that of meaning which is being lost or threatened on all sides but simply awaits the breath of the Spirit to be reborn. Now all that is needed is this breath to recreate stage by stage Ezekiel's experience in the valley of the dead:

The hand of the Lord was upon me, and he brought me out by the Spirit of the Lord, and set me down in the midst of the valley; it was full of bones. And he led me round among them; and behold, there were very many upon the valley; and lo, they were very dry. And he said to me, 'Son of man, can these bones live?' And I answered, 'O Lord God, thou knowest.' Again he said to me, 'Prophesy to these bones, and say to them, O dry bones, hear the word of the Lord. Thus says the Lord God to these bones: Behold, I will cause breath to enter you, and you shall live. And I will lay sinews upon you, and will cause flesh to come upon you, and cover you with skin, and put breath in you, and you shall live; and you shall know that I am the Lord.'

So I prophesied as I was commanded; and as I prophesied, there was a noise, and behold, a rattling; and the bones came together, bone to its bone. And as I looked, there were sinews on them, and flesh had come upon them, and skin had covered them; but there was no breath in them. Then he said to me, 'Prophesy to the breath, prophesy, son of man, and say to the breath, Thus says the Lord God: Come from the four winds, O breath, and breathe upon these slain, that they may live.' So I prophesied as he commanded me, and the breath came into them, and they lived, and stood upon their feet, an exceedingly great host (Ezekiel 37, 1-10).

NOTES

Book I

1. On the uselessness of general theories, see Georges Dumézil's preface to Mircea Eliade, *Traité d'histoire des religions*, pp. 5-9. Analogous observations are also quite frequent in the work of Claude Lévi-Strauss, E. E. Evans-Pritchard and others.
2. *Les Lois de l'imitation*.
3. The potlatch is 'the system of gift exchange in northwest America'. Marcel Mauss, *The Gift*, trans. Ian Cunnison, London: Cohen & West, 1970.
4. *Violence and the Sacred*, pp. 11-28.
5. Ibid., pp. 56-67.
6. For the relation of doubles, see 'Acquisitive Mimesis and Mimetic Desire', p. 283.
7. Philippe Lacoue-Labarthe, 'Typographie,' in *Mimesis*, pp. 231-250. On the irreducible incoherence of mimesis in Plato, see note 8 of 'The Double Session' in Jacques Derrida, *Dissemination*, pp. 186-187.
8. Thomas Rymer, 'Against Othello', in Frank Kermode, ed., *Four Centuries of Shakespearean Criticism*, pp. 461-469. On Cervantes, see Cesareo Bandera, *Mimesis conflíctiva*.
9. Claude Lévi-Strauss, *L'Homme nu*, pp. 559-621.
10. Pierre Manent, *Contrepoint* 14, 1974, p. 169: 'Once the murder is accomplished, there is no reason that violence should not begin again *immediately*. Human beings can only become acquainted with peace through their familiarity with a common world: René Girard's theory isolates human beings after the murder: there is simply one less among them. Human beings cannot know peace unless something exists outside of them that by virtue of its greatness and transcendence has the right to demand their obedience and the ability to appeal to their desire.' The quote sums up a common misunderstanding of the founding murder, which here is thought of as an *idea* rather than as the only *mechanism* capable of structuring, for all its cultural descendants, a common world and a 'transcendence' thought to 'require their obedience'.
11. Leviticus 16, 5-10.
12. Claude Lévi-Strauss, *L'Homme nu*, pp. 600-610.
13. See Book I, Chap. 4.
14. *Les Formes élémentaires de la vie religieuse*, pp. 49-58.

15. pp. 104-116, 302-306.
16. *The Golden Bough*, pp. 662-664.
17. Luc de Heusch, *Essai sur le symbolisme de l'inceste royal en Afrique*, pp. 61-62.
18. Claude Lévi-Strauss, *L'Homme nu*, pp. 600-610.
19. Lacoue-Labarthe, *Mimesis*.
20. *Gesammelte Werke* XVI, p. 195.
21. E.E. Evans-Pritchard, 'The Divine Kingship of the Shilluk of the Nilotic Sudan', *Social Anthropology and other Essays*, p. 205.
22. pp. 119-125, 281-284.
23. N. G. Munro, *Ainu Creed and Cult*; Carleton S. Coon, *The Hunting People*, pp. 340-344.
24. Alfred Métraux, 'L'Anthropophagie rituelle des Tupinamba', *Religions et magies indiennes d'Amérique du Sud*, pp. 45-78, *Violence and the Sacred*, pp. 274-280.
25. On hunting and hominization, see Serge Moscovici, *La Société contre nature*.
26. p. 32.
27. *Totem und Taboo, Gesammelte Werke* IX, pp. 5-25.
28. Lévi-Strauss is perfectly aware that the exchange of women does not differ from the exchange of alimentary and other goods, but then he considers all these 'objects' as if they were commodities in the modern sense. As always, he eliminates or minimizes the role of religion in the genesis of human institutions.
29. A. M. Hocart, *Kings and Councillors*, pp. 262ff.
30. See 'The "Radical" Elimination', p. 105.
31. *Sociologie et anthropologie*, p. 152ff.
32. Francis Huxley, *Affable Savages*, p. 242.
33. See 'The Metaphor of the Tomb', p. 163.
34. For a recent overview of these topics, the reader might consult the essays gathered in the volume *L'Unité de l'homme*, as well as the very lively work by Edgar Morin, *Le Paradigme perdu: la nature humaine*. Both works contain bibliographic references.
35. 'Tools and Human Evolution', *Culture and the Evolution of Man*, pp. 13-19.
36. '*Ecology and the Protohominids*', *Culture and the Evolution of Man*, p. 29.
37. Weston La Barre, *The Human Animal*, p. 104.
38. Edgar Morin, *Le Paradigme perdu*, p. 213ff.
39. pp. 154-155.
40. Konrad Lorenz, *Das sogenannte Böse: Zur Naturgeschichte der Aggression*, Chap. 11.
41. pp. 34; 58-59.
42. pp. 18-28. In *Totemism*, the analysis of myths is determined by the principal purpose of the book, which is to discredit the notion of 'totemism'. However it no less typical of Lévi-Strauss's method, as is shown by the very similar analyses in *Mythologiques*, particularly in those I have chosen

for my own analysis. Lévi-Strauss himself links the Ojibwa and Tikopia myths; in each case he comes to the same conclusion (*The Raw and the Cooked*, pp. 50-55).

43. p. 230.
44. *Totemism*, p. 26; *The Raw and the Cooked*, p. 52; p. 53.
45. See 'Sexual Prohibitions and the Principle of Exchange', p. 73.
46. In the original edition, an extract from Theodor Koch-Grünberg, *Zwei Jahren unter den Indianen. . .*, pp. 292-293 appeared here.
47. C. Maloney, ed., *The Evil Eye, passim.*
48. *The Raw and the Cooked*, p. 53.
49. *Dictionnaire Littré*, 'émissaire'.
50. 'La Structure mythico-théâtrale de la royauté japonaise,' *Esprit*, February 1973, pp. 315-342.

Book II

51. pp. 19-22, 86; 475-476; 492-495. Obviously Max Weber's theses must be compared with that of Nietzsche in *The Anti-Christ* and elsewhere.
52. 54-72. Criticism of the cult of sacrifice by pre-exilic prophets is played down by the majority of commentators, whether they are religious or irreligious by persuasion, Jewish or Christian, Protestant or Catholic. People attempt to show that the prophets are only opposed to a 'cultural syncretism' which they believe to be unorthodox and that their principal aim is to centralize worship at Jerusalem. But in fact the texts are too many in number and too explicit for there to be any room for doubt. See for example: Isaiah 1, 11-16; Jeremiah 6, 20; Hosea 5, 6; 6, 6; 9, 11-13; Amos 5, 21-25; Micah 6, 7-8.

To combat sacrifices, these prophets have recourse to historical arguments. They draw a distinction between the profuse sacrifices of their own decadent times and the ideal period for the relationship between Yahweh and his people, which was that of the life in the desert when the absence of livestock made sacrifices impossible. And the deep-seated reason for their refusal comes to the surface in the link between animal sacrifice and the sacrifice of children, in Micah, for example—he perceives behind the increasing practice of sacrifice an escalation which, in the final analysis, always involves reciprocal violence and mimetic desire:

> With what shall I come before the Lord,
> and bow myself before God on high?
> Shall I come before him with burnt offerings,
> with calves a year old?
> Will the Lord be pleased with thousands of rams,
> with ten thousands of rivers of oil?
> Shall I give my first-born for my transgression,
> the fruit of my body for the sin of my soul?

> He has showed you, O man, what is good;
> and what does the Lord require of you
> but to do justice, and to love kindness,
> and to walk humbly with your God? (Micah 6, 6-8).

The prophet contrasts the grotesque and threatening escalation of burnt offerings with the quintessence of the law, which is love of one's neighbour.

If Ezekiel takes a sacrificial position, once again, this is because in his period sacrifices quite clearly had nothing more than a ceremonial and archaeological value. The mimetic crisis stays 'sacrificial' in the broader sense; but it is no longer sacrificial in the strict sense, it is no longer directly centred on the question of sacrificial rites properly speaking.

53. 'Der Erstgeborene Satans und der Vater des Teufels', *Apophoreta*, 70-84.
54. See 'Death and Funeral Rights', p. 80.
55. P. Wendland, 'Jesus als Saturnalien-König', *Hermes* XXXIII, 175-179.
56. Frazer, *The Golden Bough*, Pt VI (*The Scapegoat*) pp. 413-414.
57. The Acts of the Apostles, 69 (Anchor Bible).
58. Ephesians I, 170-183 (Anchor Bible).
59. Jean Daniélou, *Origène*, p. 265.
60. *The Quest of the Historical Jesus*, pp. 330-403 and *passim*.
61. p. 69.
62. *Eros et Agape*.
63. p. 55.
64. *Theology of Culture*, p. 66.
65. On the subject of collective violence in the Psalms and the other books of the Bible, see the excellent analyses by Raymund Schwager in a work entitled *Jesus, der Sohn Gottes als Sündenbock der Welt*.
66. In some patristic writings we can find resistance to the sacrificial reading. Here for example is a characteristic passage from Gregory Nazianzus:

> Why would the blood of his only Son be agreeable to the Father who did not wish to accept Isaac offered as a burnt offering by Abraham, but replaced that human sacrifice by that of a ram? Is it not obvious that the Father accepts the sacrifice not because he insists upon it or has some need for it, but to carry out his plan: it was necessary for man to be sanctified by the humanity of God, it was necessary for he himself to free us by triumphing over the tyrant through his force, and for him to call us back to him through his Son. . . Let us pass over the rest in reverent silence.

Quoted by Olivier Clément, 'Dionysus et le ressuscité', *Évangile et révolution*, p. 93. Original text in *Patrologiae Graecae* XXXVI, Oratio XLV, 22, 654.

In the article on 'sacrifice', the *Dictionnaire de théologie catholique* by Vacant and Mangenot recognizes that the gospel text, as regards sacrifice 'is very sober . . . the word sacrifice is not pronounced there.' Nonetheless the author comes down in favour of sacrifice on the strength of Christ's 'total gift of himself'. The total gift of oneself is precisely what has to be interpreted in a non-sacrificial light. Or if you absolutely must have the word 'sacrifice', then you must do without it in the case of all forms of sacrifice except the Passion, which is clearly impossible.

67. p. 131.

68. *La Source grecque*, pp. 57-64 and *passim* in several of her other works.

69. Our present concern is to point out that people are basically unresponsive to the gospel text as a revelation of the scapegoat mechanism; and this unresponsiveness is shared by the semiotic method and all the other methods of analysis. In this connection, the second part (entitled 'Sémiotique du traître') pp. 97-199, in Louis Marin's work, *Sémiotique de la passion*, acquires a special importance. The present remarks are also influenced by my conversations with Gérard Bucher of the University of New York at Buffalo. The fact that they are restricted to their principal objective makes them neglect not only the positive aspects of the work specifically in question, but also implicitly a number of other essays which claim to use the same method or similar methods. The author would like to emphasize that these aspects have not passed him by. He is responsive to the effects of rigour and the general establishment of order produced by these methods, as well as to the remarkable insights of the researchers who make use of them, always in a very personal fashion.

This goes not only for *Sémiotique de la passion* but also for *Le Récit évangélique* by Claude Chabrol and Louis Marin. There is also a great deal of value in the essays collected together in *Analyse structurale et exégèse biblique*, particularly in two fine studies, one by Roland Barthes, 'La Lutte avec l'ange', pp. 27-39, and one by Jean Starobinski, 'Le Démoniaque de Gerasa', pp. 63-94. [R.G.]

70. Vladimir Propp, *Morphology of the Folktale*.

71. Joseph Klausner, *Jesus of Nazareth*.

72. On the question raised here, there is a great deal of material from the technical, political and sociological angles. But philosophical and religious interpretations are almost non-existent. There are certainly a great many allusions but they usually come down to a few sentences trotted out in a banal way. The works which must be read are those by Hannah Arendt and also Karl Jaspers, *La Bombe atomique et l'avenir de l'homme*. Above all, see Michel Serres, *La Traduction*, pp. 73-104.

73. *Foi et compréhension*. See especially the essay on 'Histoire et eschatologie dans le Nouveau Testament', pp. 122-127. On the same problems seen from an angle which is often very different, see the essays collected in *Herméneutique et eschatologie*, ed. Enrico Castelli. See also Joseph Pieper, *La Fin des temps*.

74. On all these themes, it is important to look at what Jean-Marie Domenach says in *Le Retour du tragique*.

75. Jean Brun, *Le Retour de Dionysos*.

76. Martin Heidegger, *Introduction to Metaphysics*, p. 127.

77. Ibid., p. 134.
78. Ibid., pp. 123-135; 'Logos', *Essais et conférences*, pp. 249-278.
79. *From Stone Age to Christianity*, p. 371.
80. Raymond Brown, *The Gospel According to John*, I,4 (Anchor Bible).
81. Henri de Lubac, *Exégèse médiévale*; Paul Claudel, *Introduction au livre de Ruth*, pp. 19-121. See also the outstanding essay by Erich Auerbach, 'Figura', *Scenes of European Literature*, pp. 11-76.
82. *Eros et Agape*.
83. p. 133.

Book III

84. Gregory Bateson, 'Toward a Theory of Schizophrenia', in *Steps to an Ecology of Mind*, pp. 201-227. See also the other articles in this work, particularly 'Minimal Requirements for a Theory of Schizophrenia', pp. 244-270, and 'Double Bind, 1969', pp. 271-278.
85. *Naven*, pp. 175-197.
86. Paul Watzlawick *et al.*, *Pragmatics of Human Communication*, pp. 73-230.
   Anthony Wilden makes an interesting attempt at comparing communication theory with the work of the French structuralist school, in particular Jacques Lacan, showing where they diverge and where they might be reconciled with one another; most of these essays are brought together in his *System and Structure*.
87. This is why Lévi-Strauss has been right up to this point to claim that a scientific approach, in anthropology, would be unable to take account of desire.
88. *Within a Budding Grove, Remembrance of Things Past* I, p. 846.
89. Émile Benveniste, *Le Vocabulaire des institutions indo-européennes*, II, pp. 57-69; *Violence and the Sacred*, pp. 152-154.
90. *Le Paradigme perdu*, pp. 109-127.
91. *The Devils of Loudun*.
92. Among the numerous works of Charles Pidoux, see in particular: *Les États de possession rituelle chez les mélano-africains*, L'Evolution psychiatrique, 1955, 11, pp. 271-283.
93. It is well worth consulting Henri F. Ellenberger's masterly work, *The Discovery of the Unconscious*, New York: Basic Books, 1970; also Dominique Barrucand's interesting study, *Histoire de l'hypnose en France*, PUF, 1967.
94. Pierre Janet, *Névroses et idées fixes*, pp. 427-429.
95. See on this issue Claude M. Prévost's excellent study, *Janet, Freud et la Psychologie clinique*, Payot, 1973.
96. Henri Faure's first work on this subject is summed up in his book: *Cure de sommeil collective et psychothérapie de groupe*, Masson, 1958. Since then there has been a great deal of research done under his supervision in the Bonneval psychiatry centre for children and juveniles, but this has not yet been published.

97. I.M. Lewis, *Ecstatic Religion*, pp. 73-75. Michel Leiris, *La Possession et ses aspects théâtraux chez les Éthiopiens de Gondar*. It is also important to consult Chapter VIII of *Psychologie collective et analyse du moi* on the relationship between the passion of love and hypnosis: 'Veriebtheit und Hypnose', in Freud's *Gesammelte Werke* XIII, pp. 122-128. Freud's first writings on hypnosis are collected together in Vol.I of the *Standard Edition*.

98. R.A. Hinde, 'La Ritualisation et la communication sociale chez les singes Rhésus'. *Le Comportement rituel chez l'homme et l'animal*, p. 69; Konrad Lorenz, *On Aggression*, pp. 130-131.

99. Mircea Eliade, *Rites and Symbols of Initiation*, pp. 68-72.

100. 'Dostojewski und die Vatertötung', *Gesammelte Werke* XIV, pp. 397-418.

101. *Gesammelte Werke* XIV, pp. 407-408.

102. *Deceit, Desire and the Novel*.

103. *Oeuvres* II, p. 810.

104. *Gesammelte Werke* X, 154. *Standard Edition* XIV, p. 88.

105. *Gesammelte Werke* XIII, 75-161 (*Massenpsychologie und Ich-Analyse*); pp. 237-289 (*Das Ich und das Es*): *Violence and the Sacred*, pp. 169-192.

106. Gilles Deleuze and Félix Guattari, *Anti-Oedipus*.

107. *Gesammelte Werke* X, p. 154.

108. *Gesammelte Werke* X, pp. 155-156. Standard Edition XIV., p. 89.

109. Sigmund Freud and Lou Andreas-Salomé, *Briefwechsel*; Paul Roazen, in his *Brother Animal, The Story of Freud and Tausk*, opens the way to a more complete investigation of the interdividual relationships within Freud's circle. There are many suggestive remarks about these relationships in Marthe Robert, *La Révolution psychanalytique*. On the subject of narcissism, the contributions of André Green, Guy Rosolato, Hubert Damisch and many others to *Narcisses* (*Nouvelle revue de psychanalyse 13*) seem to me to be full of insights, which are often very striking. But they come within a framework which we are in the process of criticizing. See also François Roustang, *Un destin si funeste*.

110. *Gesammelte Werke* XII.

111. *Within a Budding Grove, Remembrance of Things Past* I, pp. 845-856.

112. R. Girard, 'Perilous Balance: A Comic Hypothesis'. On the elements of 'sacrificial revelation' in the thinking of Baudelaire, see: Pierre Pachet, *Le Premier Venu*.

113. Gallimard, 1952, 3 vols.

114. *Gesammelte Werke* XIV, pp. 415, 418.

115. *Swann's Way, Remembrance of Things Past* I, pp. 72-73, 129-145.

116. *Deceit, Desire and the Novel*, pp. 45-46.

117. *Jean Santeuil* III, pp. 66-73.

118. Jacques Lacan, *Ecrits*.

119. *Gesammelte Werke* XIII, 14. *Standard Edition* XVIII, 16.

120. *Beyond the Pleasure Principle*, 15-16; *Gesammelte Werke* XIII, 20-21.

121. See 'How do you reproduce a Triangle?', p. 356.

122. Michel Serres, *La Traduction*, pp. 73-104.
123. See 'The Metaphors of Desire', p. 382.
124. Francisco Zorell, *Lexicon Graecum Novi Testamenti*, pp. 1206-1207.
125. *Ancien Testament* (Pleiade Edition), I, p. 348; *Bible de Jérusalem* (French edition), p. 125.
126. See Book I, Chapter 4.
127. R. Girard, 'Superman in the Underground', *MLN*, December 1976, pp. 1169-1185.

To conclude

128. *The Savage Mind*,
129. pp. 305-9.
130. See 'The Double Semantic Sense of the Word "Scapegoat" ', p. 130.
131. André Glucksmann, *Les Maîtres penseurs*; Bernard-Henri Levy, *La Barbarie à visage humain*.
132. *The Guide of the Perplexed*, XXXII, pp. 322-327.
133. Even more remarkable, it should be stressed, is 'the well-known Talmudic apophthegm', also quoted by Emmanuel Levinas in *Difficile Liberté*, p. 119: 'The day that people speak the truth once again without concealing the name of the person who spoke it for the first time, the Messiah will come.'

BIBLIOGRAPHY

Albright William Foxwell, *From the Stone Age to Christianity*, New York: Doubleday, 1957.

Arendt Hannah, *The Origins of Totalitarianism*, New York: Harcourt, 1966.

—*On Violence*, New York: Harcourt, 1970.

Auerbach Eric, *Scenes from the Drama of European Literature*, New York: Meridian Books, 1959.

Balandier Georges, *Anthropologie politique*, Presses universitaires de France, 1967.

—*Sens et Puissance*, Presses universitaires de France, 1971.

Bandera Cesareo, *Mimesis conflictiva*, Madrid: Gredos, 1975.

Barth Karl, *Das Wort Gottes und die Theologie*, Munich: Kaiser, 1925.

Barth Markus, *Ephesians*, Anchor Bible, New York: Doubleday, 1974, 2 vols.

Barthes Roland, 'La Lutte avec l'ange', *Analyse structurale et exégèse biblique*, Neuchâtel: Delachaux et Niestlé, 1971.

Bartholomew Jr., George A., and Joseph Birdsell, 'Ecology and the Proto-hominids', *Culture and the Evolution of Man*, New York: Oxford University Press, 1962.

Bateson Gregory, *Steps to an Ecology of Mind*, New York: Ballantine Books, 1972.

—*Naven*, Stanford University Press, 1972.

Benveniste Émile, *Le Vocabulaire des institutions indo-européennes*, Minuit, 1969, 2 vols.

Bernheim Hippolyte, *Hypnotisme et suggestion*, Doin, 1910.

Brown Raymond, *The Gospel according to John*, Anchor Bible, New York: Doubleday, 1966-1970. 2 vols.

Brun Jean, *Le Retour de Dionysos*, Desclée, 1969.

Bultmann Rudolf, *Foi et Compréhension*, Seuil, 1969.

—*Primitive Christianity*, New York: Meridian Books, 1956.

Burkert Walter, *Homo Necans: Interpretationen altgriechischen Opferriten und Mythen*, Berlin, New York: De Gruyter, 1972.

Caillois Roger, *L'Homme et le Sacré*, Gallimard, 1950.

—*Les Jeux et les Hommes*, Gallimard, 1958.

—*La Dissymétrie*, Gallimard, 1973.

Camus Albert, *La Chute*, Gallimard, 1956.

Caplow Theodore, *Two against One, Coalitions in Triads*, Englewood Cliffs, New Jersey: Prentice-Hall, 1968.

Castelli Enrico, ed. *Herméneutique et eschatologie*, Aubier, 1971.

Chabrol Claude and Louis Marin, *Le Récit évangélique*, Aubier, 1974.

Charcot J.-M., *Leçons du Mardi à la Salpêtrière*, Progrès médical, 1892.

Claudel Paul, 'Du sens figuré de l'Écriture', *Introduction au livre de Ruth*, Gallimard, 1952.

Clément Olivier, 'Dionysos et le ressuscité', *Évangile et Révolution*, Centurion, 1968.

Coon Carleton S., *The Hunting People*, Boston: Little, Brown, 1971.

Cullmann Oscar, *Christologie du Nouveau Testament*, Neuchâtel: Delachaux et Niestlé, 1968.

Dahl N.A., 'Der Erstgeborene Satans und der Vater des Teufels', *Apophoreta* (Maenchen Festschrift), Berlin: Töpelmann, 1964.

Damisch Hubert, "D'un Narcisse à l'autre", *Nouvelle revue de psychanalyse 13*, Gallimard, 1976.

Daniélou Jean, *Origène*, Table ronde, 1948.

Darwin Charles, *The Origin of Species*, Sixth Edition, London: John Murray, 1888.

—*The Expression of the Emotions in Man and Animals*, The University of Chicago Press, 1965.

Deleuze Gilles and Félix Guattari, *L'Anti-Œdipe*, Minuit, 1972; Athlone Press, 1984.

Derrida Jacques, *Dissemination*, trans. Barbara Johnson, London: Athlone, 1981.

Dodd C.H., *The Interpretation of the Fourth Gospel*, Cambridge University Press, 1953.

Dols Michael W., *The Black Death in the Middle East*, Princeton University Press, 1977.

Domenach Jean-Marie, *Le Retour du tragique*, Seuil, 1967.

—*Le Sauvage et l'Ordinateur*, Seuil, 1976.

Dostoyevski Fiodor, *L'Eternel Mari*, in *l'Adolescent*, French trans. Boris de Schloezer, Gallimard, Bibliothèque de la Pléiade, 1956.

Douglas Mary, *Purity and Danger*, Penguin Books, 1970.

Durkheim Émile, *Les Formes élémentaires de la vie religieuse*, Presses universitaires de France, 1968.

Eliade Mircea, *Rites and Symbols of Initiation*, New York: Harper, 1965.

—*Traité d'histoire des religions*, Payot, 1970.

Evans-Pritchard E. E., *Social Anthropology and Other Essays*, New York: Free Press, 1964.

—*Theories of Primitive Religion*, New York: Oxford Press, 1965.

Faure Henri, *Hallucinations et Réalité perceptive*, P.U.F., 1969.

—*Les Appartenances du délirant*, P.U.F., 1966.

Firth Raymond, *We, the Tikopia*, Allen & Unwin; Beacon Press, 1936.

—*Tikopia Ritual and Belief*, Allen & Unwin; Beacon Press, 1967.

Flaubert Gustave, *Œuvres*, Gallimard, Bibliothèque de la Pléiade, 1952; 2 vols.

Foucault Michel, *The Order of Things*, trans. Alan Sheridan, London: Tavistock, 1970.

Frazer James George, *The Golden Bough*, London: Macmillan, 1911-1915; 12 vols. Pagination in the notes follows *The Golden Bough*, one-vol. edition, New York: Macmillan, 1963.

—*Folklore in the Old Testament*, New York: Hart, 1975.

Freud Sigmund, *Gesammelte Werke*, London: Imago, 1940-1952. 17 vols.

—*The Standard Edition of the Complete Psychological Works*, ed. and trans. by James Strachey, London: Hogarth, 1953-1966. 24 vols.

—*Essais de psychanalyse*, trans. S. Jankélévitch. Payot, 1963.

Freud Sigmund and Lou Andreas-Salomé, *Briefwechsel*, Frankfurt: Fischer, 1966.

Girard René, *Deceit, Desire and the Novel*, trans. Yvonne Freccero, Baltimore: Johns Hopkins Press, 1965.

—*Critique dans un souterrain*, Lausanne: L'Age d'homme, 1976.

—*Violence and the Sacred*, trans. Patrick Gregory, Baltimore: Johns Hopkins Press, 1977.

—'Myth and Ritual in A Midsummer Night's Dream', *The Harry F. Camp Memorial Lecture*, Stanford University, 1972.

—'Perilous Balance: a Comic Hypothesis', *MLN*, 1972, 811-826.

—'Vers une définition systématique du sacré', *Liberté*, Montréal, 1973, 58-74.

—'Discussion avec René Girard', *Esprit* 429: novembre 1973, 528-563.

—'The Plague in Literature and Myth', *Texas Studies XV* (5), 1974, 833-850.

—'Les Malédictions contre les Pharisiens et l'interprétation évangélique', *Bulletin du centre protestant d'études*, Geneva, 1975.

—'Differentiation and Undifferentiation in Lévi-Strauss and Current Critical Theory', *Contemporary Literature XVII*, 1976, 404-429.

—'Superman in the Underground: Strategies of Madness—Nietzsche, Wagner and Dostoevsky', *MLN*, 1976, 1161-1185.

Glucksmann André, *Les Maîtres penseurs*, Grasset, 1977.

Green André, 'Un, autre, neutre: valeurs narcissiques du même', *Nouvelle revue de psychanalyse 13*, Gallimard, 1976, 37-79.

Gregory Nazianzus, Oratio XLV, 'In Sanctum Pascha', *Patrologiae Graecae XXXVI*, ed. J. P. Migne, Garnier, 1886.

Hastings James, *Encyclopaedia of Religion and Ethics*, New York: Scribner's.

Heidegger Martin, *Essais et conférences*, Gallimard, 1958.

—*Introduction to Metaphysics*, trans. R. Manheim, Oxford University Press; Yale University Press, 1959.

Heusch Luc de, *Essai sur le symbolisme de l'inceste royal en Afrique*, Bruxelles: Université libre, 1958.

Hinde R. A., 'La ritualisation et la communication sociale chez les singes Rhésus', *Le Comportement rituel chez l'homme et l'animal*, ed. Julian Huxley, Gallimard, 1971.

Hocart A. M., *Kings and Councillors*, University of Chicago Press, 1970.

Huxley Aldous, *The Devils of Loudun*, Chatto & Windus; Harper, 1952.

Huxley Francis, *Affable Savages*, New York: Capricorn, 1966.

Huxley Julian, ed., *Le Comportement rituel chez l'homme et l'animal*, Gallimard, 1971.

Janet Pierre, *Névroses et idées fixes*, Alcan, 1898. 2 vols.

Jaspers Karl, *La Bombe atomique et l'avenir de l'homme*, Buchet Chastel, 1963.

Kermode Frank, ed., *Four Centuries of Shakespearean Criticism*, New York: Avon, 1965.

Klausner Joseph, *Jesus of Nazareth*, translated from Hebrew by Herbert Dandy, Boston: Beacon Press, 1964.

Kourilsky Raoul, André Soulairac and Pierre Grapin, *Adaptation et Agressivité*, Presses universitaires de France, 1965.

Kraüpl Taylor F. and J.-H. Rey, 'The Scapegoat Motif in society and its Manifestations in a Therapeutic Group', *International Journal of Psychoanalysis* XXXIV, 1953, 253-264.

La Barre Weston, *The Human Animal*, University of Chicago Press, 1954.

Lacan Jacques, *Écrits*, Seuil, 1966.

Lacoue-Labarthe Philippe, 'Typographie', *Mimésis des articulations*, Aubier-Flammarion, 1975.

Laplanche J. et J.-B. Pontalis, *Vocabulaire de la psychanalyse*, Presses universitaires de France, 1967.

Van der Leeuw G., *La Religion dans son essence et ses manifestations*, Payot, 1970.

Leiris Michel, *La Possession et ses aspects théâtraux chez les Éthiopiens de Gondar* (L'Homme: Cahiers d'ethnologie, de géographie et de linguistique), Plon, 1958.

Leroi-Gourhan André, *Le Geste et la Parole*, Albin-Michel, 1964. 2 vols.

Lévi-Strauss Claude, *The Elementary Structures of Kinship*, trans. James Harle Bell, John Richard von Strumer and Rodney Needham, Boston: Beacon Press, 1969.

—*Totemism*, trans. Rodney Needham, Merlin Press: London, 1964.

—*The Savage Mind*, London: Weidenfeld and Nicolson, 1966.

—*The Raw and the Cooked*, trans. John and Doreen Weightman, New York: Harper & Row, 1971.

—*L'Homme nu*, Plon, 1971.

Levinas Emmanuel, *Difficile Liberté*, Albin-Michel, 1963.

—*Quatre Lectures talmudiques*, Minuit, 1968.

Lévy Bernard-Henri, *La Barbarie à visage humain*, Grasset, 1977.

Lewis I. M., *Ecstatic Religion*, Penguin Books, 1971.

Lorenz Konrad, *Das sogenannte Böse: Zur Naturgeschichte der Aggression*, Vienne: Borotha-Schoeler, 1963.

On Aggression, New York: Bantam Books, 1967.

Lubac Henri de, *Exégèse médiévale: les quatre sens de l'Écriture*, Aubier, 1959-1964. 4 vols.

Maïmonide Moïse, *The Guide of the Perplexed*, trans. Shlomo Pines, University of Chicago Press, 1963.

Maloney Clarence, ed., *The Evil Eye*, New York: Columbia University Press, 1976.

Manent Pierre, 'R. Girard, *La Violence et le Sacré*', *Contrepoint 14*, 1974, 157-170.

Marin Louis, *Sémiotique de la passion*, Aubier, 1971.

Mauss Marcel, *The Gift*, trans. Ian Cunnison, London: Cohen & West, 1970.

Métraux Alfred, *Religions et magies indiennes d'Amérique du Sud*, Gallimard, 1967.

Monod Jacques, *Chance and Necessity*, trans. Austyn Wainhouse, New York: Knopf, 1971.

Montagu M. F. Ashley, ed., *Culture and the Evolution of Man*, New York: Oxford University Press, 1962.

—*Man and Aggression*, New York: Oxford University Press, 1973.

Morin Edgar, *Le Paradigme perdu: La nature humaine*, Seuil, 1973.

—and Massimo Piatelli-Palmarini, ed, *L'Unité de l'homme* (Centre Royaumont pour une science de l'homme), Seuil, 1974.

Moscovici Serge, *La Société contre nature*, Union générale d'éditions, 1972.

—*Hommes domestiques et hommes sauvages*, Union générale d'éditions, 1974.

Müller Jean-Claude, 'La Royauté divine chez les Rukuba', *l'Homme*, janvier-mars 1975, 5-25.

Munck Johannes, *The Acts of the Apostles*, The Anchor Bible, New York: Doubleday, 1967.

Munro N. G., *Ainu Creed and Cult*, New York: Columbia University Press, 1963.

Narcisses, Nouvelle revue de psychanalyse 13, Gallimard, 1976.

Neher André, *L'Existence juive*, Seuil, 1962.

Nietzsche Friedrich, *The Anti-Christ*, in *Twilight of the Idols* and *The Anti-Christ*, trans. R. J. Hollingdale, Penguin, 1968.

—*Œuvres philosophiques complètes*, Gallimard, 1974-1977, vol. I and vol. VIII.

Nohl Johannes, *The Black Death*, London: Allen and Unwin, 1926.

Nygren Ander, *Eros et Agape*, Aubier, 1958. 3 vols.

Otto Rudolf, *Le Sacré*, Payot, 1968.

Oughourlian Jean-Michel, *La Personne du toxicomane*, Toulouse: Privat, 1974.

Pachet Pierre, *Le Premier Venu: essai sur la politique baudelairienne*, Denoël, 1976.

Pieper Joseph, *La Fin des temps*, Desclée, 1953.

Propp Vladimir, *Morphology of the Folktale*, trans. Laurence Scott, Texas University Press, 1968.

Proust Marcel, *Jean Santeuil*, Gallimard, 1952. 3 vols.

—*Remembrance of Things Past*, trans. C.K. Scott Moncrieff and Terence Kilmartin, Penguin, 1983, 3 vols.

Ricoeur Paul, *La Philosophie de la volonté*: vol. 2, *La Symbolique du mal*, Aubier, 1976.

—*De l'Interprétation: Essai sur Freud*, Seuil, 1965.

—*Le Conflit des interprétations*, Seuil, 1969.

—*La Métaphore vive*, Seuil, 1976.

Roazen Paul, *Brother Animal: The Story of Freud and Tausk*, New York: Random House, 1969.

Robert Marthe, *La Révolution psychanalytique*, Payot, 1964. 2 vols.

Rosolato Guy, 'Le Narcissisme', *Nouvelle revue de psychanalyse 13*, Gallimard, 1976.

Roustang François, *Un destin si funeste*, Minuit, 1977.

Rymer Thomas, *A Short View of Tragedy*, London: R. Baldwin, 1963.

Schwager Raymund, *Glaube, der die Welt verwandelt*, Mainz: Matthias-Grünewald, 1976.

Schweitzer Albert, *The Quest of the Historical Jesus*, New York: Macmillan, 1961.

Serres Michel, *La Traduction* (Hermès III), Minuit, 1974.

Shoham Shlomo, 'Points of no Return: some Situational Aspects of Violence', *The Emotional Stress of War, Violence and Peace*, Pittsburgh: Stanwix House, 1972.

Sow I., *Psychiatrie dynamique africaine*, Payot, 1977.

Spicq C., *L'Épître aux Hébreux*, Gabalda, 1952. Vol. I: Introduction.

Starobinski Jean, 'Le Démoniaque de Gerasa: Analyse littéraire de Marc 5, 1-20', *Analyse structurale et exégèse biblique*, Neuchâtel: Delachaux et Niestlé, 1971.

Tarde Gabriel, *Les Lois de l'imitation*, Alcan, 1895.

Tiger Lionel, *Men in Groups*, Random House; Nelson, 1969.

Tiger Lionel and Robert Fox, *The Imperial Animal*, New York: Holt, Rinehart and Winston, 1971.

Tillich Paul, *Theology of Culture*, New York: Oxford University Press, 1964.

Vacant A. and E. Mangenot, *Dictionnaire de théologie catholique*, Letouzey, 1935-1972.

Walsh Maurice N., ed., *War and the Human Race*, Amsterdam: Elsevier, 1971.

Washburn Sherwood L., 'Tools and Human Evolution', *Culture and the Evolution of Man*, ed. Ashley Montagu, New York: Oxford University Press, 1962.

Watzlawick Paul, Janet Beavin, Don Jackson, *Pragmatics of Human Communication*, New York: Norton, 1967.

Weber Max, *Ancient Judaism*, trans. H.H. Garth and D. Martindale, Glencoe, Illinois: Free Press, 1952.

Weil Simone, *La Source grecque*, Gallimard, 1953.

Wendland P., 'Jesus als Saturnalien-König', *Hermes XXXII* (1898), 175-179.

Wickersheimer Ernest, 'Les Accusations d'empoisonnement portées pendant la première moitié du XIVe siècle contre les lépreux et les juifs: leur relation avec les épidémies de la peste', *Comptes rendus du quatrième congrès international d'histoire de la médecine*, ed. by Tricot-Royer and Laignel-Lavastine, Antwerp, 1927.

Wilden Anthony, *System and Structure*, London: Tavistock, 1972.

Yamaguchi Masao, 'La Structure mythico-théâtrale de la royauté japonaise', *Esprit*, February 1973.

Ziegler Philip, *The Black Death*, John Day; Collins, 1965.

The Anchor Bible, ed. by W. F. Albright and D. N. Freedman, New York: Doubleday, 59 vols.

La Bible: L'Ancien Testament, ed. Edouard Dhorme *et al*, Gallimard, Bibliothèque de la Pléiade, 1956-1959, 2 vols.

The Holy Bible, commonly known as the King James Version, New York: American Bible Society.

The Jerusalem Bible, London: Chapman, 1971.

Nouveau Testament, Traduction oecuménique de la Bible, Cerf, 1972.

Novum Testamentum Graece et Latine, ed. Eberhard Nestle, Ewin Nestle and Kurt Aland, Stuttgart: Würtembergische Bibelanstalt, 1964.

Peake's Commentary on the Bible, ed. Matthew Back and H. H. Rowley, London: Thomas Nelson, 1962.

Zorell Francisco, *Lexicon Graecum Novi Testamenti*, Lethielleux, 1961.

INDEX